Room 40

ROOM 40

British Naval Intelligence 1914–18

by

PATRICK BEESLY

HBJ

Harcourt Brace Jovanovich, Publishers

San Diego   New York   London

Requests for permission to make copies of any
part of this work should be mailed to:
Permissions, Harcourt Brace Jovanovich, Publishers,
757 Third Avenue, New York, NY 10017.

Library of Congress Cataloging in Publication Data

Beesly, Patrick, 1913–
Room 40: British naval intelligence 1914–18.

Bibliography: p.
Includes index.
1. World War, 1914–1918 — Cryptography. 2. World War,
1914–1918 — Secret service — Great Britain. I. Title.
II. Title: Room forty.
D639.C75B43 1983   940.4′86′41   83-234

Printed in the United States of America

To WRH and JHG
and to
the men and women of 40 OB, BP and OIC

Contents

List of Maps

drawn by Patrick Leeson

Illustrations

Acknowledgements

To try to piece together the history of a highly secret Intelligence organisation after the lapse of nearly seventy years has called for a certain amount of detective work. My task has been made easier by the kindness and help of many people who share my view that the time has now come when the story should be told as fully as possible. I am, therefore, very grateful to all those who have responded to my requests for help. Some have contributed a great deal; others have perhaps only been able to supply a single clue which has, nevertheless, led me on to the solution of a major problem which would otherwise have eluded me. To all of them I say thank you.

I must make it clear that I alone am responsible for any views expressed, unless directly attributed, and that if any errors have crept in, the responsibility is mine.

I would first of all like to express my gratitude to Judge Edward Clarke, Robin Denniston, Michael Lloyd-Hirst and Faith Stubbs (*née* Hall) for lending me their fathers' papers.

I am particularly indebted to Professor Walter Bruford (so far as we both know the last surviving member of Room 40), to David Kahn, to Matti Mäkela and to Captain Stephen Roskill, who have each read and commented on individual chapters and have supplied me with very helpful information and suggestions. I must also pay tribute to the great kindness of the late Professor Arthur Marder, who went to much trouble to select and send me information from his own files.

I should like to thank Dr Christopher Andrew, J. R. D. Brown and his staff in the Naval Historical Branch of the Ministry of Defence, Mrs (Ella) Cochrane, Commander M. Craig-Waller, H. M. Denham and the staff of the Public Record Office, Roger de Grey, Professor R. V. Jones, Lieutenant-Commander P. K. Kemp, Dr R. J. Knight of the National Maritime Museum, Lieutenant-Commander F. L. Phillips, Miss Brenda Russell Clarke, Marion M. Stewart of the Churchill College Archive Centre, Mrs Somers-Cocks, Walter Serocold, Rear-Admiral Thring and Commander A. R. Wells.

I am grateful to Sir Frank Cooper, C. F. Cresswell, J. F. Rickard and J. F. Smith for their courtesy and help in speeding up the declassification of Room 40's voluminous records which have been one of my indispensable sources.

In America I owe a very special debt to John F. Light for giving me access to his unique collection of material about the sinking of the *Lusitania*, for drawing my attention to many files in the Public Record Office directly and indirectly concerned with the disaster and for his detailed comments on my chapter on the subject. He has been exceptionally generous because not only was he the first to persuade the British authorities to make a limited release of Room 40 records, but he is himself writing a book which I believe will be the definitive account of the tragedy. I must also thank Dr Ronald E. Swerczek, Richard T. Gould and the staff of the National Archives, Washington DC, for their help and courtesy.

In Germany I am once again indebted to Professor Dr Jürgen Rohwer of the Bibliothek für Zeitgeschichte, Stuttgart, and to Dr Kehrig of the Bundesarchiv, Freiburg, and to Dr Walle of the Militärgeschichtes Forschungsamt. I am also most grateful to Rainer Matthä who has made a considerable study of German World War I codes and has also given me most helpful information about the escapades of Herr Wassmuss in Persia.

Dr R. J. O'Neill, Head of the Strategic and Defence Studies Centre, Australian National University, took great pains to unravel the story of the capture of the HVB code and of the part played by Dr Wheatley. I thank him and the staffs of the Department of Historical Research, Department of Defence, of the Australian Archives and of the Australian War Memorial. I am also grateful to Lieutenant James Goldrick RAN for comments and suggestions.

I am grateful to the Trustees of the National Maritime Museum for permission to quote from *The Recollections of Admiral of the Fleet Sir Henry Oliver*, to Hutchinson Books Ltd for permission to quote from A. W. Ewing's *The Man of Room 40: The Life of Sir Alfred Ewing*, to The Hamlyn Publishing Group Ltd for permission to quote from W. S. Churchill's *The World Crisis 1911–18*, and to Methuen & Co Ltd for permission to quote from W. James's *The Eyes of the Navy*.

This book could not have been written at all without the tireless co-operation of Mary Pain and her unrivalled ability to track down the most elusive records. She has dealt with all my importunate requests charmingly and efficiently.

Analise Hamilton has again managed to decode my dreadful typing and produce a plain language text for my publishers and has even declared that she has enjoyed the process.

The British Isles and the North Sea

CHAPTER ONE

Splinters are Bound to Fly

At midnight on 4 August 1914 Great Britain declared war on Imperial Germany. For the next few months, indeed for the next four and a quarter years, the attention of the nation and of the whole world was concentrated on the vast and bloody struggles on land. The British Grand Fleet disappeared into the mists of the North Sea and the second Trafalgar, longed for by the Royal Navy, confidently expected by the British public and fearfully anticipated by Wilhelm II, never took place; the two main fleets met only once in the indecisive Battle of Jutland. But control of the sea does not necessarily depend on a single smashing victory and, if blockade and counter-blockade were not the stuff to inspire many headlines, British seapower nevertheless played as vital a part in the defeat of the Kaiser as it had done one hundred years before in that of Napoleon and was to do again, twenty-five years later, in the downfall of Hitler. Had the Royal Navy ever lost control of the sea routes, the tiny British Expeditionary Force of 1914 could never have expanded into the mighty armies which defeated the Central Powers in 1918; the German nation's will to resist would not have been broken and the Imperial Navy would not have gone down to mutiny and then to ignominious surrender[1] at Rosyth on 21 November 1918.

What is perhaps not generally realised is the debt owed by the Royal Navy, and therefore by the country as a whole, to its Director of Naval Intelligence, Captain Reginald Hall, and to his tiny band of code-breakers in what has come to be known, from the number of the room which they occupied in the Old Building of the Admiralty, as '40 OB' or 'Room 40'. Few people nowadays can be ignorant of the work of Room 40's successors at Bletchley Park in World War II, but Room 40's achievements and influence on the outcome of World War I were every bit as great as those of BP in the second conflict. But for Room 40, the Battles of the Dogger Bank and

[1] Technically internment.

Jutland would probably never have been fought at all, the Irish Easter Rebellion might possibly have succeeded, the U-boats would not have been mastered when they were, and above all a reluctant America would not have been dragged into the war in April 1917. Good Intelligence was the keystone of victory.

The foundations of Room 40's tremendous success were laid swiftly but largely fortuitously in the first twelve weeks of the war, when five seemingly unimportant events took place quite unnoticed by the world at large. The first of them – and it was Britain's very first offensive act – stemmed from a minor decision taken by the Committee of Imperial Defence (CID) in 1912. It was, in the event of war, to cut all Germany's overseas telegraph cables. In the early hours of 5 August 1914 the cable ship *Telconia* began to dredge up and sever the first of the five German cables which ran from Emden, on the German-Dutch frontier, down the English Channel to France, Spain, Africa and the Americas. *Telconia* had no need to proceed on to the Mediterranean because all the cables there were British owned, while the only other link open to the Germans was via the German-American owned Liberia-Brazil cable. Despite typical timidity on the part of the Foreign Office, by 1915 a British cable company had persuaded its American confrère to allow this cable too to be quietly cut. From that moment on, Imperial Germany was unable to communicate by cablegram with neutral Spain, with its colonies or with any of its embassies or consulates except in a few contiguous neutral European countries such as Sweden and Holland or in allied Austro-Hungary and Turkey. Recourse had to be had to letters – slow and in constant danger of interception by the ubiquitous Royal Navy – or to wireless. It is true that the meanings of such messages could be concealed and protected from the enemy by means of codes and ciphers. Whether the Committee of Imperial Defence intended to do more than cause the Germans inconvenience and delay, is not clear: certainly few steps were taken to intercept, to pluck from the ether, the increasing flow of wireless messages, or to institute an efficient system of censorship of mails,[1] or most important of all, to set up an organisation to decode any disguised messages that were obtained. These omissions, as will be recounted later, were swiftly remedied by the Admiralty's Intelligence Division.

[1] So far as the censorship of mails and cables was concerned, it is clear that the CID were thinking defensively, not offensively; to prevent information reaching the enemy, rather than to obtain information for Britain.

Wireless Telegraphy (W/T) was of course a very recent invention in those days, and although by 1914 it was widely used by all warships and many merchantmen, no one had fully envisaged the enormous increase in wireless traffic which war conditions would bring. Disguising the meaning of messages by codes and ciphers was known to the ancients, and by the first decade of the twentieth century the fighting services of all countries were coding their messages to protect them from the prying eyes and ears of unauthorised persons. Curiously enough, Britain was not the only nation to have failed to set up a code-breaking organisation before the war. Germany had none; Russia no naval one (indeed as Tannenberg and Lemburg were to show, she was incapable of encoding all her own army signals); France had only re-established a Military Cabinet Noir in 1912, and the sole major belligerent with a long tradition of military code-breaking was the supposedly inefficient Austro-Hungarian Empire. So, although Room 40 was established within ten days of the outbreak of war, and although coded German messages were by then beginning to pile up on the desk of the Admiralty's Director of Intelligence, there was no plan, no experience, no expertise to deal with the situation.

Luck, however, was with the British. The German Navy started the war with three principal codes. Within four months the British Admiralty was in physical possession of copies of all three of them. Room 40 had, very nearly by pure chance, secured the essential knowledge that would immediately lay open to it the whole of the Imperial German Navy's wireless traffic, and which would eventually also enable it to crack German diplomatic messages.

The first German code-book to fall into British hands was captured on the other side of the world – in Australia. On 11 August the German-Australian steamship *Hobart*, unaware that war had been declared, was seized off Port Philip heads, Melbourne. The affair was managed with some guile. The boarding party, under Captain J. T. Richardson RAN, were in plain clothes and successfully represented themselves as being merely a quarantine inspection group. Richardson allowed the German master considerable latitude in the hope that, thinking himself unobserved, he would attempt to destroy his confidential papers and so betray their whereabouts. The plan worked. In the early hours of the morning the skipper crept from his bunk, slid back a secret panel in his inner cabin and withdrew the precious documents. But Richardson was right behind him and, at pistol point, compelled the luckless German to hand them over. They included the *Handelsverkehrsbuch* (HVB), the code used by the *Admiralstab* (the German Admiralty) and warships for communication with their merchantmen. Even more important, it was also extensively used within the *Hochseeflotte* (the High Sea Fleet) itself. Captain Richardson had secured a prize of much greater value than he can have anticipated, or, apparently, his superiors, because it was not until 9 September that Naval Board, Melbourne, informed the Admiralty in London of its success. A copy was then made and sent to England, but in those days even the fastest steamer took many weeks to make the voyage so that it was not until the end of October that the HVB code finally reached its destination. By that time Room 40 was already in possession of another and even more secret code, the *Signalbuch der Kaiserlichen Marine* (SKM).

On 25 August two German light cruisers, *Augsburg*, wearing the flag of Rear-Admiral Behring, and *Magdeburg*, with accompanying destroyers were carrying out an armed reconnaissance of the entrance to the Gulf of Finland. It was probably a mistake to have sent *Magdeburg* on such a hazardous mission, to within two hundred miles of the Imperial Russian Navy's main base at Kronstadt. Although she was only three years old, *Magdeburg* was not fully operational; one of her three turbines had broken down and been removed, and her crew was a scratch one: she could not be compared with her sister ship, *Breslau*,[1] who only a fortnight earlier had accompanied the battlecruiser *Goeben* in the famous dash from the Mediterranean to Constantinople, which was to bring Turkey into the war on the side of the Central Powers. Be that as it may, Admiral Behring's little squadron encountered thick fog and became separated. Early on 26 August, *Magdeburg* ran hard aground on the Island of Odensholm off the coast of Russian Estonia. Despite all efforts the ship could not be got off and her commanding officer, Korvettenkapitän Habenicht – very junior for such a command by British standards – was fortunate that one of the destroyers, V.26, came to his assistance. Orders were given to prepare to blow up the ship after her crew and confidential papers had been transferred to the destroyer. Unfortunately, before these measures could be properly completed, the fog began to lift and two Russian cruisers, *Pallada* and *Bogatyr*, appeared in the offing and opened

---

[1] One of *Breslau's* junior officers was a certain Karl Dönitz. It is interesting to speculate how the course of history might have been affected had he been serving in *Magdeburg*.

fire. Confusion reigned; the explosive charges were set off too soon, and seem to have done almost as much harm to the crew as to the ship; only part of the crew could be transferred to V.26 before she had to make off; the confidential books were not effectively disposed of, and after four hours Habenicht and fifty-seven of his men were made prisoners by the Russians.

Precisely what happened to the confidential papers is not clear. Winston Churchill, at that time First Lord of the Admiralty, recounts that the Petty Officer charged with the destruction of the most secret SKM code-book was killed and blown overboard. Next day, so the story goes, the Russians recovered his body with 'these priceless sea-stained documents' still clasped faithfully to his bosom. It makes a romantic story, but unfortunately the book itself, Copy No. 151 of the SKM, now in the Public Record Office in London, shows no signs of immersion in the salt waters of the Baltic. The official German account also claimed that most of the secret papers, including the signal books, were thrown overboard, although acknowledging that some of the less vital documents were left in a seabag on the cruiser's quarterdeck. Count Constantine Benckendorf, son of the Russian Ambassador in London, and at that time an officer of the Imperial Russian Navy, stated in his autobiography that he was told that the Russians found the signal book in its 'customary place in the charthouse'. What is undeniable is that, from one place or another, the Russians did retrieve the code-book, the current key, a copy of the German naval gridded chart for the Baltic, the bridge log and the ship's War Diary. The German Kaiser, on being told of the destruction of one of his cruisers remarked blandly: 'Well, splinters are bound to fly at a time like this.' He did not know what damage those splinters were going to do.

The Russians themselves made good use of their booty, but with uncommon good sense and in a spirit of co-operation which was not repeated in World War II, instructed their Naval Attaché in London to inform the British Admiralty of their splendid capture and of their willingness to present one of the code-books to their ally if the Royal Navy would be good enough to send a ship to North Russia to collect them. HMS *Theseus* left Scapa Flow on this mission and arrived at Alexandrovsk (Polyarno) on 7 September. Due to not untypical misunderstandings with the Russians, she did not sail again until 30 September. Her cargo also included six trunks of clothes belonging to Princess Louis of Battenberg, wife of the 1st

Sea Lord. Count Benchkendorf claimed that it was he who brought the code-book to England, in a Russian Volunteer Navy ship to Hull; he may have brought another copy[1] or he may, unwittingly, have been serving as a decoy, although both seem improbable (which casts some doubt on the authenticity of his information about where the SKM was actually found). It is, however, quite clear from contemporary British Grand Fleet records that the *Magdeburg's* invaluable documents were first brought to England in the care of Captain Kredoff and Commander Smirnoff of the Imperial Russian Navy, who arrived at Scapa Flow from Polyarno on board HMS *Theseus* on 10 October. They handed their precious charge over to the 1st Lord, Winston Churchill, on 13 October. It was a gift just as priceless as the reconstructed version of the German Enigma Machine presented to the British by the Poles in 1939.

The receipt of *Magdeburg's* book may just possibly have led within four days to the first successful operational use by the British Naval Staff of Room 40's new-found source of knowledge, and within weeks to the recovery of the third code-book, the *Verkehrsbuch* (VB).

By the middle of October, with the Battle of the Marne won, the so-called 'Race for the Sea' had taken place, and some sort of a continuous line had been formed on the Western Front by the armies of the two sides all the way from the Swiss frontier to the southernmost piece of the Belgian coast. The first Battle of Ypres was about to begin. Antwerp had been lost and the Belgians and French were struggling desperately to hold Dixmude and Dunkirk. The Royal Navy was doing all that it could to help by bombardment from the sea. A German attempt to interfere with these operations was anticipated, and news of activity by their destroyer flotillas in the Heligoland Bight began to reach the Admiralty. Whether this news came from Room 40 is not clear. What is certain is that, early on 17 October, Captain Cecil Fox was ordered to take his newly commissioned light cruiser *Undaunted* and the destroyers *Lance*, *Lennox*, *Legion* and *Loyal* to sea and sweep north up the Dutch coast. When Fox was approaching The Texel, the scene of Duncan's great victory over the Dutch one hundred and seventeen years before – almost to the day – he sighted four old German destroyers

[1] It appears that *Magdeburg* was carrying three copies of SKM, Nos. 145 and 974 as well as No. 151, but only one, No. 151, was sent to Britain. For a description of the construction and use of this code, *see* Ch. 3.

steaming south in line abreast. Their mission was to lay mines in The Downs. The Germans were outnumbered and outgunned and turned about, but two of their ships were quickly reduced to a sinking condition and when the other two most gallantly turned back to the assistance of their sisters, they too suffered the same fate. By 4.30 in the afternoon, S.115, S.117, S.118 and S.119 were all at the bottom of the North Sea. It had been a minor if very successful action – a few more 'splinters', perhaps the Kaiser would have called it. But the senior German officer in S.119, before she had been sunk had quite correctly jettisoned all his secret papers in a lead-lined chest. The British did not know it, and the Germans probably thought no more about it.

However, in those now far-off days, harmless fishing boats were not bombed and machine-gunned off the face of the sea by aircraft as they were during World War II; despite occasional attacks by U-boats and the risk of capture by enemy destroyers, they were able on the whole to continue to ply their peacetime trade. On 30 November a British trawler, fishing off The Texel, fortuitously[1] dragged up the lead-lined chest and its load of secret documents. By 3 December it was in the hands of Room 40. When opened it proved to contain not only a mass of extremely valuable papers but a copy of the *Verkehrsbuch* (VB), the third and last Imperial German Naval code. Quite why this code was issued to the destroyers is not clear, unless it was for the purposes of communicating with the German Army, for it was rarely used at sea except by Flag Officers. It was such treasure trove, however, that Room 40 always referred to the incident as 'The Miraculous Draught of Fishes', worth even more than Duncan's glorious Camperdown. The capture of the SKM and HVB codes had already begun to enable Room 40 to provide the Naval War Staff with better information about the movements and intentions of their opponents than any other military command had ever possessed. Now the process was complete, and virtually any wireless signal made by the German Navy which could be intercepted, was to become equally available to Winston Churchill, Admiral 'Jacky' Fisher (now 1st Sea Lord) and their immediate subordinates. No one, on either side, had anticipated such a swift and overwhelming intelligence defeat for the Germans; it was one from which the Imperial German Navy was never to recover.

---

[1] Hall claims deliberately, but this seems doubtful.

CHAPTER TWO

Room 40 is Born

What then was Room 40? How was it created and how did it fit into the British Naval Staff? The Naval Staff was, in 1914, a recent concept, and was still largely in a process of gestation. The Royal Navy remained, as it had been for hundreds of years, a very autocratic organisation, centred on the professional head of the Navy, the 1st Sea Lord, and its political head, the 1st Lord. Churchill had been made 1st Lord in 1911 partly to compel the Admiralty to set up an efficient Naval Staff, and had encountered much opposition from the Sea Lords, who regarded staff work with distrust, not to say contempt. It was not, in their view, the job of junior officers of commander's and captain's rank to think about the higher conduct of war; that should be left to the 1st Sea Lord and the Commanders-in-Chief at sea. As Winston himself remarked: '. . . at the outset of war we had more captains of ships than captains of war.' There was, therefore, little decentralisation, no delegation of responsibility, and effective control even of minor day to day operations remained concentrated in the hands of a very few senior officers; the 1st Lord himself to whom, despite his avowed object of creating a proper staff, this was most welcome; the 1st Sea Lord (from the end of October) the volcanic but septuagenarian Jacky Fisher and the Chief of the War Staff (COS) (from November), Rear-Admiral H. F. Oliver.

Oliver, one of Fisher's men, was the creator of Room 40 and was to play a large part in its history. In August 1913, at the age of forty-nine, he had been appointed the Director of the Intelligence Division (DID), the senior Division of the Naval Staff. His extreme taciturnity had earned him the nickname of 'Dummy', and he was reputed to be the worst dressed officer in the Navy. He had little charm but was a tremendous worker. Edward Bell, Secretary of the American Embassy throughout the war, commenting on half a dozen Englishmen who had impressed him, remarked: 'I didn't understand him at all. He works twenty-three hours a day.' It was both his strength and his weakness. Oliver was an intelligent and able man – when he died at the age of 100, he was an Admiral of the Fleet – but the same cannot be said for his principal deputy, the Director of the Operations Division (DOD), Captain Thomas Jackson. A boorish, self-opinionated man, he was, in the words of the late Professor Marder, a 'disaster'. One other very senior officer had something to do with the work of Room 40, Admiral Sir Arthur Wilson. A former 1st Sea Lord, and before that Commander-in-Chief of the Channel Fleet, he was a dedicated, tough and very practical seaman. Known to the Lower Deck as 'old 'Ard 'Art' and to his fellow officers as 'Tug', he had retired from the Service in 1912 on reaching the age of seventy but with characteristic selflessness returned in an unofficial and unpaid capacity in November 1914. He was as silent and taciturn as Oliver, with whom he was great friends.

Although the Royal Navy had only one wireless station, Stockton, to intercept enemy wireless messages, as soon as war broke out other stations belonging to the Post Office and to the Marconi Company, and also a few private individuals (radio hams, in modern parlance) at once began to pick up and record coded messages apparently of German origin. These messages found their way to the Director of Intelligence in the Admiralty. Oliver realised their potential value but had no staff who were not already fully occupied and certainly none with the slightest idea of how to set about the problem of code-breaking. One day in the first half of August, Oliver was walking across to the United Service Club in Pall Mall for lunch in the company of his friend the Director of Naval Education (DNE), Sir Alfred Ewing. 'It struck me,' Oliver recounts, 'that he was the very man I wanted . . .' He knew that Ewing had some interest in ciphers, because the latter had recently talked to him about what Ewing described as 'a rather futile ciphering mechanism' which he had devised, and they had gone on to discuss 'novel methods of constructing ciphers'. Oliver pointed out that the development of Naval education would obviously receive little priority until the war was won, and offered the task of devising means of code-breaking and of setting up an organisation to do so to Ewing, who promptly accepted. It was assumed that he would have no difficulty in combining his two functions for the few months which it was thought that the war would last.

Ewing was at this time aged fifty-nine. His son in his biography of his father describes him as 'a short thick-set man with keen blue eyes overshadowed by ill-kept shaggy eyebrows and with a disarmingly quiet Scottish voice [who] might well resemble a benign physician or a guile-less dominie.' Son of a Church of Scotland clergyman he was married to an American, a great-great-niece of George Washington. He had won an engineering scholarship to Edinburgh University to which he returned, after some years' practical experience with cable firms, on engineering research. Appointments as Professor of Engineering at Tokyo and Dundee Universities followed, and in 1890 he was offered the Chair of Mechanical Engineering at Cambridge. Five years later he was awarded the Gold Medal of the Royal Society for his work on Magnetic Induction in Iron and other Metals. In 1902, when Jacky Fisher first became 1st Sea Lord and, with Lord Selborne, the 1st Lord, began to introduce their radical reforms in the recruitment, education and training of officers for the Royal Navy, he persuaded Ewing to accept the newly created post of Director of Naval Education. He was such a success that he was made Companion of the Bath in 1906 and advanced to Knight Commander of the Order in 1911. 'Careful at all times of his appearance, his suits were mostly grey, added to which he generally wore – whatever the prevailing fashion – a white piqué stripe to his waistcoat, a mauve shirt, a white butterfly collar and a dark blue bow tie with white spots.' He was a brilliant and successful man, but not unconscious of his position and dignity and not, it would seem, without a prickly side to his nature, '– too distinguished a man' in Oliver's view 'to be placed officially under the orders of the Director of Intelligence or Chief of Staff, although he procured intelligence that was used by both.' Nor, like his friend Oliver, does he seem to have been one who could inspire the admiration and devotion of his subordinates. He was, however, the 'Father' of Room 40, and if he owed a great deal of his subsequent reputation to the folly of the Germans and to the truly extraordinary efforts of the remarkable band of individuals who eventually constituted the staff of Room 40, it must always be remembered that Ewing, virtually single-handed, was the midwife who presided over that organisation's birth.

He was the first to admit that in August 1914 he was woefully ill equipped to solve the problems which Oliver had thrust upon him. In a lecture given in 1927 to the Edinburgh Philosophical Institution (a lecture which incidentally aroused the ire of the authorities because it was the first semi-official disclosure of the extent of Room 40's successes), he recalled how 'in the first few days I visited Lloyd's, the General Post Office and the British Museum to see their collection of code-books . . . Admitted into the great Library behind the British Museum, conducted to the appropriate shelves and left to prowl among dusty code-books, I was able to glean from them certain general notions, about how codes were or might be built up.' It was obvious that this could not continue to be a single-handed task. As Director of Naval Education, Ewing had of course been in close touch with the Royal Naval Colleges of Osborne and Dartmouth. A number of the older cadets – fifteen- and sixteen-year-olds – were being appointed to sea (many to be tragically lost in the old cruisers *Cressy*, *Aboukir* and *Hogue*, torpedoed by a single U-boat on 22 September, and others to go down with Admiral Cradock at the Battle of Coronel on 1 November), and in any case the Colleges were on holiday in August. Their masters were therefore an obvious source at least of temporary help. Like Ewing himself, they knew nothing of codes and little of naval routine and operations, but they were available and anxious to serve their king and country in any way they could, and as quickly as possible. Moreover, they possessed the prime qualification for the job – their discretion could be relied upon absolutely, and some of them were German linguists.

Among the first of these volunteers (for a purely temporary job, as they thought) was Alastair Denniston, who had been teaching German at Osborne. Denniston was thirty-three, like Ewing a Scotsman and short in stature. He was a great athlete, having represented Scotland in the Olympics at hockey, and had been educated at the Sorbonne and Bonn Universities. He, too, was very quiet, with, according to his daughter, a rather pawky sense of humour. Unknown to him, he had now found an entirely new career – by virtue of ability and seniority in Room 40 he soon became second in charge. After World War I he became head of Room 40's successor, the Government Code and Cipher School (GC&CS); there, with half a dozen other old Room 40 hands, he kept alive its traditions and expertise in the face of the neglect of the authorities and the parsimony of the Treasury. He laid the foundations of Bletchley Park's immense successes in World War II, and continued as its chief until 1942, when partly as a result of ill health he had to hand over the naval and military side to his second in command. His country owed him a great debt for more than thirty years of devoted service to Intelligence, for which the OBE awarded him in 1937 and the CMG in 1942 were very inadequate recognition.

There were two others who were to become permanent members of the staff; R. D. Norton, an ex-member of the Foreign Office and

a company promoter, about whom little else is now known, and
Lord Herschell, son of one of Mr Gladstone's Lord Chancellors.
Aged thirty-eight, he was a typical member of the Edwardian
Establishment. Educated at Eton and Magdalen College Oxford,
he had served as private secretary to his father on an international
commission and to the Lord Lieutenant of Ireland. He had been
Lord in Waiting to Edward VII and then to George V. He had
travelled much, especially in the less frequented parts of Persia
(Iran) and had formed an interesting collection of Persian arms and
armour; a lover of music, he was a talented amateur pianist. How he
came to be recruited is something of a mystery; he seems an unlikely
acquaintance for Ewing, but he was a linguist and probably offered
his services to the Admiralty on that basis.

Various other Osborne and Dartmouth schoolmasters served
until the Colleges restarted towards the end of September, including the Headmaster of Osborne, Charles Godfrey, elder brother of
a young naval officer, John Godfrey, who was to head the Naval
Intelligence Division with great distinction for four years in World
War II. Some returned again during subsequent holiday periods and
a few ultimately became permanencies, but in those early weeks the
numbers of the staff could be counted on the fingers of two hands.
Some help was given by two members of Ewing's staff, Naval
Instructors Parish and Curtis and by Professor Henderson, a scien-
tist and mathematician from Greenwich Naval College, but this was
only when they could be spared from their other duties. They all had
to use Ewing's cramped office and to retire to the cubby hole
occupied by his secretary, Mountstephen, when visitors came to see
Sir Alfred in his capacity as DNE. Nor were they able to make any
real progress on German codes, an alleged copy of one of them,
supplied by the Secret Service, having proved in Denniston's words,
to be 'a pup of the poorest class'. However, the War Office was also
receiving intercepted coded messages and Colonel Macdonagh, of
Military Intelligence, called on Ewing and suggested that his staff
should co-operate with a similar small body which had just been set
up in the War Office under Brigadier Anderson, who had had some
experience of cryptography in the Boer War. So work continued in
the Admiralty and the War Office by day, Denniston, Norton and
Herschell being seconded to the latter, as watchkeepers. Those in
the Admiralty at least identified a code used in messages sent by the
German high power station, Nauen, to German West Africa and
elsewhere. They knew nothing of wireless procedure, but with the

help of Mr Bradfield, Manager of the Marconi Company, began to identify various call signs. Over in the War Office the would-be code-breakers were equally unsuccessful, confusing naval with military messages, and very pleased with themselves if they were able to make any sense of the not infrequent messages intercepted *en clair* (plain language). But they all learned how to analyse and file, and after a time how to differentiate codes from ciphers.

Then, about the middle of September, the French provided the Army with the method and key of the German military ciphers and actual deciphering became possible for the first time. Denniston recalls that '. . . the signs of jealousy were not absent even in this small section of men drawn from many branches of civil life . . . the messages all concerned the Western Front and were of immediate value to the Intelligence Section of General Headquarters, whither they were transmitted by wire and by daily bag. But it must also be remembered that they were also deciphered and translated in the Admiralty . . . It is said that a climax was reached when the all highest on one side of Whitehall was told of a translation of great interest (actually proposals for treatment of Indian prisoners of war) by his opposite number *before* his own section had managed to get the information through to him.' One can well imagine the glee of that ex-subaltern of Hussars, Mr Winston Churchill, now a 'Naval Person', in scoring off the head of his old Service, the great Lord Kitchener, a phenomenon not unknown in World War II.

In the meantime, the number of intercepts of all sorts had been increasing. The work of the Post Office and Marconi stations and of the single Admiralty 'police' station, Stockton, had been supplemented by three enthusiastic amateurs. Early in September a friend of Ewing, Russell Clarke, a barrister by profession, called on him and told him that he and his friend Colonel Hippisley, a Somerset landowner, had been receiving German intercepts on their sets in London and Wales. As Denniston remarked, 'It is not clear why the police or the Post Office had not sealed up their apparatus but it can well be imagined that some rash official had tried his best on Russell Clarke and had been forced to retire the worse for wear.' He quickly persuaded Ewing that, given reasonable conditions, he and Hippisley could produce a great deal more. They were promptly installed in the coastguard station at Hunstanton, on the Norfolk coast of The Wash, ideally situated from a reception point of view and already equipped with wireless. They were joined by a friend, another radio ham, Leslie Lambert, later

better known as the BBC broadcaster A. J. Allen. Hunstanton and
Stockton were the core of a 'Y' service (Interception service) which,
together with the Marconi and Post Office stations, grew rapidly so
that eventually it was able to intercept and record almost every
naval wireless message, and diplomatic, consular and commercial
messages as well, which were transmitted by the German authorities.

Towards the end of September 1914, most of the schoolmasters
returned to their naval Colleges and the staff seems to have dwin-
dled to Denniston, who had obtained leave from Osborne, Herschell and Norton, with part-time help from Henderson, Parish and
Curtis. The last three knew something of mathematics but little
German; the others were German linguists but no mathematicians.
Not much was achieved. Then, on 13 October, came the quite
priceless gift of *Magdeburg's Signalbuch der Kaiserlichen Marine*
(SKM).

Unfortunately, it was quickly found that possession of the SKM
only permitted a small number of German signals, weather reports,
to be decoded; the great majority of intercepts were obviously
subjected to some form of reciphering, and this completely baffled
Ewing and his men. The man who saved the day was Fleet Paymaster (Paymaster-Commander) C. J. E. Rotter, the Naval Intelligence Division's German expert. His Christian names (or at least the
third one, Ehrhardt), would, as one of his colleagues subsequently
remarked, undoubtedly have raised the gravest suspicions in the
minds of the counter-espionage department, MI5, had they known
it, since they later objected to the recruitment of a civilian called
Sandbach until reminded that it was the name of an English village!
Rotter was transferred to Ewing's staff, ensconced in Mountstephen's tiny office, and directed by Sir Alfred to decode the
intercepted messages according to the code-book, a process which
Ewing does not seem to have realised could only result in gibberish
until the key to the recipherment had been found. Rotter, however,
understood better than his chief what was involved, and as he not
only spoke faultless German but, unlike all the others, had some
knowledge of naval language and procedure, set to work to break
the keys. The material he had to work on was a series of numbered
messages sent out by the German naval high power transmitter at
Norddeich.

The Germans, whose folly was even greater than the ignorance of
the British, reciphered the numbers of these messages, thus offering

to their enemies the simplest and surest entry into their reciphering tables. Within a week, Rotter had solved the puzzle, and was then able to instruct the others in the correct use of the code-book. It was then found that Norddeich's high power signals were merely intelligence reports of Allied shipping which were broadcast by the German Naval Staff – interesting information to the British but quite uninformative about the *Hochseeflotte* itself. By good fortune, Russell Clarke happened to come into Ewing's office and saw some of the intercepts waiting to be decoded. He immediately proclaimed that he could intercept hundreds of such messages daily on short not long waves. At the time there was only one aerial at Hunstanton, still doing good work on military traffic. Ewing was, according to Denniston, loath to lose this valuable stuff for a 'pig in a poke' but eventually agreed to a weekend trial. This proved conclusive, and it was obvious that Ewing and his men would be able to follow every movement of the *Hochseeflotte* provided always that it used the same key, call signs and code-book. Denniston recounts that: 'It was now clear that the Admiralty cryptographic section had found a task which concerned the Navy alone and that there might be an enormous outlet for their energy. The watchkeepers were therefore recalled from the War Office and started to keep a continuous watch on naval signals . . . Relations between the two offices were already somewhat strained and as the new activities in the Admiralty were a closely guarded secret [and as Hunstanton presumably abruptly ceased to intercept military traffic] a definite breach occurred which endured till the spring of 1917 . . . the loss of efficiency to both departments, caused originally by mere official jealousy, is the most regrettable fact in the development of Intelligence based on cryptography.'

The next development, on 6 November, was the much overdue provision of proper accommodation for the cryptographers, sparked off, in all probability, by the august Assistant Secretary to the Admiralty being refused admittance to Sir Alfred's room by a civilian cryptographer ignorant of his identity and importance. The seven-man staff, Rotter, Henderson, Curtis and Parish as day men and Denniston, Herschell and Norton as watchkeepers, were moved to Room 40 on the first floor of the Old Building, in the same corridor as the Admiralty Board Room and the 1st Sea Lord's office,[1] and only a few steps from the 1st Lord's Residence.

[1] Fisher transferred his office to the West Block, well away from the Board Room in the Old Building.

Although soon to become overcrowded in its turn (it was just over twenty-four feet by just under seventeen feet) it looked out on an inner courtyard, was quiet and remote from the hurly-burly of the rest of the Admiralty, and so was well placed to escape the attention of inquisitive eyes, for from the outset its activities were to be shrouded in the greatest secrecy.

Winston Churchill and Fisher had undoubtedly been kept fully informed by Oliver of all that had transpired, and were immediately conscious of the immense potential importance of the weapon now placed in their hands and of the vital need to prevent the slightest suspicion reaching the Germans of the tremendous defeat they had suffered. On 8 November, Churchill drafted in his own hand the following 'Charter' for Room 40 OB, as the organisation soon came to be called. It was headed 'Exclusively Secret' (although Excessively Secret would have been a more accurate description), and was addressed to the Chief of Staff (by this time Oliver) and the Director of Education; not, be it noted, to the newly appointed Director of Intelligence, Captain Reginald Hall. It read as follows:

> An officer of the War Staff, preferably from the ID [Intelligence Division] should be selected to study all the decoded intercepts, not only current but past, and to compare them continually with what actually took place in order to penetrate the German mind and movements and make reports. All these intercepts are to be written in a locked book with their decodes, and all other copies are to be collected and burnt. All new messages are to be entered in the book, and the book is only to be handled under direction from COS [Chief of Staff].
>
> The officer selected is for the present to do no other work.
>
> I shall be obliged if Sir Alfred Ewing will associate himself continuously with this work.

The instruction was initialled 'WSC' in the famous red ink, and 'F' (Fisher) in the equally well-known green ink.

Oliver at once passed the missive on to Hall for consideration and consultation with Ewing. Hall replied next day:

> I have consulted with Sir Alfred Ewing and propose that Fleet Paymaster Rotter be detailed exclusively for this work (he discovered the code). The system at present in force is as follows. All intercepts are decoded immediately they are received. The original intercept is then filed and kept under lock and key. The

translation is entered in a book which is kept under lock and key. Two copies only are made out of the translation – one sent by hand and given personally to COS, the other given to DID [Director Intelligence Division]. This sytem ensures that the information is at once given to the responsible people, the COS to act as necessary, the DID to compare with information from other sources. DID's copy is kept under lock and key and is seen by no one but DID. In future, the envelopes will be marked 'To be opened only by . . .' I would point out that to carry the book round will entail much delay and will not save copies being taken as so many messages are being received. I would therefore propose that the work be continued under the direction of Sir Alfred Ewing on the lines indicated above.

The system, although it may have suited Churchill and Oliver splendidly, because they liked to keep all the threads in their fingers (Fisher was less subject to this fault) and did indeed meet the vital need to secure secrecy, had a number of disadvantages which were to come more and more apparent as time went on. The first was that it appeared to make Ewing and 40 OB responsible to Oliver, COS, and failed to define their relationship with the DID, Hall, who was their natural overlord. Not only was Oliver far too busy a man to give any supervision to Room 40's organisation and general efficiency, but he himself had stated that Ewing was too distinguished a man to be placed even under the Chief of Staff. Ewing was therefore in fact responsible to no one, an obvious weakness and a potential source of friction with the head of the department intimately concerned with all sources of intelligence, Hall. This situation was further aggravated by the ukase that no one in the Intelligence Division, other than Hall himself, might even know of the existence of the decodes, thus completely cutting the Division off from its most valuable source of information. Second, the very proper provision for security within the Admiralty was carried too far, and for this one must blame Churchill and Oliver. Oliver has recorded that 'only the First Lord, the First Sea Lord, the Second Sea Lord, the Secretary [of the Admiralty], Sir Arthur Wilson, me and Hall, the DOD [Director Operations Division], the Assistant Director and my three Duty Captains were supposed to be aware [of Room 40's work] in the Admiralty. Churchill may have told the Prime Minister but I never had any evidence that the rest of the War Cabinet knew.' Many will agree that politicians, bracketed with diplomats, are the last people to be trusted to keep these sort of secrets, but the best of information is quite useless unless it can be put to practical use. As Ronald Lewin has stated in his admirable book *Ultra Goes to War*, 'for Intelligence, Battle is the Pay Off', and to leave the dissemination of this most priceless information in the hands of so few individuals, burdened with a thousand and one other important problems, was a very serious error. Room 40 was to remain for far too long Oliver's private cryptographic bureau and not a proper Intelligence Centre, a weakness avoided in World War II thanks to the far-sightedness of John Godfrey and 'Ned' Denning.

Of course, modifications to the system perforce began to be made almost before the ink was dry on Winston's original charter. The idea that Rotter should be the officer to study all the intercepts, to act as an 'Intelligence Officer', studying, analysing and appreciating the true significance of the translated decodes, was quickly abandoned; he was far more usefully employed on cryptographic work, and a substitute had to be found. The choice fell, by great good fortune, on Commander Herbert Hope, an officer on the active list, a wonderful selection made by the newly arrived Hall. Hope, together with two other regular commanders, was engaged on the very humdrum task of plotting the positions, as known from scanty and inaccurate reports, of enemy warships, in the Admiralty 'Chart Room', something which as he himself said could have just as well have been performed by three intelligent clerks.

He was sent for by Hall and subsequently wrote that:

he first impressed on me the need for absolute secrecy, and then informed me that German Naval W/T [Wireless Telegraphy] messages were being decoded in the Admiralty; the First Lord had decreed that an Executive NO [Naval Officer] was to be appointed to sift the messages and extract the juice, and I was detailed for this purpose. I was put in a little room by myself [in the area occupied by the Intelligence Division in the West Block of the Admiralty, and therefore very remote from Room 40] and was told that the messages would be brought to me. I sat there for a few days and about half a dozen messages at the outside per diem were brought to me. These messages were not, in themselves, of great importance and in some cases were not very intelligible. However, I did my best by writing remarks on them which I sent to Admiral [in fact at that time Captain] Hall. I found out afterwards that he sent my remarks to the First Lord who sent them on to the COS. I quite realise now that at that early stage my remarks were very amateurish and beside the point, and must have added to the worries of the COS, who by that means got prejudiced (in addition to other reasons) against my work and myself; it took a long time to break down this prejudice. I realised that if I was to make anything out of these messages it was absolutely necessary that I should be in close touch with the producers, and that I must have access to the Holy of Holies where these messages were produced. I approached [Captain Hall] in this matter and though he saw my point, he was powerless to help me, as the production of the messages was not under his direction and the feeling for the necessity of secrecy was such that it was considered inadvisable by the powers that be that I should have access to the mystery. I had been isolated in this manner for a short time when, one day the door opened and in came Lord Herschell with Lord Fisher. It appeared that the former was on his way to me with a message from the Holy of Holies, but was unable to find me and was wandering round the passages of the Admiralty [when he] happened to meet Lord Fisher who asked him what he was doing; when Lord Fisher learnt what was the matter, he said, 'Oh, I know where Hope is, I'll take you there.' I had never met Lord Fisher before and he enquired about my work. I siezed the opportunity to tell him I ought to be in close touch, he quite agreed and went away to give orders to that effect there and then; he also told me that I was to visit him twice daily with copies of the messages, a course which I pursued not only with him but with his successors Sir Henry Jackson and Sir John Jellicoe . . . and so I was introduced into the Mystery on 16 November 1914. This was the beginning of a sphere of work which was probably unique, was absorbingly interesting and which threw me into a close relationship with probably as fine a set of fellows as it would be possible to meet.

Hope was just the right man for the job; quiet, modest and unassuming, he claimed to know no German and nothing of cryptography, but William Clarke, who joined Room 40 early in 1916, has stated that 'if one took him a version of a German signal, which one had carefully prepared, he would often say "I don't like that, can it not be . . . ?" and he was practically always right. His appreciation of situations seemed always right and if those at the top had only realised this instead of forming their own opinions, the war at sea might have been better managed. He inspired a devotion in those who worked under him which can seldom have been equalled . . .'

Hope's job was to supply the naval knowledge inevitably lacking in Room 40's civilian volunteers and to be the organisation's first 'intelligence' as opposed to cryptographic officer. He did this work superbly until posted to sea in 1917, where he gained a DSO in the Adriatic. He finally reached the rank of Rear-Admiral. He was, in effect, the real head of Room 40, which, despite all it owed to Ewing and to the brilliance of men like Denniston and later civilian recruits, would never have achieved so much without the leadership of three regular naval officers, Hall, Hope and Rotter.

On 29 November Churchill issued a further instruction: 'The intercepted telegrams should not be copied, one copy only being made for circulation – the record preserved in the secret book. Commander Hope is to study the telegrams with a view to finding out the general scheme of the enemy, and tracing how far reports of the telegrams have in the past been verified as recorded facts, but it is not necessary for him to write views on each telegram as it arrives and not to transcribe large portions of these messages. The telegrams when intercepted will go direct and exclusively to COS who will mark them 1st Sea Lord, [and] Sir A. K. Wilson, it being understood that deliveries are not to be delayed through the temporary absence of any of the addressees.' Once again one can see the emphasis on secrecy, the over-centralisation (no copy apparently for the DID), the restriction of the knowledge to a tiny magic circle. Churchill instinctively realised the inestimable value of these golden eggs and the need to protect the goose that laid them. Equally characteristic is the fact that he himself drafted the instructions for their handling, that he insisted on seeing them all himself and that he was not prepared to leave arrangements to the staff whose duty it should have been to deal with such matters.

So, by the middle of November, Room 40 was a going concern, still understaffed, inexperienced and lacking in the finesse which it later acquired, but, right from the outset, supplying Churchill, Fisher and Oliver with an unprecedented flow of information about the movements of the *Hochseeflotte*.

CHAPTER THREE

Codes and Ciphers

It may be helpful at this stage to say a little about codes and ciphers in general, and German naval ones in particular. Nowadays, the art or science of codes and ciphers, the old 'secret writing' is called cryptology, a term which covers both the construction and the breaking of concealed messages. Cryptography means the construction and cryptanalysis the breaking of codes, while to decipher or decode a message is usually taken to mean the transformation of a disguised message into plain language by the intended recipient, while if the same process is performed by an unauthorised person, he is said to be decrypting a message. If the cryptanalyst can 'unbutton' a message without much delay, i.e. as quickly or nearly as quickly as the authorised recipient, he is said to be 'reading it currently'. In World War I, however, the word cryptanalysis had not been coined, and cryptography, decode or decipher were used to describe both the authorised and unauthorised transformation of concealed messages into plain language.

The expression 'coded message' is often loosely used of communication by either code or cipher, but there is an essential difference for the cryptographer between a code and a cipher. To send a message in Code, an agreed *code-book* is required by both sender and recipient. This is a sort of dictionary in which, in one half, for encoding, words, numbers, dates and sometimes whole phrases (like military or naval commands) are listed in alphabetical order, with the code-group opposite each, like the foreign words in a bilingual dictionary. In the other half (for use in *decoding*) these code equivalents are listed, also in alphabetical order if they consist of groups of letters, in numerical order if it is a numerical code. (Codes are much easier to 'break' if in the 'encode'-half the code-groups are not jumbled in their order, 'hatted' as cryptographers say, i.e. as if taken out of a hat, and not alphabetical, – or in numerical order, if they are groups of numbers.)

To send a message in *cipher*, no elaborate (and possible bulky) tool of this kind is needed. Instead, the message, as expressed in plain language, or in technical terms *en clair*, is enciphered, by either *substitution* or *transposition* (or a combination of both). Substitution is the systematic replacement of one letter of the alphabet by another throughout the message, or of each successive pair of letters ('bigrams') by a different pair, following in each case the *key* held by both sender and recipient. In the British Playfair Cipher the bigram substitution-table can be constructed from a memorised key-word. 'Transposition' means the systematic scrambling of the letters composing the 'clear' in an agreed manner. A very effective system is what the Germans called a 'Chi' (from CHIffre). Substitution or transposition of some kind is often applied, as a further precaution, to the groups of an encoded message, as in the case of the *Verkehrsbuch*. The code message is then said to have been *reciphered*. Probably the safest method of recipherment, applicable only to figure-codes, is to add a continuous string of figures (from a key-pad held by both sender and recipient) to the string of figure-groups in the encoded message. Exactly the same string of figures has then to be subtracted from the groups received at the other end. If a genuinely 'one-time pad' is used such a recipherment is unbreakable. All three German Naval codes, the *Signalbuch der Kaiserlichen Marine* (SKM), recovered from *Magdeburg*, the *Verkehrsbuch* (VB), the Miraculous Draught of Fishes, and the *Handeslverkehrsbuch* (HVB), seized from *Hobart*, were subjected to additional recipherment, the keys to which were changed from time to time.

The SKM (sometimes referred to in German documents as the SB), the most secret of the three codes, was only issued to a few formations, and was principally used during or in connection with major operations. It was a three-letter code; for example the order '*Musterung auf der Gefechtstation*' was represented by the letters 'ODI'. Each plain text meaning could only be represented by one code group, and words not in the book had to be spelt out with a second substitution table after a warning group. The book had a full alphabet plus umlauts and Alpha, Beta, Gamma, Delta and Epsilon, but there was no means of coding the name of a ship except by reference to a number in a list. Ships' call signs were indicated by a group of two letters prefixed by Beta. The book itself was bulky, fifteen inches by twelve inches by six inches, something explained by the fact that it included large sections dealing with Flag, Semaphore and Lamp signalling. In fact it had been originally designed for visual signalling – for speed in emergencies rather than with the needs of security in mind. Moreover, it contained no fewer than 34,304 three-letter groups, many of which were obsolete, such as GÜK, *'Feindlichen Flaggschiff Rammen'* ('Ram Enemy Flagship') while there was no group at all for aeroplane. As Room 40 remarked, it was cumbersome and 'full of various complications which were all of a nature to puzzle the German coder and assist the English decipherer . . . Had the White Knight in Alice Through The Looking Glass carried about a code-book, it would no doubt have been of such a nature.'

The technical difficulty of providing any replacement for a code-book of 34,000 groups was obviously much greater than for a book of only 10,000 or 5,000 groups, which would have given a perfectly adequate vocabulary. Frequent replacement of codes is essential to security in wartime, but the SKM was kept in force until May 1917, two years and ten months after the start of the war! The SKM had further disadvantages. It was a single encode/decode book, and it contained no alternative groups for the same word and no dummy groups, all factors of immense help to Room 40's cryptanalysts. It is true that the SKM was reciphered, a fact in which the Germans obviously placed great faith, but the keys for the reciphering were, for a long time, not changed as frequently as once a month, nor were these keys difficult for Room 40 to solve. The key, or substitution-table, was not made on any arbitrary basis, but, for ease of ordering the periodical changes, was made by reference to an ingenious system of slides. The letters of the alphabet were fitted vertically into certain compartments, the nature of which could be indicated by a series of numbers and were then drawn out horizontally. The order of drawing them out would give the key. No change was made in this method until 1916. Until towards the end of the war, the Germans seem to have had no conception at all of the requirements of signal security. Orders for the change of key were announced by wireless and, due to poor staff work, often came into force before all ships were supplied with or could understand the necessary information. Signals therefore had to be repeated again using the old key or sometimes even another code. This was yet another factor which considerably lightened the load for the night watch in Room 40.

Perhaps even more extraordinary than the intrinsic weaknesses of the SKM itself was the fact that the *Admiralstab* [German Naval Staff] totally ignored responsible suggestions that it might have been compromised by the loss of *Magdeburg*. On the very day of her

destruction, the officer commanding the squadron, Rear-Admiral
Behring, had signalled 'SKM key not certainly known to have been
destroyed', while at the Court Martial proceedings on 17 September
1914 it was expressly stated that the possibility that the signal book
itself, its key and other papers, might have been recovered from the
sea by the Russians could not be completely excluded. It is true that,
immediately after the first suggestion that the key had been compromised, the *Admiralstab* ordered the printing and distribution of
a fresh key, but due to delays and fears about further compromise, it
was not until 20 October that a fresh key effectively came into use,
and another three months were allowed to elapse before this was in
turn replaced. The *Admiralstab* stuck to the opinion they had
expressed only two days after the sinking: 'No fears of dangerous
consequences are entertained here through the possible loss of the
signal book.'

Despite this, some far-sighted officers were unconvinced and, on
19 February 1915, Prince Henry of Prussia, Commander-in-Chief
Baltic, and brother of the Kaiser, wrote to the Commander-in-Chief
Hochseeflotte as follows: 'The very searching legal enquiry into this
matter has shown that at least certain naval charts in use . . . were
lost; it must be assumed with virtual certainty that these charts were
fished up by the Russians who came on the scene immediately
afterwards. It is probable that an SKM Key similarly fell into the
hands of the Russians; finally the possibility must be envisaged that
the Russians recovered one of the signal books from the clear and
not deep water by diving. The War Diary was probably captured by
the Russians . . .'

However, the suggestion that a thorough revision of the reciphering system should be put in hand was rejected, and throughout 1915
changes in the Keys continued to be made at long intervals, for
example, only six times between the beginning of March and the
end of the year. Prince Henry continued to press for the production
of a new code but this was rejected not only by the *Admiralstab* but
by the *Hochseeflotte* as well.

In 1916 Key changes were at last speeded up and dummy groups
issued for the first time, although these were most foolishly inserted
at fixed intervals in the sequence of the book, a procedure which
persisted until 1918. Ironically, when, in the summer of 1916, the
Admiralstab did produce an entirely new book the Fleet refused to
use it as it was too cumbersome and complicated. It was not until
May 1917 that the SKM code was finally replaced by a completely

new three-letter code, the *Flottenfunkspruchbuch* (FFB). Although this certainly caused Room 40 a good deal of difficulty, and the almost current reading previously possible was often succeeded by considerable delays in breaking keys, the book itself was gradually reconstructed. The initial break-in was achieved by a careful study of Baltic traffic; the Germans had not, as they could and should have done, produced two books, one for the Baltic and one for the North Sea, although they did for the first time issue separate encoding and decoding books. Room 40 subsequently remarked: 'Even after four years of war, the German Admiralty got no further than to devise a key which could be solved in three or four days but was kept in force for ten days and allowed books to remain in force for a year which could effectually be compromised in two months and, in fact, were generally readable within the period.'

After the war the German Navy gradually came to realise the crucial importance of the loss of *Magdeburg*'s signal book. In 1934 Korvettenkapitän Kleikamp concluded a secret paper on 'The Influence of Wireless Intelligence on Operations in the North Sea 1914–1918' (which incidentally demonstrated that, as so often, the only people permanently kept in ignorance of British Intelligence achievements were the British public), with these words: 'The loss of signal books in war is always a possibility to be reckoned with. But it [the loss of *Magdeburg*'s book] proved so completely disastrous for us because, due to lack of preparations for war, no effective action was taken after the loss of the signal books, in spite of the high probability of their capture by the enemy.'

The HVB (*Handelsverkehrsbuch*) was originally intended for communication between warships and merchantships. It was first issued in 1913 to all warships fitted with W/T, to various naval commands and coastal stations, and to the head offices of the eighteen principal German steamship companies, who in turn issued copies to all their vessels fitted with W/T and, in some cases, to their more important overseas offices. If messages were to be transmitted by W/T, four-letter groups were employed – for example, 'König' would be represented by the group 'SCZR'. There were, however, alternative ten-letter groups for use in cables (possibly to comply with cable company regulations) – in such event 'König' became 'MUKOPEMARI'. In some ways it was a better code than the SKM, because there were groups for proper and ships' names, and adequate alternative groups for the same meaning. It contained no fewer than 456,976 potential groups, although by no means all of

them were used. It also had an appendix containing silhouettes of all
the principal German and foreign warships. Not surprisingly, it was
almost as bulky as the SKM – thirteen inches by nine inches by one
and a half inches. In its reciphered form it was used by all units of the
Imperial Navy, almost exclusively so by all small craft such as patrol
boats and mine-sweepers and for the ordering of coastal lights to be
switched on or off, and for net barriers and other anti-submarine
defences to be opened and closed. Its keying was simple although
changed at intervals. Room 40 derived an immense amount of
valuable information from the routine messages constantly made by
and to the humblest vessels in the German Navy in the Baltic and
the Heligoland Bight.

But, the HVB was also used by U-boats and Zeppelins, both of
which were of course constantly engaged on operations in which
capture and compromise of codes were sooner or later inevitable. In
the case of U-boats, reliance was placed on using different and more
complicated reciphering processes. Their keys, however, necessarily had to remain in force for considerable periods and frequently a
change in cipher would not coincide with a change in key. This
meant that the old key had to be used for U-boats already at sea,
with the result that the new cipher could immediately be broken by
Room 40. Moreover, the complications caused to the Germans by
these keys led to mistakes in their distribution, and frequently
messages had to be repeated in another key, a further source of
compromise. When a new method of keying was finally introduced
with the AFB, very nearly enough material was sent in practice
signals to compromise the key before it was actually used to cipher
serious signals. What is even more astounding is that, if the Germans, or some of them, suspected that the SKM *might* have been
compromised, they *positively* knew, as early as November 1914,
that the HVB code had been! On 25 November a wireless message
to the Governor of German South West Africa informed him that
'Imperial Colonial Office cipher is in hands of enemy, likewise HVB
and key', while between 22 and 27 November repeated signals were
sent to the cruiser *Karlsrühe*, at that time in the South Atlantic,
which included the information that the HVB code was compromised although, in this case, it was suggested that the secret key might
not have been. The entire failure to replace this very widely used
code until 1916, is totally inexplicable.

The replacement for the HVB was the *Allgemeinefunkspruchbuch* (AFB), which was issued in the early part of 1916. It was issued

to an even larger number of shore authorities including organisations throughout the Middle East, in Turkey, Bulgaria and Russia,
as well as to small craft, Zeppelins and U-boats. It was a two-letter
code, for example, 'UP' represented 'Shore batteries'. It was again
an encode/decode book and was even larger than its predecessor.
The first copy to be captured was from a Zeppelin, within months of
the code being brought into service, but numerous other copies
were thereafter recovered from sunken U-boats. In general it
presented Room 40 with no more difficulty than had the HVB.

In some ways the *Verkehrsbuch* code (VB) was the best of the
three original codes. It was a five-numeral code, for example,
'Embargo' would be represented by the figures 38256. It was
intended principally for communication by cable with warships
overseas, and with Naval Attachés and some Embassies, Consulates and agents abroad. It was used at sea, with special recipherment, as a Flag Officer's code, and it is by no means clear why the
destroyer sunk on 17 October, from whose jettisoned chest it
reached Room 40, was carrying it. If used by senior officers it was
reciphered with key Lambda, and some of Scheer's messages during
the Battle of Jutland may have been transmitted by this variation of
the VB code. It contained 100,000 groups. In 1917 it was replaced –
but only for Flag Officers' use – by a code known to Room 40 by its
key as Nordo, but although only seventy messages were made in this
code it was duly broken by Room 40. For other uses, the VB code
remained in use throughout the war. Room 40, commenting on the
VB, says that it was rarely 'used for fleet work, so that the Germans
were deprived of the use of additional or subtractional keys, which if
properly varied and concealed, would have been easy to manage
and hard to break.'

Professor W. H. Bruford, who joined Room 40 in 1917 and
worked on the messages in the VB code between Berlin and the
Naval Attaché in Madrid, and is now probably the last surviving
member of the Room 40 staff, writes as follows:

> The code was elaborately reciphered by an ingenious system of
> transposition which the Germans called a 'Chi', (from Chiffre or
> Cypher). The effect was to redistribute all the figures of the
> encodement in what seemed a completely random order . . . The
> key was different for each message, but it was made up each time
> quite simply by a pre-arranged procedure from three short ele-
> ments. One of these was the five letter word in the ABC Commer-

cial Telegraph Code that followed (in that code) the same figure
as the serial number of the message being transmitted. For
example, Message No. 568 – MAPOL or whatever it might be in
the ABC. The other two elements were something like the date
and month (in German), e.g. vierzehn Mai. The three elements
(say MAPOL/vierzehn/Mai) written one after another gave a
series of letters (the total number of them varying from message
to message between about ten and twenty) which was turned into
a series of numbers by writing '1' under the first letter of the
alphabet which occurred in the series of letters, then '2' under the
next and so on. This series of jumbled figures, e.g. 9, 1, 13, 12, 8,
15, 6, 3, 14, 16, 4, 5, 11, 10, 2, 7, was copied out on squared paper,
and under it a space was marked out containing exactly as many
squares as there were figures in the encoded message. These
figures, the code-book groups obtained from the VB, were copied
horizontally into the diagram, beginning at the top left and
continuing from line to line until all the squares were occupied.
The final reciphered text was read off vertically beginning at the
top of the column marked '1' in the key, continuing with column
'2' and so on. This text was divided into five-figure groups for
transmission. To decipher, the process was reversed . . . This was
a good reliable system if properly used, and suited the Germans
better than a 'subtractor' key system because there was no safe
way of transmitting the long key-tables it would have required
from Berlin to Madrid. When in 1918 the key system was
changed, (they were using the same three elements to make up
the key, but in a different order), I managed after several days to
find out the nature of the change, but only because we received
two messages of exactly the same length from Madrid, one of
which we could read, because it was on the old system, and one
we could not, and assumed, correctly as it turned out, to be on the
new system. This was of course a stupid mistake of a cipher clerk.

The great value of the VB to the British was almost certainly the
ability it gave them to read the Naval Attaché traffic between
Berlin, Madrid, Washington, Buenos Aires and Peking, and between the German Admiralty and Constantinople. Although the
best-constructed code of the three, it was no more proof against the
skill of Room 40 than were the SKM or the HVB.

Room 40's postwar verdict on German code-making was that it
was 'bad, lacking in the first essentials of secrecy, brevity and speed

of replacement. Their ciphering methods were laborious and difficult . . . Their efforts were at first careless and bad; latterly they were good but in the wrong direction. They never aimed consistently at the goal of frequent changes of difficult books with ciphers which should have been easy to manage or none at all. Only by very frequent changes of key can real success in cryptography be obtained.'

Kleikamp commented in 1934 that the fact 'that it took three years to recognise and deal with the dangers of wireless traffic shows a remarkable failure on the part of our operational leadership and organisation. Only careful preparation in peacetime, in particular through the instruction of the higher staff by specialists with many years' experience, will avoid similar mistakes in the future.' His words of wisdom seem to have fallen largely on stony ground, for the Germans repeated many of their World War I errors in World War II.

The Room 40 appreciation does, however, go on to point out that 'no state had sufficiently allowed for what might happen in time of war', and remarked that not only was the British Merchant Navy Code extremely simple (the Germans seem to have broken or captured its first edition very early in the war) but 'the British Fleet itself used codes and ciphers of ridiculous simplicity, more fitted for the playthings of schoolboys than for the dissemination of orders during important operations.' They paid tribute to the successes of their German opposite numbers (of whom more later), and instanced in particular the successes of the German U-boats in the Mediterranean which, they claim, were due in no small measure to accurate knowledge of Allied shipping movements. That the British were almost as unprepared for the wireless war as the Germans is shown by the fact that when, in October 1914, Winston Churchill hurriedly despatched a force of Marines in a futile attempt to bolster up the Belgian defence of Antwerp, their commander, General Paris, was sent off with no codes or ciphers at all! On 7 October, the Admiralty's War Registry received the following note from Eddie Marsh, Winston's Private Secretary: 'Please send this *en clair*. First Lord to General Paris, Antwerp. Endeavour obtain cipher from British Minister Ostend. If unsuccessful use Playfair's code following War Office practice as to key word.'[1] Paris replied next day that

---

[1] Churchill was in fact confusing code and cipher. The Playfair *cipher* was an ingenious and well-known system devised by an Englishman, Charles Wheatstone in 1854, and eventually used by the British Army.

he could not obtain a cipher, but it is not clear whether this and subsequent signals in which Paris reported he was having to withdraw his lines because of the destruction of some of the Belgian forts (for which he was very sharply and characteristically castigated by the 1st Lord), were made as directed in Playfair's cipher or *en clair*. Improvements in British codes were made slowly. Room 40 state that they were not really satisfactory until 1917, a curious foretaste of the situation in World War II when both British and German ciphers were again compromised. On the latter occasion also, the error was recognised and eventually put right by the British but never by the Germans.

It is by no means clear in the following passage from the Room 40 appreciation already quoted, whether the authors intended to refer to British or German practice when they remarked, 'History, that has few tears to shed, may be permitted one broad smile at the spectacle of an Admiral and an Admiralty elaborately hiding from subordinates facts and intentions which, at least for three quarters of the war, they failed to conceal from the enemy.' History has probably continued to smile for sixty-seven years at the successful efforts of the British authorities to conceal the facts from the British public.

Apart from the intrinsic weaknesses of their codes, the Germans contributed to their insecurity by excessive and quite unnecessary use of wireless. They fell into this trap partly because of the very excellence of their transmitters, which were not only better than those of the British but better than the Germans themselves realised. The range of their main high power transmitters was, for those days, amazing. Nauen, operating on 800 metres, could reach the Mediterranean, the Adriatic, America, South-West Africa and even China. Their U-boats, on 400 metres, soon found they could receive and transmit signals over several hundreds of miles, rather than, as had been supposed before the war and was the case for a long time with British submarines, merely within a maximum range of fifty or sixty miles. This encouraged the U-boats of the *Hochseeflotte* and the U-boat Command to be unduly garrulous, although this did not apply to the smaller Flanders boats operating in the Channel.

Kleikamp, in his appreciation referred to earlier, comments on the very successful operational use made by Admiral Scheer of low power wireless at Jutland – orders were quickly and clearly transmitted and as quickly received and executed. Room 40, however, noted that German reception of their own signals was not always good, and because of the need for repetition they were often decoded by the British sooner than by their German recipients. Certainly the German Navy in all arms of the Service made far greater use of wireless than did the Royal Navy, which preferred whenever possible to give orders by visual signals, either flag, lamp or searchlight, a system which gave the German cryptanalysts fewer opportunities, but which 'signally' failed in the heat and confusion of actual battle. On the other hand, the German reliance on wireless was carried to excess in their practice of issuing routine orders to patrol craft, minesweepers, light vessels, boom ships and so on. These were, it is true, sent on low power which the Germans did not believe could be intercepted by the distant British land stations. They were much mistaken, and Room 40 thereby acquired a detailed knowledge of all German movements not only in the Bight but also in the Western Baltic, and were often able to detect impending sorties of the *Hochseeflotte* from such trivial and routine messages. By the end of the war, signals on 200 metres between German ships in port were being easily picked up. Room 40's comments are once again to the point; 'Efficient staff work would have obviated the necessity for using what the Germans well knew to be a dangerous method of communication. However, the staff work was bad, those responsible for it lived in depot ships out of visual range of most of the units of the Fleet, and the volume of wireless traffic was enormous.'

British interception of enemy wireless traffic developed very rapidly from August 1914, although there had been virtually no organisation in existence for this purpose previously. It was not an easy task and, to start with, many intercepts were missed or incomplete or garbled, and even later on it was often necessary for several intercepts of the same signal to be obtained in order to secure a complete and correct version. Nevertheless, by 1916 the great majority, and by 1917 all, of the messages from the Bight were being successfully intercepted. However, the ratio for the Baltic was not nearly so high, while, for various reasons, little was at first achieved by the British from the Mediterranean (although the French were successful there). It was estimated after the war that, after making due allowance for duplicates, useless fragments and so forth, something like 20,000 German signals reached Room 40 in those four and a quarter years, and the majority of them were decrypted. It was an astonishing feat.

The Germans too had their successes in decoding, but on nothing like the British scale. Their first decode of British naval signals was, in fact, achieved by a Bavarian Army cryptographic post at Roubaix on the Franco-Belgian frontier sometime late in 1914. Having time on their hands, the soldiers amused themselves with intercepting and decoding messages originated by the Dover Command. Apparently as a result of this rather fortuitous event, the German Navy set up its own *Entzifferungsdienst*, (E. Dienst) or Decrypting Service, at Neumünster, halfway between Kiel and Hamburg. This, as Kleikamp points out, was a mistake. It was too far from any operational command and should have been located either with the *Admiralstab* in Berlin or with the *Hochseeflotte* Command at Wilhelmshaven. Nor, for a long time, was its potential importance recognised by the operational authorities. At first, the department seems to have been manned largely by naval signal ratings, but eventually a number of academics were posted to it. Kleikamp claims that the most these men could achieve was analysis, because they entirely lacked operational experience, a handicap which, incidentally, did not for long prevent the academics of Room 40 from proving their worth! It does seem to be a fact that Neumünster took some time to develop the art of code-breaking, but the E. Dienst did nevertheless grow, with a separate organisation centred on Libau for the Baltic, and another for the Mediterranean in the Austrian Adriatic port of Pola. In the West, Neumünster's most important substation was at Bruges, which continued to maintain close liaison with the Army post at Roubaix.

Kleikamp, however, considered that the E. Dienst was slow and generally unsuccessful and instances the case of a signal from the British submarine E 23, reporting that she had torpedoed the battleship *Westfalen* during the sortie of the German Fleet on 18–19 August 1916. Bruges intercepted and decoded this signal promptly, but it took five hours before the decode reached Neumünster (and presumably longer still before it was received by Admiral Scheer at sea).

The E. Dienst did achieve successes in penetrating Royal Navy codes, for example during the Battle of Jutland, but partly because they were not technically as proficient as their British counterparts and partly because of the British insistence on maintaining wireless silence at sea to the maximum possible extent, these successes were, on the whole, meagre. In consequence, and because also of Neumünster's remote location, the German Service tended, for far too long, to be neglected by the *Admiralstab* and the *Hochseeflotte* Command. It suffered from a further disadvantage, probably because of its isolation; its decodes were transmitted by wireless without any attempt at disguising their source. Room 40 commented that although Neumünster achieved some successes,

> The very serious error was made . . . of using and publishing freely to the [German] Fleet the results of Neumünster's researches. Thus the English and Russian authorities could often be aware of the failures of their efforts to secure secrecy by code. The climax was reached in 1917 when decipherings of the English code were sent unciphered alongside the equivalent group in the German code-book, which had only lately come into force [presumably the FFB]. Not only was it evident to the English authorities that great progress had been made in the decipherment of one of their codes, but also the sense of certain meanings of the German code-groups could be ascertained on this side merely by looking them up in the English code-book!

It is however fair to point out that the E. Dienst did study some of the weaknesses of the German coding system, and had some influence on the belated efforts made by the *Admiralstab* to rectify them. For example, on 19 March 1918, Neumünster, no doubt to the wry amusement of Room 40, instructed all ships to use more dummy groups than hitherto, to send as few routine signals as possible, to tune carefully on to the correct wave length and to send on as low power and as seldom as possible.

On neither the British nor the German side was there adequate liaison between the code-makers and the code-breakers, but as has been said of war in general, victory comes to the side that makes the fewest mistakes, and the Germans made many more in the Wireless War than did the British.

CHAPTER FOUR

A Clear Case of Genius

We must now return to Room 40 in October 1914, and start by introducing that extraordinary character Captain William Reginald Hall – Reggie to his many friends, 'Blinker' to the rest of the Navy. The nickname came from his habit of constantly blinking his eyes, something his daughter ascribes, together with a chronically weak chest, to the appalling food at his preparatory school, where the boys had to creep out at night to get turnips from the fields to fill their little bellies.

Blinker Hall was born in 1870, the eldest son of Captain William Henry Hall RN, the first Director of the Intelligence Division, who died in 1895 as he arrived to take up the post of Superintendent of Pembroke Dockyard. Reggie joined his father's Service in 1884. He specialised in gunnery and was promoted Commander in 1901 and Captain only four yours afterwards, having earned himself an enviable reputation as a strict but very enlightened disciplinarian. Fisher in his first term at 1st Sea Lord, picked him to be Inspecting Captain of the new Mechanical Training Establishments, where he again enhanced his reputation. In 1908 he was appointed Captain of the cadet training cruiser, *Cornwall*. During a visit to Kiel he had his first experience of covert Intelligence work. The Admiralty were particularly anxious to discover how many building slips the Germans had, but access to them was naturally impossible for foreigners. Hall managed to borrow a very fast motor launch from the Duke of Westminster, who was also visiting Kiel in his large steam yacht. Disguised as a yachtsman, he roared up and down Kiel Fjord until he contrived a convincing breakdown just off the building slips. While 'repairs' were being effected, two of his officers, concealed in the cabin, took photographs which revealed all that the Admiralty wished to know. A small episode, but one which Hall loved to recount, and which shows his natural aptitude and enthusiasm for 'cloak and dagger' work.

Hall was next appointed to the armoured cruiser *Natal*. She was already about the best gunnery ship in the Navy at the time when enormous strides were being made in the science, but Hall managed to improve on *Natal's* previous record. He again showed himself a marvellous 'man manager', although a strict one, and demonstrated that he was also a splendid seaman by his rescue of the sailing ship *Celtic Rose* in a gale so severe that even the lifeboats could not put to sea. For this he received a presentation of a silver centre-piece from the owners and underwriters.

After a short spell as Assistant to the Controller at the Admiralty, Hall was given the command of the brand new battle cruiser *Queen Mary*. Once again he raised his ship to the very highest level of efficiency and at the same time introduced a number of far-reaching and far-sighted reforms, such as the three watch system, the abolition of the Ship's Police, the first cinema in a man o'war, the first book stall, and also the first chapel. He also refitted the petty officers' mess to enhance their prestige, and improved out of recognition the stokers' washing arrangements. His second in command, and later biographer, Admiral Sir William James,[1] has testified that in that élite force, the Battle Cruiser Squadron of the Grand Fleet, 'the ship's company's response was immediate, and there has seldom been such a loyal, hard-working, and happy ship's company as that manning the *Queen Mary*.' She was also, incidentally, the best gunnery ship in the Squadron. It was therefore not surprising that his friend and commanding Admiral, the dashing Sir David Beatty, was very upset when, after only two months of war, Hall's health broke down and he had to ask to be relieved of his command.

Hall's career up to this point had been a successful if fairly straightforward and conventional one. He had shown himself to be a first class sea officer; like Nelson, a strict but humane and forward looking disciplinarian, concerned with the welfare of his men and capable of inspiring their loyalty and affection; no respecter of out-of-date traditions which hindered rather than helped efficiency; dedicated to the Navy and to the service of his country, but, like most of his fellow officers with few obvious contacts or interests outside his own profession. Had his health not given way he might have gone to the top, although it is far more probable that he would

---

[1] Known throughout the Navy as 'Bubbles' because, as a child, his portrait had been painted by his grandfather, Sir John Millais, blowing soap bubbles. The picture was subsequently purchased by the Pears Soap Company and widely used in their advertisements.

have gone down with his ship and over 1200 of her complement at Jutland, in which case no one now would know his name. Even as it was, he seemed destined, in October 1914, either for retirement or some obscure post ashore. But fate decreed otherwise. On 14 October Oliver became Naval Assistant to the 1st Lord and next month Chief of the War Staff, and Hall was chosen to replace him as Director of the Intelligence Division (DID). According to Oliver, Mrs Hall wrote to him when he became Churchill's Naval Assistant because she was so concerned about her husband's health; as a result Oliver persuaded Winston and Prince Louis of Battenberg, still 1st Sea Lord at that time, to appoint Hall to Oliver's vacant post. However the decision was made, it was an inspired one, demonstrating as did the appointment in 1939 of Hall's World War II successor, John Godfrey, that the Royal Navy can, on occasions, place very round pegs in vital round holes.

In attempting to describe Hall, it is difficult to avoid the use of hyperbole and overworked expressions such as 'charisma', but he was indeed a man whom even the most unobservant person could not ignore. I met him only once, when, about 1936, I was invited by his daughter Faith to a dinner party at his house in the New Forest before a local hunt hall. It was not the sort of occasion when young men pay a great deal of attention to their 'aged' hosts, but Admiral Sir Reginald Hall made an impression on me that evening which I can truthfully say I have never forgotten. He did not conform to my rather stereotyped ideas of a retired British admiral. Small (like Nelson, it is true), the top of his imposing head was bald but, over his ears and at the back, his white hair was unfashionably long (Faith said that the only way to get him to the barber was to tell him he was beginning to look like Lloyd George!). He wore a ruffled shirt, a blue, as opposed to the conventional black, dinner jacket with white silk facings and gold buckled evening shoes. Not very extraordinary nowadays, but highly unusual in those conformist times. But it was his face and eyes that caught one's attention. A majestic nose over a rather tight-lipped mouth and a firm, cleft chin made one feel instinctively that this was not a man with whom one could take liberties. He looked rather like a peregrine falcon, an impression which was reinforced by his penetrating eyes, darting round the assembled company. He had a short incisive way of talking. Over the port, that night in 1936, I made some rather trite remark to the effect that no one wanted another war. The Admiral pounced. 'War, my boy? Of course we want another war! We didn't finish off the last one properly. We shall have to teach that fellow Hitler a lesson. You young men had better get used to the idea!' I thought, at the time, that this sounded rather like Low's celebrated cartoon character, Colonel Blimp, but he was right, of course (as so often was Blimp), and curiously, his remarks were not made in such a way as to make me feel small but rather that I had made a useful and intelligent contribution to the conversation. I do not remember the rest of the evening, but I never forgot my formidable but charming host.

A young man's recollections of a single meeting with a retired admiral are not of course of any great significance, but Blinker Hall, as Director of Intelligence from 1914 to 1918, made an equally striking impression on many more mature and better informed contemporary observers. The United States Ambassador, Dr Walter Hines Page, admittedly a rather besotted Anglophile in the opinion of some Americans, including his friend President Wilson, wrote to the latter in 1918, 'Hall is one genius that the war has developed. Neither in fiction nor in fact can you find any such man to match him . . . The man is a genius – a clear case of genius. All other secret service men are amateurs by comparison . . . I shall never meet another man like him; that were too much to expect . . . For Hall can look through you and see the very muscular movements of your immortal soul while he is talking to you. Such eyes as the man has! My Lord! I do study these men here most diligently who have this vast and appalling War Job. There are uncommon creatures among them – men about whom our great-grandchildren will read in school histories; but of them all, the most extraordinary is this naval officer – of whom, probably they'll never hear . . .' His biographer, James, also considered him 'a genius, and his genius was given full play because he had a quite remarkable gift for drawing everything that was best from his fellow men. This gift, which made him one of the outstanding sea-captains of his time, was even more conspicuous when he found himself in a world which was quite strange to a man who had so far spent his life at sea.'

Hall was to arouse the admiration and indeed the devotion of the staff of the Intelligence Division, but he had a very ruthless side to his nature and could on occasions be frighteningly angry. His sense of humour was sometimes sardonic, not to say cruel. When a German spy, in whose arrest he had played a part, was given a very light sentence by Mr Justice Bray, on the grounds that he was only passing back to Germany the location of British factories, which the learned judge considered to be 'targets of no military importance', Hall was furious and took care to send back a report to Germany, in the spy's name, which gave the position of the judge's country house as the site of another factory. Not long afterwards Hall found himself seated at dinner next to Mr Justice Bray, who was bemoaning the fact that his house had been subjected to a rain of bombs from marauding Zeppelins, and that he had narrowly escaped with his life! Hall's delighted rejoinder was, 'Well, it was not a target of any military importance, was it?' The story may well be apocryphal, but it is revealing that it was one which Hall himself was fond of telling.

His very attractive wartime secretary, Ruth Skrine, gave this pen-portrait to James:

He seemed to have all the qualities for the head of such a Department [The Intelligence Division]. He was uncannily quick at sizing up a man – of almost seeing into his mind, and I am sure – unknowingly often – he exercised a sort of hypnotism on some of the unfortunate victims who fell into his hands. Jimmy Bone, the London Editor of the *Manchester Guardian*, once said to me: 'Your great little Chief is half Machiavelli and half school-boy', and this was true; the Machiavelli in him could be cruel, and the 'means' he used often 'justified the ends' in many a battle he fought in the murky world of Intelligence. But the school-boy was always round the corner, and his love of the dangerous game he, and all of us, were playing would bubble out, and the fun and hazard of it all would fill him with infectious delight. 'Adventures are for the adventurous,' he would chant, rubbing his hands and grinning like a crafty little French Abbé. He was a gambler. One of his favourite sayings was: 'Mistakes may be forgiven, but even God himself cannot forgive the hanger-back.' We all followed with a blind devotion the risks he took, because we were sure he would win.

Hall was certainly a marvellous choice to head a department which had not yet properly found its feet, but which was destined to play such a vital role in the Navy's and the nation's affairs in the next four years. Unconventional, an innovator, ambitious for success, less for himself than for his service and his country, willing, indeed anxious, to assume any amount of responsibility, he was prepared to use any methods which seemed likely to achieve his objectives. Despite the poor health which had compelled him to give up command afloat, his energy, incisiveness and imagination were equalled only by those of Churchill and Fisher, and were in striking contrast to the rather lack-lustre qualities of some of the rest of the senior officers at the Admiralty. Perhaps the most remarkable thing of all was the way in which he instinctively and immediately threw himself into 'The Great Game', using all the weapons of deception, disinformation, double-agents, bribery, blackmail and general skullduggery which we now associate with Intelligence but which, over half a century ago, were quite foreign to the experience of the generally conventional officer corps of the Royal Navy. It must, therefore, have been frustrating for him to find, on taking up his new appointment, that he was not his own master, that his immediate superior was his predecessor in office who would deny him, for more than two years, full control over the most fruitful source of factual information about the enemy that any Intelligence chief could possibly desire. It is typical of the man that he never lost his enthusiasm, his burning energy or his sense of purpose, and that he succeeded in imbuing all his staff with a similar sense of mission.

*

Room 40 had not got off to a good start. Undermanned, with no previous experience of code-breaking, and, with the exception of Hope and Rotter, totally ignorant of naval procedure and parlance, mistakes were inevitable. Denniston gives two examples of rather trivial errors in the very early days which unfortunately aroused the distrust and contempt of hidebound officers such as Jackson, and even Oliver, who should have shown more understanding. 'Owing to poor interception and lack of knowledge on the part of the staff, a signal was circulated alleging that the [German] light cruiser *Ariadne* was proceeding to the Jade. The Operations Division knew that *Ariadne* had been sunk in the Battle of the Heligoland Bight [on 28 August]. Further, any signal which could be read was circulated without comment [this was before the arrival of Commander Hope] . . . the Operations Division cannot be blamed for their lack of enthusiasm for the times at which the Kiel barrier was opened . . .' The German signals were impeccably translated but not, unfortunately, into navalese and even the 1st Sea Lord, Fisher, pointed out that ships do not 'run' they 'proceed'. William Clarke gives the following example of the sort of message which caused the lips of regular executive officers to curl: 'The 2nd Battle Squadron will run out at 2 p.m. and return to harbour athwartwise at 4 p.m.'

Things began to improve in this respect as soon as Hope was installed in Room 40. He constituted himself a censor of messages, of which an increasing number were now being intercepted and decoded each day, and decided which should be circulated and which logged but not circulated. It is of course a common mistake to suppose that almost any decode of an enemy signal will, on its own, provide valuable information. In fact, in both World Wars, the great majority of decodes were of messages of a routine and humdrum nature, meaningless in themselves, but, when carefully collated and compared, capable of revealing matters of far greater significance than their own individual content. It was typical of Churchill's flair that he had at once realised this fact, and demanded the appointment of an officer to devote himself solely to this duty.

Hope says that

the first task I set myself was to make out the organisation of the [German] Fleet; in this we were very much helped by a thorough and extensive W/T exercise which the Germans used to carry out every night; this chiefly consisted in each squadron and unit being called up in succession, the individual ships having to answer by their call signs. I was soon able to obtain their complete organisation . . . The next thing to be tackled was the channels of egress and ingress from and to the three river mouths of the Jade, Weser and Elbe. The Germans had divided up the North Sea into a number of little squares, about six by six miles, each of which was numbered. Whenever any of their vessels was at sea, she was continually signalling her position by saying what square she was in. By plotting all these positions on a chart, we were soon able to establish clearly defined channels, and furthermore, it was soon seen that there were large numbers of squares in which no ship ever reported herself and which remained conspicuously blank on the chart; it was only reasonable to suppose that these blank spaces were mined areas. As soon as sufficient information was obtained, a chart was made out and circulated . . . the Germans were exceedingly methodical in their methods and a large number of routine signals were made day after day which were of great assistance in solving a new 'key' to the code when it was shifted. One day in December a new type of message appeared about certain orders to the lightships [off the islands and the mouths of the rivers, which were not normally lit]. This was followed immediately by the Scarborough raid. When subsequently in

January similar messages again appeared we were able to warn DOD [Director of Operations] that probably some operation was in progress and this proved to be the case – the Dogger Bank. On all subsequent occasions it was found that messages which were not according to routine, were to be looked on with the greatest suspicion, and in this way we were able to build up a large number of signs and portents and were able always to warn the Staff when anything out of the ordinary was on the tapis . . . In a very few months we obtained a very good working knowledge of the organisation, operations, and internal economy of the German Fleet. Had we been called upon by the Staff to do so, we could have furnished valuable information as to the movements of submarines, minefields, mine-sweeping etc. But the Staff was obsessed by the idea of secrecy; they realised that they held the trump card and they worked on the principle that every effort must be made to keep our knowledge up our sleeves for a really great occasion such as the German Fleet coming out in all their strength to throw down the gage of battle. In other words the Staff determined to make use of our information *defensively* and not *offensively* [Hope's italics].

These criticisms by Hope, a most sober and modest man, are very significant; they represent the view held by all in Room 40 that it was not until the last year of the war that the best operational use was made of the purely naval decodes. It must nevertheless also be pointed out that the problem was entirely new, and when one comes to examine the amount of information based on decodes which Oliver (for he alone drafted almost every signal in his own hand) did send out – sometimes 'straight', as to Jellicoe, and one or two other senior officers, but also in bowdlerised form to many more – one is staggered by the volume of information that one man was in fact able to assimilate and disseminate. That it might have been done better, that mistakes might have been avoided, that Room 40 could have provided even better information if they had been permitted access to other sources and to knowledge of British plans and movements (as was the case in the Operational Intelligence Centre in World War II), cannot be denied. Centralisation and secrecy were carried far too far, but the results were nonetheless of the greatest importance.

Hope was not the only one to have doubts about the system of dissemination of information derived from decodes. On 9 November Admiral Jellicoe had sent the following signal to the 1st Sea Lord; 'Captain Kedroff [sic] Russian Navy had acquired me [sic] a list of documents regarding German Navy he brought for me from Russia. They include their signal books cipher position squares etc. May I be furnished with originals or copies immediately. The information I may intercept would be of extreme value if we can decipher it at once and will probably lose all value if we have to wait until Admiralty decipher and send it to me. This matter seems of most urgent importance to me.' Despite the urgency of his request Jellicoe received no reply, and on 9 December he sent a reminder. This too brought no response, so ten days later he renewed his request: '. . . Strongly urge that signal books, ciphers brought for me from Russia may be sent to me by special messenger. Time saved by receiving and deciphering on board instead of awaiting news from Admiralty would be of incalculable value – it is of vital importance that delay caused by deciphering at Admiralty and transmitting should be avoided. There are always strong probabilities of messages not reaching me in time for complete action.' Winston minuted on his copy of this signal, marking it to Fisher and then to Oliver, 'Surely he ought not to talk about this in this open way. How was this telegram sent – in what cipher? Who has seen it? Please report. It looks most reckless.' Oliver replied to the 1st Lord's enquiry by assuring him that Jellicoe's signal had been sent in the C-in-C's own code, and although it had been decoded in the War Registry and had received only a very limited circulation he had removed the original. He agreed that Jellicoe should not have telegraphed in this manner, adding, 'It does not augur well for the secrecy which will obtain when he gets the books.' These last words seem to have been decisive, because although Winston replied to Jellicoe, 'I agree with your view and steps are being taken to meet it, but it was very dangerous to telegraph so explicitly on such a subject. We should have understood by reference to your preceding telegrams', Herschell was in fact given a commission as a Lieutenant Commander in the RNVR (Royal Naval Volunteer Reserve) with the intention of sending him to the flagship to handle decoding, but the plan was never put into effect. Herschell remained in the Admiralty, and Jellicoe had to be content with the information which Oliver personally sent him, supplemented from time to time by special messages from the 1st Lord and 1st Sea Lord.

The final decision was undoubtedly correct, although whether it was taken for the right or the wrong reasons is open to question.

Jellicoe obviously did not realise the tremendous volume of decodes that Room 40 soon began to handle, the number of intercepting stations required, nor the fact that a large and experienced staff would be needed to break changes in keys and fresh codes, and to analyse and make sense of the results. Where he was right was in his instinctive fear that the Admiralty would not in the event supply him swiftly with all the information that came into its possession. Had he had his own cryptanalysts on board during the Battle of Jutland, it is just possible that the dreadful Intelligence failures which then occurred might have been avoided. Centralised Intelligence is both necessary and desirable, but only if it ensures that all information does always reach those who are in a position to act on it fully and without delay.

As Room 40 rapidly mastered the SKM and HVB codes, and as the number of intercepts grew thanks to the setting up of more Y stations by Russell Clarke and Hippisley, the need for an increase in staff numbers became very apparent. It was not eased by the fact that Hall commandeered Herschell to translate the documents – said to be of great interest – recovered with the VB code in the Miraculous Draught of Fishes. Hall thought so highly of Herschell that he did not return him to Room 40 when the work was finished but retained him as the first of his two Personal Assistants, the other being Claud Serocold, a most successful stockbroker, of whom more later. Whether Hall or Ewing was responsible for the new recruits to take Herschell's place and permit, in addition, the institution of a two man watch, is not clear. These recruits included Lord Monk Bretton, a former private secretary to Joseph Chamberlain, H. A. Morrah, a southern Irishman and former President of the Oxford Union, W. H. Anstie, another Dartmouth schoolmaster, H. W. Lawrence, an expert on furniture and art, and Commander Fremantle, scion of a famous naval family; a pretty mixed bunch, most probably found by means of that much derided system, the 'old boy network', which has, with certain fearful exceptions, served Britain so well in two world wars. 'None of these men,' wrote Denniston, 'had more qualifications than the original men.

They knew ordinary literary German fluently and they could be relied on. But of cryptography, of naval German, of the habits of war vessels of any nationality they knew not a jot. Their training was of the shortest before they were told off into watches of two men each and given the responsibility of looking after the Ger-

man Fleet. Worse than that, they had to learn the intricacies of
the office routine. They probably had more than their fair share of
log writing, they had to sort and circulate. They had to turn the
German squared chart into latitude and longitude of which they
had not heard since the geography class of their school days . . .
There was no traditional routine to be followed. New methods
had to be evolved to meet new problems . . . Hope and Rotter
were present daily from 9 a.m. till 7 p.m., the former dealing with
the translated messages, the latter working up the many fragments and examining the unknown. The [men] on watch had to
sort, decode and translate the new. Hunstanton, Stockton,
Leafield and Hall Street [Y stations] had direct lines to the
Admiralty and there was a never ending stream of postmen
delivering bundles of intercepts. In a few months these men were
replaced by an automatic tube which discharged the goods into a
basket with a rush which shook the nerve of any unwitting visitor,
and very much disturbed the slumbers of the night-watchman
taking his time off. In the very early days *every* message which
appeared to give sense to the man on duty was 'logged' and 'sent'.
That is, the translation was written in the current log book and
three copies were made for circulation, one for the COS, one for
DID, and one for Hope . . . But still there was a vast number of
fragments of messages which failed to satisfy the fastidious
German of the watchkeepers, or messages in unknown codes and
languages. All these were bundled into a tin on which was painted
large and black, NSL. It was a very important tin, nearly always
full in those days . . . Truly NSL only meant 'neither sent nor
logged'. When the war was finished there was still a box called
NSL when there had been no log for the last two years! NSL was a
living thing . . . and it is recounted how a night-watchman woke
trembling in a sweat – he had dreamed he had been dropped in the
NSL and got lost! The log became an object of hatred before long.
The 1st Lord had called into being that particular form of filing
current work and it was over two years, its originator being
elsewhere, before a more labour saving and less soul destroying
method was allowed to replace it. In the days when a watchkeeper
averaged twelve messages it could be written up, though even
then it was the fashion to let the messages accumulate and allow
the new watch to write it up and thus appreciate the situation! But
it was beyond a joke when naval actions were pending or Zepps
fluttering and the watchkeeper had twelve to twenty pages of the

book to write up . . . When 1915 began 40 OB was already a cheerful party [and] fairly pleased with itself in its innocence . . . all naval signals were read even if without intelligence . . . no attempt was made to develop any Intelligence side of the work, beyond Hope's duty of instructing the authorities on the real meaning of certain signals. The request that 40 OB should be allowed to keep a flagged chart of the German coast was vetoed as an unnecessary duplication of the work in the Operations Division. [Nor was Room 40 permitted to have any knowledge of British operations let alone future plans, knowledge of which would, of course, have made the interpretation of German actions and reactions much easier] . . . True it is that in certain cupboards there were increasing piles of 'stuff' which was not read, but it was not naval German. The art of reading other people's telegrams was still in extreme infancy; no one then imagined that all these files contained telegrams possibly of the greatest interest which could be read and, in 1915 it may be said, read without extreme difficulty.

There, perhaps, we should leave Room 40 for the time being; inexperienced, overworked, unable for these reasons and because of the faulty system imposed upon it to realise its full potential, but full of not unjustified confidence that it could play a vital part in the war at sea. The early results of Room 40's newfound source of knowledge will be examined in the next chapter.

CHAPTER FIVE

The First Fruits

Only weeks before the outbreak of war the Royal Navy had reluctantly decided that, because of the threat from the torpedoes of German destroyers and U-boats, and of mines in the comparatively shallow waters of the Heligoland Bight, it would have to abandon its traditional policy of close blockade of the enemy's ports and rely instead on a distant blockade. Geographically, Britain was ideally placed for such a strategy, lying as it does like 'a breakwater athwart the approaches to Germany'. At the southern end of the North Sea the Strait of Dover is a mere twenty miles wide, while in the north the distance from Scotland to Norway is not much more than two hundred miles. Unfortunately, the Royal Navy's three principal bases, Chatham, Portsmouth and Devonport (Plymouth) had been developed to deal with the ancient enemies, Spain, Holland and France; they were ill-suited for operations against the new foe. Harwich was only capable of accommodating light forces, and the Grand Fleet, with nearly thirty dreadnoughts and battle cruisers and its squadrons of cruisers and flotillas of destroyers not only required a well-equipped dockyard but a vast stretch of water as an anchorage. The considerable commercial port of Hull was unsuitable for various reasons; Rosyth, in the Firth of Forth was slowly, very slowly, being developed, but equally had a number of drawbacks[1] and the choice for a fleet base finally seemed to boil down to Cromarty Firth in the far north of Scotland or Scapa Flow in the Orkneys. Both were totally undefended anchorages with no base facilities at all, but, *faute de mieux*, the choice fell on Scapa Flow for the battleships and Cromarty for the battle cruisers of the Grand Fleet.

The Imperial German Navy's main base was Kiel, at the western end of the Baltic. Until the construction of the Kaiser Wilhelm

---

[1] Prevalence of fog in the case of Rosyth and insufficient water at Hull, where the Fleet could only get in and out during about two hours each side of high water. Nevertheless, the Fleet did eventually move to Rosyth.

Canal, connecting Kiel with Brunnsbüttel on the estuary of the Elbe, German warships could only be transferred from the Baltic to the new North Sea naval bases of Wilhelmshaven, Cuxhaven and Emden by the long passage through the Danish Belts and out through the Skagerrak. In 1906, with the launching of HMS *Dreadnought*, battleships of all navies began to increase in size to such an extent that the newly constructed canal could not accommodate them, and had to be widened. This process was not completed until 1914, and even then the latest classes of German dreadnoughts could only get through after partially emptying their coal bunkers. On the other hand, the German North Sea bases were well sighted; approach to them by a hostile fleet was hazardous due to the treacherous and shifting sandbanks of the Frisian Islands and the great fortress of Heligoland, while they themselves were nearer to the coast of Norfolk than was Scapa Flow.

Both sides, therefore, had real problems which were, as it turned out, compounded by imaginary fears about the intentions of their opponents, fears which better intelligence would at once have dissipated. The Germans were quite unaware, for some months, that the British had abandoned their policy of close blockade. The *Hochseeflotte*, although superbly constructed and well trained, was inferior in numbers to the Grand Fleet and, with no tradition behind it, suffered from a distinct inferiority complex vis à vis the Royal Navy. It expected to see the Grand Fleet come storming into the Heligoland Bight within days of the declaration of war, an impression quickly reinforced by the confused and poorly co-ordinated Battle of the Heligoland Bight on 28 August in which Commodore Tyrwhitt's Harwich force of light cruisers and destroyers, supported in the nick of time by Beatty's battle cruisers, managed to sink three German light cruisers without loss to themselves. The *Hochseeflotte*'s strategy was dictated to it by the Army's formidable General Staff and the Kaiser. The former, confident that the Army could win the war on its own, required the Navy merely to secure Germany's coastal waters and protect its flanks; the Kaiser, the creator of the *Hochseeflotte* and an avid if not very intelligent student of the widely read American naval historian Mahan, was obsessed with the idea of a 'Fleet in Being', to be used as a bargaining counter in the final peace conference. Admiral von Ingenohl, the Commander-in-Chief, was therefore forbidden to take any risks with his main forces until such time as the British superiority had been whittled away by ambush of isolated squadrons, by mines or torpedoes. The few

German ships overseas were hostages to fortune; the *Goeben* and the *Breslau* only escaped from the Mediterranean to Constantinople through British ineptitude, while despite Admiral von Spee's courageous handling of the East Asiatic Squadron it was only a matter of time before his ships, and the few other cruisers and auxiliary cruisers in the Atlantic and Indian Oceans were run down and destroyed by superior British forces. In the Baltic alone was German pre-eminence assured; that sea became a German lake, where German mastery was only challenged by a few British and Russian submarines.

Curiously, if the Germans completely misread British intentions, the British suffered from similar illusions about their opponents. The War Office, confused by the propaganda of the advocates of universal military service, by Erskine Childers' splendid yarn *The Riddle of the Sands*, by Saki's *When William Came* and by even more lurid romances by William Le Queux and French and German writers, had persuaded themselves that Germany would at once launch an invasion of the east coast of England. The Admiralty were very sceptical, but could not guarantee to intercept a small 'bolt from the blue' before it could be thrown ashore; they were, however, certain that its transports would then quickly be destroyed and all reinforcements annihilated. Two Divisions were therefore withheld from the original British Expeditionary Force to guard against this completely non-existent threat, and considerable naval forces were tied up on purely local anti-invasion duties. To the Navy, on the other hand, it seemed quite inconceivable that the *Hochseeflotte*, so rapidly created in the last fifteen years, and the principal cause of the marked deterioration in Anglo-German relations, would not at once come out and challenge Jellicoe's Grand Fleet; by attempting to interfere with the movement of the BEF to France or by attacking British trade in the North Sea or even the Atlantic. Both the Royal Navy and the public felt certain that a major clash between the two Fleets would occur within a few weeks, and that it would result in a second Trafalgar and so end the war. This view completely ignored all the lessons of history; it took ten years of blockade and the disastrous campaign in Russia to defeat Napoleon after Trafalgar. It is hard to see now why anyone should have supposed that the German Fleet, significantly outnumbered, should willingly throw down the gauntlet except under conditions entirely favourable to itself.

Jellicoe's problem was that Scapa Flow was over 500 miles away trom Wilhelmshaven and that without first class British Intelligence the Germans could be off the British coast, or anywhere in the North Sea, before he could bring the Grand Fleet to the scene. The relative geographical positions were such that he virtually had to sail at the same time as his adversary if he was to have any hope of intercepting him. Intelligence was *not* available, and in the first three months of the war the Grand Fleet steamed thousands of miles on fruitless sweeps of the North Sea, wearing out ships and men to no advantage and constantly risking being caught in the act of coaling at a critical moment. The dangers were exemplified by the events of 4 November, when Admiral Hipper, covering a mine-laying operation with his four battle cruisers, bombarded Yarmouth with impunity and then returned safely to Wilhelmshaven before Beatty's force from Cromarty could catch him. It will be rembered that it had taken Room 40 some weeks to master the SKM code, and that the HVB had only been received at the end of October, while the VB code was still lying at the bottom of the sea; nor had Commander Hope been admitted to the 'mystery'. So, if Room 40 did have any clue to the attack on Yarmouth, no practical use was made of it.

Von Ingenohl was encouraged by this success and by the know-ledge that at least two of Beatty's battle cruisers had been rushed off by Fisher to the Falkland Islands to avenge the defeat of Coronel. He therefore determined to repeat the operation, this time with a bombardment of the Yorkshire towns of Scarborough and Hartle-pool, again in conjunction with minelaying by the light cruisers. But this time he determined to support Hipper with his battle squad-rons, which would advance to the middle of the North Sea. He hoped that if Beatty did not get caught by the newly laid minefield he might be lured into the very unfriendly arms of the *Hochseeflotte*. The plan was for Hipper to sail early on 15 December, followed by the main force the same evening, so that the bombardment could start at first light on the following morning. On 14 December Hipper wirelessed a request for extensive reconnaissance by airships and aeroplanes to the west, north-west and north on the 15th and 16th, adding that German forces would be at sea, leaving the Jade at 0330 and passing Heligoland at 0530 (German time). He also called for lights to be lit and additional minesweeping to be carried out.

By now, however, Room 40 was getting into its stride, and Hipper's signals, some of which were almost certainly made in the HVB code, were decoded and laid before Oliver.

Hope's rough notes indicate that at first it was thought this movement was no more than an extended exercise, but further information or closer study resulted in a more correct appreciation being made. Churchill's account, vivid as always, suggests that it was A. K. Wilson who was responsible for the change of view.

At about 7 o'clock Sir Arthur Wilson came to my room and asked for an immediate meeting with the First Sea Lord and the Chief of Staff. It took only a few minutes to gather them. He then explained that his examination of the available evidence indicated the probability of an impending movement which would involve their battle cruisers and perhaps – though of this there was no positive evidence – have an offensive character against our coasts. The German High Sea Fleet, he stated definitely, appeared not to be involved. [It is difficult to understand why Wilson should have been so positive; his appreciation can only have been based on the negative fact that there was no information of any sort at all about the intentions of the German main fleet.] The indications were obscure and uncertain. There were gaps in the argument. But the conclusion reached . . . was that we should act as if we knew that our assumptions and suppositions were true. It was decided not to move the whole Grand Fleet. A great deal of cruising had been imposed on the Fleet . . . and it was desirable to save wear and tear of machinery and condensers as much as possible . . .

A number of things are interesting about this account. It shows the extent to which purely operational decisions had to be referred to the 1st Lord, and how very few people were involved in taking them – Churchill, Fisher, Wilson and Oliver; neither the Director of Naval Intelligence, nor Sir Alfred Ewing nor any member of Room 40 were summoned to give their opinions about the interpretation of the available evidence; no officers from the Operations Division were present and when, later, Jellicoe wished to take the whole Grand Fleet to sea, he was overruled. On the other hand, Churchill does bring out clearly the difficulties in interpreting enemy intelligence correctly, the gaps which even cryptanalysis always leaves in completing the 'jigsaw' puzzle, a factor so often ignored by those who claim that Ultra won World War II. Churchill also proclaims, for the first time – what Rodger Winn, the famous head of the Admiralty's World War II Submarine Tracking Room, called a 'working fiction' – the decision that Operations must accept Intelligence's best 'guess' as factual and act upon it, unless and until it is proved wrong.

The difficulty with which the 1st Lord and his three professional advisers were confronted on 14 December 1914 was that, accepting that a raid on the English coast was intended, there was no means of ascertaining which particular part of it was threatened – it could be anywhere from Harwich up to Newcastle. There was, therefore, little chance of being able to prevent it. But, if it did take place, there was every hope of being able to intercept and destroy the raiding squadron on its return passage.

Oliver drafted and sent the following signal to Jellicoe, which was received just before midnight on the 14th:

> Good information has just been received showing that a German cruiser squadron with destroyers will leave the Jade on Tuesday morning early [15 December] and return on Wednesday night. It is apparent from our information that the battleships are very unlikely to come out. The enemy will have time to reach our coast. Send at once, leaving tonight, the Battle-Cruiser Squadron and Light Cruiser Squadron [Beatty, at Cromarty] supported by a battle squadron, preferably the Second [Warrender with the most powerful dreadnoughts at Scapa]. At dawn on Wednesday [16th] they should be at some point where they can intercept the enemy on his return. Tyrwhitt with his light cruisers and destroyers [the Harwich Force] will try to get in touch with the enemy off the British coast and shadow him, keeping the Admiral informed From our information the German cruiser squadron consists of four battle cruisers and five light cruisers and there will probably be three flotillas of destroyers.

Jellicoe was no doubt mindful of Nelson's dictum, 'only numbers can annihilate', but had to accept Churchill's orders to send only the 2nd Battle Squadron; he did, however, select the perfect rendezvous for Warrender and Beatty at first light on 16 December. It was to be off the south-east corner of the Dogger Bank, on an almost direct line from Scarborough, the Germans' actual objective, to Heligoland; 180 miles from the former and 110 miles from the latter.

So the scene was set. Unknown to each other, both sides were to be presented with opportunities for an important victory which were not to re-occur in the same way again, – for the *Hochseeflotte* to destroy two powerful but isolated squadrons of the British Grand

Fleet, thus at a stroke putting themselves on equal terms with the
Royal Navy; for the British to wipe out the German battle cruiser
squadron, the élite force of the Imperial German Navy and establish, once and for all, a crushing superiority in the North Sea.
  Churchill continues:

> On the morning of 16 December at about half-past eight I was in
> my bath, when the door opened and an officer came hurrying in
> from the War Room with a naval signal which I grasped with a
> dripping hand. 'German battle cruisers bombarding Hartlepool.'
> I jumped out of the bath with exclamations. Sympathy for
> Hartlepool was mingled with what Mr George Wyndham once
> called 'the anodyne of contemplated retaliation.' Pulling on
> clothes over a damp body, I ran downstairs to the War Room.
> The 1st Sea Lord had just arrived from his house next door.
> Oliver, who invariably slept in the War Room and hardly ever left
> it by day, was marking the positions on the map. Telegrams from
> all naval stations along the coast affected by the attack, and
> intercepts from our ships in the vicinity speaking to each other,
> came pouring in two or three to the minute. The Admiralty also
> spread the tidings and kept the Fleets and flotillas continuously
> informed of all we knew . . . The bombardment of open towns
> was still new to us at that time. But, after all, what did that matter
> now? The war map showed the German battle cruisers identified
> one by one within gunshot off the Yorkshire coast, while 150
> miles to the eastward *between them and Germany*, cutting mathe-
> matically their line of retreat, steamed in the exact positions
> intended, four British battle cruisers and six of the most powerful
> battleships in the world . . . only one thing could enable the
> Germans to escape annihilation at the hands of an overwhelming-
> ly superior force . . . while the great shells crashed into the little
> houses of Hartlepool and Scarborough, carrying their cruel mes-
> sage of pain and destruction to unsuspecting English homes, only
> one anxiety dominated the thoughts of the Admiralty War Room.
> The word 'visibility' assumed a sinister significance . . .

The great men in the War Room were right to be worried; visibility
was perfect at that moment but, as so often in the North Sea, it was
soon to deteriorate markedly and play a part in robbing the British
of the victory which, to some extent, they deserved. 'We went on
tenterhooks to breakfast,' says Churchill. 'To have this tremendous
prize – the German battle cruiser squadron whose loss would fatally

mutilate the whole German Navy and could never be repaired – actually within our claws, and to have the event turn upon a veil of mist was a racking ordeal.'

But the Admiralty, as so often, did not know *precisely* what was happening in the North Sea; above all they remained totally ignorant of the fact that Admiral von Ingenohl, with most of the *Hochseeflotte* had been within a few miles of Warrender's 2nd Battle Squadron, steaming south to meet Beatty's four battle cruisers. It was not the Germans who had been in danger of annihilation but the British! In the darkness just before dawn on the 16th, Warrender's advance screen had run into one of von Ingenohl's destroyers. A confused action between the rival flotillas and cruisers ensued. The Germans retired on their main fleet, and von Ingenohl, mindful as so many German admirals were to be in both World Wars of the inhibiting orders of the 'All Highest', and believing himself to be confronted by the whole of the Grand Fleet, turned about almost at once and legged it for home. Hipper and the 1st Scouting Group were left to fend for themselves. Ingenohl thereby missed the greatest opportunity the German Navy was ever to have. Warrender, on the other hand, does not seem to have given any consideration at all to the significance of the encounter. He continued steadily onwards to his rendezvous with Beatty, without, so far as can be ascertained, making any signal to the latter, to Jellicoe, or to the Admiralty. Beatty, on intercepting the reports of the British light forces, immediately steered at high speed towards the sound of the guns, little realising that he was chasing the whole might of the *Hochseeflotte* to the eastward. Very fortunately for him, both he and Warrender soon received the news of the attacks on Scarborough and Hartlepool and in their turn reversed course to steer west in order to find and destroy Hipper's battle cruisers.

Hipper, a bold and skilful commander, his mission successfully accomplished, was in fact steering a reciprocal course directly towards Warrender and Beatty, oblivious to the fact that his commander-in-chief had deserted him and was now well on his way home. The two forces were approaching each other at a combined speed of nearly forty knots, but the wind and sea had increased, and pouring rain rendered visibility very poor. In spite of this, at 1124, Beatty's cruisers made contact with Hipper's and it seemed as if the trap had been successfully sprung. There then occurred an incident which unfortunately was to prove typical of British signalling performance throughout the war. A badly phrased signal sent by

Beatty[1] by searchlight, intended only for two of the cruisers of the
1st Cruiser Squadron, was wrongly assumed by Commodore
Goodenough to apply to his whole squadron; he broke off the action
and resumed his station ahead of the battle cruisers. The enemy
disappeared into the mist and contact was lost. It was briefly
regained three quarters of an hour later when Warrender's cruisers
sighted those[2] of Hipper, but the latter, alerted by accurate wireless
reports, was able to alter course before he himself was sighted and
so elude his more powerful opponents.

The quadrumvirate in the War Room had not been able to
contribute very much to all this. Although Room 40's records show
that a considerable number of German signals, starting with the
report from von Ingenohl's destroyer of the encounter in the dark
with Warrender's screen, were intercepted, it is by no means certain
that many of them were decoded in time to be of operational use.
Certainly the first signal that Oliver sent out was to Warrender at
1030 on the morning of the 16th: 'Enemy is probably returning
towards Heligoland. You should keep outside the minefield and
steer so as to cut him off.' This of course referred to Hipper, not to
von Ingenohl's battleships. At 1325 Warrender and Beatty were
given the position of the German battle cruisers at 1215 and the fact
that they were steering east by south at twenty-three knots. It was
not until 1350 that it was at last realised that the German main force
was also at sea, and a signal was made to Warrender, Beatty,
Jellicoe and to Commodore (Submarines) Keyes, 'High Sea Fleet is
out, and was in 54.30 North 5.55 East [eighty miles west of Heligo-
land] at 1230 today. So do not go too far to the eastward', but even
then it was not appreciated that von Ingenohl was retreating not
advancing. However, it gradually became clear that the great
opportunity to catch Hipper had been missed. Churchill, who had
been to the War Committee of the Cabinet, returned to the War
Room. 'The shades of a winter's evening had already fallen. Sir
Arthur Wilson then said, in his most ordinary manner, "Well, there
you are, they have got away. They must be about here by now", and
he pointed to the chart on which the Chief of Staff was marking the
positions every fifteen minutes.' Churchill would not accept defeat.
Keyes, Commodore (Submarines) was at sea with two destroyers in

---

[1] The fault was that of his Flag Lieutenant, Ralph Seymour, who made similar
unfortunate mistakes on at least three other occasions.
[2] The German cruisers had previously seen the British recognition signals and
made good use of this knowledge to aid their escape.

order to overcome the very short range of the wireless sets of the British submarines and so maintain communication with the boats which he had deployed to try to intercept the Germans. At twelve minutes past eight Oliver gave Keyes this 'forlorn hope' order; 'We think Heligoland and Amrum Lights will be lit when ships are going in. Your destroyers might get a chance to attack about 2.00 a.m. or later on the line given you.' This was, of course, based on the decoded German wireless instructions to the Light Vessels concerned, but Keyes, who had been longing for just such an order all afternoon, had finally decided that it would never come, and was already far on his way back to base. One of his submarines in fact got in a shot at von Ingenohl's leading dreadnought, but because of the heavy sea it ran too deep and missed. Just before noon on the next day, 17 December, Oliver informed Jellicoe that 'Everything is quiet and the German ships have returned to the Elbe and the Jade. Send 1st and 3rd Flotillas back to Harwich.'

So ended, to the deep frustration of all concerned, the Scarborough raid. Beatty wrote to Jellicoe, 'There never was a more bitterly disappointing day . . .' Fisher considered that 'all concerned had made a hash of it' and swore that heads should roll. Jellicoe was '*intensely* unhappy'. Churchill, confronted with howls of rage from the great British public that undefended towns had been bombarded with impunity, had 'to bear in silence the censures of our countrymen. We could never admit for fear of compromising our secret information where our squadrons were, or how near the German raiding cruisers had been to their destruction. One comfort we had, the indications upon which we had acted had been confirmed by events.'

The Germans were no less furious at their own failures. Gross Admiral Tirpitz, the father of the *Hochseeflotte*, wrote a few weeks afterwards, 'Ingenohl had the fate of Germany in the palm of his hand. I boil with inward emotion whenever I think of it.' The captain of one of the German battle cruisers was even more caustic about von Ingenohl. He maintained that the commander-in-chief had turned back 'because he was afraid of eleven British destroyers . . . Under the present leadership we will accomplish nothing.' But, as Churchill had pointed out, British Intelligence had won its spurs; it may not have been able to paint the complete picture for Wilson and Oliver, or they may not have drawn all the deductions from it which they should have done, but it had shown that it could provide reliable advance warning of at least some German moves. If only the Germans would come out again it might do even better and luck, next time, might be wholly not just partially with the British.

Both sides reviewed their arrangements in the light of the unsatisfactory outcome of the Scarborough raid. The Kaiser and the *Admiralstab* issued fresh instructions to von Ingenohl that he was not to risk his ships in any rash enterprise, although he was given discretion to make limited forays against any inferior British force which could be located. On the other hand, the *Admiralstab* became increasingly nervous that the British intended some major operation such as an attempt to block the mouths of the Jade, Elbe or Ems. It is a fact that at this time Churchill and Fisher were still debating with their advisers and with Jellicoe the possibilities of seizing the islands of Borkum or Sylt, or of a combined operation against Zeebrugge or even – Fisher's pet plan – the despatch of the Fleet into the Baltic. Whether rumours of these discussions reached the Germans or whether they fed on their own fears is hard to say, but they were in a highly nervous state.

The British equally credited their opponents with a bolder spirit than they in fact possessed. In a long signal on 20 December, drafted by Oliver and approved by Churchill, Jellicoe was instructed to send the Battle Cruiser Squadron and four of the fastest light cruisers to Rosyth 'in view of another possible raid at an early date, which may probably be to the southward.' After assuring Jellicoe that if this should materialise he should take his Fleet to sea and 'assume complete charge of the whole operation', the message then set out a number of qualifications; the Admiralty would promulgate an intercepting position to which the Battle Cruiser Squadron would immediately proceed; 'all information received subsequently by the Admiralty as to the enemy's position would be communicated simultaneously to you and to the Vice-Admiral, Battle Cruiser Squadron'; the Harwich Force would continue under Admiralty orders until it could be decided whether it should join either Jellicoe's own Battle Fleet or Beatty's battle cruisers; Keyes's submarines would remain under the orders of the Admiralty. The signal concluded by stating that 'The possibility must be kept in mind of the enemy breaking through the Straits of Dover and making a raid on Ireland and the French and British Western patrol squadrons, which are slow and weak, afterwards returning by the west coast of Ireland and north of Scotland.' This latter possibility was crediting the Germans with a degree of enterprise which they certainly did not possess. The instruction is also interesting in showing the dawning realisation that the Admiralty's priceless Intelligence would be of little value unless it could reach *all* those who would have to act upon it. But it fell short in theory, and was to fall far shorter in practice, of giving the Commander-in-Chief the complete control he desired and which he should have been accorded in what was, after all, a comparatively restricted potential area of operations. It was not only von Ingenohl who was restricted by the conviction of an 'All Highest', that he 'knew best'. This fatal tendency to refuse to leave decisions to the man on the spot, after providing him with all the information available on shore, was to have serious consequences in the future, and was even less justifiably inherited by Sir Dudley Pound, the 1st Sea Lord in World War II (and by Churchill).

German fears of a British attack were greatly strengthened when on 19 January, a German seaplane sighted Beatty's battle cruisers and 'close upon a hundred small craft' sixty miles off Heligoland on an easterly course. Beatty was in fact only covering an operation by the Harwich Force against German patrols in the area, but this was at once interpreted by the Germans as the anticipated 'blocking operation'; but when nothing further developed the *Admiralstab* assumed that it had been postponed and von Ingenohl relaxed the state of readiness of the *Hochseeflotte* and sent his most modern and powerful battle squadron to the Baltic for exercises. His Chief of Staff, Admiral Eckermann, however, prevailed upon him to send Hipper's battle cruisers to carry out a reconnaissance of the Dogger Bank area, to try to find out what the British were up to and perhaps gobble up a few of their light cruisers and destroyers. 'No special preparations are needed; an order issued tomorrow morning to the Senior Officer Scouting Forces would be sufficient – "Proceed out at night, arrive in the forenoon, return in the evening."' Von Ingenohl somewhat reluctantly agreed. The orders were issued *by wireless* to Hipper, who promptly proceeded to execute them. They were as promptly intercepted by the British and decoded by Room 40.

On this occasion there could be no doubt about the scale, timing, objective and area of the German operation. The ordering of coastal lights for the night departure, the warning to German U-boats that their own forces would be at sea, the choice, left to Hipper, of the two destroyer flotillas which were to accompany him, all signalled, one would suppose, in different codes (SKM and HVB), were now as simple for Room 40 to unbutton as for their official recipients. Russell Clarke's new Y stations were missing

little. It is true that earlier in the month the Germans had made the
first change in the key to the SKM code. Such a change had been
fearfully anticipated for some time. Denniston recalls:

> Now the dreadful change had come! All the available staff were
> summoned by telephone and after a night-long struggle the new
> key was obtained to the joy and admiration of all concerned. The
> 1st Lord called early next morning and congratulated the experts
> who had solved the key so promptly. In the course of the day it
> was discovered that the key had *not* changed but that the existing
> key had been 'slid' and that the actual work involved need not
> have taken five minutes. This discovery 40 OB kept to itself and
> when a few days later the key really did change, the new one was
> produced quietly and without much trouble in a few hours. Two
> years later when the key changed every night at 12 o'clock the
> night watchmen were greeted with the cold contempt of their
> relief had they failed to solve the new key.

Fisher was laid up with a cold on 23 January, and Churchill went
over to his quarters in the Admiralty to talk over their many
problems. When he returned just before noon, he tells us, 'I had
hardly sat down when the door opened quickly and in marched Sir
Arthur Wilson unannounced. He looked at me intently and there
was a glow in his eye. Behind him came Oliver with charts and
compasses. "First Lord, those fellows are coming out again."
"When?" "Tonight. We have just time to get Beatty there."'
Churchill goes on to say that 'a raid on the British coast was clearly
to be expected', but this is nonsense; the decoded signal from von
Ingenohl to Hipper read: 'First and Second Scouting Groups,
Senior Officer of Destroyers and two flotillas to be selected by the
Senior Officer Scouting Forces are to reconnoitre the Dogger Bank.
They are to leave harbour this evening after dark and to return
tomorrow evening after dark.'

After what Churchill describes as nearly an hour but what in fact
was more than two hours, the following signal was sent at 2.10 p.m.
to Jellicoe, Beatty, Tyrwhitt (at Harwich) and Bradford (Vice-
Admiral Commanding 3rd Battle Squadron): 'Four German battle
cruisers and six light cruisers will sail this evening to scout on
Dogger Bank probably returning tomorrow evening. All available
battle cruisers, light cruisers and destroyers from Rosyth [Beatty]
should proceed to a rendezvous in 55.13 N 3.12 E arriving at 7 a.m.
tomorrow. Commodore T [Tyrwhitt] is to proceed with all available

destroyers and light cruisers from Harwich to join VA *Lion* [Beatty] at 7 a.m. at above rendezvous. If enemy is sighted by Commodore T while crossing their line of advance they should be attacked. W/T is not to be used unless absolutely essential.' The last restriction should be particularly noted. Although neither the British nor the Germans had at this time developed an efficient Direction Finding organisation, it was possible for ships at sea to detect the presence of a nearby enemy by the strength of the reception of the latter's wireless messages. There was also the danger that too much British chatter would interfere with Room 40's reception of the priceless German signals. Finally, there was the fear that Neumünster (Room 40's opposite number) might be also eavesdropping. Further signals swiftly followed – to Keyes to take four submarines and two destroyers to sea towards Borkum; to the 3rd Battle Squadron, Bradford, to proceed so as to be able to cut off the Germans if they should try to escape to the northward; and, at 2.45 p.m. to Jellicoe to take the main battle fleet in the same direction and to 'act as you feel best to intercept the enemy'. He, too, was specifically enjoined to 'avoid using wireless if possible until after daylight tomorrow or until enemy is reported'.

Jellicoe subsequently claimed that there was unnecessary delay in issuing these orders, and that had he been warned earlier he could have sailed sooner and been in a better position to intercept Hipper on the following day. It has not so far been possible to establish exactly when the relevant German signals were decoded in Room 40, but it is very probable that there was justification for the complaint. In the event Jellicoe was 140 miles from Beatty when the battle was fought. Had Room 40 been permitted to send para-phrased versions of the German decodes direct to Jellicoe, or had Oliver and Wilson done so without waiting to discuss the counter-action to be taken with Churchill, the Grand Fleet would certainly have been able to get to sea sooner, and the results might have been very different.

Nevertheless, it did look as if this time a trap had been laid from which Hipper could not escape. Beatty had with him not only three ships of the 1st Battle Cruiser Squadron, *Lion* (flag), *Tiger* and *Princess Royal*, but also Rear-Admiral Moore's 2nd Battle Cruiser Squadron consisting of *New Zealand* and *Indomitable*. Hipper had but three battle cruisers, *Seydlitz* (flag), *Moltke* and *Derfflinger* plus the much weaker and slower armoured cruiser, *Blücher*. 'In December,' wrote Winston, 'we had hardly credited our sources of information. All was uncertain. It had even seemed probable that nothing would occur. Now with that experience wrought into one's being, only one thought could reign, battle at dawn! Battle for the first time in history between mighty super-Dreadnought ships! And there was added a thrilling sense of a Beast of Prey moving stealthily forward hour by hour towards the Trap. We were afoot the next morning while it was still dark. Fisher, Wilson, Oliver and I were all in the War Room when daylight began to grow out of doors . . . Suddenly, with the sureness of destiny and the punctuality of a parade, a telegram intercepted from the Fleet was laid before us.' It was the first sighting report by Beatty's light cruisers of Hipper's force. Other intercepted British signals followed. Churchill goes on:

> There can be few purely mental experiences more charged with cold excitement than to follow, almost from minute to minute, the phases of a great naval action from the silent rooms of the Admiralty. Out on blue water in the fighting ships amid the stunning detonations of the cannonade, fractions of the event unfold themselves to the corporeal eye. There is the sense of action at its highest; there is the wrath of battle; there is the intense, self-effacing physical or mental toil. But in Whitehall only the clock ticks, and quiet men enter with quick steps laying slips of pencilled paper before other men equally silent who draw lines and scribble calculations, and point with the finger or make brief subdued comments. Telegram succeeds telegram at a few minutes' interval as they are picked up and decoded, often in the wrong sequence, frequently of dubious import; and out of these a picture always flickering and changing rises in the mind, and imagination strikes out around it at every stage flashes of hope or fear.

No matter what doubts one may have about the accuracy of some of the details in Mr Churchill's histories, no one could conceivably paint a more vivid picture than this of the atmosphere in a naval operations room, whether as in this case during the Battle of the Dogger Bank, or during Jutland in 1916, or during the pursuit of the *Bismarck* in 1941 or the disaster of Convoy PQ 17 in 1942.

But, sadly, the smashing victory which seemed within Beatty's grasp again eluded him. The trap was superbly set but the jaws failed to close completely. In the chase to the south-east, *Lion*, *Tiger*, *Princess Royal* and *New Zealand* drew away from the slower *Indomitable*, and by the time she too was able to open fire, *Lion* was beginning to suffer badly from the accurate shooting of Hipper's battle cruisers, accuracy aided by a mistake in fire direction by *Tiger*, which left *Moltke* to concentrate her fire unmolested on Beatty's flagship. After an hour and a quarter, with both engines badly damaged, *Lion* began to drop out of the line. Beatty signalled his ships to close the enemy as rapidly as possible and instructed *Indomitable* to finish off the poor *Blücher*, the last and slowest ship in the German line, already on fire and helpless, though still fighting bravely. The odds were still in favour of the British – *Princess Royal*, *Tiger* and *New Zealand* against *Moltke*, *Derfflinger* and *Seydlitz*; the last named had received eight hits from *Lion* and *Tiger* of which one, from *Lion*, had hit her quarterdeck, penetrated the barbette armour of the after turret and caused an enormous explosion which put both turrets out of action. The ship would almost certainly have been blown to pieces like *Queen Mary* and *Invincible* were to be at Jutland, had not her after magazines been promptly flooded. She was in a very poor state to continue a running fight. *Derfflinger* had also been hit by the three leading British ships, suffering, according to her signal after the battle, 'considerable' though not vital damage.

Then, at 1054, when *Lion* was already two miles astern of the rest of the British ships, U-boats were reported on her starboard bow and Beatty, who claims himself to have seen the track of a torpedo, ordered his whole force to turn away almost at right angles to the enemy's course, thus temporarily slowing the pursuit. This manoeuvre was the standard counter to submarine attack, but in fact the reported U-boats were an hallucination. Just over two hours later, at 1310, Oliver signalled Beatty and Moore that 'enemy submarines are in the following positions – 54.9N 5.16E, and – 54.17N 5.35E', forty miles south of the scene of the action. Hope in Room 40 knew well enough which U-boats were at sea, and with a fair degree of accuracy where they were. One can, with hindsight, perceive the folly of the quadrumvirate in the Admiralty (or in this case, triumvirate, for Fisher was not there) constituting themselves into a little Intelligence and Operations Centre remote from the real sources of information. To someone with personal experience of the World War II Operational Intelligence Centre, the failure to provide those at sea with such vital information in good time is hard to understand, but one must acknowledge these were very early days, and it was to take another twenty-five years before the lessons finally sank in.

There then occurred another fatal error in British signalling which may have saved Hipper from destruction. *Lion* had now dropped well astern of the other ships, her wireless shot away and her searchlights out of action. Beatty signalled Moore by flag to 'Attack the rear of the enemy', but the signal 'Course North-East' – for the turn away to avoid the mythical U-boats – was still flying and when both were hauled down together,[1] Moore thought Beatty intended that all four British ships should concentrate on the wretched *Blücher*, now little more than a blazing hulk but bearing north-east from him at the time. Moore was no Nelson, and the chase was abandoned. Despite serious weaknesses in British fire control and the inadequacy of the side armour of Beatty's battle cruisers, *Seydlitz* at least should have been sunk and probably *Derfflinger* also. It is not impossible that the whole German squadron would have been wiped out. It was hailed as a victory in Britain, but it was not the triumph which it should have been.

When von Ingenohl received Hipper's despairing calls for help, he ordered the 1st Battle Squadron to raise steam and replied to Hipper *en clair*, 'Main Fleet and flotillas are coming', adding in code 'as soon as possible'. This and the fact that a destroyer attack was planned, but could not be carried out by Hipper's boats because of shortage of fuel, were promptly signalled to Beatty. A Zeppelin reported the fate of *Blücher* and the subsequent concentration of British forces round the damaged *Lion*, but in the end *Lion* was got safely back to Rosyth and *Seydlitz*, even more seriously damaged and with 159 dead, to Wilhelmshaven.

It *had* been a triumph for Room 40. That Jellicoe was not given earlier warning of what was known to be afoot, that the position of the U-boats in the North Sea was only made clear so late in the day to Beatty, and then in only a partial form, was not Room 40's fault. It was the result of a system which concentrated the dissemination of intelligence, not in the hands of the experts best qualified to pass it on immediately to those at sea, but in the hands of the 1st Lord, the two septuagenarians, Fisher and Wilson, and the Chief of Staff, Oliver, who, according to Winston never left the War Room, night or day; he would have been super-human if he had not sometimes become both physically *and* mentally exhausted.[2]

---

[1] Seymour again.

[2] On 23 March 1915 Fisher wrote to Churchill, 'AKW and dear Oliver are mules! Besides they concentrate for days on some side issues . . . Oliver so overburdens himself he is 24 hours behind with his basket of papers.'

CHAPTER SIX

Alarums and Excursions

An immediate result of the Battle of the Dogger Bank was the relief of Admiral von Ingenohl as Commander-in-Chief by Admiral von Pohl, who came under renewed pressure from the Kaiser to be more cautious than his predecessor in permitting forays by the German Battlefleet. In Professor Marder's words, 'Over a year was to pass before the German capital ships dared show themselves in the North Sea again.' This is of course perfectly true, but it was not something that could be anticipated by the British Admiralty. On the contrary, as Room 40's expertise and detailed knowledge of every German movement increased, there were continual 'alarums and excursions'; scarcely a week passed during the next four months without the Grand Fleet being brought to short notice, and frequently ordered to sea, as the result of the detection of some apparent excursion by von Pohl and Hipper. Churchill, Fisher, Jellicoe and Beatty were wracking their brains for schemes which would tempt the *Hochseeflotte* to come out and provide the opportunity for the decisive action for which they all longed, and which they still could not bring themselves to believe the Germans would refuse.

On 21 February Oliver informed Jellicoe that the Germans were aware of the despatch of British pre-dreadnoughts to the Mediterranean, and that the Admiralty intended to send in addition dummy battle cruisers there to 'make them believe that we are weak at home and to tempt their fleet out. In this event it would be best to postpone this cruise and keep all your heavy ships coaled and ready in harbour during the next week.' On 1 March the Commander-in-Chief was informed that 'It is necessary that during the next three weeks the whole Fleet should be kept in readiness for immediate action.' Then on 10 March came a most interesting message from Churchill to Jellicoe: 'All German forces have been ordered to be in a high state of readiness from 11 March onwards and no underwater repairs are to be begun. Whether this is *because they are afraid that*

we are going to attack them or because they know how many ships
are in the Mediterranean and *mean to attack us is not certain*
[Author's italics]. We have sent two dummy battle cruisers out to
Carden [at the Dardanelles] and have advertised our strength out
there as much as possible. Therefore you must be ready. I grudge
Orion [Grand Fleet dreadnought] going away for a refit now.'
Behind this, one begins to discern the dissembling hand of Blinker
Hall, but we will return to this point later. Hope's notes are
revealing. Reporting on 'The Outing of the Fleet on March 6' (note
the already proprietorial attitude, common to all Intelligence
officers, towards the enemy), Hope wrote: 'On this occasion there
was plenty of notice that the Fleet was coming out; there were also
indications that they would use the Southern Channel because
barrier breakers [converted and strengthened merchantmen designed to explode unlocated mines] had been busy off the Ems and
two submarines were ready at Borkum. The movable light ship had
been sent out on the afternoon of the 5th and the barrier was to be
opened from 8 till 11.30 p.m. [German time]. On the 5th, Measures
A and B were ordered. The first actual indication that the Fleet were
out was on the morning of the 6th. A message . . . to the Officer
Commanding the 2nd Destroyer Division and the 2nd Flotilla
informing these vessels that the main body was going to steer SW
from 7 a.m. until 10 a.m. was intercepted . . .' Signals continued to
be intercepted and decoded, giving full information about the
movements of the battle fleet, flotillas, light vessels, barriers etc,
throughout the day, and were, of course, passed on to Jellicoe until
it became clear that the *Hochseeflotte* was returning to harbour.

During the second half of March, Hope produced a further report
from which it is worth quoting because, although the operation
again came to nothing in the end, it does reveal exactly what sort of
information Room 40 was now able to supply, and also shows the
extent of German fears of some major British move against them.
Headed 'Very Secret. The Episode of March 15 (New Moon)', it
contains marginal remarks by Fisher with frequent and typical
underlinings and exclamation marks. After noting that the German
1st Battle Squadron had been transferred on 22 February to the
Baltic for exercises, on the strict understanding that it should return
by 8 March in accordance with some order whose code-name has
been heavily crossed out, the report details the request made and at
first refused for an extension of the exercises. On 5 March the
Squadron was granted an additional three days. 'Where were our

submarines? Echo answers where!' scrawled Fisher in the margin.[1]

On the return of the 1st Battle Squadron to Wilhelmshaven on the 12th, Hope noted that the *Hochseeflotte* in the North Sea consisted of the 1st, 2nd, 3rd and 4th Battle Squadrons, and the 1st, 2nd, 3rd and 4th Scouting Groups; 'All there!' notes Fisher with heavy underlining. The *Seydlitz's* repairs would be completed by 15 March, added Hope, and a request to send a battleship to Kiel for repairs was refused, von Pohl having, on 9 March ordered that the Fleet be ready for emergencies after the evening of the 11th. Barrier breakers and extensive aerial reconnaissance were ordered for the 14th, but fog caused a forty-eight hour postponement. Heligoland and Borkum were instructed to make weather reports for the 15th and 16th, and at 9 a.m. the *Hochseeflotte* was told to be in a state of readiness by 9.30 a.m. on the 16th, subsequently increased to an 'enhanced state of readiness' by 4.30 a.m. on the 16th. (Much heavy underlining by Fisher.) Further instructions followed from von Pohl, and a later addition to Hope's report notes that two transports escorted by destroyers had left Kiel for a now illegible destination on the 11th. By 7.30 a.m. on the 16th it was all over; the *Hochseeflotte* was ordered to revert to a normal state of readiness and ships were to return the envelopes containing Very Secret Order No. 1150 of 15 March. Hope pointed out that, in some cases, Room 40 had decoded instructions cancelling orders without having intercepted the original orders themselves, and added the warning that 'too much dependence should not be placed on all orders being received by us', which caused yet more underlining by Fisher. Hope then went on to set out the arguments in favour of the intended operation having had an offensive character, against which Fisher noted, 'The sooner we get Admiral Bethel's three ships and his two light cruisers and Stuart Nicholson's three ships and the 1st Cruiser Squadron under Arbuthnot at the Humber the better – with the Patrol Destroyers. In another paper this is proposed, doing gunnery en route at the Swin. The gunnery practice much required.' Fisher was obviously nervous of another East Coast raid. But Hope then went on to suggest that the German preparations may in fact only have been defensive, because, he said, 'the order for the Fleet to be in a state of readiness from the 11th was prefaced by the words: "In consequence of Information received."'

[1] The British submarines E 1 and E 9 had reached the Baltic as early as October 1914, and were operating with the Russians from the Gulf of Finland.

The British Admiralty continued, apparently, to favour the 'offensive' theory. On 20 March Jellicoe was informed that: 'Now that you have had your exercise cruise we hope you will not find it necessary to go to sea again during present critical period. Loss from submarines may easily be incurred and Fleet should be kept at its fullest strength and highest state of readiness.' On 1 April he was told that it was desirable to have the Grand Fleet ready for eventualities by 8 April, and on that day that 'there were indications of a movement about Saturday'. This was followed two days later by the following signal; 'Several important signs pointing to movements of the main German Fleet on Monday or Tuesday. You should be cruising on Tuesday on Longitude 2 East between Latitude 58 and 59 North. Wireless on power should be stopped by Fleet. *Iron Duke* can be recognised making W/T signals and position located by Directionals' [Direction Finding]. (Ten days later Hope drew attention to a decode to Nordholz, one of the new German direction finding stations: 'The Germans seem to be taking this directional method up very much, and we shall have to compete with it in future.')

British alarm grew. On 14 April Churchill sent a personal message to Jellicoe: 'You should return at once to coast and wait in constant readiness. Enemy's movements have been checked by seeing some of our submarines but it seems to be intended later.' On the 17th everyone went to panic stations. Oliver signalled Jellicoe: 'Enemy are about to carry out the secret plan which they have purported since 12th instant. This plan seems to involve 1st Scouting Group and 1st and 3rd Battle Squadrons. A flotilla [of destroyers] has been attached to each of the above and light ships for sailing are being lit at 10 p.m. tonight. We do not know what they intend but if a coast raid it seems clear that their two dreadnought Battle Squadrons will be at hand to deal with our battle cruisers. You should therefore proceed to 3rd Battle Squadron rendezvous with main fleet as early as possible on 18th. You are not debarred from crossing the suspected area east of the Dogger Bank if you consider it necessary at any time.' All minesweepers and local patrol craft from Aberdeen down to Dover were urgently recalled to harbour[1] and submarines, with attendant destroyers to provide means of communication, were stationed off the mouth of the Thames. Twenty-four hours later the *Hochseeflotte* was back in port – another false alarm.

[1] This order was intercepted and decoded by the German Army post at Roubaix.

The scares continued throughout April and into May. On 25 April Jellicoe was informed that: 'It is desirable to make a demonstration each time that the High Sea Fleet puts to sea so that our Fleet may also be reported at sea in due course by neutral merchant ships.' The signal went on to suggest that the nine 'Special Service' ships (dummy warships) might be used for this purpose to save much wear and tear on the Grand Fleet, and that a couple of small guns should be mounted on each of them. 'If,' the signal rather callously concluded, 'unfortunately one of these ships were sunk it would further mislead the enemy.'

On 17 May Churchill, in the midst of the crisis caused by Fisher's resignation and the signs that his own political position was in great danger, sent a personal message to Jellicoe stating that, 'It is not impossible that tomorrow may be the day. All good fortune go with you.'

What *was* all this about? Von Pohl and the *Admiralstab* had *no* offensive plans at all; *no* intentions to provoke a major action in the North Sea let alone raid the British coast! Why should the British have half hoped, half feared that they would? Sometime in March, the British seemed to have suspected that the Germans were on the point of invading neutral Holland. This may have been occasioned by continued German reactions to fears of a British attempt to block their river mouths or to descend on one of the Frisian Islands or on Zeebrugge. Then, in the second half of April, the Germans received reports, which they at first distrusted but finally felt compelled to accept, that the British were going to invade Schleswig-Holstein, and for these at least Hall was in part responsible. In one of the five draft chapters of his unpublished autobiography, Hall gives some details of successful attempts he made to mislead the Germans with partially true and partially false information. He first recounts how he and Lieutenant Colonel Drake, of MI5, the counter-espionage service, planted faked photographs on the Germans which persuaded them that repairs to Beatty's flagship *Lion*, after the Dogger Bank action, were far more extensive and would take far longer than was in fact the case. As a result, Hall claims, U-boats waiting off the mouth of the Tyne to attack her when she left, were withdrawn, thus permitting *Lion* to rejoin the Grand Fleet unmolested after the speedily effected repairs had been completed.

Hall had made contact with Drake very early on and had formed a high opinion of his ingenuity, and their co-operation became extremely close. Hall suggests that it was in April that he and Drake concocted another scheme to deceive the Germans, by sending them reports purporting to come from their agents in Britain whom Drake had in fact long since arrested (a ruse which most people have hitherto thought was first practised in the Double Cross system in World War II). It is difficult now to disentangle just what did go on, but it seems highly probable that the 'information' received by the Germans in March, referred to by Hope, actually emanated from Hall's and Drake's fertile brains. Hall's autobiography states that: 'For some little time, we knew German agents had been reporting to Berlin elaborate preparations on our part for an attack in great strength on the Belgian coast. Actually any such plan had been abandoned at the end of January. Measures were taken, however, to keep the enemy well supplied with reports of this nature. 'Evidence' was even provided to show that an early invasion of Schleswig was contemplated. And these measures were not without results. There came movements of German troops which were only explicable on the assumption that they were expecting some such move on our part. What, then would they think of a sudden stoppage of all traffic between this country and Holland?' The intention of this and earlier ruses was to persuade the Germans that the British forces which they were bound to learn were being sent to the Dardanelles, would not cause any diminution in the strength of the BEF in France or permit them to concentrate forces against the BEF. The first landings in Gallipoli were planned for 25 April and on 19 April all traffic between Britain and Holland was indeed stopped. This, incidentally, caused something of a storm in England because a number of well-known and well-meaning ladies, who had made arrangements to attend a Women's International Peace Conference at The Hague (largely a German propaganda affair), were unable to do so, much to the relief of the British Foreign Office, but to the embarrassment of the Home Secretary who had reluctantly stated that they could do so and had issued them with the necessary passports. Hall developed a diplomatic cold at this point and could not be questioned by the Press or by the Home Secretary!

The German Official History records that reports of some British moves had been received in mid-April; they had at first been disbelieved, but then on 23 April a 'reliable' agent's report of an expedition against Schleswig-Holstein had come in, followed by accounts of '50 warships and 63 transports' being assembled in the Thames and its closure to all civilian traffic. Other reports suggested that the whole of Kitchener's new army was to be shipped to France or the Dardanelles from Liverpool and hitherto unused West country ports. The General Staff demanded that the *Admiralstab* take immediate action. The results were not exactly as Hall and Drake had anticipated. The movements of German troops were interpreted by British Military Intelligence (apparently blissfully unaware of the Drake/Hall deception plan) as portending a descent on Britain, and both Army and Navy anti-invasion forces were put on a high state of alert. The German Navy, far from despatching the *Hochseeflotte* to attack the British on the other side of the North Sea, stood ready only to defend its own coasts. To meet the Army's call for offensive action, the *Admiralstab* eventually sent all available ocean-going U-boats to the northern North Sea and some round Scotland to the western English Channel and the Irish Sea, while the smaller Flanders boats were concentrated on the east coast from Yarmouth down to Dover, instructions which at least so far as the ocean-going boats were concerned were quickly intercepted by Room 40. It was one of these ocean-going boats which was to sink the *Lusitania* off the south coast of Ireland on 7 May! As Sir Walter Scott wrote: 'Oh what a tangled web we weave, when first we practise to deceive.'

The problem for the British was that Room 40's information was now so good, that signs of any German movement could be detected in advance and could not be ignored if the Grand Fleet was to be sailed in time to intercept any offensive operation. That the movements, throughout 1915, always turned out in the end to be purely local ones, to cover minesweeping in the Heligoland Bight, or to guard against possible British attacks, could rarely be ascertained until the *Hochseeflotte* was already on its way back to port. It was all most frustrating both for those who credited the Germans with more aggressive intentions than they in fact possessed, and equally for those longing to bring on the great naval battle which would ensure Britannia's supremacy once and for all.

*

Something should now be said about the British development of Direction Finding. The German Kleikamp thought that the British organisation antedated the German and was much superior to it. In fact, both seem to have started about the same time – the early part of 1915. On the British side the initiative came from a certain Captain Round of the Marconi Company, who had carried out successful experiments for the Army in France. Hall was informed, and Round was quickly instructed to set up a station at Chelmsford, but the site proved unsuitable and the station was moved to Lowestoft. Other stations were brought into service at Lerwick, Aberdeen, York, Flamborough Head, Lowestoft, and Birchington, all under Hall's direct control. Some of these stations also acted as Y stations, intercepting German messages for Room 40 as well as taking bearings of the transmitting units. By May 1915, Oliver was able to tell Jellicoe that, thanks to 'Directionals', they had success-fully followed the track of a U-boat right across the North Sea, and as the system expanded and gained in expertise there is no doubt that its accuracy, probably because of its wider base line, was considerably greater than that of the Germans. This could be seen by Room 40 because the Germans used their system extensively to aid the navigation of their Zeppelins, whose messages were of course easily read by the British. As the U-boat war spread further afield, five stations were set up in Ireland under the control of Vice-Admiral Queenstown, while yet other stations in Britain and overseas were administered by Admiral Commanding Reserves, presumably because, after much argument, a Naval Shore Wireless Reserve was created. This divided control seems curious to those of us with experience of the World War II DF organisation, which was so successfully developed and administered by a combined Intelli-gence and Signals Division section of the Admiralty's Operational Intelligence Centre. It is, however, clear that despite these apparent weaknesses, the British DF organisation provided a great deal of highly valuable information to Room 40, where eventually a sepa-rate section was created to plot the bearings and determine the resulting 'fixes'. It is also probable that, as in World War II, the code-breakers were often able vastly to improve the accuracy of the DF plotters and also use the latter as a cover for promulgating their own even more secret information.

The British Naval Staff (which in fact means Oliver and Wilson), continued throughout 1915 to impress on Jellicoe the need to conceal the source of Room 40's knowledge. The Commander-in-Chief was repeatedly enjoined to be most careful in passing on the fruits of its work even to his most senior subordinates and, again and again, to restrict the use of wireless by the Fleet when at sea. Messages to Jellicoe when in Scapa were sent to him in a special cipher, 'B', or if at sea, on the lowest possible power from the nearest shore station, often addressed to a private ship, the signal being prefaced with the coded instruction that the signal concerned was only for the C-in-C and was not to be decoded by the ship concerned. Messages sent to Scapa were always marked 'Not by W/T'. In May the records show that an additional method of passing information to Jellicoe when at sea was brought into force – the so called 'Henry' messages. On 4 June, for example, the following signal was made:

> Cypher B. Admiralty to Afloat Aberdeen. Despatched 7.45 p.m. Received 7.50 p.m.
> Priority. 142. Private and Personal from 1st Sea Lord. HENRY. MOUSE. RAPID.

This was a simple code designed to indicate which German units were at sea or in port or in the Baltic. It was replaced by the William and Mary code in July 1916 in which, for example, WILLIAM meant IN HARBOUR, MARY IN PORT, FORGE 1st SQUAD-RON, WASTE TWO SUBMARINES, and so on. Many of these signals were prefaced 'Clear the line', indicating the utmost urgency. The signals were highly secret, were seen only by the Commander-in-Chief and his Chief of Staff and received no circulation in the Admiralty.

These precautions were certainly entirely successful in preventing the Germans from entertaining any suspicion of the extent to which their W/T communications were entirely open to their enemy. When, in 1917, the *Hochseeflotte* itself became more circumspect in its use of wireless, it was almost certainly due more to fear of direction finding than to the realisation that its codes were hopelessly compromised because small craft, U-boats and Zeppelins continued to chatter as much as ever. But, of course, a price had to be paid by the British for this security. Hope has recorded that the regular statements of the dispositions of the German Fleet, prepared by the Intelligence Division for the use of Flag Officers in the Grand Fleet and elsewhere, at first came to him for vetting in the light of his much greater and more accurate knowledge. Then this was deemed inadvisable, and the statements were no longer corrected by Room 40 before promulgation, thereby losing greatly in value. On 14 June 1915 the process was taken still further, and the 1st Sea Lord sent a personal message to Jellicoe to say that the daily return showing movements of enemy ships would not be supplied to Flag Officers other than the Commander-in-Chief himself, and requested him to inform his Flag Officers accordingly. Similarly, charts of Germans minefields based on Room 40's information received very restricted circulation, often only to Jellicoe personally. Although Oliver did signal a greal deal of intelligence to Jellicoe and also at times to Beatty, Tyrwhitt at Harwich and Keyes and his successor as Commodore (Submarines), Jellicoe for one was not satisfied that Beatty was getting all the information he should. On 31 March 1915 he 'submitted for consideration desirability of VA BCF [Beatty] being supplied with cypher B for communication with Admiralty and myself', and on more than one occasion subsequently expressed his concern to Oliver that he himself was not getting all the information as quickly or as fully as was possible. It was certainly the post-war view of Room 40 that these sort of complaints were justified, at least up to 1917 when Hall began to gain control and to start to turn Room 40 from a purely cryptographic bureau into a proper Intelligence centre.

*

We must now leave Home Waters and retrace our steps to recount the course of events in the distant oceans. The Germans had, before the war, maintained, largely for prestige purposes, a small but powerful cruiser squadron in the Far East, based on Tsingtao, in their small colony of Kia Chow in China. It consisted of two modern armoured cruisers, *Scharnhorst* and *Gneisenau*, and three light cruisers, *Leipzig*, *Nürnberg*, and *Emden*, and was under the command of one of the boldest and most skilful German admirals, Graf von Spee.

Realising that Tsingtao was doomed, von Spee who was in the German Caroline Islands in the Pacific at the outbreak of war, first of all detached *Emden* to attack British shipping in the Indian Ocean, and then set off himself for the west coast of South America where German interests were strong and where he could expect to find colliers and supply ships organised for him by the *Admiralstab*'s efficient *Etappenkommando*. The British Admiralty were at first unsure of von Spee's intentions and were much concerned to provide protection for Australian and New Zealand troop convoys, but gradually the impending threat to British interests in South America became clear as isolated reports of von Spee's somewhat leisurely progress started to come in.

Fisher had not, at this time, been recalled from retirement and the 1st Sea Lord was Prince Louis of Battenberg (the late Earl Mountbatten's father), unkindly dubbed 'I concur' by the Naval Staff as this seemed to be his invariable comment on any propositions put to him. Devoted to the Royal Navy, and a splendid seaman, his supreme achievement had been to cancel the dispersion of the Reserve Fleet after the test mobilisation and Royal Review in July 1914. Thereafter he seems to have been content to leave most decisions to his 1st Lord, who was of course the irrepressible Churchill, and to the Chief of the War Staff, Admiral Sturdee. Whoever was in fact responsible, the actual results were that two British squadrons, both individually weaker than von Spee, who had been reinforced by the arrival of the light cruiser *Dresden* from the West Indies, were left to face the music: Rear-Admiral Stoddart on the east coast and Rear-Admiral Cradock on the west coast of South America. Other dispositions were made in case von Spee should double back on his tracks, but in fact the real danger point was clear, and the steps taken to deal with the situation were almost bound to lead to disaster.

Disaster soon occurred when Kit Cradock, a fighting admiral if ever there was one, encountered von Spee off Coronel on the southern coast of Chile on 1 November. Disdaining to run for it, Cradock at once accepted the unequal battle. In under four hours it was all over. Cradock's two elderly armoured cruisers, *Good Hope* and *Monmouth*, had been sunk with all hands and his two other ships, the light cruiser *Glasgow* and the armed merchant cruiser *Otranto*[1] were fleeing as fast as possible to the south through the Magellan Straits for the somewhat doubtful safety of the Falkland Islands. It had been a repetition of the early frigate actions of the war of 1812, when an over-confident British Admiralty (and British captains) had confidently expected weaker ships to stand up against heavier and better trained American ones; the blow to British prestige was no less severe, although the final results were no more serious.

Up to this point intelligence had been defective on both sides. Communications were difficult and slow. Wireless reception off the southern tip of South America was notoriously difficult if not impossible. British Admiralty practice was to cable to Montevideo or the Falkland Islands and to rely on the latter's wireless station to pass messages on if British squadrons were at sea in the South Atlantic; for the Pacific coast cables could equally be sent to Valparaiso and passed on from there to various points up and down

---

[1] Cradock had been sent an obsolete battleship, *Canopus*, but had not taken her with him, probably because of her slow speed. Her fighting value was in any case doubtful.

the Chilean coast, where they would have to wait until a British warship called to collect them. Even the more efficient German long range wireless could not guarantee always to reach von Spee, and it is not possible to say with certainly which signals and what information despatched from London or Berlin actually reached the intended recipients. The Germans were of course using the *Verkehrsbuch* code for communication between Berlin and von Spee, and the *Handelsverkehrsbuch* code for communication between him and his supply organisation. German Embassies, Consulates and agents were also communicating in these two codes. But the HVB code had only reached London from Australia at the end of October, and the VB was to remain a closed book to Room 40 for another four weeks. Obviously, nothing could have been gleaned in London from German overseas messages before the beginning of November.

In Australia, however, the situation was different. Although, as already noted, the Naval Board at Melbourne took four weeks to notify the Admiralty that they had captured the HVB from *Hobart*, a delay which is hard to understand, they did proceed quite quickly to set up their own local version of Room 40 and they did so in exactly the same way that Oliver had done in London; they appointed a Ewing of the Southern Hemisphere to tackle the problem.

In January 1914, Frederick William Wheatley, a graduate of Oxford and Adelaide Universities, had been appointed Senior Naval Instructor at the RAN College Geelong. He was a fluent German speaker, and on the outbreak of war had been immediately seconded to the War Staff at the Navy Office and put in charge of all intercepted wireless messages. Most of them were in an unknown code (probably the VB), but the booty from *Hobart* had included not only the HVB but also its first wartime key. Unfortunately, the early HVB messages intercepted, contained, according to Dr Wheatley, little of great interest. When the British Naval Intelligence Officer Montevideo, presumably the Naval Attaché, acting on Admiralty instructions, began at the end of October to cable copies of messages – which evidently came from von Spee's squadron – to Wheatley, he found that the key had changed. It took him three days, working day and night, to discover the new key. Writing in 1926, he describes how 'on the third day, which happened to be Melbourne Cup Day [3 November], I was so wearied and fuddled that at 2.30 I made up my mind to go and see the Cup run. I was back at the office at 4.30 and at 6 o'clock was satisfied that I had solved the problem. All that night had to be spent in decoding and translating the messages which . . . were all from the German Pacific Squadron[1] and gave their itinerary through the Magellan Straits, up to the Abrolhos Islands off Brazil to meet the *Elinore Wöhrmann* [a collier] (afterwards sunk by the *Australia*) and then to West Africa. That night the Admiralty was informed by cable and Lord Fisher immediately ordered the *Invincible* and *Inflexible* to . . . proceed to the Falkland Islands. They reached there a few hours before the German Squadron and the *Scharnhorst, Gneisenau, Nürnberg* and *Leipzig* were sunk.'

While it is established that Wheatley did manage to break the HVB key exactly as he states, and that the fact was at once cabled to the Admiralty, an official report which he made in 1915 in no way substantiates his later claim that this success was responsible for the decision taken by Fisher and Churchill to send the two battle cruisers to the South Atlantic. None of the messages which Wheatley quotes in his first report gave any indication that Spee was about to leave the west coast of South America and proceed round the Horn. The decodes were concerned rather with the movements of German supply ships on the west coast and, as late as 1 December, in response to an enquiry from the Naval Board, the Admiralty refer to an 'overheard conversation' which suggested the possibility that the German squadron might be proceeding to the South Atlantic. On 5 December there was a rather obscure reference in one of Wheatley's decodes to the Abrolhos Rocks (off the coast of Brazil), but by this time the *Invincible* and *Inflexible* were only two days' steaming away from the Falkland Islands. Nor do the other steps taken by the Admiralty suggest that they had any precise knowledge of von Spee's intentions. One can only conclude that, with the passage of time, Wheatley forgot the exact sequence of events and genuinely believed that his brilliant decoding had played a larger part in Fisher's bold decision than was in fact the case. He would not have been the last cryptographer to make this mistake.[2] The Admiralty were delighted at Wheatley's success in breaking the key, and at their request he made 200 copies of the code within ten days, of which 100 were sent to the Admiralty, fifty to the Comman-

---

[1] More correctly, von Spee's East Asiatic Squadron.

[2] *See* the author's *Very Special Intelligence*, and the genuine belief held by Bletchley Park that the decoding of the Athens telegram was responsible for the final interception and sinking of the *Bismarck* in 1941.

der-in-Chief of the America and West Indies Station, and others to individual ships of the China Squadron and Royal Australian Navy. One is struck by the contrast between the excessive secrecy surrounding Room 40 and the very liberal distribution given to the HVB overseas.

The first news of Coronel had reached the Admiralty, from German sources, early on 4 November (an indication of the slowness of communications; Coronel was fought on the evening of 1 November). Battenberg had just resigned as the result of a vicious campaign in the Press about his German ancestry, and Jacky Fisher had replaced him. It is clear from the accounts of Churchill and others that he and Fisher considered that at least four options were still open to von Spee, and they took action to meet all of them. They considered that he might either continue north up the Chilean coast and even pass through the Panama Canal to attack trade in the West Indies and off the eastern American seaboard; alternatively, he might return across the Pacific; or he might round the Horn and endeavour to support the Boer rising in South Africa and the German troops in what was then German South-West Africa.[1] But the most likely course of action certainly seemed to be that he would make for the east coast of South America and it was for this reason that, on that very morning of 4 November, Jellicoe was ordered to detach *Invincible* and *Inflexible* forthwith. After a very hurried refit at Devonport, they sailed on 11 November under the command of Admiral Sturdee whom Fisher had refused to keep as COS. They reached the Falkland Islands on 7 December. Next morning von Spee, totally ignorant of their presence in the South Atlantic, also approached this remote British coaling station with the intention of destroying the coal stocks and capturing the Governor. This time the tables were turned. It was the Germans who were completely outclassed and *Scharnhorst*, *Gneisenau*, *Leipsig*, and *Nürnberg* were all sunk with heavy loss of life, including that of the gallant von Spee. Only *Dresden* managed to escape.

One of the mysteries about the battle of the Falkland Islands is why von Spee ever decided to try to attack them. Although without shore defences and in no sense a proper naval base, they were, it is true, an important British coaling and wireless station and in consequence constantly used by the Royal Navy's ships. Even

---

[1] The Germans did indeed have plans to mobilise German reservists in South America and for von Spee to transport them to South-West Africa, but the German and rebel Boer forces there were defeated before these plans could be put into effect.

before Coronel von Spee had been exchanging messages with the *Admiralstab* about the possibilities of a break for home and the arrangements for coal and supplies that would be needed, and agents in both North and South America were active in furthering these plans. Cradock achieved at least one thing at Coronel; he caused von Spee to use up a lot of ammunition, and this was something that could only be replaced from Germany. After that battle the die was cast; the East Asiatic Squadron had *no* option but to try to return to the Fatherland. Why then add to the dangers of an already perilous voyage by an attack on the Falklands? Certainly, there was much needed coal there and its destruction would be another blow to British prestige. On 15 November the German Consul at Punta Arenas informed Valparaiso that all British warships had left the Falklands, and that a German attack was feared. Although Valparaiso did not believe this report and did not forward it to von Spee, there is some evidence that he in fact received it from elsewhere, and a few days later he certainly instructed the commanding officer of one of his auxiliaries to try to find out if the British had abandoned the islands. Now, in some post-war notes by Hall for a lecture on Intelligence we find under the heading Propaganda: 'Can be used for various purposes. 1. To deceive the enemy in order to lead him to take a certain course for which you are prepared (Falkland Islands) . . .' It seems at least possible that the rumours were another 'plant' by Hall; if so he certainly made a major contribution to Sturdee's victory because, had von Spee not so rashly approached the islands, it is quite likely that Sturdee would never have intercepted him at all. Whether von Spee could have successfully eluded all the other forces which would then have been hunting for him, is another matter.

There is a postscript to the story of von Spee's destruction, and one that again demonstrates the weakness of the HVB keys, in which the Germans placed so much faith. It will be remembered that the only German ship to escape was the light cruiser *Dresden*. For months she eluded her pursuers in the maze of badly charted channels and inlets from the Straits of Magellan up the Chilean coast to Coronel and further north. More than once she only got away by the skin of her teeth, but coal was essential and coal was now much more difficult to come by. Finally, her captain decided to make for Cumberland Bay in Juan Fernandez Island (Robinson Crusoe's island), some four hundred miles out in the Pacific due west of Valparaiso, an anchorage used more than once by von Spee.

He sent a signal to this effect to the collier which the German Naval Attaché in Chile had organised to supply him. The Senior Officer of the British ships which had conducted such a frustrating and hitherto fruitless search for *Dresden*, was Captain Luce, of *Glasgow*. He and his ship's company had a particular score to pay off, but the chase since the Falklands had been a long one. There had even been a case of scurvy among the crew, a reminder that, in 1915, despite all the changes and innovations in the Royal Navy made by the incredible Jacky Fisher, the Service was still in some respects closer to the age of Nelson than to that of Cunningham. Then at last, in the words of Vice-Admiral Harold Hickling, at that time a Sub-Lieutenant in *Glasgow* 'our luck turned. We intercepted a signal in Telefunken, the German wireless with its distinctive note . . . Earlier on we had captured the German merchant vessel code . . . The code book lay on the captain's dining table [perhaps supplied by Wheatley] and every officer spent a few hours a day trying to solve the puzzle. [Obviously *Glasgow* had not been supplied with the current key.] A few days later Charles Stuart, the Signal Officer, bounced up on the bridge: 'I think I've got it, sir.' . . . 'Am proceeding Juan Fernandez meet me there 9 March very short of coal.'" That was all Luce needed. With *Kent* and the Armed Merchant Cruiser *Orama*, he thankfully left the forbidding fjords of Patagonia and by 14 March arrived at Cumberland Bay. Sure enough, there was *Dresden*, at anchor, some of her crew ashore cutting wood for fuel. After a couple of rounds in the old French fashion ('for the honour of the flag'), she hauled down her colours and blew herself up. That was the end of the saga of Coronel and the Falklands. The Admiralty were anxious to discover just how Stuart had managed to break the key, and their enquiry and Luce's full explanation can now be seen in the files of the Public Record Office.

The German *'guerre de course'* with surface ships was now virtually over. *Emden* had been caught and destroyed on 9 November by HMAS *Sydney* when attempting to destroy the wireless station at Cocos Keeling Island in the Indian Ocean. *Karlsrühe*, *Dresden*'s relief in the West Indies, had sunk after an internal explosion, although it was some months before the British Admiralty became sure of the fact. The few armed merchant cruisers had either been sunk or driven into internment in neutral ports. There remained only the light cruiser *Königsberg*, which had taken refuge in the Rufigi River in German East Africa (Tanganyika), where she was blockaded by British ships based on Zanzibar. *Königsberg* was ably commanded and cunningly situated, and she repulsed all attacks until light draught monitors were brought out to effect her destruction on 11 July 1915. Efforts to supply her had not been aided by the fact that her captain's messages to Germany, sent via Portuguese Lourenço Marques to accommodation addresses in Holland, Switzerland and Sweden, were regularly intercepted and decoded by Room 40. It is of interest that Hall allowed some of the letters to reach their destinations, after reading their contents, in order to keep the line open and so obtain further information. A number of wireless signals, some in VB and some in HVB, were also intercepted and ensured the destruction of the supply ship *Rubens* sent out from Germany,[1] and the detection of a row of mines laid off the mouth of the river. One of *Königsberg*'s reports, probably dated 24 May ran as follows: 'It must be regarded as certain the cipher [i.e. key] has been in the hands of the enemy for some time, every signal from *Möwe* and auxiliary ship was transmitted to Zanzibar by blockading squadron. I have satisfied myself by means of a fictitious cipher telegram which was to lure the enemy to Mikindini that enemy must be in possession of our Reserve Key A. Several enemy cruisers were at Mikindini exactly at the time specified in the faked telegram. I beg you to send by W/T new Reserve Key A via Windhuk in the last group but one of a cipher telegram with unintelligible contents.'

Once again it would seem that the British were far less circumspect in their handling of cryptographic material overseas than they were at home. After her destruction, *Königsberg*'s survivors fought with the German Governor of East Africa, von Lettow-Vorbeck, who was never completely defeated and did not surrender until the Armistice in 1918. The German Navy has every reason to be proud of the achievements of its overseas cruisers in World War I.

There was, however, another overseas theatre in 1915 which was foremost in the attention of Churchill and the Naval Staff – the

---

[1] On 7 April Oliver signalled the C-in-C at Zanzibar: 'Supply steamer was in 12S 44E on 6 April and expects to arrive rendezvous in 6S 45E early on 8 April. Rendezvous is same as that given in my 116 of 5 April. *Königsberg* intends to break out and complains that blockade is strict.' *Königsberg*'s own signals were intercepted by the blockading squadron and cabled to England, not always very securely, as one message started in the British code, then included a passage in the German code, concluding with another section in British code. Oliver reported to the 1st Lord that it had been sent by W/T to Zanzibar and thence by cable, but he had instructed the C-in-C that in future all intercepts must be spelt out letter by letter in British code no matter how lengthy this made the signal.

Dardanelles. We are here only concerned with the part played by Room 40 and Hall in this epic tragedy. It might well have been a larger one if there had been any liaison between British and French naval Intelligence, but unfortunately there seems to have been none at all at this stage.[1] The French in fact intercepted a large amount of German traffic in the Mediterranean quite early on (though whether as early as March 1915 is not clear). The material available to the British, on the other hand, was small and Room 40's staff too hard pressed for much to be achieved.

However, according to his own account, Hall nearly managed to render the Dardanelles campaign unnecessary. As early as January 1915, he had despatched a Mr George Griffin Eady, who had been in Constantinople at the beginning of the war working for the contracting firm of Sir John Jackson Ltd, Gerald Fitzmaurice, formerly of the British Embassy and Edwin Whittall, a member of one of the leading British merchant houses in Turkey, to open negotiations with Talaat Bey, the Minister of the Interior in Enver Pasha's Young Turk government, to try to persuade or bribe the Turks to break with Germany and allow the Royal Navy a free passage through the Dardanelles. Hall provided Whittall and Eady with a letter giving his own personal guarantee of three million pounds, with discretion to go to four million, if the Turks would agree. The Chief Rabbi in Turkey was acting as an intermediary but negotiations, although seemingly taking a favourable course, dragged on and were not helped by the fact that secret promises had been made by the Foreign Office to Russia promising her Constantinople and other Turkish European territory to various Balkan countries. By March, time was getting short, because the attempts by the British and French Fleets to force the Dardanelles, which had begun in the second half of February, were being resumed with redoubled force.

Hall's own account then goes on:

> On 13 March there was brought to me the German Emperor's telegram [a VB decode by Room 40], and it seemed to me of such importance that I took it at once to the 1st Sea Lord's room. Lord Fisher, I learned, had gone to the 1st Lord's room and there I

[1] Room 40 subsequently commented that: 'Our Allies were regarded as untrustworthy, or at least liable to indiscretions. In fact both the French and the Italians had broken an Austrian code and sent a copy to the Admiralty where it lay untouched for two years!' The position was not rectified until 1917 when Hall visited the Mediterranean. This is rather an indictment of Ewing's control of Room 40.

found him standing with Mr Churchill before the fireplace. 'First Sea Lord,' I said, 'we have just received this.' [The message read: 'From Nauen to Constantinople. 12.3.15. Most Secret. For Admiral Usedom [the German Inspector-General of Coast Defences and Mines at the Dardanelles], HM the Kaiser has received the report and telegram relating to the Dardanelles. Everything conceivable is being done to arrange for the supply of ammunition. For political reasons it is necessary to maintain a confident tone in Turkey. The Kaiser requests you to use your influence in this direction. The sending of a German or Austrian submarine is being seriously considered. By command of All Highest. v. Muller.']

'Lord Fisher took the message, read it aloud and waved it over his head. 'By God,' he shouted, 'I'll go through tomorrow!' Mr Churchill, equally excited, seized hold of the letter and read it through again for his own satisfaction. 'That means,' he said, 'they've come to the end of their ammunition.' 'Tomorrow,' repeated Lord Fisher, and at that moment I believe he was as enthusiastic as ever Mr Churchill had been about the whole Dardanelles campaign. 'We shall probably lose six ships, but I'm going through.' The 1st Lord nodded. 'Then get the orders out.' And there and then Lord Fisher sat down at Mr Churchill's table and began to draft out the necessary orders. I was about to return to my room when Mr Churchill turned to me and asked for the latest news from Whittall and the others, and it was then that I told him of the large sum of money I had personally guaranteed. He stared at me. 'How much?' 'Three million pounds,' I replied, 'with power to go to four millions if necessary,' and as I mentioned these figures they did seem to be extraordinarily large. He was frowning. 'Who authorised this?' he demanded. 'I did, 1st Lord.' 'But – the Cabinet surely knows nothing about it?' 'No, it does not. But if we were to get peace, or if we were to get a peaceful passage for that amount, I imagine they'd be glad enough to pay.'. . . Mr Churchill turned to Lord Fisher who was still busily writing. 'D'you hear what this man has done? He's told his people they can go up to four million to buy a peaceful passage! On his own!' 'What,' cried Lord Fisher, starting up from his chair. 'Four millions? No, no. I tell you I'm going through tomorrow, or as soon as the preparations can be completed.' He turned to me. 'Cable at once to stop all negotiations. No, let the offer for *Goeben* remain. But nothing else. We're going through.'

There was nothing to be done but obey orders . . . The necessary cables were sent . . . they not only rendered any future discussions useless but also destroyed the belief in Turkish minds of our good faith. . . . Ironically enough, when the gallant attempt of March 18 had proved unsuccessful, the Cabinet were asking me to spare no expense to win over the Turks. Unfortunately, it was then too late.

This may seem a somewhat unbelievable story, but then so are most of the stories about Hall, and most of them are true! There certainly *were* sub rosa negotiations with the Turks at this time, and the Usedom telegram *was* decoded by Room 40 on 13 March. On 14 March Carden,[1] at that time the British Admiral in charge of the Dardanelles operations, *did* receive a telegram from the 1st Lord (not Fisher). It stated that the Admiralty 'had information that the Turkish forts are short of ammunition, that German officers have made despondent reports and have appealed for more. Every conceivable effort is being made to supply ammunition, it is being seriously considered to send a German or an Austrian submarine, but apparently they have not started yet . . . All this makes it clear that the operation should now be pressed forward methodically and resolutely by night and day. The unavoidable losses must be accepted. The enemy is harassed and anxious now. The time is precious as the interference of submarines [Turkey had none] is a very serious complication.'

The attack was resumed vigorously on 18 March. It was on the point of succeeding when two British and one French battleships ran into a small minefield. The Fleet withdrew to await the landings of the troops and the next act in the Gallipoli tragedy. In retrospect, it would seem that four million pounds would have been a very cheap price to pay for such a great prize.

The arrival of U-boats on the scene was not long delayed. U 21 sailed from Germany on 25 April, a fact at once detected by Room 40 although her destination was not immediately apparent. On 19 May, having reached the Austrian Adriatic port of Cattaro (Kotor), she was informed by the *Admiralstab* of the position of English battleships bombarding Gallipoli. This information, too, was at

---

[1] Carden resigned on 16 March due to ill health. Generally regarded as not man enough for the job, I recall him during his post-war retirement in Lymington as a delightful and distinguished old gentleman, the very epitome of a British Admiral, and a very good hand in my father's small sailing boat.

once passed on to Admiral de Robeck, now in charge, but despite this warning two pre-dreadnoughts were sunk, at anchor, by U 21 – HMS *Triumph* on 25 May and HMS *Majestic* on 27 May.

It is to the U-boat war that we must now turn.

CHAPTER SEVEN

Lusitania: Foul-up or Conspiracy?

1.45 p.m. Excellent visibility, very fine weather. Therefore surface and continue passage; waiting off the Queenstown Banks seems unrewarding.

2.20 p.m. Sight dead ahead four funnels and two masts of a steamer steering straight for us (coming from the SSW towards Galley Head). Ship identified as a large passenger steamer.

2.25 p.m. Dive to periscope depth and proceed at high speed on an intercepting course in the hope that the steamer will alter to starboard along the Irish coast. Steamer alters to starboard and sets course for Queenstown so permitting an approach for a shot. Proceed at high speed until 3 p.m. in order to gain bearing.

3.10 p.m. Clear bow shot from 700 metres (G. Torpedo set for 3 metres depth, inclination 90 degrees, estimated speed 22 knots). Torpedo hits starboard side close abaft the bridge, followed by a very unusually large explosion with a violent emission of smoke (far above the foremost funnel). In addition to the explosion of the torpedo there must have been a second one (boiler or coal or powder). The superstructure above the point of impact and the bridge are torn apart, fire breaks out, a thick cloud of smoke envelopes the upper bridge. The ship stops at once and very quickly takes on a heavy list to starboard, at the same time starting to sink by the bow. She looks as if she will quickly capsize. Much confusion on board; boats are cleared away and some of them lowered into the water. Apparently considerable panic; several boats, fully laden, are hurriedly lowered, bow or stern first and at once fill with water. Owing to the list fewer boats can be cleared away on the port side than on the starboard side. The ship blows off steam; forward the name *Lusitania* in gold letters is visible. Funnels painted black, no flag on the poop. Her speed was 20 knots.

3.25 p.m.   As it appears the steamer can only remain afloat for a short time longer, dive to 24 metres and proceed out to sea. Also I could not fire a second torpedo into the mass of people saving themselves.

4.15 p.m.   Come up to periscope depth and take a look round. In the distance astern a number of lifeboats; of the *Lusitania* nothing more can be seen. From the wreck the Old Head of Kinsale bears 358 degrees 14 miles. Wreck lies in 90 metres of water. (Distance from Queenstown 27 miles.) Position 51 degrees 22'6 N 8 degrees 31' W. The land and lighthouse very clearly visible.

This laconic and somewhat cold-blooded description of one of the world's most famous maritime tragedies is an extract (Author's translation) from the fair copy log of Kapitänleutnant Walther Schwieger, the commanding officer of U 20. There is no reason to suppose that, in essentials, it is not an accurate description of his actions. It was first published in an article in the French journal *L'Illustration* in 1920.

Why then should controversy concerning the exact circumstances surrounding the loss of the *Lusitania* have arisen almost from the moment on that sunny afternoon of 7 May 1915 when she sank off the southern coast of Ireland within eighteen minutes of being struck by U 20's single torpedo? The death of 1195 civilians,[1] ninety-four of them children and 140 of them neutral American citizens, outraged a world not yet accustomed to the idea of total war involving innocent men, women and children. It seemed inconceivable, sixty-six years ago, that the Imperial German Navy could be so ruthless, despite clear warnings that such behaviour was intended. It seemed almost equally unbelievable that one of the largest and most modern liners in the world, holder, with her sister ship *Mauretania*, of the Blue Riband of the Atlantic, should go to the bottom far more quickly than the *Titanic* had done when half her

---

[1] Including Mr Paul Crompton, a cousin of the author's father and of the Chairman of the Cunard Line, his American wife and their six children aged fourteen years to five months, who were making a visit to their relatives in England.

side had been ripped out by an iceberg three years previously. Was the *Lusitania*, as the British maintained, a harmless passenger ship for whom the Germans had laid a deliberate and deadly trap? Or was she, as the Germans soon proclaimed, an armed auxiliary of the Royal Navy carrying Canadian troops and a lethal and contraband cargo of munitions and so, despite her civilian passengers, a legitimate target for any German warship? Whichever version was true, why had the Royal Navy not taken effective steps to ensure her 'safe and timely arrival'? Or was her loss due to the wilful negligence of her Master, Captain William Turner, in failing to obey Admiralty instructions? Was the appalling loss of life due to the ship being hit by more than one torpedo, probably fired by more than one U-boat – another British claim – or was it caused – the German version – by the explosion of her cargo? Was the construction of the ship to blame, or was it the fault of the incompetence of the crew? Was the Cunard Company responsible? Or was the disaster, and this is the most sinister suggestion of all, really the result of a machiavellian plot by Winston Churchill, aided and abetted by Fisher, Wilson, Oliver and Hall, deliberately to bring about her sinking in order to involve the United States in the war against Germany?

All these theories have been advanced in articles, books and at least one television programme which have appeared in the last sixty years. It must be said that there is some evidence, good, bad and indifferent, positive and negative, which can be made to support any one of them. Advocates of these rival and contradictory statements each profess to have found the definitive answer. This account makes no such claim, although it is based on examination of a number of files only released to the Public Record Office since 1976, and on a very great deal of information most generously supplied by the man who undoubtedly knows more about the subject than anyone else now alive, the American, John Light. Light actually owns the *Lusitania*'s wreck and has made over thirty dives on it. He has spent nearly twenty years on research and has an unrivalled collection of documentary evidence, some of it unique. His findings are still to be published, but, when they are, they will surely dispel many myths. No one, however, can now cross-question the principal personalities involved (or who might have been involved) to obtain their explanations of why certain things were or were not done, and without such cross-examination even the most detailed records cannot possibly tell the whole story. To make matters worse, the records, at least those available to the public, are not complete. The very unsatisfactory nature of the official enquiry held in June 1915 and the refusal then, and for the next sixty-six years, of the British authorities to disclose all the information in their possession, has only succeeded in fuelling suspicions that they have had something discreditable to conceal. German and American records are also remarkable for the absence of certain papers which once existed but which can no longer, apparently, be produced.

Was the loss of the *Lusitania* the result of an unforgivable 'foul-up' (so often the true explanation of the otherwise inexplicable), or was it an even more unforgivable conspiracy?

Before attempting to suggest some possible answers to these questions, it is necessary to look back at the U-boat war and Britain's reactions to it since August 1914. We must also bear in mind the events described in the previous chapter and the preoccupation of the 1st Lord and his advisers with those events.

Before the outbreak of war, neither the British nor the Germans had thought of the submarine as anything more than a purely defensive weapon, formidable perhaps off its own coasts against an invading or blockading fleet, but incapable of operating far afield or keeping the sea for any length of time. A. K. Wilson considered the submarine to be 'underhand, unfair and damned unEnglish' and when Fisher, with his amazing percipience, wrote, 'I don't think it is even *faintly* realised *the immense impending revolution which submarines will effect as offensive weapons of war*' no one believed him, any more than they did when he later forecast that the Germans would use them ruthlessly and indiscriminately against merchant shipping.

Early in August, both sides quickly discovered that their pre-war ideas had been wrong and that their submarines were indeed 'offensive weapons of war'. U-boats soon reached as far north as Scapa Flow and within five months had sunk four cruisers, a battleship and a primitive aircraft carrier. The Grand Fleet had been forced for a time to abandon its chosen anchorage until it could be made secure. British submarines maintained patrols in the Heligoland Bight, made the long and difficult passage to the Baltic in October, causing alarm to German admirals there, and in April 1915 forced their way through the Dardanelles to the Bosphorus and the Black Sea. The submarine did not take long to come of age. Both surface fleets suffered from severe attacks of 'submarinitis'.

The difficulty for both sides was that little thought had been given to anti-submarine weapons. The ram and the gun were reasonably effective if a submarine could be caught on the surface, but this was not a frequent occurrence. As long as a submarine could stay submerged it was virtually undetectable and invulnerable; there were no depth charges, no hydrophones, no sonar; the most deadly counter-measure was the mine and that, of course, had to be laid in the right place.

The reason why Churchill and his 1st Sea Lord, Battenberg, had rejected Fisher's warning in 1913 that the Germans would use U-boats in a ruthless '*guerre de course*', was that Germany would have to flout International Law and the accepted customs of the sea (as expressed in the Hague Conferences of 1899 and 1907), in order to do so. It was acknowledged by all nations that enemy merchant ships should not be sunk unless they had first been stopped, visited and searched to establish their identity and the nature of their cargo; furthermore, provision had to be made for the safety of the crew and passengers (merely to permit passengers and crew to take to the ship's boats was not considered adequate). These rules had of course been established when commerce raiders were all surface ships, which could either put a prize crew on board and bring the captured vessel into port, or possibly themselves take on board their prisoners. But neither of these measures was really practicable for a submarine; both she and her crew were too small. Moreover, a submarine, stopped on the surface, was very vulnerable even to an unarmed merchantman, let alone to one armed with a defensive gun, a practice hallowed by ancient tradition. It was not long before both the U-boat commanders and the *Admiralstab* began to chafe under these restrictions, and cases occurred, whether deliberately or not, of merchant ships being sunk by torpedo without warning and without the slightest provision being made for the safety of the crew. Nevertheless, up to the end of January 1915, only ten British merchantships had been sunk by U-boats and the Admiralty did not regard the danger to British trade as being in any degree insupportable.

British merchant shipping was not, at this stage, tightly controlled, the whole emphasis being on 'business as usual'. Admiralty Instructions were advisory not mandatory[1] and were concerned, in the main, with how to escape if a U-boat was sighted, and the use of neutral flags and markings (a recognised '*ruse de guerre*'). Routes to be followed were suggested, but it was left very much to the

[1] Although if these instructions were ignored the War Risk Insurance was invalid.

masters of merchant ships whether to reject or accept this advice. The main emphasis was on persuading owners to keep their vessels operating by means of the official War Risk Insurance scheme. Convoy, the time honoured defence against a *'guerre de course'*, was rejected as unnecessary and impractible by both naval and mercantile opinion, although troopships were always, and valuable individual merchantships sometimes given escort. The great majority of modern destroyers, the most suitable type of ship for protecting fast vessels against U-boats, were tied up screening the Grand Fleet or operating with the Harwich Force or the Dover Command, so that the defence of British coastal waters devolved largely on the Auxiliary Patrol, a miscellaneous collection of yachts, trawlers and motor boats manned by the RNR and RNVR. Many of them were not fitted with wireless, some of them were very lightly armed, and hardly any of them possessed sufficient speed to overtake a surfaced U-boat. They may have had some deterrent effect but otherwise achieved very little. Although some merchant ships had been fitted with one or two 4.7-inch guns at the beginning of the war as a defence against German armed merchant cruisers, the need for defence against surface ships soon vanished.

To sum up the position at the beginning of 1915, it may be said that British shipping was still operating largely on a peacetime basis, unconvoyed, unarmed and uncontrolled. The Royal Navy's anti-U-boat measures were confined to 'offensive' patrolling of suspected danger areas by destroyers when available or by the Auxiliary Patrol when they were not; in neither case was such patrolling effective.

By the end of January, German naval and military opinion was strongly in favour of abandoning adherence to the 'Prize Law', and was pressing for the institution of a sink at sight U-boat campaign against shipping. The British blockade was beginning to bite and there now seemed no prospect of an early end to the war on land. Retaliation was called for, and this could not be provided by the Hochseeflotte, but only by the U-boat arm. The German Foreign Office, well aware of the damage being done to Anglo-US relations by the British blockade and fearful that American wrath would be turned against Germany if American lives or property were lost, at first demurred but finally gave way. On 4 February 1915, Germany announced that with effect from 18 February all the waters round the British Isles, except for a route north of Scotland, would become a 'War Zone', in which all ships 'would be destroyed even if it is not possible to avoid thereby the dangers which threaten the crews and passengers'. The announcement added that, 'owing to the British misuse of neutral flags', neutral shipping might also be endangered. In a clumsy attempt to deflect the anger of the United States, they issued a statement on 19 February that it had been confirmed by 'an intercepted wireless message' that British submarines were under orders to sink the first American ship encountered and throw the blame on the Germans. Needless to say, this was pure invention; even the Germans would not have been so foolish as to broadcast to the world their ability to decode such a British signal had they in fact done so. It is, of course, true that only a week earlier Churchill had written to the President of the Board of Trade, Walter Runciman, that it was 'most important to attract neutral shipping to our shores, in the hopes especially of embroiling the United States with Germany. The German formal announcement of indiscriminate submarining has been made to the United States to produce a deterrent effect on traffic. For our part we want the traffic – the more the better; and if some of it gets into trouble, better still . . .' Churchill, like many other Englishmen (and not a few Americans, such as Walter Hines Page, the Ambassador in London), could not understand why President Wilson somehow seemed incapable of realising that Britain and France were defending democracy and freedom, all that America held most dear, against a ruthless, uncivilised power, bent on world domination. Of course Churchill would have welcomed American involvement on the Allied side (provided, naturally, that it did not result in any diminution of British power and influence). But the letter to Runciman can hardly be adduced as proof that the 1st Lord was prepared to go so far as to order the Royal Navy to sink neutral American ships in order to bring this about.

By the end of 1914, Room 40 were well informed about the strength and general location of the U-boat fleet. In January 1915 Hope began submitting a daily return to Churchill, Fisher, A. K. Wilson and Oliver which set out the last known position of every U-boat mentioned in decodes. Thanks to the frequent wireless reports made by German coastal stations, by the senior officers of flotillas, and by the FdU himself (Senior Officer, U-boats), Hope had already built up an accurate idea of the composition of each flotilla, and so of the total operational strength, of the location and state of readiness of every individual boat if in port, and when and if it put to sea. The total threat was thus clearly known. Moreover, the wireless reports from coastal stations that 'U. so and so' had sailed, usually included the words 'to the west' or 'to the north-west' and sometimes added 'for a distant operation', thus giving some clue as to the boat's intended patrol area. Nor was this all. Orders from the *Hochseeflotte* to the FdU or from that officer to flotilla commanders were sometimes even more precise, while Neumünster's regular broadcasts, addressed to 'All ships' but obviously intended for the benefit of U-boats, reported British shipping movements and frequently the latest Admiralty advice and instructions. If this information referred to areas hitherto clear of U-boats it provided a pretty good indication that the enemy was either on his way there or had already arrived. As the Germans began to realise that wireless transmission and reception by U-boats was possible at a far greater range than they had previously supposed, it became the custom for U-boats to test communications by sending position reports, sometimes every two or three hours, for the first two days of their outward passage. This of course gave the British precise information about their course and speed of advance. However, at this stage, transmission and reception was only considered possible for a distance of two or three hundred miles, so that when U-boats began to push out into the Atlantic this source of information ceased. It was then a question of 'by guess and by God' both for the British and German authorities in estimating the exact position of an individual U-boat at any specific moment, until, on its homeward voyage and once more within wireless range of its base, it announced its position, estimated time of arrival and a list of sinkings.

To sum up, it can be said that, early in 1915, Room 40 knew the total strength of the U-boat fleet, the rate at which it was growing, the number of U-boats at sea or in port, losses, as evidenced by the failure of a U-boat to return, and, in most cases, the size of the threat in any particular area. It was information of enormous value, but it did not mean that the position of each and every U-boat on patrol could be pin-pointed with any degree of accuracy; the sea was vast, weather and other conditions were unpredictable, and the decisions of individual U-boat commanding officers impossible to guess.

It must be emphasised that Room 40 was not an Intelligence centre; it was not operating as the Admiralty's World War II Submarine Tracking Room did, producing a continuous plot based on information from every possible source and working in close co-operation with the Trade Division to route merchant ships clear of danger. Room 40 was not permitted to keep a plot of British warships, let alone of merchant ships and therefore could have no idea whether a decoded U-boat position posed or did not pose an immediate threat to any British or Allied vessel or formation. The Director of the Trade Division (DTD), Captain Richard Webb, was probably not even aware of Room 40's existence; he certainly had no direct access to the information it produced. Nor for that matter did the staff of the E 1 (German) section of the Intelligence Division. Although by the spring of 1915 at least some of the staff of E 1 were doing their best to follow the movements of U-boats, it must have been a case of the blind leading the blind so far as any advice which they could give Webb and his men. In any case, with so few merchant ships equipped with wireless and no convoy system, the problem of controlling the hundreds of ships sailing independently and diverting them from known danger areas was well nigh insuperable.

Hope's daily returns were, however, closely studied by Churchill who initialled them regularly unless he was absent from the Admiralty, and often sent them back to Hope with comments and enquiries scrawled in the margin. For example, on 15 March, when Hope had reported that U 33 was 'preparing for a distant operation. Ready 16 March,' Churchill wrote in the margin, 'Watch this carefully.' Doubtless he was anxious about the despatch of a U-boat to the Dardanelles, disclosed in the Usedom Telegram. In fact, Oliver and Wilson were the only people able to study Hope's returns and the individual decodes in depth, and to decide what action if any should be taken as a result. In so far as the information from Room 40 seemed to affect the Grand Fleet or other Royal Navy formations or ships, the authorities were kept promptly and very fully informed; it must be remembered that, until the German announcement in February, warships and to some extent troopships were the U-boats' primary targets. Strenuous efforts were made by means of indicator nets, minefields and patrols to render the passage of the Strait of Dover impassable by U-boats, thus denying them the ability to attack military and other traffic to France or the focal points through which all British overseas shipping had to pass – the entrance to the English Channel, or the entrance to the St George's Channel and the Irish Sea. The North Channel, giving access to the Clyde and an alternative approach to Liverpool not only seemed beyond the range of a U-boat coming southabout Britain, but was in fact closed to British shipping because of the

Tory Island mine field laid by the disguised German minelayer *Berlin* in October 1914. Although, for the reasons already given, the general control and protection of merchant shipping was extremely difficult, Oliver did take energetic steps to ensure the safety of particularly important individual merchant ships, when danger seemed to threaten, by holding them in port, diverting them or even providing destroyer escort.

The first U-boat to penetrate as far as the Irish Sea was U 21, towards the end of January 1915. Her departure from Germany and passage down the English Channel had been at once detected by Room 40, and her patrol area revealed by Norddeich (Neumünster) giving information about conditions off Barrow-in-Furness. As a result Oliver sent the following signal to a large number of authorities, some of them quite minor commands:[1] 'It has been ascertained on reliable authority that a German submarine is proceeding down [the English] Channel to go up Irish Channel[2] and operate in the vicinity of Barrow-in-Furness. Her subsequent movements are not known.' The Cunard liners *Transylvania*[3] and *Ausonia*, carrying two 14-inch naval gun barrels and mountings from Bethlehem Steel in the States, were diverted to Queenstown to await destroyer escort. Destroyers were detached from the Grand Fleet to sweep down from the north and from the Harwich Force to come up from the south. U 21 after shelling Walney Island (Barrow-in-Furness) on 29 January and being fired on by an armed yacht and after sinking three ships in Liverpool Bay, started her return passage. Although this was anticipated by Oliver and Wilson, who warned Dover, it could not be confirmed until she reported by wireless on 6 February. She reached the Ems on 8 February, when a fairly detailed report of her experiences was intercepted by Room 40.

In the meantime Kapitänleutnant Schwieger had been operating in the English Channel where he sank three ships without warning, and fired a torpedo, which missed, at the hospital-ship *Asturias*,

[1] The actual addresses were SO Cruiser Force G, C-in-C Grand Fleet, Admiral Queenstown, SO Cruiser Force E, SNO Belfast, SNO Liverpool, SNO Larne, Captain Supt Pembroke, *Targ* via War Signal Stations Mull of Kintyre and Tor Head.

[2] The Irish Sea, sometimes referred to at this time as the Irish Channel, is the water between Ireland and England, bounded on the north by the North Channel and on the south by the St George's Channel. It does not include the waters south of Ireland from the Fastnet to Waterford.

[3] Commanded at this time by Captain William Turner.

[4] He was under instructions to sink any ships in this area as it was considered that they must either be troopships or supply ships for the BEF.

claiming that he mistook her for a transport. He returned to the Ems on 8 February after some hair-raising experiences with one of the anti-submarine nets in the Strait.

The British reaction to this was to order the fitting out of Q ships,[1] the defensive arming of 100 ships in the coastal trade, and to instruct merchant ships if attacked by a U-boat from ahead to steer straight for it to compel it to dive – the so called 'ramming' order, although this word was carefully omitted from the instruction. This order was intercepted by Neumünster and U-boats were informed, something which naturally did not encourage their commanding officers to take any chances.

The western English Channel and the Irish Sea did not remain clear of U-boats for long. On 11 February Room 40 learned that U 30 was about to leave for an operation 'to the west', and instructions were immediately passed to Dover to try to intercept her. She was due to be followed shortly by U 8, a smaller type destined only for the eastern part of the English Channel. However, the threat to the Irish Sea caused the Admiralty to strengthen the North Channel patrol by four more destroyers. It was 17 February, and the unrestricted campaign was about to start in earnest. Norddeich issued instructions, intercepted by Room 40, that certain American ships were not to be attacked. The use of neutral flags and the wholesale defensive arming of merchant ships seemed even more desirable to the British. By 20 February U 30 had reached the Irish Sea and sank two ships. As a result two steamers carrying horses for the Army from America to Liverpool were diverted into Queenstown and held there pending the provision of escorts despite the fact that the horses were dying. By 25 February U 30 had started her return voyage, but on the same day two more U-boats, U 27 and Schwieger's U 20 were signalled as having left on 'distant operations'. U 27 incidentally, was the first U-boat to carry out wireless experiments while crossing the North Sea. As a result Jellicoe was given her position and the information that she seemed to be making for Fair Isle at ten knots. U 27 was destined for the Irish Sea northabout, but it was learned that U 20 had had to put into Bruges for minor repairs, and so she would reach her patrol area via the English Channel. U 27 was sighted off the Orkneys as expected.

On 3 March Norddeich broadcast that the *Lusitania* was expected

---

[1] Merchant ships with naval crews equipped with a good but concealed gun armament to lure U-boats into attacking them.

to reach Liverpool from New York on 4 or 5 March. Trade Division, apparently at the Cunard Company's request signalled *Lusitania* as follows: 'Owners advise keep well out. Time arrival to cross bar without waiting.' Oliver, despite the fact that at this time there was a grave shortage of destroyers, ordered two to be sent out to escort the *Lusitania* and the first Q ship HMS *Lyons*, was sent to cruise in Liverpool Bay. In the event, the senior officer of the destroyers detailed to escort *Lusitania* had the greatest difficulty in ascertaining either from the Cunard Company or the Admiralty just when the liner could be expected or on what precise route, and then failed to make contact because he had not been issued with the Merchant Navy code; *Lusitania*'s master, Captain Dow, who did not of course hold any naval codes, refused to disclose his position *en clair*. South of Ireland, the cruiser HMS *Essex* and three Canadian troops ships, which were also carrying civilian passengers, were diverted into Queenstown to await destroyer escort; a good example of the ease with which a convoy with warship escort could be controlled. In the English Channel U 8 was caught in nets in the Strait of Dover and all her crew captured. They were treated, on Admiralty instructions, as 'accused persons' awaiting trial and subjected to harsh treatment until reprisals by the Germans and Churchill's and Fisher's departure from the Admiralty caused a modification to this policy.

Schwieger reached the Bristol Channel and pushed on up the Irish Sea. After sinking one ship, he decided to start his return via the North Channel, but claimed to have encountered very strong patrols and to have been forced to lie on the bottom for the whole of one night. Always a prudent commander, to put it charitably, he therefore went back the way he had come, via the English Channel. U 27 however, went northabout and reached port safely. U 29, which had been operating in the English Channel and was also returning northabout, attempted to attack the Grand Fleet off Scapa; she was rammed by HMS *Dreadnought*, and sank with all hands including her commanding officer, Weddingen, who had sunk the *Cressy*, *Aboukir* and *Hogue* in the previous September. Before this had happened and before it had become known to the British that U 20 had also left the Irish Sea, concern had been felt about the *Lusitania* due to sail again for New York on 10 March, a fact broadcast as usual by Norddeich. Oliver directed that she be held in port until 20 March when it was certain that the area was clear.

On 27 March Room 40 decoded a Neumünster broadcast which

confirmed that the Germans were currently reading the Merchant Navy Code in which advice and instructions were regularly sent to British Merchant Ships. Oliver immediately signalled C-in-C Devonport Cruiser Force E and Cruiser Force G that 'wireless messages should not be made to merchant vessels giving them directions as to routes. It only informs German submarines where to look for them. Unless signals can be made visually they should not be made.' This instruction does not seem to have been passed to Queenstown, which continued to use a code known by Oliver to be compromised.

Despite the sinking of U 8 in the English Channel, Churchill was much displeased with what he and Fisher considered the failure of Hood, his former Naval Secretary, now commanding at Dover, to prevent U-boats traversing the Strait more or less at will. Hood was summarily removed from his command and sent instead to Cruiser Force E at Queenstown. Cruiser Force E consisted of a number of obsolete cruisers and ocean-boarding vessels which, in turn, acted as station ships off south-west Ireland. They were in no sense anti-submarine ships, indeed they were tempting targets for any U-boat. Their mission was to act against any armed merchant raider or bold blockade breaker which might appear, and to pass on directions to inward-bound British merchant ships. In February Force E's patrol area had been shifted two hundred miles to the west of the Fastnet in order to minimise any risk to them from U-boats.

On 28 March, for the first time, a U-boat began to operate off the south-eastern coast of Ireland; U 28 sank the SS *Fallaba* close to the Coningbeg Light Vessel, which marks the western entrance to the St George's Channel. 104 lives were lost. U 28 was followed by U 32. U 32 had, contrary to Churchill's views, experienced such difficulties in passing through Hood's defences that when she started her return voyage she not only did so northabout but, when again in communication with base, sent in a report which caused the Germans to give instructions that the English Channel route was to be abandoned and that all U-boats operating in the North-Western and South-Western Approaches were to proceed northabout in future. The change in routing soon became apparent to Room 40. Churchill recognised that he had done Hood an injustice, and one of his last acts before leaving the Admiralty was to appoint him to command the 3rd Battle Cruiser Squadron of the Grand Fleet. He perished when his flagship, *Invincible*, blew up at the Battle of Jutland.

On 15 April the North Channel was declared free of mines, but for some reason permission to use it was not at once given to merchant ships. Two days later the *Lusitania*, now under the command of Captain William Turner,[1] sailed on what was to be her last westbound crossing; she arrived in New York on 24 April. These dates are of significance because, in the Admiralty's Trade Division, Captain Webb had been busy preparing fresh instructions for merchant ships to meet the rapidly growing danger from U-boats. These instructions included, for the first time, the advice that merchant ships should follow Royal Navy practice and zigzag when in known danger areas. The instructions had to be referred to Churchill for final approval which was not given until 25 April, but distribution outside the Admiralty did not even start until 13 May. They therefore cannot possibly have been in Turner's possession when he sailed from New York on the *Lusitania*'s final fatal voyage on 1 May, despite definite and repeated claims by the Admiralty, and it must be said, somewhat confused and hesitant admissions by Turner, to the contrary.

We must now remind readers of the fears of the Germans throughout the first four months of 1915, that the British were intending to carry out some major offensive operation against their coasts, culminating in the information planted by Hall and Drake that Schleswig-Holstein was to be invaded. On 19 April cross-channel traffic to Holland was halted, and the Germans became convinced that 'D.Day' was imminent.

U-boats, including Schwieger's U 20 were held ready for operations in the Heligoland Bight despite the fact that normal refit and rest time had not been completed. On 24 April the Germans received Hall's planted reports that there were heavy sailings of troop transports from British west and south coast ports, resulting in the demand from the General Staff for something more than merely defensive measures. On 25 April, U 30 sailed to replace another U-boat destined for the Irish Sea, U 22, which had returned due to engine trouble. Bauer, FdU (Senior Officer, U-boats) recorded in his War Diary that orders were received for all available U-boats, large and small, to be sent immediately to attack shipping off British ports, the smaller Flanders boats from Yarmouth down to the English Channel, and the ocean-going boats to the northern North Sea, to attack possible invasion transports sailing from Hull, and to lie in wait for the Grand Fleet. Yet others were to proceed north-about Scotland to British west and south coast ports allegedly being

[1] The Cunard Company did not appoint masters permanently to their large liners, but shifted them from ship to ship as convenient.

used to transport British troops to France or the Dardanelles. Such was the urgency that U 30 had been under way only a few hours when fresh orders were signalled to her, changing her area of operations from the Irish Sea to Dartmouth. Around midday on 25 April, Room 40 intercepted a signal to U 30 telling her that large movements of English troops were to be expected from southern and western coasts of England. U 30 was to proceed by the fastest route round Scotland to the English Channel and to take up a position off Dartmouth. She was to stay on patrol as long as supplies lasted and was to attack transports, merchant shipping and warships. She was also informed that U 20 and U 27 were being ordered to the Irish Sea and Bristol Channel. Bauer makes clear in his War Diary that Dartmouth was regarded as the least important target area, and because there was some doubt about whether U 30 would receive these wirelessed instructions she was allocated this area, leaving the most vital points to the other two U-boats who had not yet sailed and to whom orders could be issued in writing.

Oliver thus had clear warning of the precise areas which were threatened and, by this time, sufficient experience to estimate with some accuracy when the U-boats concerned were likely to arrive on station. In striking contrast to the action taken on previous occasions, the only warning passed to the commands affected was a signal made by Admiralty on 29 April to Larne, Glasgow, Liverpool and Queenstown (not Devonport), repeating alleged sightings of U-boats that day well out in the Atlantic to the west of northern Ireland, and off St Kilda, west of the Hebrides. The signal added that 'auxiliary patrols and west coast should be informed and cautioned that submarines may be expected from north passing westabout.' It should be particularly noted that the information available about U 30's movements was not even passed to Jellicoe, who was normally kept completely au fait with such reports. U 30 had in fact been sighted two days earlier and unsuccessfully hunted in the Fair Isle Channel (between the Orkney and Shetlands), but it cannot be established whether the later sightings were or were not genuine. It is possible that one of them may have been of U 21, which had left Germany on 25 April bound for the Mediterranean. Her departure was immediately known to Room 40, but her destination, although suspected because of the Usedom Telegram, could not be at once established. It so happened that U 30 was by chance steaming south on the track used by the Grand Fleet colliers thirty miles off the west coast of Ireland, and had sunk three of them and a Russian collier between 28 and 30 April. As soon as reports from their survivors that details of the secret route had been captured were received, it was altered and further losses avoided. U 30 reached the Scillies in the western entrance to the English Channel on 1 May and torpedoed the US tanker *Gulflight*, which was being forcibly escorted to the Channel Islands by British patrols. The ship did not sink, but the master had a fatal heart attack and two members of the crew jumped overboard and were drowned. The newly commissioned Q ship *Baralong*[1] had been warned of the likelihood of a U-boat operating off Dartmouth, but she and *Lyons* were not informed of the sinkings near the Scillies and remained inactive in Torbay. U 30's fuel was low if she was to return westabout rather than up the English Channel, and after sinking another ship near the Scillies, she started her return passage on 3 May. Although she hoped to pick up more colliers she failed to find any because of the change of route to the North Channel and the Minches. Neither FdU nor Room 40 were aware of her whereabouts, until on 8 May she made her first report from the middle of the North Sea, announcing her estimated time of arrival at base, and adding that she had been unable to reach Dartmouth due to insufficient fuel.

So much for U 30. By 29 April the *Admiralstab* had responded further to the Army's demand for offensive action and four ocean-going boats left on operations. They were U 35, U 36, U 39 and U 41. Next day, 30 April, Oliver signalled Jellicoe that 'Four submarines sailed yesterday from Heligoland. They are proceeding from Horns Riff to Buchannes and thence probably north. Two to Lindesnes and then probably Fair Isle. They appear to be making good 12½ knots. Do not divulge exact source of information in any steps you take.' This was followed two hours later by the news that two further U-boats had left Borkum on a north-westerly course and that Rosyth had been informed of the possibility of extra U-boat activity. The U-boats in question were U 28 destined for the North Sea and U 20 bound for the Irish Sea. Oliver was well aware of the destination at least of Schwieger's U 20 but despite the warning to Jellicoe, and to Rosyth, no information was sent to Liverpool, Queenstown or Milford Haven. On 2 May Oliver did

---

[1] Her captain, Godfrey Herbert, later sank U 41 and shot the survivors in a most cold-blooded fashion. British opinion was of course much inflamed by the loss of life involved in the sinking of the *Lusitania* and other passenger ships, but Herbert was, with some justice, regarded as a 'war criminal' by the Germans.

suggest to Jellicoe that the sailing of the battleship *Orion*, which had just completed a refit at Devonport and was urgently required back with Grand Fleet, be temporarily deferred, and when she did in fact sail, on 4 May, she was given an escort of four destroyers and instructed that because of submarines operating off west and south coasts she was to keep at least fifty miles from the Scillies, 100 miles from the Irish coast and sixty miles to the west of the Hebrides. Similarly, the cruiser *Gloucester* returning from Gibraltar was ordered to pass sixty miles west of Cape Finisterre, to cross the parallel of 50 North in Longitude 9 West and then steer a mid-channel course up the Irish Channel. After passing 49N she was to maintain a speed of not less than twenty knots and to zigzag. The old battleship *Jupiter*, returning to Barrow for repairs after a trip to North Russia, was given a destroyer escort and routed in through the North Channel. It can be seen that the potential threat to warships was clearly recognised and precautions taken. The same cannot be said for merchant shipping. The North Channel had been declared free of mines on 15 April, but it was not until 2 May that Captain Webb was informed that masters of merchant ships could be advised of this provided the circumstances seemed to warrant it. One can only assume that this meant provided no merchant ships had been recently attacked there or if this route appeared safer than that via the St George's Channel because, as Webb had no access to Room 40, he can only have become aware of the location of any U-boat after it had disclosed its presence by a sinking or by being sighted.

The second U-boat destined for the southern half of the Irish Sea, U 27, had been delayed and did not sail until 4 May. On 5 May a decoded position report placed her outwardbound in the North Sea, but this information was not passed to Jellicoe.

On 4 May the following memo was issued in the Admiralty: 'The arrangements proposed for the issue of warning signals are fully described in orders to C-in-C Devonport and VA Queenstown. With regards to information available only at the Admiralty [i.e. from Room 40's decodes] it is suggested that under ordinary circumstances the Director of Trade Division should be the recognised medium of communication between Admiralty and Shipping Intelligence Officers, and that information of importance to the Mercantile Marine in the possession of other Divisions of the War Staff should as a rule be communicated through Trade Division. *In case of urgency the proper authorities would as at present communi-*

cate with *C-in-C Devonport and VA Queenstown.*'[1] This was a thoroughly bad instruction. Trade Division had at least some knowledge of where British merchant ships might be, but no contact with Room 40. Room 40 knew nothing of the whereabouts of British merchant ships and had no authority to communicate their knowledge about U-boats to anyone except Wilson and Oliver. If the Intelligence Division were at this time trying to keep a plot of U-boat movements, they also were denied the benefit to Room 40's priceless information. So far as the Intelligence Division and Trade Division were concerned it was a case of the blind leading the blind. Although some sort of a plot was kept in the War Room, it is extremely unlikely that, at this stage, it included the positions of all merchant ships and even more unlikely that it permanently recorded the known and estimated positions of all U-boats;[2] these were only marked up on charts in the personal care of Oliver and A. K. Wilson. By 2 May the Admiralty were aware of the German warning which had appeared in American newspapers that passengers should not travel in British ships.

Two other points need to be noted before we turn again to the exploits of Kapitänleutnant Walther Schwieger. Back on 29 March, the Admiralty had informed the Canadian authorities that no further convoys of Canadian troops could be received after 7 May due to the difficulty of providing ocean escorts, a very thin excuse. On 23 April, after traffic between England and Holland was halted, all other overseas troop movements to and from the British Isles were also stopped with one exception, the movement of X Division[3] from Dublin to Liverpool, which was to start on 27 April and was to last for eight nights under destroyer escort. This movement was duly completed on 5 May and the destroyers concerned, *Legion* (whom we last met off The Texel on 17 October 1914), *Lucifer*, *Linnet* and *Laverock* were instructed to proceed from Dublin to Milford Haven and await further orders.

---

[1] Author's italics. 'The proper authorities' must mean Oliver.

[2] According to Oliver, there was an immense chart of the world in the War Room, 'with pins and flags showing the positions of all ships but my first task after visiting Churchill each morning (sitting up in bed with a big cigar working at papers and telegrams) was to shift the flags showing the places of any important movements to incorrect places. This was necessary because Churchill and Fisher and other dignitaries brought in MPs and Lords and Cabinet Ministers and Bishops and all sorts of club gossips and editors, etc. to see the Map and an incorrect map impressed them just as much. I kept the correct charts covered up on a table in my office . . .'

[3] A freshly raised Irish Division destined for the Dardanelles.

Schwieger had sailed during the forenoon of 30 April; he tested wireless communications and reported his progress across the North Sea no fewer than fourteen times during the next twenty-four hours; none of these position reports were passed to Jellicoe. Schwieger then ceased transmitting because he began himself to pick up British signals whose increasing strength warned him that enemy forces were not far off. Avoiding patrols hunting off Peterhead, he passed through the Fair Isle channel during the forenoon of 2 May, sighting but not being seen by further destroyers and patrol craft. That night he sighted a large neutral passenger steamer with her name illumin-ated, a Dane bound for America, or so he thought, but was too far off to attack. It is clear from his log entry that he would have done so had he been able! Next evening he tried to torpedo a 2000-ton steamer flying the Danish Flag, which his ex-merchant navy reserve quartermaster[1] considered to be in fact British. The torpedo tube jammed and the ship escaped. Throughout that day he continued south down the west coast of Scotland and Ireland, generally in poor visibility. On the evening of 4 May he again attacked what he describes as a neutral Swede, the *Hibernia*, but missed. It is clear that he was perfectly prepared to attack vessels without warning whether they were neutral or not. By the afternoon of 5 May Schwieger, now proceeding east along the south coast of Ireland, had reached the Old Head of Kinsale. He sighted what he at first took to be a large sailing vessel. On approaching closer, however, he found that she was a small three-masted schooner. Seeing no gun and apprehending no danger, he this time allowed the five-man crew time to take to their boat before sinking the ship, *The Earl of Lathom*, by bombs. The crew rowed ashore and by 9.30 that evening the news of the sinking had reached Queenstown and the Admiralty. Proceeding further eastward, Schwieger encountered yet another 'neutral' steamer near Daunt's Rock off Queenstown. The vessel was in fact the British *Cayo Romano*. Schwieger's torpedo missed, and the *Cayo Romano* reached Queenstown and reported the incident. This news was passed to the Admiralty before midnight. Both Queenstown and Admiralty therefore had positive and open proof that a U-boat was within twenty miles of Queens-town on the main shipping route for Atlantic trade to and from Liverpool.

---

[1] Highly praised by Schwieger for his ability to recognise British merchant ships and advise on their normal speed.

At 10.30 p.m. Queenstown broadcast a message *en clair*, warning merchant ships that a U-boat was active off the south coast of Ireland – a rather vague statement in the light of the precise knowledge available. Shortly after midnight (5–6 May) the usual general advice was broadcast to all homeward-bound British merchant ships as had been done every night since March. It read: 'Between South Foreland and Folkestone keep within two miles of shore and pass between the two light vessels. Take Liverpool pilot at Bar. Avoid headlands. Pass harbours at full speed. Steer mid-channel course. Submarine off Fastnet.' The only variation on this occasion was the last sentence, and the reason for its inclusion and the failure to include information about the *Earl of Lathom* and *Cayo Romano* incidents, is difficult to understand. No specific information or instructions were sent to *Lusitania*.

The visibility, which had been deteriorating now got worse, and Schwieger proceeded on submerged. Schwieger's Log entries show that he was a most cautious commander, attacking on the surface only if he considered there was absolutely no risk to his boat. When he surfaced next morning (6 May) he had reached the vicinity of the Coningbeg Light Vessel. During the forenoon, in variable visibility, he chased the British SS *Candidate* and eventually compelled her after several hits by gunfire to stop and abandon ship. As a torpedo then did not cause her to sink, he finished her off with more gunfire. The *Candidate*'s survivors were eventually picked up by patrol craft and landed at Milford Haven whence the news reached both the Admiralty and Queenstown at the latest by 3.40 a.m. on 7 May. Soon after sinking the *Candidate*, another steamer appeared out of the fog heading straight for U 20. Schwieger thought she was a White Star liner of 14,000 tons (she was the *Arabic*), but he was unable to get off a torpedo at her. That afternoon, however, he was luckier and sank another ship, the *Centurion*, with two torpedoes. *Centurion*'s survivors were also picked up and landed later that night. The news of this sinking had certainly reached Admiralty and Queenstown by 8.55 a.m. on the 7th. No immediate attempt to broadcast warnings of U-boat activity in the St George's Channel was made by either authority.

Let us try and look at the position as it might have appeared to Oliver. On 29 April a rather vague warning had been sent to the appropriate authorities that U-boats might be expected from the north passing westabout. Room 40's more precise information about U 30, U 20 and U 27 may have influenced this signal, but it was the *only* warning that was issued. By 1 May the sinkings off the Scillies must have made clear that U 30 was in the western English Channel. Previous experience would have indicated that she would not be able to remain there for more than a few days. Her return passage either south of Ireland, or possibly via the Irish Sea must have been anticipated; either route posed a threat to all shipping bound to or from Liverpool. U 20's departure was accurately known and her arrival south of Ireland could be calculated as being sometime between 4 and 5 May. So there were definitely two U-boats to be reckoned with somewhere between Dartmouth to the east and the south-west tip of Ireland to the west. Why was no firm appreciation of the positive threat given to Queenstown or Devonport – or Liverpool? The danger to *Lusitania* was obvious, if from nothing else then from Norddeich's regular broadcasts; the last was made on 6 May, informing all U-boats that she was due to sail again from Liverpool for New York on 15 May. The sinking of the *Earl of Lathom* and the attack on *Cayo Romano* off Daunt's Rock were open proof of the presence of a U-boat in the Queenstown area, facts known to the Admiralty by the late evening of 5 May. It should surely have been realised that these two incidents were most likely to have been caused by U 20, whose destination was known to be the Irish Sea. The threat to shipping in the St George's Channel by early on the 6th ought to have been obvious, not so much to Queenstown, who had *not* been told about U 20, but certainly to Oliver. Even Queenstown only had to work out the U-boat's furthest on position from the *Earl of Lathom* sinking to realise that there was danger. *Lusitania* was at this time some 750 miles west of the Fastnet, steaming east at twenty-one knots. The absence of any specific individual warning to her contrasts with the anxiety felt for HMS *Orion* in Devonport. Hood, in the old cruiser *Juno*, was returning to Queenstown having been relieved in the normal course of events by the ocean-boarding vessel *Partridge*. By 5 May the movement of X Division from Dublin to Liverpool had been completed, and *Legion*'s division of destroyers were instructed to proceed to Milford Haven. They arrived at their destination the following afternoon (6 May), and were later instructed to pick up the battleship *Colossus* at 12.30 p.m. on 8 May and escort her to Devonport.

In the usual nightly broadcast to all British merchant ships on the following night (6–7), the reference to a U-boat off the Fastnet was dropped possibly because it was felt by Queenstown that the report was false, which it was. However, by 1.30 a.m. on the 7th, at the latest, news of the sinking of the *Candidate* had reached Milford Haven (where the survivors had been landed and where four destroyers were lying idle) and both Admiralty and Queenstown. It has not been possible to establish whether either *Candidate* or *Centurion* or the ships which picked up their survivors had reported the facts earlier by wireless, because all the relevant papers are missing. Even if no wireless messages were received from any of these ships, the fact remains that the loss of one of them was known to the naval authorities at the very latest only an hour and a half after midnight, and that the loss of both of them was common knowledge to the Liverpool public by breakfast time. Once again there is no surviving record of any specific action being taken. There is, however, evidence that between 5 and 7 May five official radio telegrams were sent to and acknowledged by the *Lusitania*, that one message was received from her, and that two messages to her were received by the wireless stations but could not be sent because communication with her could not be established. Copies of these messages were forwarded by the Post Office (who operated the wireless stations) to the Admiralty on 2 June 1915. No trace of them can now be found, but there is some reason to suppose that they included a request from Turner to divert to the North Channel rather than use the St George's Channel, and that this request was refused. Such a diversion would have been possible because at 5.00 a.m. on 7 May *Lusitania* was still 120 miles west-south-west of the Fastnet, when she passed *Partridge* on patrol. Moreover, Webb had been informed on 2 May that the North Channel was at last open to merchant shipping if the circumstances seemed to warrant it.

At 12.40 p.m. on 7 May Queenstown informed Admiralty that one of the Auxiliary Patrol had sighted a U-boat five miles south of Cape Clear at 10.00 a.m., proceeding west. The Admiralty claimed that this information had been simultaneously passed to *Lusitania*. The veracity both of the report (which certainly could not have been of a German submarine) and of the receipt of the information by *Lusitania*, is very much open to question. Nevertheless, auxiliary patrols were ordered to hunt in this area, while no similar action was ordered in the St George's Channel.

By this time a number of reports of U-boats being sighted in widely separated areas had been coming in, most if not all of them quite baseless. Webb may have been confused; nor do we know whether he had any authority to divert shipping on his own initiative. Oliver, on the other hand, must have known by now that only

U 20 could be off southern Ireland and that she had been within
twenty miles of the Coningbeg Light Vessel at midday on the 6th,
and so could not be more than eighty miles away from that position
by the following forenoon. He might well have thought that she was
proceeding north up the Irish Sea to Liverpool, and could arrive
there at the same time as the *Lusitania* if she came in through the
North Channel. On the other hand, it ought to have been apparent
to him that the danger would be even greater if the liner overhauled
the U-boat in the St George's Channel or the southern Irish Sea. In
either case, why did he do nothing at all? Destroyers were available
either to hunt the U-boat or to escort the liner both at Liverpool and
Milford Haven. *Lusitania* could have been instructed to make at
maximum speed for Queenstown. So far as the available records
show, nothing was done even to give her the latest information until
11.15 a.m. on the 7th when a message from Admiral Queenstown
was broadcast to all British merchant ships, stating the U-boats
were 'active in southern part of Irish Channel.[1] Last heard of twenty
miles south of Coningbeg Light Vessel.' This message could have
been sent at least eight hours earlier. That it was sent at all was
probably due to the fact that Alfred Booth, Chairman of the Cunard
Company, had been much alarmed at breakfast time, when in
common with everyone else in Liverpool, he had learned of the
sinking of the *Candidate* and the *Centurion*. He had gone at once to
the Senior Naval Officer, Liverpool, and enquired whether any
special warning had been sent to his famous ship, and begged the
SNO to see that something was done.

What was the cautious Walther Schwieger doing at this moment?
His log records the following:

6 May. 3.15 p.m. [German time – one hour ahead of British time].
Thick fog. Dived to 24 metres. Course 240 degrees in order to
keep out at sea. Decided not to proceed further towards Liverpool, the proper operational area, for the following reasons:
1) With the thick fog, the lack of wind and the state of the
   barometer during the last two days, no expectation of clearer
   weather in the next few days.
2) Timely sighting of the expected strong enemy patrols of
   destroyers and trawlers in the St George's Channel and Irish
   Sea not possible in thick weather; therefore continual danger
   necessitating submerged passage.

[1] Not, be it noted, off the south coast of Ireland.

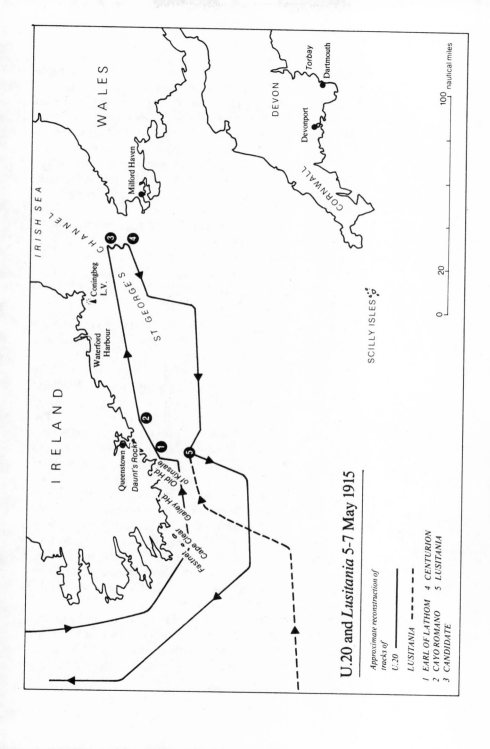

U.20 and *Lusitania* 5-7 May 1915

Approximate reconstruction of tracks of

U.20 ——————

LUSITANIA - - - - - -

1 *EARL OF LATHOM* 4 *CENTURION*
2 *CAYO ROMANO*   5 *LUSITANIA*
3 *CANDIDATE*

0   50   100 nautical miles

IRELAND

WALES

DEVON

CORNWALL

IRISH SEA

ST GEORGE'S CHANNEL

Milford Haven

Waterford Harbour

Coningbeg L.V.

Queenstown
Daunt's Rock
Old Hd. of Kinsale
Galley Hd.
Fastnet
Cape Clear

Devonport
Torbay
Dartmouth

SCILLY ISLES

3) Surface action against transports leaving Liverpool impossible except in clear weather at night, because escorting destroyers cannot be sighted in time. And it must be assumed that transports leave Liverpool at night and are escorted.

4) Passage to St George's Channel has already consumed so much fuel that return from Liverpool southabout Ireland would no longer be possible. I shall commence return passage when down to 2/5ths fuel, avoiding the North Channel if at all possible because of the type of patrolling experienced there by U 20 on her previous operation.

5) Only three torpedoes left, of which, if possible, two must be kept for the return passage.

Have therefore decided to remain to the south of the Bristol Channel and attack steamers until down to 2/5ths fuel, particularly as there are greater attacking opportunities here with less opposition than in the Irish Sea off Liverpool . . .

Schwieger might have thought differently had not *Legion*, *Lucifer*, *Laverock* and *Linnet*, not to mention the Q ships *Baralong* and *Lyons* all remained inexplicably inactive.

When Schwieger surfaced early on 7 May he found the visibility still poor, and decided to start his return passage south of Ireland without further ado, excusing himself in his log by saying that he would try to push into the North Channel from the north if the weather permitted. At 11 o'clock (German time) he sighted a fishing boat, which he thought might have been a patrol vessel, and as the weather suddenly cleared, he decided that discretion was the better part of valour, dived and made off. Shortly after this, he heard a ship pass over him at high speed. Allowing ten minutes to elapse, he came to periscope depth and saw in the distance an old cruiser zigzagging at high speed towards Queenstown. She was in fact Hood's *Juno*, maximum speed sixteen and a half knots, returning from station and zigzagging because of warnings specifically sent to her at 7.45 a.m. of U-boat danger off Queenstown.[1] One and a half hours later Schwieger sighted the *Lusitania*, with the results described at the beginning of this chapter.

Room 40's post-war verdict was that, 'There has never been any direct evidence to prove that submarine officers were ordered to sink the *Lusitania*, but from prisoners' statements it is clear that in German naval circles a view prevailed that Schwieger had definitely

---

[1] This signal was repeated to the Admiralty.

been order to lie in wait with a view to torpedoing her . . .' While it is perfectly obvious now that the encounter, where and when it happened, was purely fortuitous, the repeated broadcasts from Norddeich concerning her scheduled arrivals at and departures from Liverpool[1] show quite definitely that she, in common with other large liners also mentioned in the broadcasts, was considered by the *Admiralstab* as a prime and legitimate target for U-boats from the moment that unrestricted warfare was announced.

The Commander-in-Chief of the *Hochseeflotte*, who directly controlled the operations of U-boats in British waters, was informed by a wireless message at 8.15 p.m. on the evening of the sinking, that *Lusitania* had been sunk by a torpedo. This signal was intercepted by Room 40, but the originator could not be made out. It was probably derived from press reports, rather than from a signal made by Schwieger himself. There is no good evidence that U-boats could communicate with base or tried to do so from such a distance at this time, and the message was in a totally different form to the usual reports of successes made by U-boats. Moreover, the Germans themselves were not aware which U-boat had been responsible until Schwieger first re-established wireless contact with German wireless stations on the morning of 12 May, when he had re-entered the North Sea and was only 200 miles from Wilhelmshaven. He then signalled, 'Have sunk one sailing vessel, two steamers and *Lusitania*.' A later signal added that *Lusitania* had been sunk by *one* torpedo. The German response was immediate and unprecedented. Five hours later the C-in-C signalled U 20: 'My highest appreciation of commander and crew for success achieved of which *Hochseeflotte* is proud and my congratulations on their return.' The exchange of signals between Schwieger and his superiors was considered so important by the British that Ewing was instructed to obtain signed copies of the encoded messages from the Y station operators who had intercepted them. The copies, duly signed and certified as correct by Hippesley and the 'Chief censors' attached to the Post Office and Marconi stations, were returned to Ewing between 18 and 20 May. Subsequent German suggestions that Schwieger had acted without the approval of his superiors and that he was thereafter almost in disgrace, were no doubt produced by the belated realisation of the effects of the tragedy on non-

[1] Her scheduled sailings were regularly advertised in Lloyd's List and the British and American press.

German opinion. They were as hypocritical and as self-interested as the immediate attempts of the British authorities to throw all the blame for the disaster on the master of the *Lusitania*, the unfortunate Captain Turner.

Before considering what these British reactions to the disaster were, let us consider briefly what Oliver could or could not have done to avert it in conformity with action taken in similar circumstances in the past and in the future. He could have diverted *Lusitania* north of Ireland at any time up to about 6.00 a.m. on the morning of 7 May. He could have alerted Vice-Admiral Coke at Queenstown to the real danger threatening his area from 25 April onwards. He could have ordered *Legion*'s division of destroyers out from Milford Haven either to proceed to Queenstown to escort *Lusitania* when within range, or, at least, have sent the destroyers to search in the St George's Channel after the news of *Candidate*'s sinking came in on the night of 6–7 May. He could have given instructions for special warnings to be sent to *Lusitania* to increase to full speed and make for Queenstown. He could have positioned *Baralong* and *Lyons*, the two Q ships, more effectively. Neither he, nor anyone else, did any of these things. What he could not do, as has been suggested, was to order the obsolete cruiser *Juno* or the ocean-boarding vessel *Partridge*, to escort *Lusitania*; they were far too slow and never had been intended for such a task. That such a procedure might, in the event, have been sufficient to scare off the over-prudent Schwieger could not have been anticipated. The fact remains that none of these precautions were taken. To rely on the general instructions to all British merchant ships to steer a mid-channel course and to avoid making landfalls by approaching prominent headlands or light vessels, was patently absurd. The waters south of Ireland are *not* a 'channel'. These instructions were designed to cover the English Channel or the St George's Channel. Merchant ships eastbound from America, including the *Lusitania* on previous voyages, regularly made landfall off the Fastnet and then, as often as not, obtained a firm fix of their positions by a sight of the Old Head of Kinsale before entering the first 'channel', the St George's Channel, an area notorious for fog where accurate navigation depended, in those days before electronics, entirely on a clear observation of some established point on land. That such considerations were not forgotten by Oliver and Wilson, is shown by the detailed instructions as to the course they should follow sent to *Orion* and *Gloucester*. Why should it have been supposed that the master of a merchant ship should require less guidance than a post-captain of the Royal Navy?

The first in the rush to keep his own particular yard-arm clear, was Vice-Admiral Coke at Queenstown. As soon as the first news that *Lusitania* had been torpedoed was received he had ordered *Juno*, who had only just returned, to sail again and she did so in a commendably short time. However, before she had even cleared Queenstown harbour, and therefore long before she was in sight of the scene of the disaster, further reports came in showing that the liner had sunk and that numerous small craft had been ordered to the area to search for survivors. *Juno* could have done nothing constructive, and would merely have provided a sitting target for any U-boat commander bolder than Schwieger, who might have remained near the scene waiting for just such an opportunity. Coke therefore, very properly, recalled *Juno*. At 6.25 p.m. he reported to the Admiralty: 'Kinsale War Signal Station reports 20 boats of *Lusitania* in vicinity of place ship was sunk. Ship was especially warned that submarines were active on south coast and to keep mid-channel course avoiding headlands also position of submarine off Cape Clear at 10.00 a.m. was communicated by W/T to her . . .'

The hunt for a scapegoat was on, and the obvious candidate was Turner. That same evening Fisher directed that all reports of U-boat movements and sightings were to be collected into a special *Lusitania* file. Webb, perhaps with a guilty conscience, signalled Coke that he presumed Queenstown was sending warning messages of U-boats to merchant ships, and received a reply in the affirmative. It was a little late in the day! It was obvious that a full enquiry would have to be held, and Webb at once set about preparing the case which Churchill would present to the Cabinet. On one of Webb's many memos Fisher wrote, with characteristic underlinings, 'As the Cunard Company would not have employed an *incompetent* man it's a certainty that Captain Turner is not a fool but a knave. I hope that Captain Turner will be arrested immediately after the enquiry *whatever* the verdict.' Admittedly Fisher was within three days of the brainstorm leading to his resignation, but Churchill replied two days later, 'I consider the Admiralty's case against the Captain should be pressed by a skilful counsel and that Captain Webb should attend as a witness if not employed as an assessor [Judge and jury too!]. We will pursue the captain without check.' They did indeed! Two of the most eminent lawyers of the day, the Attorney General, Sir Edward Carson, and the Solicitor

General, F. E. Smith,[1] presented the Government's case. The Wreck Commissioners' enquiry, which opened on 15 June, was presided over by Lord Mersey, who had conducted the investigation into the loss of the *Titanic*, assisted by four assessors, an admiral and a lieutenant commander of the Royal Navy and two Merchant Navy captains, it having been decided in the end that it would be better if Webb did not appear in person. No doubt it was concluded that all concerned would do as they were told.

The Admiralty and the British Government were confronted with several problems in deciding what evidence should be laid before Lord Mersey's enquiry. It was due to open on 15 June. By this time both Churchill and Fisher had left the Admiralty, the former having been replaced as 1st Lord by A. J. Balfour, while Admiral Sir Henry Jackson had become 1st Sea Lord. Both of them were of course as fully informed of Room 40's activities as their predecessors had been, and were equally aware of the vital necessity of maintaining complete secrecy. There could be no question of disclosing the extent of British knowledge about the movements of U-boats. Quite apart from the security aspect, however, any such revelations would immediately have given rise to very awkward questions about why no precautions had been taken to protect *Lusitania*. There was also the lesser question of the security of the Merchant Navy Code and Naval codes in which relevant signals had been despatched. Room 40, and therefore Oliver and those others privy to its secrets, knew that the Merchant Navy Code had been compromised (and indeed a new version was issued shortly after the tragedy), but such an admission would not have helped the Admiralty's image if this fact and also the fact that Queenstown had continued to use the code (not having received orders to desist), had become public knowledge.

The main points at issue were to establish publicly the cause of the sinking and why it had occurred so unbelievably quickly, and secondly to determine whether the Admiralty, the Cunard Company or the master and crew were responsible for or could have done anything to mitigate the disaster. There was absolutely no doubt that the *Lusitania* had been torpedoed; the Germans did not deny it. This was a tremendous propaganda weapon for the British but only if the German claims that she had carried a lethal cargo of munitions could be refuted. Virtually all witnesses agreed that there had been a second explosion after Schwieger's torpedo had struck.

[1] Later lord Birkenhead.

It would obviously be advantageous to the British to try to establish that this second explosion was the result of a second torpedo or even a third, or at the very least due to the explosion of the liner's boilers or coal. By the middle of May, Room 40 knew very well that only U 20 had been involved, and that Schwieger's first wireless reports from sea, before any pressure could have been put upon him by his superiors, had stated unequivocally that he had only fired one torpedo. But of course none of those directly engaged in preparing the Admiralty's case – Webb and the civil servants in the Admiralty and the Foreign Office and Board of Trade – were aware of this. What they did know was that the *Lusitania*, in common with other fast Cunard liners, had for some time past been regularly carrying shells and other munitions ordered principally from the Bethlehem Steel Corporation in the States on every eastbound voyage. They also knew where these munitions were stowed, and could have established precisely their exact nature. The munitions were stowed, according to a telegram from Cunard's General Manager in New York to their General Manager in Liverpool, dated 29 June 1915, 'in the trunkway of meat boxes and 2 baggage deck . . .' this 'trunkway' was on the lower orlop deck below the bridge and just forward of the foremost bulkhead of the four boiler rooms – the exact point of impact of the torpedo observed by Schwieger, conforming precisely with the unusual second explosion which he recorded.

The British account, produced to the Enquiry, and accepted by Lord Mersey, was that these munitions consisted of 4,200 cases of rifle ammunition, which it was claimed would not explode as a result of careless handling, shock or fire; 1,250 cases of 3.3-inch shrapnel shell cases, unfilled and therefore also harmless; and eighteen cases of percussion fuses, which, it was claimed, were stowed separately, aft, in the *Lusitania*'s own magazine. John Light has conclusive evidence that the shells were not empty cases; they were filled although not fused. Unlike shipments of 'trial' cases for proof purposes, which had invariably been consigned to the 'Superintendent of Experiments at Shoeburyness', these were consigned, as were all regular munitions shipments, to the 'Royal Arsenal, Woolwich'. It should be noted, again according to Cunard's New York General Manager, in a telegram to Liverpool, that *Lusitania* on her previous voyage had carried 'Special shipments, Bethlehem, 18 cases fuses, 1466 cases shrapnel shells *filled*,[1] . . . two Orlop and two

---

[1] Author's italics. Light has the original and possibly only surviving Cunard files concerning the sinking of the *Lusitania*.

refrigerator hatch . . .', exactly where the munitions were again stowed on her last voyage. This cable specifically stated that the shells were filled and that the fuses were stowed in the same space as the shells. The fuses consisted of fulminate of mercury, a highly sensitive substance. There is no obvious reason why they should have been stowed in any different manner on *Lusitania*'s next voyage.

But to admit all this would have been to concede the German claim that the liner sank so quickly, and with such appalling loss of life, only because her cargo, contraband in German eyes, exploded. Filled shells, even unfused, might conceivably have been caused to explode by the one torpedo; if the fulminate of mercury fuses were also in the same area, an enormous explosion would have been inevitable. Such facts would not only have blunted the revulsion of the world against German brutality, it would have raised questions about the British policy of shipping dangerous munitions in passenger vessels carrying civilian, not to mention neutral, passengers. Worse still, it would inevitably have meant that the American authorities and the Collector of Customs at New York, officially responsible for the enforcement of the American Neutrality Laws, would have had to enforce those laws rigidly instead of turning a blind eye, as was done, to breaches of the rules. Britain was in the midst of a munitions crisis which was endangering the position of Mr Asquith's Government; the Army in France was desperately short of shells. Any curtailment of the by now considerable flow of munitions, transported in the fastest ships available, would have been disastrous.

This, then, was the second fact that had to be concealed. It had somehow to be shown that the second, very large explosion, testified to by one and all, had nothing to do with *Lusitania*'s cargo. The only way to do this was to produce 'evidence' that it occurred much further aft than in fact was the case. Could not the second explosion have been caused by a second torpedo, or by a boiler explosion? There were survivors from all three boiler rooms; none of them mentioned any explosion and some of them reported that water had first entered No. 1 Boiler Room through the bulkhead at its foreward end. None of them were called to give evidence. A large proportion of the liner's seamen were working in the passengers' luggage store, just above where the ammunition was stored. Not surprisingly, not a man survived. When she was hit the ship began to sink immediately and very rapidly by the bows, which is

Acting Vice-Admiral Sir Henry Oliver, Chief of War Staff 1914–18

SMS *Magdeburg* as the Russians saw her on the morning of 26 August 1914

Copy No. 151 of the *Signalbuch der Kaiserlichen Marine* recovered from *Magdeburg* and now in the Public Record Office, Kew

Copy No. 369 of the *Handelsverkehrsbuch* recovered from SS *Hobart* and now in The Australian Archives, Brighton, Victoria

Vom H. V. B. getrennt aufzubewahren.

Geheim.   **Nr. 369.**

Chiffreschlüssel zum H. V. B.

A. Chiffrieren.

Gebrauchsanweisung.

1. Schlage im H. V. B. die Codewörter bzw. Verkehrsgruppen für die Bedeutungen des Telegrammes auf.

2. Suche jeden Buchstaben dieser Codewörter bzw. Verkehrsgruppen in Spalte 1 der nebenstehenden Chiffriertafel (schwarze Buchstaben) und setze dafür den in Spalte 2 stehenden roten Buchstaben ein.

Unchiffriert bleiben:

die Telegrammadresse,

das Kennwort — **havanbe** —,

bei dem chiffrierten Inhalte vorauszusetzende Codewort bzw. die Verkehrsgruppe für die Bedeutung: »Das folgende ist chiffriert mit dem Chiffreschlüssel zum H. V. B.« — **kisahaciba** — PCZA —.

Beispiel:

Ablösungstransportdampfer Neckar will unter Benutzung des Chiffreschlüssels dem Admiralstabe der Marine seine Ankunft in Schanghai mitteilen.

Im H. V. B. ist aufzuschlagen:	Umgesetzt nach Chiffriertafel:
für Admiralstab der Marine	hanibynixe	zivolevora
bin eingetroffen	kukiburohi	bybolytuzo
15. Juni	mifobalyri	comulineto
Schanghai	fysucixonu	mewydoruvy
Neckar	bugikarecu	lyxobitady

Das abzusendende Telegramm würde lauten:

Lloyd Bremen

havaube   kisahaciba

zibolevora   bybolytuzo   comulineto

mewydoruvy   lyxobitady

Chiffriertafel.	
1	2
a	i
b	l
c	d
d	s
e	a
f	m
g	x
h	z
i	o
k	b
l	n
m	c
n	v
o	u
p	g
r	t
s	w
t	f
u	y
v	p
w	k
x	r
y	e
z	h

The 'Charter' of Room 40 drafted by Winston Churchill in his own hand and initialled by him and Admiral Fisher on 8 November 1914

Sir Alfred Ewing, Director of Naval Education 1902–17, and first head of Room 40

'Blinker' Hall, Captain of HMS *Queen Mary,* 1914

RMS *Lusitania,* westbound two miles off The Old Head of Kinsale, 1911

Opposite: Battle squadrons of The Grand Fleet at sea, *c.* 19

Kapitänleutnant Schwieger's U 20

'Colonel McBride' and the skipper of SY *Sayonara*

entirely consistent with Light's discovery from his dives on the wreck that her bottom forward of the bridge had been blown *outwards*, and her bows nearly severed from the rest of the hull.

Fortunately for the authorities there were, as always in such cases, plenty of reports claiming that something very different had happened; that the 'first' torpedo had struck not forward of the first funnel and below the bridge, as in fact it did, but between the second and third funnel – i.e. well away from the munitions; that a 'second' torpedo had almost certainly struck the ship even further aft; that yet a 'third' torpedo had missed the ship and that this had been fired from the port, not the starboard side thus indicating that more than one U-boat had been involved. The witnesses who gave this 'evidence' were no doubt completely sincere in their assertions, as were those who claimed to have seen a submarine on the port side an hour before the disaster – although with the *Lusitania* steaming at that time at eighteen knots no submarine could have kept sufficiently close to her to have been in a position to take a part in her sinking. Such confused and contradictory reports, even from trained observers (which none of them were), are commonplace after disasters, especially ones which happen as swiftly as this one had done. But no matter how convincing these stories were made to sound, the hard facts are that the liner sank immediately and acutely by the bows, that there were no survivors from the baggage room, and that there were survivors from all three boiler rooms (the fourth and aftermost boiler room was out of commission), that none of them reported any explosion in the compartments in which they were working, and that water entered through the foremost bulkhead of No. 1 Boiler Room. This did not prevent Lord Mersey and his Assessors from accepting the evidence of those witnesses who were actually called and from finding that the ship was hit by two torpedoes, one between the first and second funnel and one, the cause of the second explosion, somewhere near the third funnel. This of course effectively disposed of any unwelcome suggestions that the cargo might have exploded!

The first coat of whitewash had therefore been liberally applied but, on its own, did nothing to disguise the fact that the Admiralty had entirely failed, whether by design or accident, to prevent the *Lusitania* being torpedoed, irrespective of whether she was hit by one or more torpedoes fired by one or more U-boats.

The obvious scapegoat was the luckless Captain Turner, selected as early as the evening of the disaster by Admiral Coke in his signal to the Admiralty. Turner, the Enquiry was told, had been specifically warned of the presence of U-boats; he had been instructed to proceed at full speed, to avoid headlands and prominent landfalls and to keep a mid-channel course, to zigzag and to time his arrival off the Liverpool Bar in darkness. He had, Webb reported, done none of these things except the last. In the highly suspicious absence of any trace of the signals exchanged by the Admiralty with *Lusitania* between 5 and 7 May, one cannot demolish all the charges against Turner with certainty, but some facts can be stated. First of all, he cannot possibly have received the advice to zigzag. Secondly, he was not *specifically* warned of U-boat danger. Such warnings as were sent out (and they were far less precise and far more dilatory than they should have been) were sent to all British merchant ships, not specifically to *Lusitania*. What did they consist of? That a U-boat had been reported off the Fastnet on 5 May; that U-boats were operating off the south coast of Ireland; not that the *Earl of Lathom* had been sunk off the Old Head of Kinsale and that a U-boat had been off Queenstown on 5 May; not, until late on the forenoon of 7 May, that ships had been sunk near the Coningbeg Light Vessel on the afternoon of 6 May. Thirdly, let us examine the advice to keep a mid-channel course. The waters south of Ireland are not a 'channel'. The advisory instructions were clearly intended to refer to the much narrower waters of the English Channel and particularly the Strait of Dover, and to the St George's Channel. This is the way Captain Turner understood them, and this is what anyone now reading them would equally do. Fourthly, the advice to maintain full speed. *Lusitania*'s full speed was twenty-four and a half knots, but, for reasons of economy, the Cunard Company had, some months back, closed down one of the four boiler rooms and reduced the number of stokers carried, with a resulting reduction in maximum speed to twenty-one knots. Early on the morning of 7 May, *Lusitania* had run into thick fog and Turner had prudently reduced speed to fifteen knots. By about 11.00 a.m. he had run out of the fog and had increased speed to eighteen knots. It was at once suggested that he should have reverted to his maximum speed of twenty-two knots[1], or even have brought in the stokers off watch and have lit the six boilers in No. 4 boiler room to raise steam for twenty-four and a half knots. Let us just note that, simple as it would have been to signal him specifically to do so, no such instructions

---

[1] This was the Admiralty's claim, but in fact *Lusitania's* maximum speed on nineteen boilers was twenty-one knots.

were sent; the contrast with the detailed orders sent to *Orion* and *Gloucester* is glaring. Let us also note that eighteen knots was faster than that of many warships and of almost all merchant ships at that time.[1]

Turner was one of Cunard's most experienced masters. He had commanded the *Lusitania* before and was in no sense a 'relief' skipper. He had gone to sea as a boy before the mast and had worked his way up to the top of his profession on his merits as a fine seaman, but obviously without the benefit of much formal education. He was a sailor of the old school, deeply conscious of his responsibilities for the safety of his crack liner but, like so many others, less appreciative of the fact that, in May 1915, the ordinary perils of the sea were no longer the only ones he had to face. He was making a landfall after six days at sea, and was doing so after running through thick fog. He was concerned to fix his position accurately before laying off a course to bring him safely through the narrow waters of the St George's Channel and make the run up the Irish Sea in darkness and, quite possibly, in renewed fog (a reason given by Schwieger for leaving that very area!). Mindful of the Admiralty's advice, he kept much further from the Fastnet than normal but, when the weather cleared, felt he must close the land to establish his exact position with certainty. In peacetime it had been the custom for Atlantic liners to pass within two miles of the Old Head of Kinsale. Turner kept a good twelve miles off this point (a fact confirmed both by Schwieger at the time and Light when he dived on the wreck, and accepted also by Room 40 in their reconstruction of Schwieger's cruise). Turner considered that such a distance was in conformity with the Admiralty messages to avoid headlands.[2] The Admiralty must have shared his view, because, despite Turner's statements that he was at least thirteen miles to seaward, the Enquiry was persuaded that the distance was much closer, perhaps only eight miles – although how this was supposed to have been established is not clear. It was, however, a useful point against him.

Turner, that simple seaman, did not stand much of a chance in the witness box against the array of legal talent mobilised to prove him guilty. His own counsel had to drag statements from him favourable

[1] Only nine other ships in the British Merchant Marine had a maximum speed of more than eighteen knots.

[2] He was justified in this view because only vessels passing *within* five miles of headlands were reported to the Admiralty for having ignored instructions.

to his case, and suggested to Lord Mersey that he was a poor witness. Mersey disagreed; he considered he might have been mistaken in his actions on the fatal day, but that he was an honest man and was telling the truth to the best of his ability. It will be remembered that Turner's last information about U-boats had been that one had been sighted that morning proceeding west off Cape Clear. The *Lusitania* had passed this supposed danger safely. It was not until nearly noon that he was warned of the presence of a U-boat twenty miles south of the Coningbeg Light Vessel on the previous day, i.e. that a U-boat had been operating very nearly in the *middle* of the channel through which he would have to pass! Turner therefore decided to steer as close as possible to the Light Vessel and the rocks which it marked, rather than keep further out to sea; yet another reason for accurate navigation.

The evidence which he gave was certainly somewhat muddled. For example, when pressed, he admitted that he must have seen the zigzag order, although he did say that it sounded very different when read out by Carson. Of course it did: he must have confused it with something else, because, as has been shown, he cannot possibly have received it. He was not zigzagging when torpedoed, but was steering a steady course while endeavouring to obtain a four-point fix on the Old Head of Kinsale. Obviously, in Fisher's words, he was a knave! Although certain questions about what instructions he had received had been included in the Board of Trade's original draft, these were omitted from the final version on the insistence of the Admiralty. Why? Turner stated at the Coroner's Court at Kinsale, two days after the disaster, that he had received instructions from the Admiralty, but refused to disclose what they were. There are indications that he had asked permission, while there was still time, to change course for the North Channel, by now open, but had been refused. There is also evidence that he had been making for Queenstown, not Liverpool – such as the fact that the crew were getting up the passengers' baggage, the remarks to a member of the US Embassy and the recollections of the quartermaster on duty – but it is no longer possible positively to confirm this.

In the end, Lord Mersey, strongly supported by his Merchant Navy assessors, but to the evident displeasure of the Naval ones and of the Admiralty, found that Turner had not acted imprudently. This verdict has been described as the whitewashing of Captain Turner. In fact, it was about the only finding of the Enquiry which was *not* whitewash. Suggestions that the *Lusitania* was an armed auxiliary of the Royal Navy, a warship, and so a legitimate target for Schwieger, that she was carrying Canadian troops and that her cargo included a large consignment of gun cotton, are equally wide of the mark. The Limits of Liability trial in New York in 1917, after the United States had entered the war, also absolved both the Cunard Company and Turner of negligence, but was, in other respects, just as unsatisfactory an enquiry as Lord Mersey's.

So who *was* responsible for *Lusitania*'s loss? There is obviously no shadow of doubt that the immediate culprit was Schwieger, acting on the instructions of the German Navy and Government to sink all ships, whether passenger liners or not, encountered in the War Zone. His War Diary, the repeated signals sent out by Norddeich concerning *Lusitania*'s movements and the immediate congratulations sent by the Commander-in-Chief of the *Hochseeflotte* make it crystal clear that *Lusitania* was regarded as a desirable not to say prime target. The declaration of the War Zone was a distinct and ruthless breach of hitherto accepted International Law, not least because a blockade is not legal[1] unless effective (and this the U-boat campaign was not). For all this the *Admiralstab* and German Government must accept full responsibility.

On the other hand it is highly probable that the ship, hit forward by a single and not particularly powerful torpedo,[2] might not have sunk, and certainly would not have sunk so quickly, but for the second explosion. All the evidence supports the view that this explosion was among the munitions carried on the orlop deck. Was the British Government justified in arranging for munitions to be carried in passenger liners (for the *Lusitania* was only one of several Cunarders and other fast vessels engaged both before and after her loss in so doing)? The point is debatable. At the time the public, had they known that such cargoes were being carried in this way, would probably have strongly condemned the practice. On the other hand, the British Army in France was appallingly short of ammunition; supplies simply had to be provided by the swiftest possible means. The American authorities were well aware of what was going on, and winked at it.

In the circumstances, it is easy to understand why the British

---

[1] A fact admitted by the German Foreign Office in a telegram to their minister in Buenos Aires, in 1917.

[2] The G Torpedo contained 278 lbs of explosive. It is significant that *Candidate* had to be sunk by gunfire after one torpedo had failed to do the trick, and that *Centurion* required two torpedoes.

Government, and probably the United States Administration as well, were anxious to keep the true facts quiet. The attempt to make Turner the scapegoat by suppressing, not to say fabricating, evidence was thoroughly discreditable, but Churchill, Fisher, Oliver, Wilson and Hall were all ruthless men when they considered the safety of their country was at stake. They would not have worried too much about the reputation of a man like Turner. After all, it was widely supposed, even before the *Lusitania* was sunk, that such an event would bring America into the war against Germany. The dreadful loss of life, including that of so many Americans, must have made the probability seem even greater, but American reaction would have been somewhat different had the true facts been allowed to emerge.

By far the most difficult question to answer is just why no effective steps were taken to protect the *Lusitania*. Why, in stark contrast to the information sent to naval authorities on previous occasions when U-boats were operating in the Irish Sea, and to the partial information sent to Jellicoe and others in May if warships were threatened, was nothing passed to Queenstown and Liverpool? Why was this ship with its cargo vital to the war effort and the hundreds of human beings on board, not diverted? Why were no destroyers sent to Queenstown or even to the St George's Channel? Why did Coke at Queenstown do so little, even on the basis of the contradictory and often very dubious information which he did have? He was relieved[1] as soon as Balfour became 1st Lord, but no one else paid any penalty for what, at the best, can only be described as gross negligence.

One would of course prefer to believe that the disaster was due to negligence, even to gross negligence, rather than to conspiracy—to the faulty system which prevented one department in the Admiralty knowing what another was doing, to the concentration of knowledge and decision making in the hands of only Churchill, Fisher, Wilson and Oliver. Were these men so preoccupied with the dangers from the *Hochseeflotte* and, even more, with the problems of the Dardanelles campaign that they simply failed to see the perils threatening the *Lusitania?* Oliver certainly lapsed frequently in his handling of Room 40's information, notably at Jutland, but in the case of Jutland these lapses all occurred within a period of thirty-six hours, when he was subjected to immense mental and physical strain. The action,

---

[1] By Admiral Bayly at the suggestion of Jellicoe and Beatty, but with greatly increased authority and responsibilities.

or absence of action, in respect of the *Lusitania* was spread over ten days! Can one really accept a foul-up as the complete explanation?

But if it was no foul-up, then it *must* have been a conspiracy, and a great deal that is otherwise inexplicable would fall into place. Of course the German suggestion that the British themselves sank the *Lusitania* can be dismissed.[1] It was a torpedo from U.20, not one from a British submarine, which struck the ship. One must also say that *if* there was a plot by Winston and his advisers to engineer an encounter between U.20 and the *Lusitania*, it left an enormous amount to chance. Although Room 40's knowledge of the movements and intentions of German U-boats at this time was much greater than has previously been supposed, it was *not* precise; neither U.30 nor U.20 was in fact where their intercepted orders would have led Oliver to believe that it would be. An encounter between the U-boat and the liner depended on the thousand-to-one chance of the U-boat being, not just within ten or twenty miles of the *Lusitania*'s actual route but within a few hundred yards and on a bearing suitable for an attack. Certainly no one could have anticipated that Schwieger's single torpedo would strike in the one position that would cause the great liner to sink with such fearful rapidity and with such horrible loss of life. Indeed, had not Schwieger overestimated her speed by four knots, it would not have done so.

But having said this, one still has to answer the question *why* precautions to ensure *Lusitania*'s safety, which had been taken on previous occasions and which could and should have been taken on her last voyage, were conspicuous by their absence. As Schwieger wrote in his log, 'It is remarkable that today [7 May] there should have been so much traffic despite the fact that two large steamers

---

[1] It may, however, be remarked that on 15 July 1941, when America was still neutral but when the US Navy was escorting British ships, Admiral Little, head of the British Admiralty Delegation in Washington, wrote to Admiral Pound, the 1st Sea Lord, as follows: '. . . the brightest hope for getting America into the war lies in the escorting arrangements to Iceland, and let us hope that the Germans will not be slow in attacking them.' He went on to add, perhaps only jokingly, 'Otherwise I think it would be best for us to organise an attack by our own submarines and preferably on the escort!' Churchill himself was determined to involve the USA in the war and only six weeks earlier, when the *Bismarck's* consort, the heavy cruiser *Prinz Eugen* was being hunted in the Atlantic, he thought he had found the opportunity for which he was seeking. He told Pound and Alexander, the 1st Lord: 'It would be better for instance that she should be located by a US ship as this might tempt her to fire on that ship, thus providing the incident for which the US Government would be so thankful . . .'

[2] Indeed, had Schwieger not overestimated her speed by four knots it would not have done so.

were sunk south of the St. George's Channel yesterday. It is also inexplicable that the *Lusitania* was not routed in via the North Channel.' Nothing, *absolutely nothing* was done to ensure the liner's safe arrival.

The mysterious signals which passed between the Admiralty and the *Lusitania* between 5 and 7 May may well hold the answer. The file seems to have been in the possession of the Admiralty as recently as 1972. Now it has vanished again!

The reader must form his or her own judgement on the basis of the facts I have recounted: all the evidence that is available at the time of writing. For my part, unless and until fresh information comes to light, I am reluctantly driven to the conclusion that there *was* a conspiracy deliberately to put the *Lusitania* at risk in the hopes that even an abortive attack on her would bring the United States into the war. Such a conspiracy could not have been put into effect without Winston Churchill's express permission and approval.

The sinking of the *Lusitania* did not mark the end of the first phase of the unrestricted U-boat campaign. Nor did it result in an American declaration of war on Germany. It did cause a considerable relaxation of American pressure on Britain to modify her blockade policy, and it was a severe blow to German standing as a civilised power in the eyes of world opinion. Ambassador Page was disappointed in his President's reactions, and so were the British public and those Americans already Anglophile. One might say it was a disappointment to all concerned; to Schwieger, who later felt he was in disgrace, and to the German Foreign Office, who correctly saw that it had brought the United States a step nearer to the Allied side. Much more, however, was needed before the whole of America would be singing 'The Yanks are coming . . .' President Wilson protested, and the Germans excused themselves and brought counter-accusations against the British. The U-boat campaign was to continue for another four months, not with the success that the *Admiralstab* had promised, but at least with results which should have warned the British Admiralty that their counter-measures were largely ineffective.

CHAPTER EIGHT

My Name is Hall

Early in 1915 it had become obvious, not least to Blinker Hall, that Room 40 was still too understaffed to handle all the material that was becoming available. Baltic naval traffic did not get all the attention it deserved, and even the naval attaché traffic in the VB code was not being attacked as consistently and regularly as it should have been. Any messages which appeared to be in a hitherto unbroken code simply could not be tackled at all. Fresh recruits had therefore to be found, and both Ewing and Hall shared in this task.

Unfortunately, it is not now possible to establish with any exactitude how or when the new men were found, but in the next twelve months the staff grew from ten or twelve to around thirty. Some of them came from the universities, principally Cambridge, a few more were released from Osborne, while yet others had diplomatic backgrounds. The first recruits in 1915 were probably two naval schoolmasters, Edmund Green and G. L. N. Hope. Those from the Diplomatic Service were B. F. Talbot, P. A. Somers-Cocks and George Young. Of these, Young seems to have been the most remarkable. An expert on the Near East, he had been serving in Lisbon at the outbreak of war. Although at that time already forty-two he at once resigned and returned to Britain to find some more 'active' appointment. He was probably recruited by Hall, who put him in charge of the new diplomatic section of Room 40 where he did extremely well. This, however, was still not active enough for him and, at the end of 1917, he managed to enlist in the army and then secured a commission in the Royal Marines. Who was the first of the remarkable band of academics is not at all clear, but it may have been 'Dilly' (Dilwyn) Knox. Aged thirty-one, he was the third son of the Bishop of Manchester[1] and had been educated at Eton,

---

[1] His brothers were Edmund, later a famous editor of *Punch*, Wilfred, a Church of England theologian, and Ronald, the brilliant Roman Catholic divine who translated the New Testament for Catholics.

where he was a Scholar and at King's, Cambridge where he was elected a Fellow in 1909. Although he had a passion for mathematics, he was in fact a classicist. According to his niece, Mrs Fitzgerald, the arguments he put forward in his Fellowship dissertation on the prose rhythms of Thucydides were regarded as unacceptable but so brilliant that they could not be contradicted.

Room 40 itself was beginning to bulge at the seams, and other nearby rooms were commandeered. Dilly, no doubt, after apprenticeships as a watchkeeper, and having proved himself a brilliant, intuitive crypanalyst, was given Room 53, no larger than a 'bathing box', as his office, despite the fact that somehow the Admiralty had been persuaded to instal a bath there for the use of the men after night duty. This, apparently, did not matter to Dilly, who claimed to do his best work in the bath, in a steamy, soapy atmosphere. The results, according to Mrs Fitzgerald, were presented as they had been at Eton, 'in inky scribbles on sheets of dirty paper'. He was extremely forgetful and, if one is to believe the light-hearted skit written by his great friend Frank Birch, *Alice in ID 25*, kept his spectacles in his tobacco-case to remind himself that he had put the tobacco in the spectacle-case but had then changed the latter for a ham sandwich in case he should forget that he was hungry. He was Room 40's most brilliant but most unpredictable cryptanalyst.

Frank Birch was another Etonian and also a Fellow of King's, an Exhibitioner in modern languages and a double First in History. Seven years younger than Knox and a keen yachtsman, he had enlisted in the RNVR at the outbreak of war and had served at sea in the Atlantic and at the Dardanelles. His hobby was amateur dramatics and he delighted in playing 'the Widow Twankie' in professional pantomimes in the Christmas vacations. He seems to have found his way to Room 40 at the end of 1915 or early in 1916, and was one of the few inmates at that time in naval uniform. He and Knox shared a house in Chelsea. Birch's strength was not so much cryptanalysis as analysis and appreciation of the intelligence gained from the decodes.

King's supplied yet a third don, Frank E. Adcock, lay Dean of the college but a contrast to the two eccentric and incalculable Etonians as he came from Wyggeston Grammer School and a Methodist background. He won all possible distinctions as an undergraduate, and never deviated from the straight and narrow way to the Cambridge Chair of Ancient History.

Another man of a totally different type was the Rev. William

Montgomery from Westminster Presbyterian College, Cambridge,[1] who, in 1917, helped to solve the notorious Zimmermann telegram. Montgomery was aged forty-four and the author of studies of St Augustine and a brilliant translator of Schweitzer. He came to Room 40 from the Censorship. There was also Edward Bullough from Caius College, Cambridge. Bullough was thirty-five and bilingual in German and English. After education at Dresden he went up to Trinity College, Cambridge when only seventeen and obtained first class honours in Modern Languages. His favourite language from childhood had been Italian and he married the daughter of Eleonora Duse. From London University came Professor L. A. Willoughby, a German specialist. This list of university recruits is probably incomplete and other distinguished academics were recruited later, some of whom will be mentioned in subsequent chapters.

But Hall had seen that not only Room 40 but also he himself and his Intelligence Division, faced with a hundred and one problems never foreseen in peacetime, needed a very considerable injection of civilian talent. This might now seem unremarkable and obvious, but if one remembers Hall's very conventional naval background and the general attitude of Service officers at that time to anyone who had not gone through the same mill that they had, it is an indication of his breadth of view and instinctive grasp of what was needed to deal with unprecedented tasks.

Hall must have realised from the outset that he himself lacked contact with the world outside the Navy, with the universities, the City, the business, banking, Press, diplomatic and social life of Britain. We have already seen how, in December 1914, he 'cut out' Herschell from Room 40 and made him into a trusted personal assistant. Herschell moved in Court circles and was no doubt in touch with the diplomatic world, but probably less so with the City, and to fill this gap, Hall chose a very successful stockbroker, Claud Serocold. Serocold was also an Etonian, three years older than Herschell and may have been introduced to Blinker by him, although it is possible that Hall already knew him. Curiously, like so many others, Hall himself, Ewing, Denniston and others, he was a small man. He had been cox of the Eton VIII for three years, probably a record, and then went up to New College Oxford, where he coxed his College crew for a year, before abandoning the University for the City. He was the youngest son of a rather large

[1] Not part of the University.

and staid family and was considered by them to be slightly 'raffish'; he loved the good things of life and was not averse to attending the Empire and other music halls of the period. He was also a lover of good music and good paintings. He spoke French well and was a successful and devoted racing yachtsman, and a member of the Royal Yacht Squadron. He had enormous charm and was popular with all with whom he came in contact. Unfortunately, Serocold left no records of his work for Hall, nor did he talk about it to his family, but there is no doubt that he and Herschell were extremely close to the Director and shared most of his secrets. A clue can be found in the advice Hall gave to John Godfrey when the latter became Director of Naval Intelligence in February 1939. This was that he had found Serocold so invaluable that Godfrey ought to try to find a similar personal assistant. The result was the recruitment of Ian Fleming.

Both Herschell and Serocold were, so to speak, honorary members of Room 40, but they were not regular members of the team, any more than Ian Fleming took any part in the affairs of the Operational Intelligence Centre. Hall also recruited a number of other very talented men to the Intelligence Division, as opposed to Room 40; among them were L. G. Wickham-Legg, a Fellow of New College, Oxford and later Editor of the *Dictionary of National Biography*, George Prothero, editor of the *Quarterly Review*, Algernon Cecil the historian, Thomas Inskip, KC, later a Conservative politician and as Lord Caldecote, Lord Chancellor, and Sir Philip Baker Wilbraham, a Fellow of All Souls, Oxford.

There were, however, other recruits whom Hall directed into Room 40. One of the most successful was the young Nigel de Grey. Yet another Etonian, he had not gone on to university but had studied languages with a view to entering the Diplomatic Service. Apparently he failed the examination because, although fluent in French and German, his Italian did not meet the required standard. He therefore joined the publishing firm of William Heinemann, but on the outbreak of war, like Frank Birch, joined the RNVR, and became an Observer in the Balloon Section of the Royal Naval Air Service in Belgium. Hall seems to have known of him, and early in 1915 de Grey found himself in Room 40, where he soon showed a real talent for cryptanalysis. He seems to have been something of a favourite of Hall who tranferred him to the Diplomatic Section, when it was formed, and then, after he had broken the Zimmermann Telegram, put him in charge of the Mediterranean Section, when this was set up in Italy later in 1917. Like many other old Room 40 hands, including Frank Birch, de Grey threw up his job as Director of the Medici Society in 1939 and rejoined the old firm at Bletchley Park.

For much of the information about the personalities of Room 40 we are indebted to W. F. Clarke, a barrister who arrived early in 1916. Son of a famous Edwardian QC, he had always loved the Navy and, by knocking ten years off his real age (thirty-three) had secured a commission as an Assistant Paymaster RNVR at the beginning of 1915. He had been educated at Uppingham and Magdalen College, Oxford, and was a fluent German speaker. Early in 1916 he came to Hall's attention and found himself, not at sea as he had wished, but a member of Room 40. Like Frank Birch, with whom he became very friendly, he was no more than an average cryptanalyst, but his legal training made him a good Intelligence Officer, and as Room 40 expanded and specialised sections began to be formed, he assisted Hope in compiling appreciations and 'working up' the raw material provided by the code-breakers. After the war he and Frank Birch were instructed to compile a secret record, from Room 40's files and information, of the activities of the German Fleet.[1] He was one of the small band who remained with Room 40's successor, the GC & CS, and kept the torch burning in the lean inter-war years. Obviously an extremely able and intelligent man, with considerable knowledge of the world and at least some knowledge of the Navy and its ways, he complemented in a down-to-earth way the eccentricities of the more extraordinary university dons, but during World War II he seems to have become rather embittered, and some of his comments on his former colleagues need to be taken with a pinch of salt. He had no opinion at all of Ewing, but, with the foregoing caveat, must be regarded as a most valuable witness.

If Old Etonians and Fellows of King's seemed to have predominated in the first two years, a marked exception was Lionel Fraser, a friend of Serocold, but one with a very different background. His father had been a butler and his mother also in domestic service. They were devoted parents and their son rapidly made his own way in the City. A keen Territorial, he had survived Gallipoli, but then

---

[1] *A Contribution to the History of German Naval Warfare.* Two volumes, each in two parts, and a third consisting of a complete and most detailed Index of all the sources used. The first two volumes are at present in the Library of the Naval Historical Branch, and extracts from the index, which has hitherto been classified, are likely to be released to the PRO shortly, or incorporated into the PRO's own index of the papers released.

injured his knee playing Rugby and was about to be invalided out of the Army when Serocold got him into Room 40. He was the first of several wounded Army officers who gradually began to take over some of the more routine tasks, such as collecting the encoded messages as they thudded out of the pneumatic tube, sorting them into categories and passing them to the appropriate specialists for decoding and further study – Tubists, they were called.

Benjamin Faudel-Phillips was almost certainly another of Serocold's finds. An Etonian and the son and grandson of Lord Mayors of London, Faudel-Phillips was inevitably nicknamed The Lord Mayor. He succeeded Young in charge of the Diplomatic Section. He was not only wealthy but generous to his new colleagues and was one of the most popular members of 'The Old Gang', as those who joined at this time later called themselves.

Hall's relations with Ewing were not good. It is scarcely surprising. Hall seems to have realised the tremendous potential of Room 40 better than the Director of Naval Education, who was, perhaps, content with the task of supplying Oliver with decodes of purely naval operational interest. Hall the professional naval officer, curiously, had the greater imagination and the wider vision; he was not the type of man who would refrain from poking his nose into other people's business if he felt that he could thereby do something to frustrate the Germans' 'Knavish tricks'. He was quite prepared to act on his own authority, and in the most unorthodox ways to achieve his objects. Learning that the organisation set up under Colonel Cockerill of the War Office to censor mails was collapsing under the strain, Hall, with Cockerill's enthusiastic agreement, produced within four days a new scheme manned by members of the National Service League. This rapidly brought order into the previous chaos, but Hall had no warrant to tamper with His Majesty's mails and soon found himself hauled before the Home Secretary, Mr Reginald McKenna, to explain himself. He did this to such good effect that, after the matter had been referred to the Prime Minister, Mr Asquith, Hall's arrangements were approved and a War Trade Intelligence Department created. A tremendous amount of information about German attempts to secure supplies from overseas eventually flowed in, which was of great importance to the enforcement of the British blockade. Whereas the pre-war censorship plans had been directed primarily to preventing information reaching Germany from this country, Hall saw at once that it could be made into a most useful source of intelligence about

Germany and the activities of German agents overseas. Intercepted letters passing between Germans in neutral countries began to be regularly intercepted, and as many of them were in code or cipher found their way in due course to Room 40. But, as already remarked, Room 40 could not cope properly with the purely naval wireless messages, let alone with non-naval ones, whether contained in wireless messages or letters in unbroken codes. As Denniston remarked, 'no one [had] then imagined that all these files contained telegrams possibly of the greatest interest which could be read and, in 1915 it may be said, read without extreme difficulty'. It was subsequently found that, due to total lack of liaison with the Censorship in the early days no fewer than 176 cablegrams *passing through England* from German Naval Attachés in North and South America from the outbreak of war until May 1915 had been intercepted but had never reached Room 40, and so had never been decoded. Most of these messages had dealt with the movements of German cruisers overseas and their supply ships. They were later found to include much information about von Spee's movements and intentions to try to break for home after the Battle of Coronel!

However, although progress was made with the VB code, other encoded messages in Room 40's possession proved unbreakable. All that could be said about them was that they did not appear to be naval messages. They were in fact German Foreign Office coded signals, and Birch and Clarke in their post-war history remarked that German diplomatic codes were considerably more ingenious and difficult to crack than those of the Imperial Navy. Once again luck and lack of security by the Germans came to the aid of the British – a copy of one of these codes was captured and once more the Germans, who should surely have been aware of the possibility, did not, for far too long, take any effective steps to replace it.

It is just possible that two copies were secured almost simultaneously, but doubts remain about the value of the first 'pinch'. When the Germans had occupied Brussels they had taken over a powerful wireless transmitting station and had employed a young student, Alexander Szek to repair it. Szek, whose parents were Austro-Hungarian, held dual British and Austrian nationality, because he had been born in Britain. His father had returned, not long before the war, to Vienna, but either his mother or sister had remained in England. It seems that through one or other of them the British Secret Service made contact with Szek and with great difficulty persuaded him to make copies, page by page, of the code the Germans were using and pass the results, one at a time, to a British agent. Szek's nerve began to fail, and the British decided that he must be removed before he broke down and betrayed the facts to his German masters. This was, apparently, sometime in the spring of 1915. The unfortunate young man was never seen again. After the war his father claimed that the British had had him shot, while the latter protested that it was the Germans who had carried out the execution. Captain Roskill has recently revealed[1] that it was in fact the British who were responsible. In conversation with Roskill in the fifties, Oliver several times said, 'I paid £1,000 to have that man shot'! Quite why Oliver, by this time COS, rather than Hall the DID or Cumming, the head of the Secret Service, should have authorised Szek's liquidation is hard to understand, but it does suggest that in this, as in so much else, he was reluctant to allow his successor full authority in matters which were really no longer his direct responsibility. Szek, when he disappeared, is supposed to have had in his possession the last pages of the code which he was retaining until he had been safely spirited out of Belgium. Presumably his assassin would have recovered them and forwarded them to London, but there is no confirmation that this was done or that Szek's dangerous work was of any use to the British. It seems possible that this was the code secured by the Secret Service which Denniston referred to as a 'pup of the poorest class'.

What is clear is that, at about the same time, a complete copy of one of the German diplomatic codes was captured by the British, but that this occurred in Persia not Belgium. Herr Wassmuss, the former German Vice-Consul at Bushire on the Persian Gulf, was despatched from Constantinople in February 1915 to incite the Persians to embark on a Holy War against the British, and to sabotage the Anglo-Persian oil pipe line, a vital source of supply for the Royal Navy. Arrested by a Persian Khan on 6 March, Wassmuss managed to escape from the local gaol just as a British party arrived to haul him off into permanent captivity. His departure was so precipitous that he did not have time to take with him his baggage, piled in the courtyard. With this the disappointed British had to be content. It eventually found its way to the India Office in London (for the Government of India was at this time responsible for British affairs in the Persian Gulf). It was dumped in one of the cellars

[1] *Admiral of the Fleet Earl Beatty*, Collins, 1980.

where it might have remained indefinitely but for a typical flash of Hall intuition. Chatting one day in April to a young naval officer who had been in the Persian Gulf at the time, Blinker heard the story of Wassmuss's hairbreadth escape and the loss of his baggage; Hall was like a terrier who has smelt a rat. Within hours one of his staff, Cozens-Hardy, had retrieved the bundle from the India Office and brought it back to his Director. When this fourth treasure trove was opened it proved to contain a copy of one of the German diplomatic codes. (This story is based on the accounts given by James (*The Eyes of the Navy*) and Barbara Tuchman (*The Zimmermann Telegram*). However, in the revised edition of Tuchman's book (1966) she quotes from an article by C. J. Edmonds, 'The Persian Gulf Prelude to the Zimmermann Telegram' which appeared in *The Journal of the Royal Central Asian Society* in January 1960. In 1915 Edmonds had been Acting British Vice-Consul in Bushire. He states that the attempt to capture Wassmuss was quickly followed by the 'arrest' by the British of the German Consul at Bushire, Dr Helmuth Listemann, and goes on to say that 'two dictionary ciphers' were found 'wrapped up in several pairs of long woollen underpants.' This certainly implies that whatever codes were captured in Persia by the British came from Listemann rather than Wassmuss.

Another version, for which I am indebted to Herr Rainer Mathä of Stuttgart, is that, before his hurried escape, Wassmuss entrusted his papers to a Persian who loyally passed them on to Listemann, which would account for the codes being found in the latter's 'longjohns'. Hall, on the other hand, in a sworn affidavit in connection with Amos Pealee's investigations into German responsibility for the Black Tom explosion and other acts of sabotage in neutral America, made in 1926, stated unequivocally that 'The German cipher book covering this system of ciphering [that used between Berlin and the German Embassy in Washington] is in our possession, it having been captured by the British authorities in the baggage of a German consul named Wasmuss [sic] who was stationed at Shiraz while Wasmuss was engaged in an endeavour to cut a British oil pipe line.'

Herr Mathä also points out that Wassmuss had originally been appointed to lead a German mission to Afghanistan and that all the arrangements for this mission were made by the German Embassy in Constantinople. Now we know that Constantinople was one of the embassies furnished with code 13040, a code in use at least since

1905. The Embassy may well have thought that this was a suitable code to issue to the leader of a semi-diplomatic mission, and, like the *Admiralstab*, who issued the secret VB code to S.119 in October 1914 (see Chapter 1), have ignored the very obvious risks of its falling into enemy hands. In the event, after Wassmuss had left Constantinople, leadership of the expedition was handed over to Hauptman Oskar Niedermayer, whose brother accompanied the party as its doctor. Wassmuss went along as far as Baghdad and then left on his attempt to stir up trouble in Persia and blow up the pipe line. Dr Niedermayer recorded in his diary that after Wassmuss's narrow escape from capture the British had found in his baggage 'a complete list of members of the expedition . . . all his papers, including his code.' If this version is true, then the codes found by Edmonds must have been different ones.

To make confusion worse confounded, Birch and Clarke refer to 'the capture of code 89734 [which] revealed that many diplomatic code-books were in reality merely keys of one archetype and that possessing one, or having worked one out, the enemy might in a few hours work out another . . .' They do not state where or when 89734 was captured, but there is no available evidence to suggest that more than one German diplomatic code was captured throughout the war. Unfortunately David Kahn, author of *The Codebreakers* and the cryptological expert, writes that he has 'no record of this code [89734] as associated with either 13040 or the codes of the 18470 family. They were not related, though their construction was similar – and in both cases weak.'

All that one can say with any conviction is that *a* diplomatic code *was* captured by the British in Persia in March 1915 and that, either directly or indirectly, it quickly enabled Room 40's diplomatic section to master 13040 and so, two years later, to decode the Zimmermann Telegram (as described in Chapter 13). Unfortunately it would seem that the amount of material available for Room 40 to attack was, for many months, limited. Many of the diplomatic messages were sent by letter, not wireless, sometimes by letters to accomodation addresses in neutral countries, sometimes in the diplomatic pouches of friendly neutral countries like Sweden. It took time for the British censorship to discover all the routes used, and the liaison between the censors and those who could make sense of the encoded letters suffered, inevitably, from the secrecy surrounding Room 40; a good deal of useful information was missed. It is also obvious that, in 1915, the number of Y stations was still limited, and it is probable that by no means all the German diplomatic and secret service traffic which was sent by wireless was intercepted. For example, in November 1915 Oliver instructed the Senior Naval Officer, Persian Gulf, to detail a ship to intercept German coded and *en clair* messages between Constantinople and Isfahan, in Central Persia, giving Constantinople's call sign but not that of Isfahan and the wave length, 4,500 metres. The utmost secrecy was enjoined. Similar requests had been made earlier to ships on the South American station, and were renewed throughout the war in various areas as the existence of secret or semi-secret German transmitters was discovered.

It may now seem rather extraordinary that a purely naval department should have become so involved in intelligence matters which had only indirect connections with affairs at sea. It must, however, be remembered that, apart from the Army code-breaking organisation, which was presumably fully occupied with purely military traffic, there was no other cryptographic bureau in existence. The Foreign Office probably did not view such methods, if they even knew of their existence, with any favour and in fact only took over responsibility for the post-war Government Code and Cipher School from the Admiralty in 1922 when all the traffic was diplomatic, with considerable reluctance. But, almost certainly, it was Hall's personality and vision which led to Room 40's pre-eminence and its growing involvement in diplomatic, economic and counter-espionage matters. It also should be pointed out that very little that affected the conduct of the war was without its influence on naval affairs, and that the Royal Navy's interests and connections were world wide. Hall certainly made it his business to establish close relations with MI5, MI6, Scotland Yard, with the Press and with the City and he soon began to come to the attention not only of the 1st Lord, but of the Home Secretary, the President of the Board of Trade and of the Prime Minister himself.

Some time in the middle of 1915 Hall decided, probably on George Young's suggestion to form a separate Diplomatic Section of Room 40. This did not come under Ewing but was directly controlled by Hall. Its head was Young, and other early members were the 'Lord Mayor' (Faudel-Phillips), de Grey and Montgomery. It occupied Room 45, but continued, correctly, to refer to itself as Room 40.

Hall obviously found Ewing's more parochial and unimaginative attitude irritating and must also have chafed under Oliver's control. With Ewing he was never on Christian name terms – the few letters which have survived between them are formal, never addressed 'Dear Alfred' or 'Dear Reggie', but a note of Oliver's makes clear that their relations were in fact a great deal worse than just formal. According to Oliver, Hall 'was always trying to boss Sir A. Ewing and he would not put up with it, he was not that sort of man, and when he took on the 1st Lord had promised him a free hand. It led eventually to a row and the 1st Lord, Balfour, deputed Sir Graham Greene [Secretary of the Admiralty] and me to hold an enquiry and we spent a long afternoon restoring peace . . .' Balfour was 1st Lord from the end of May 1915 until early December 1916, so it is probable that the personal difficulties between the DID and the DNE were already fairly acute well before the end of 1915. Moreover, Ewing gave up full time control of Room 40 in October 1916, which also suggests the Oliver/Greene enquiry must have taken place well before then. It cannot have done anything to make either man's life easier, or have been conducive to the most effec-tive development of Room 40.

Hall no doubt felt that Room 40 should have been entirely under his own control. He certainly liked to keep all the threads in his own fingers, but he was no centraliser like Oliver. 'In my view,' he wrote in his autobiography, 'a Director of Intelligence who attempts to keep himself informed about every detail of the work being done cannot hope to succeed: but if he so arranges his organisation that he knows at once to which of his colleagues he must go for the information he requires, then he may expect good results. Such a system, moreover, has the inestimable advantage of bringing out the best in every one working under it, for the head will not suggest every move: he will welcome, and, indeed, insist on ideas from his Staff. And so it was, from first to last, in the Intelligence Division.'

Hall, like Godfrey in 1939, could delegate, could decide on which matters he should personally concentrate and leave well-chosen subordinates to get on with their own jobs without constantly breathing down their necks. Nor was he averse to taking the advice of his staff, whether it was Herschell, Serocold or one of the code-breakers like de Grey. He was rewarded by their devotion, tinged sometimes with feelings of awe at his ruthless methods and propensity for taking risks.

Hall's relations with Churchill seem to have been good. 'He had,' wrote Hall, both courage and vision – a brilliant man if ever there was one. But he had the defects of his great qualities; he was essentially a 'one man show'. It was not in his nature to allow anybody except himself to be the executive authority when any action of importance had to be taken. Even in matters of the extremest technicality he would insist on elaborate presentation of his own views, and his powers of argument were so extraordinary that again and again tired Admiralty officials were hypnotised – I can think of no better word – into accepting opinions which differed vastly from those they normally held. Once, I remember, I was sent for by Mr Churchill very late at night. He wished to discuss some point or other with me – alone. To be candid I have not the slightest recollection of what it was. I only know that his views were diametrically opposed to mine. He argued at some length. I knew I was right, but Mr Churchill was determined to bring me round to his point of view, and he continued this argument in the most brilliant fashion. It was long after midnight and I was dreadfully tired, but nothing seemed to tire the 1st Lord. He continued to talk, and I distinctly recall the odd feeling that although it would be wholly against my will, I should in a very short space of time be agreeing with everything he said. But a bit of me rebelled, and, recalling the incident of the broken shard in Kipling's *Kim*, I began to mutter to myself 'My name is Hall, my name is Hall . . .' Suddenly he broke off to look frowningly at me. 'What's that you're muttering to yourself?' he demanded. 'I am saying to myself,' I told him, 'that my name is Hall because if I listen to you much longer I shall be convinced it's Brown.' 'Then you don't agree with what I've been saying?'; he was laughing heartily. '1st Lord,' said I, 'I don't agree with one word of it, but I can't argue with you; I've not had the training.' So the matter was dropped and I went to bed.

This was written in 1933. Those who served closely under Churchill when he was 1st Lord and Prime Minister in World War II, would immediately recognise the truth of the story. It shows how Churchill could be weaned away from some of his more wild cat ideas by those who had the courage to stand up to him. For a mere captain from a Service whose tradition was 'theirs is not to reason why . . .', it must have taken considerable courage.

Hall also got on well with and admired Fisher; he was again called upon to display great moral courage during the crisis which arose

over Fisher's resignation on 15 May as the result of his uncontroll-
able dissatisfaction with Churchill's Dardanelles policy. The old
Admiral finally exploded and left the Admiralty without waiting for
his resignation to be accepted or a successor to be appointed.
Despite this quite indefensible behaviour there was pressure on all
sides, from the Prime Minister, Asquith, from Churchill himself and
from the Sea Lords for him to reconsider his decision.

The attitude of the Sea Lords was changed dramatically on 17
May when Room 40 observed all the usual signs of a sortie by the
Hochseeflotte. Churchill hurried back from the Cabinet, which had
been debating the Government's disastrous position arising from
the munitions crisis, but in Fisher's continued absence, the 1st Sea
Lord's duties had hurriedly to be assumed by Admiral Sir Frederick
Hamilton, the 2nd Sea Lord, who was far from au fait with the
situation. As usual, the sortie proved in the end to be no more than
an operation to cover minelaying and was all over in twenty-four
hours. Hamilton and his colleagues were deeply shocked by Fisher's
abandonment of his post at what might well have been a highly
critical moment. Hamilton sent for Hall and with some diffidence
explained to him that he wished him to do something that would
force Asquith to accept Fisher's resignation and rule out any
possibility of his returning to the Admiralty. Hamilton and the
others had been driven to the conclusion that Fisher, through age
and strain, was no longer fit to hold the post. They themselves felt
inhibited from approaching the Prime Minister but – and this is an
indication of Hall's standing and reputation after only six months as
DID – they believed that he could achieve what they could or would
not. Hall, with many private reservations, accepted the mission and
went off to decide how he could accomplish it. His first idea was a
direct approach to the Prime Minister, for whom he had a great
admiration and from whom he had already received much kindness.
Then he decided to consult the Lord Chief Justice, Lord Reading,
someone whom he did not know personally, but a man whom he
equally respected. 'He was obviously the man,' wrote Hall;

> I took Dick Herschell into my confidence, he at once agreed and
> suggested his own flat as a meeting place.' And so it was arranged.
> That afternoon Reading came round to Herschell's flat and Hall
> explained to him 'the growing difficulty at the Admiralty of
> getting organised work done. I mentioned the conditions in which
> a man like Crease [Fisher's Naval Assistant] was working and the

repeated friction between Lord Fisher and Mr Churchill. I said bluntly that in my opinion Lord Fisher was in no fit state to continue in his post, and exhorted our visitor to represent to the Prime Minister the necessity for accepting the proferred resignation without delay . . . When I had finished [Lord Reading] cross-examined me for nearly half an hour, and afterwards Dick Herschell told me that he had never heard anything like it . . . Question indeed followed question, some purely techincal, but others fashioned as to make sure of my motive . . . 'Do you yourself object to serving under Lord Fisher?' he asked. 'I'd serve under the devil,' I told him, 'if he were proficient.' 'And would that have been your answer, if I had mentioned Mr Churchill instead?' 'It would.' 'Then,' said Lord Reading slowly, 'if either of them is to leave the Admiralty, which would you suggest that it be?' I looked at him. It was the crucial question for which I had been waiting. 'Regretfully,' I told him, 'I have to say both.' 'And why? 'Because if you wish, as you must, to maintain any confidence between the Fleet and the Admiralty, you mustn't keep a 1st Lord who will appear to have driven out of office a man like Lord Fisher. The Navy would never forgive him.' Lord Reading nodded and for a moment there was silence. 'You were quite right,' he said at last, 'when you said that you were putting your future in my hands, and if you had answered my questions differently I would have broken you. But I am now satisfied that your view of what is required is correct, and I will see the Prime Minister at once. I shall not mention your name unless he asks for it. Good-bye.'

Whether Hall's distasteful and dangerous task was really necessary or not is doubtful because, within two days, Fisher, who must have been suffering from a brainstorm, destroyed himself by attempting to dictate to the Prime Minister the terms upon which he would agree to return. If the action itself was outrageous the terms themselves were even more so. Despite public outcry, the resignation was immediately accepted and Fisher was finished. Nor was there much practical likelihood that Churchill could have remained as 1st Lord. Asquith was compelled to form a Coalition Government with the Conservatives, and one of the Tory conditions for this was that Churchill should go. He was succeeded by Balfour, while Admiral Sir Henry Jackson took Fisher's place. Oliver's and Wilson's positions were not affected, but Hall would have been less than human if he had not felt at least some satisfaction at the confidence which Hamilton had displayed in him, and in Lord Reading's acceptance of the soundness of the case put to him.

CHAPTER NINE

A One Man Show

Returning now to the war at sea, we can begin to see, after the *Lusitania* disaster, a renewed attempt by Oliver and Wilson to pass out information about U-boats to those who could take action. Most attention still seems to have been concentrated on the danger to the Grand Fleet, but there was increasing emphasis on the organisation and co-ordination of patrols of destroyers and small craft to hunt U-boats to destruction when their probable movements could be forecast with any accuracy. On 4 July, for example, Jellicoe was told that 'A determined effort should be made to intercept U 39 on her return voyage with all the resources at your disposal that can be usefully employed. U 39 has been sinking ships at the entrance of the English Channel since 29 June, and will probably be starting on his return voyage very soon in which case he should be in the neighbourhood of the Orkneys about 8 or 9 July. There will probably be another submarine going the opposite way which left Ems yesterday . . .' The Commander-in-Chief was instructed to use up to half his effective destroyers in the hunt, and to accept the risk involved if the Fleet had to go to sea without them. Despite this effort, no success was achieved.

On 12 July, however, under pressure from Jellicoe and Beatty, Admiral Lewis Bayly was appointed to relieve Coke at Queenstown with the new title of Admiral Commanding Western Approaches, with responsibility for the western approaches to the British Isles, all Irish waters and the entrance to the English Channel, and the promise of a considerable reinforcement to the heterogeneous collection of Auxiliary Patrol craft, old destroyers and new sloops at his and his subordinates' disposal. On 27 July a signal was sent to Queenstown, Milford Haven, Larne, Falmouth and Stornoway, which is typical of the type of information being passed out and is somewhat surprising in its detailed nature, considering the comparatively junior rank of some of the recipients. It read: 'Submarine U 36 which sank French steamer *Danae* 80 miles NW of Cape Wrath at

11 p.m. on 23rd is probably on her way to the south of Ireland and should be there tomorrow Monday morning. Another submarine passed North of Shetland at 9 p.m. last night and may very likely try to get through North Channel during the night of 26th to 27th.' Again, on 7 August Bayly was told that two U-boats bound for the Mediterranean were passing down the west coast of Scotland at a speed of about nine knots, and would be off the Fastnet on the 9th. He was instructed to concentrate all his forces, which would be augmented by seven destroyers from Devonport, to hunt them. Information of this sort was also passed to the Senior Naval officer at Gibraltar and the (British) Rear-Admiral at Taranto. In the latter case, the Admiral was instructed to inform the Italians that two large U-boats would shortly reach Cattaro (Kotor) and to 'telegraph what steps are being taken to watch Straits of Otranto if you can ascertain them without giving offence'! The two U-boats were no doubt those about which Bayly had been warned, and which he had been unable to intercept despite all his efforts. Bayly may have been fully indoctrinated, but the other authorities cannot have been and, considering the very stringent restrictions constantly imposed on Jellicoe about the further circulation of information sent to him, these signals, by no means isolated cases, show that the problem of combining the maximum use of decoded information with the needs of security had not been properly thought out, and the rules were not being applied in a very consistent manner.

Of course, the policy of trying to hunt and destroy individual U-boats in this manner, of patrolling focal points or of instructing shipping to sail independently along predetermined 'lanes' from which the hunting forces were supposed to have driven the U-boats, was doomed to failure (just as any attempt to revive this discredited practice in the eighties is equally unlikely either to protect merchant ships or sink hostile submarines). Only the introduction of convoy could achieve both objects, and two more years were to pass and hundreds of thousands of tons of shipping were to be sunk before the Admiralty were driven to accept the logic of this argument.

By August 1915 British losses were mounting alarmingly – forty-nine ships of 135,000 tons in that month alone. However, on 19 August U 24 torpedoed the British liner *Arabic* (which had narrowly escaped from Schwieger on 6 May). Some forty lives, including three Americans, were lost. This, after all the German protestations about the *Lusitania*, was too much even for President Wilson. He protested very sharply indeed. On 30 August U-boats were forbidden to sink passenger liners, even those recognised as British, except in conformity with the Prize Laws. On 18 September the *Admiralstab* reacted to this restriction by ordering U-boats to be withdrawn from the English Channel and the Western Approaches, and the campaign in these areas petered out. This result might be deemed a 'draw'. Throughout 1915 the British lost 748,000 tons of merchant shipping by U-boat action, and a total from all causes of 855,000 tons. On the other hand, new construction had more than replaced these losses. During the same period, the Germans had lost 20 U-boats, (but few of them as a result of British anti-submarine measures); their new construction, sixty-one boats, had also more than made this good. The British Admiralty thought, most mistakenly, that it had the situation well in hand. The *Admiralstab*, for their part, were furious that American pressure on their government had caused them to call off the campaign. They had, reluctantly, to wait for another day. But not in the Mediterranean, where few if any American ships plied. It was to that sea that the U-boats were transferred; it was there, thanks to divided Allied control and the success of the *E. Dienst*, that allied shipping losses continued to mount; it was there that the real proof of the inadequacy of the Royal Navy's anti-U-boat measures should have been, but unfortunately was not, made apparent.

In the North Sea the *Hochseeflotte* remained quiescent, although the usual scares continued each time Room 40 detected a movement whose nature could rarely be confirmed in advance as a strictly local operation. By this time Zeppelin raids on England were becoming a fairly common occurrence. Room 40 was as well informed about the bases and movements of the German naval airships as it was of the U-boats. The Zeppelins used the HVB code, unreciphered, when on operations and invariably reported when they had taken off or landed, often confirming that they only had the appropriate code on board, and giving an indication of the general direction in which they were proceeding. They also often made intermediate reports if they sighted any vessels in the North Sea, and they checked their positions from time to time with the German D/F stations. As with the U-boats, instructions to and from FdL (Officer Commanding Airships) were often transmitted by wireless, but, again like the U-boats, their subsequent movements were not always predictable, due to weather, poor navigation, engine failures and so on. Nevertheless, thanks to Room 40, Oliver was often able to give warning of impending raids, as for example in this signal to North Shields and

Immingham, sent at 7.10 p.m. on 13 October: 'An air raid on Humber or Tyne or intermediate ports is probable tonight.' Commodore T at Harwich was frequently instructed to have forces at sea, in the hopes of picking up any lame ducks returning damaged or for some reason unable to maintain altitude and so a possible target for the cruisers' anti-aircraft armament. The air defence of Great Britain was a responsibility of the Royal Naval Air Service until February 1916, when it was transferred to the Royal Flying Corps, the RNAS then becoming responsible only for Zeppelins over the sea either on their outward or homeward flights. The performance of the available aircraft at the time, particularly their low ceiling and slow rate of climb, was inadequate and, like the Auxiliary Patrol with the U-boats, they were no more than a deterrent.

In August there occurred an interesting minor action which demonstrates in the clearest fashion both the strengths and limitations of cryptanalysis. German mines, unlike the British ones at this time, were extremely efficient and the Germans made good use of them, not only defensively but offensively with their new minelaying U-boats (UC-boats), and with auxiliary surface minelayers. At 9.23 on the morning of 6 August, Oliver signalled Jellicoe that 'German Armed Fleet steamer *Meteor* left Jade at 4.00 a.m. [an indication of the speed with which Room 40 was working]. Nothing is known of her intentions but it is possible that she will again take mines to the White Sea. She is more than a match for armed trawlers and should be watched for off Norwegian coast and intercepted.' Seven hours later Jellicoe was given the following additional information: '*Meteor* is believed to have laid mines at entrance to White Sea in June. Description. 1912 tons, 14 knots, 2 masts, one funnel, 2 searchlights on bridge, straight bow, 2 torpedo tubes on foc'sle. She was reported to carry guns of about 4 inch by a neutral steamer which passed her, number not known.'

Excellent as this intelligence was, it was incomplete, because *Meteor* was *not* heading for North Russia but, far more audaciously, for the Moray Firth (Cromarty) and on the night of the 7th-8th laid an extensive minefield to the north-west of Kinnaird Head without being detected. Just after completing her mission, she encountered the ocean-boarding vessel *Ramsay* and sank her before she could make any report, taking her survivors prisoner. *Meteor* had performed admirably, but at 6 p.m. that afternoon, when in the middle of the North Sea, she succumbed to the fatal German tendency to break wireless silence and report success. This was no doubt due to the need for a warning to be sent to U-boats of the dangers of the new minefield, but this could, with good staff work, surely have been left for another twenty-four hours. To make matters worse, she used the wrong key and the message had to be repeated more than once. Before midnight, Jellicoe was in possession not only of details of the minefield but of her position at 6 p.m. and the fact that she had *Ramsay*'s survivors on board. Light cruisers were immediately sailed from Scapa and Harwich. The latter force found the unfortunate minelayer at noon next day about 100 miles west of Denmark. She had no option but to scuttle herself. If only she had kept wireless silence she would undoubtedly have escaped, and her mines would probably have claimed at least some British warships as victims, instead of being incorporated in British defensive barriers. The *Admiralstab* do not appear to have learnt the lesson.

While Room 40's flow of information did not always lead to such a satisfactory outcome, it did assist the British in their own offensive minelaying operations. The first minefields had been laid off the Amrum bank in the Heligoland Bight in January 1915, and this was followed by two others in May, but Churchill regarded such operations as insufficiently offensive in character and nothing more had been attempted while he was 1st Lord.

The *Meteor*'s bold operation had, however, impressed Jellicoe and he successfully pressed the Admiralty for a riposte in kind. Room 40 knew precisely the various routes used by both U-boats and surface ships entering and leaving the Heligoland Bight, and by the end of the year a large number of minefields had been laid, although not on the scale which Jellicoe had wished. This may have been due to the fact that, having regarded the mine as a purely defensive weapon, rather beneath the dignity of the Royal Navy, the British had insufficient stocks. The situation was exacerbated by the appalling inefficiency both of the mines themselves and their mooring apparatus. One U-boat commander was said to have recovered two British mines and brought them home slung over his bows to have them cut in half to serve as punchbowls! But Room 40 could see the results; they knew whenever the Germans were satisfied, whether because the British mines had come adrift or as a result of their own sweeping, that routes were clear and could again be used. As Hope has pointed out, much better use could have been made of this knowledge, but, not surprisingly, with Oliver and Wilson acting as a two-man filter for all decoded information, with only an embryo Plans Division denied access to the 'Mystery', the enormous potential of an offensive mining policy was, for the time being, not fully realised.

1915 ended in frustration both for the Entente and the Central Powers. Gallipoli had failed and the final evacuation was about to take place; Serbia had been over-run; Russia had been driven out of Poland in disorder; despite immense sacrifices French and British offensives on the Western Front had made no impression on the Germans, who were as firmly in possession of northern France and virtually all Belgium as ever. The agonies of the Somme, Verdun, the Isonzo and the Carpathians were still to come. On the other hand, the Germans and Austrians now had to reckon with Italy as an enemy; Austro-Hungary was clearly more of a liability than an asset to Germany, and the Turkish army had been badly mauled; Russia showed no sign of collapse and the French had not been defeated, while the British Army could no longer be dubbed by the Kaiser a 'contemptible' little force.[1] Any idea of a lightning victory on the 1870 model had long since been abandoned; it was going to be a much longer war than anyone had supposed.

At sea the *Hochseeflotte* had remained strictly on the defensive for eleven months; the Grand Fleet's domination of the surface of the North Sea was even more pronounced than it had been in August 1914; German shipping had been swept from the oceans of the world and the British blockade was beginning to cause real hardship to the Central Powers; only the U-boats had achieved a measure of success until their unrestricted campaign had been called off as a result of American pressure. The British Admiralty, if unduly complacent about the threat from U-boats, was concerned about demands made on the Royal Navy to maintain and even increase its strength in the Mediterranean, where the French and Italian fleets already had an overwhelming superiority; the main feeling, both afloat and ashore, was of growing irritation at the inability of the Grand Fleet to compel its antagonist to come out and give battle. In the event, the long-sought encounter was not to be delayed for many more months.

Von Pohl, the German Commander-in-Chief was dying. On 24 January 1916 he was succeeded by Admiral Reinhard Scheer, a skilled and much more aggressive officer, who was at once given greater freedom by the Kaiser and the *Admiralstab* to pursue an offensive policy designed to whittle away the Grand Fleet's superi-

[1] This oft quoted remark about the original BEF is probably apocryphal.

ority; this was to be achieved by mining, by U-boat action and by full-scale sorties of the *Hochseeflotte* to cut off isolated and weaker British squadrons, making use of reconnaissance by the rigid Zeppelins which Britain did not possess[1] and against which they had so far failed to find any antidote.

Early in 1916 the Germans at last replaced the HVB code with the AFB (*Allgemeinefunkspruchbuch*). Attempts to reconstruct the new code soon achieved some success although the process was not entirely complete by the middle of the year. A copy recovered from a Zeppelin, L 32, on 24 September,[2] although a little charred, cannot by then have done more than enable Room 40 to fill in the less frequently used groups. The introduction of the AFB may possibly have had something to do with the successful return to Germany of the disguised merchant raider *Möwe* on 4 March after a cruise of two months, during which a minefield she laid off the Orkneys claimed the pre-dreadnought *King Edward VII* while she herself sank eleven British merchant ships. However, only six days earlier, another raider, the *Greif* had, in Hope's words, 'come to grief' within forty-eight hours of Room 40 detecting her departure. The Northern Patrol had been alerted and after a fierce action with the British AMC (Armed Merchant Cruiser) *Alcantara* – which the *Greif* managed to torpedo when she herself was in a sinking condition – she was finished off by another AMC and a light cruiser.

Cruises, such as that of the *Möwe*, although greeted rapturously by the Germans when successful, were no more than a few more 'splinters'. Scheer was not content to rely on such insubstantial means to achieve his '*Kräfteausgleich*', or equalisation of the two fleets. On 10 February he had despatched a strong force of destroyers to attack British light forces east of the Dogger Bank. They sank the minesweeping sloop *Arabis* and returned before stronger British forces could intervene. Room 40 appears to have had knowledge that some operation was pending, because on 9 February Jellicoe had been warned by Oliver that the *Hochseeflotte* might leave on the following morning for an operation to the west or south-west, and he was instructed to take the Grand Fleet to sea.

---

[1] Britain was very slow to copy the Zeppelins and produce rigid airships.
[2] Marder states in *From the Dreadnought to Scapa Flow*, Vol. III, that this 'yielded to the Admiralty the new German naval signal book (it had recently replaced the book captured from the *Magdeburg* . . .).' This of course is quite wrong. The SKM (Magdeburg) code was not changed until 1917.

Early next morning Oliver thought that the sortie was only to carry out exercises in the Bight, and the Grand Fleet's sailing was cancelled. By the late afternoon, however, Jellicoe was informed that the *Hochseeflotte* was remaining in a state of instant readiness, and that cruisers and three destroyer flotillas were 'outside the rivers'. Jellicoe was ordered to keep steam at two hours' notice until more was known and Admiral, Dover, was told to inform his French opposite number 'discreetly'. At 1.14 a.m. on 11 February, reports from German decodes came in of an engagement between British sloops and a German destroyer east of the Dogger Bank at forty minutes before midnight, and of the intention of the German battle cruisers to leave the Jade at midnight. The Grand Fleet was ordered to proceed southward. Beatty was given the same information thirty-five minutes later. By 8.15 a.m. it was all over, and the British admirals were informed that all German forces were returning to port. At 4.40 p.m. Jellicoe and Beatty were told that although all German forces except two U-boats east of the Dogger Bank had returned, they were remaining in a state of readiness. The Admiralty appreciated that 'discovery by sloops last night caused abandonment of some intended enterprise', and that although all had now reverted to normal this was unlikely to continue for many days.

A number of things are noteworthy about this little flurry. Whatever difficulties may or may not have been caused by the introduction of the AFB, Room 40 remained remarkably well informed and the possibility of offensive action by the German Fleet was fully appreciated. What was less satisfactory was the blow hot, blow cold reaction to the first report on 9 February, and the unjustifiable delay of thirty-five minutes between information of the engagement between the sloops and the Germans being passed to Jellicoe, and the same information being sent to Beatty. There seems no reason why the first signal should not have been addressed equally to Beatty. Minutes counted on this as on most such occasions. It is almost always a mistake to try to combine information and operational orders in the same signal; intelligence should be passed out the instant it is received, and then followed by operational instructions if the man on the spot cannot be trusted to act on his own judgement.

Scheer's next move was a more ambitious one, but once again the results were inconclusive. On 5 March he took the *Hochseeflotte* to sea and proceeded south to The Texel in the hopes of mopping up

British cruisers which were regularly, if ineffectively, sent out to chase returning Zeppelins. Room 40 does not appear to have obtained any advance knowledge of the movement, the first indication being a decode that the German main force was on a south-westerly course just north-east of The Texel at 5.30 a.m. on 6 March. The information was passed to Harwich at 7.31 a.m., but Jellicoe was not informed until 8.04 and orders to stop all south-bound merchant shipping were not issued until 8.33 a.m. It is again difficult to understand the reasons for such delays, although, in the absence of any advance warning of the sortie, even prompter and more co-ordinated information could not have made any difference. Oliver, of course, personally drafted every signal, which cannot have helped. At 6.40 p.m. British forces were informed that the enemy had turned back and that they should do likewise.

Three weeks later, the British attempted to lure the Germans out by a seaplane attack on what was thought to be a Zeppelin base at Hoyer on the mainland opposite the island of Sylt. It was hoped to destroy airship sheds and provoke Scheer into a sortie, but it is not clear why it should have been thought that there were any airship sheds there, and in fact there were none, as Hope well knew. Without doubt, he was not consulted about the proposed operation. In the event, it failed to achieve either of its objectives; no Zeppelins were found and three of the five planes despatched were lost. Beatty and the battle cruisers, supported further north by the Grand Fleet, were at sea for twenty-seven hours close off the German coast, but although Hipper did eventually come out, he did not get within sixty miles of Beatty and turned back, because of bad weather, nearly six hours before the British. Tyrwhitt's Harwich Force, the close covering force, was perhaps lucky to get away without loss either from the appalling weather or the enemy. One of the destroyers had been damaged in an engagement with the enemy, and Neumünster decoded British signals concerning arrangements to protect her, a fact immediately detected by Room 40. Tyrwhitt seems to have been adequately supplied with information about German destroyer and battle cruiser movements, but the whole operation was yet another disappointment.

The ball was now back in the German court, but nothing much happened for a month because the Germans anticipated another British attack of some sort between 15 and 20 April, and stood on the defensive. The grounds for this supposition are not clear, but may well have been the result of another Hall/Drake plant. On 21

April the whole *Hochseeflotte* put to sea, and Hope was puzzled
whether this was merely an exercise or a defensive measure. Beatty
wrote to Jellicoe, 'You ask me what I think? Well, I think the
German Fleet will come out *only* on its own initiative when the right
time comes . . .' He did not have long to wait, because Scheer now
planned a sudden raid on the east coast to coincide more or less with
the Irish Nationalist rising in Dublin on Easter Sunday, 23 April.
His intentions were to sail with the whole *Hochseeflotte* at midday
on 24 April in support of the battle cruisers, (temporarily under the
command of Admiral Boedicker as Hipper was sick) which were to
bombard Yarmouth, while he waited some seventy miles to the eastward. Room 40 detected an impending operation but, according
to the late Professor Marder and also to Captain Stephen Roskill,[1]
were not aware of its precise objective. However, Birch and Clarke,
in their post-war history, state that 'the orders given by the [Ger-
man] Commander-in-Chief with reference to the operation betrayed not only the inception but also the direction of the advance',
and Hope's brief contemporary notes read 'HSF under way. Special
state and readiness MSO[2] ordered. This implied an attack on
Lowestoft as it subsequently turned out . . .' although it was not
until later that decodes confirmed that the *Hochseeflotte* was actually at sea. It was perhaps natural after the constant false alarms of the
past fifteen months, that Oliver should be reluctant to order the
Grand Fleet to sea until he was absolutely sure of German movements. However, in view of the evidence quoted above, it was a pity
that the Grand Fleet was only put at two hours' notice at 3.50 p.m.
on 24 April and was not actually instructed to raise steam and put to
sea until 7.05 p.m. that evening. Oliver may, like Dudley Pound
during the Arctic convoy PQ 17 in 1942, have considered that the
information laid in front of him was insufficient, but this did not stop
him warning all local commands from Rosyth down to Dover fifty
minutes before he ordered Jellicoe to sea that 'local defence flotillas, submarines and aircraft should be in readiness for a demonstration by enemy tonight or tomorrow morning . . .' Admittedly,
the signal was prefaced with injunctions to 'be judicious in acting on
following directions and do not raise a scare as we are only preparing for an emergency which may not materialise. Do not inform
Military; they will be informed through GHQ . . .' This was not

---

[1] See *From the Dreadnought to Scape Flow*, Vol. II, and *Admiral of the Fleet Earl
Beatty*, *op. cit.*
[2] Presumably 'Most Secret Order'.

really very satisfactory; surely Jellicoe should have been instructed to put to sea at least the same time.

However, the battle cruiser *Seydlitz* struck a mine and was ordered back to port. This news, decoded by Room 40, confirmed once and for all that the projected raid was taking place. When Boedicker's battle cruisers were some sixty-five miles east of Lowestoft at 3.50 a.m. (25 April), they were sighted by Tyrwhitt's much depleted cruiser force. Tyrwhitt was in a very nasty situation, but Boedicker was no Hipper and preferred to hold on to bombard first Lowestoft and then, very briefly, Yarmouth. Having achieved this, he turned for home, before the twelve British submarines deployed off the two ports could get within range. Beatty and Jellicoe were still respectively 132 and over 300 miles away, so once again neither side managed to bring off an encounter.

It was now the British turn to serve, and a second raid on airship sheds – this time on Tondern, where they in fact existed – was carried out in the early hours of 4 May. The air raid was a failure as only one of eleven seaplanes was able to take off, and the attempt to provoke the *Hochseeflotte* was no more successful. Having cruised off the Heligoland Bight for more than six hours and with coal beginning to run low, Jellicoe decided to return to Scapa. The Germans did then come out, but from the British point of view it was too late. Beatty, unaware that on this occasion the orders to return to port had come from Jellicoe not the Admiralty, was angry. He wrote to Jellicoe: 'Why cannot the Admiralty leave the situation to those on the spot . . . ?' He then talked to Tyrwhitt about the Lowestoft raid; and was so upset that on 18 May he wrote a further long and bitter letter to his commander-in-chief, criticising the Admiralty's failures to co-ordinate the various forces properly or to work out any general plan in advance. 'The system of water-tight compartments has reached its climax. The Chief of the War Staff [Oliver] has *priceless information given to him which he sits on until it is too late* [Author's italics] for the Sea Forces to take action with any possibility of achieving a decisive result. What it amounts to is that the War Staff has developed into a One Man Show. The man is not born yet who can run it by himself . . . The 24 April [Lowestoft raid] was an object lesson which makes me weep when I think of it. There was absolutely no reason why every unit should not have been on the move 3½ hours before it was . . .' He continued in the same vein – a devastating and justified attack on the system – 'One of these days we shall be found out. The hollow mockery of our methods will be exposed, the opportunities that we have missed will be revealed. What then? . . .' Beatty, whether he knew all the facts or not, was quite right. Jutland was exactly fourteen days ahead.

CHAPTER TEN

Jutland

The Battle of Jutland was fought on 31 May 1916.[1] It was the swan song of the mighty dreadnought battleship. Thirty-five were engaged on the British and twenty-one on the German side. The *Hochseeflotte* had in addition six pre-dreadnoughts and, with armoured and light cruisers and destroyers the total number of ships in the two fleets was two hundred and forty-eight, a vast armada covering an enormous expanse of sea. The British had a clear superiority both in numbers and in weight of broadsides, and Scheer, quite rightly, had no intention of challenging the whole of the Grand Fleet to a fight to a finish. His plan was merely to repeat his previous efforts to lure the Grand Fleet into a U-boat trap and, with luck, to cut off one or two isolated British squadrons. To achieve this he needed a considerable element of surprise, so that there would be no danger of his encountering the whole Grand Fleet, but, at the same time, he had to advertise his presence at sea at the right moment to cause the British to put to sea and fall into his trap. A brief resumption of the unrestricted U-boat campaign in March had been called off in April due to American pressure, so that he had all the ocean going U-boats at his disposal. Eighteen U-boats, including three minelayers[2] were disposed in various positions from the Orkneys down to the Dutch coast to act offensively and to report British movements. In both tasks they proved largely ineffective, a serious set-back to the German plans. What, however, was worse was the indication which their sailing, on 16

---

[1] Those who wish to study the pros and cons of the actions of Jellicoe, Beatty, Scheer and Hipper in detail and to consider the materiel and other technical factors which affected the battle, are referred to Professor Marder's (Vol. III) and Captain Roskill's accounts. The brief summary given here is merely intended to provide a background against which the layman can understand the influence which Intelligence, or the lack of it, had upon the result of the only full-scale encounter between fleets of dreadnoughts which ever took place.

[2] A minefield laid by one of them was responsible for the loss of HMS *Hampshire* with Lord Kitchener on board on 4 June.

May, and subsequent failure to appear on the trade routes gave to Room 40 that another major operation was imminent.

On 28 and 29 May more precise evidence began to accumulate. At 11.02 p.m. on 28 May, Scheer ordered the *Hochseeflotte* to assume a state of special readiness, a signal probably made in the SKM (Magdeburg) code, while at 4.10 p.m. on 29 May, one of the U-boats was asked to report how far it was possible to penetrate into the Firth of Forth. Then at 9.52 a.m. on 30 May the *Hochseeflotte* was instructed to assemble in the outer Roads by 7 p.m. at the latest. Sixteen minutes later, Bruges W/T station told all submarines to reckon with their own forces being at sea on 31 May and 1 June; at least, this was the way in which Room 40 interpreted the message. In point of fact, the AFB had not then been fully reconstructed, and as it was an alphabetical book all that could then be said was that the group meant either 'own' or 'enemy' forces. The latter was later found to be the correct decode, but the inference was the same either way. An hour later, at noon British time, Jellicoe and Beatty were warned that the *Hochseeflotte* would probably put to sea sometime early on 31 May. At 3.36 p.m. Scheer signalled, 'On 31 May Most Secret 2490', obviously a reference to important written (and therefore unknown) operational orders. This was followed, at 5 p.m. by instructions that the leading ship of 3rd Battle Squadron should pass the Outer Jade Lightship at 3.30 a.m. on 31 May, followed by the 2nd and 1st Battle Squadrons, and instructions to the W/T station in Wilhelmshaven Dockyard to start using call sign DK, the C-in-C's normal call sign. Unfortunately for Room 40, this particular signal was made with an entirely new recipherment (presumably of the SKM code but possibly of the VB code), and it was ñot unbuttoned until the following afternoon (of 31 May). There were, however, other signs of what was in the wind. The Admiral Commanding the 2nd Battle Squadron (the six pre-dreadnoughts) was informed that prize crews were to be left behind,[1] an indication that offensive operations were intended. A signal announcing that the Commander-in-Chief was taking over W/T control (apparently in addition to the one noted above) was decoded, and Room 40 knew that this was standard procedure, designed to mislead British D/F stations when the *Hochseeflotte* put to sea. Taken in conjunction with the fact that, for some days past

[1] Curiously, a somewhat similar signal from *Bismark* in 1941 this time that prize crews were to be carried, confirmed to the British Admiralty that she was bound for an Atlantic commerce raiding cruise.

unusual activity by minesweepers and barrier breakers had been noted on the northern route out of the Heligoland Bight, west of Amrum Bank and up to the Horns Reef, it was quite clear that a movement up the Danish coast was going to commence in the early hours of 31 May, and that it would, in Hope's words, 'include the 2nd Battle Squadron'.

Despite this, Oliver was obsessed with the idea that the Germans might make an attempt to 'rush the Dover Straits' with their pre-dreadnoughts, against which the only available British force was the pre-dreadnought 3rd Battle Squadron in the Swin (entrance to the Thames). This squadron was without destroyers, so Oliver refused to allow the Harwich Force to sail to join the Grand Fleet as Jellicoe had previously been promised. Tyrwhitt was furious, and put to sea on his own initiative when he intercepted the first reports that the Germans had been sighted. Oliver recalled him with a peremptory signal, so that this splendid force took no part in the battle.

Oliver subsequently claimed that he did not get evidence that the German 2nd Battle Squadron was with the *Hochseeflotte* until 'very late on the night after the battle', but Hope shows that in fact the information was available on the 'afternoon' of 31 May, although by then it was probably too late to be of much value. Apart from this, it is arguable that all the preliminary indications were of a German movement to the north, and that no preparations had been made for any sortie to the south-west; had such preparations been made Room 40 would have observed them. But then, Room 40 were not asked to give *their* opinions on such matters!

At 5.40 p.m. Jellicoe had been ordered to take the Grand Fleet to sea and concentrate about 100 miles east of Aberdeen to await developments. By 10.30 p.m. that night his ships were clear of Scapa and Cromarty, and half an hour later Beatty and his battle cruisers had left Rosyth. They were respectively four and two and a half hours ahead of their adversaries. Room 40 had done all that had been asked of it, and no appreciable delays in passing out its information to the Fleet seem to have occurred. The same could not be said of Neumünster and the U-boats. It was not until 4.50 a.m. on 31 May that U 32 reported one large and two small cruisers seventy miles east of Buchan Ness. Even when, at 9.45 a.m. Neumünster passed Scheer an intercepted British weather report from the Firth of Forth and added 'Reports of this type are generally only observed when the Fleet is at sea', the German Commander-in-Chief was not alarmed; he had two U-boats in the Pentland Firth, one off Peterhead and seven off the Forth; he felt confident that, if the whole Grand Fleet was at sea, other sightings would have been made. However sceptical the men of the Grand Fleet may have been after so many abortive efforts, those in the Admiralty War Room must have felt sure that, at last, 'Der Tag' had come.

But already, according to Jellicoe, another of the series of errors in the British Intelligence system was having its effect. Jellicoe claimed afterwards that information he had received before the battle, had given him an exaggerated impression of the number of German battleships he would encounter. He had been led to believe that they might include two new battleships and a new battle cruiser. This totally false impression can only be put down to the fact that Hope had been forbidden to check the regular returns sent to the Commander-in-Chief. William Clarke, who was on duty in Room 40 throughout the Battle, has stated that the exact composition of the *Hochseeflotte* was perfectly well known there. There can be little doubt about this. The study of call signs, *including the identification of fresh ones allocated to ships joining the Fleet*, reports of transits of the Kiel Canal, of exercises in the Baltic and the Bight, of sub-calibre firing and of coaling kept Room 40 very fully informed. Indeed, on 2 May, a signal had been decoded reporting that *Bayern*, one of the new dreadnoughts which Jellicoe thought was operational and with Scheer, had achieved a speed of 22.05 knots over the measured mile. Her trials and working up continued and Clarke was somewhat irritated at having to deal with more of such decodes during all the pressure and excitement of the tremendous engagement taking place in the North Sea.

A more excusable piece of faulty information may, if it was passed to Jellicoe, have added further to his worries. On 15 May Hope had drawn Oliver's attention to a decode, saying that it 'may indicate that the Germans are developing their submarines tactically for fleet work'. Both the Germans and the British would have liked to do so, but in fact never produced a satisfactory type of submarine for this purpose throughout the war. Despite this and although no U-boats did take part in the battle thirteen sightings were reported by the British.[1]

All this was bad enough, but far worse was to come. Late on 30 May the Zeppelin detachment had reported that a reconnaissance

---

[1] If trained observers could be so mistaken, it is scarcely surprising that coast watchers, passengers and even members of the *Lusitania's* crew suffered from similar hallucinations.

would be carried out next morning, but a few hours later the FdU made a further signal stating that the state of the weather rendered reconnaissance out of the question. No further information connected with the *Hochseeflotte* reached Room 40 during the forenoon of the 31st, but shortly before noon Captain Thomas Jackson, Director of Operations, made one of his very rare visits to the Room. According to William Clarke, he had only come in twice previously, once to complain that he had cut his hand on one of the red boxes in which the decodes were circulated, and once, when a change in key had caused a temporary stoppage in the flow of decodes, to express his pleasure that he would not be further bothered with such damned nonsense! His purpose this time was to enquire where the D/F stations placed call sign DK. He was obviously not the sort of senior officer to whom one offered gratuitous advice, and he was informed that call sign DK was in Wilhelmshaven. Without further ado and without asking for an explanation or comment, the insufferable Jackson turned on his heel and left the room. All the blame for what then followed cannot however be placed on him, for it was Oliver who, as always, drafted in his own hand the following signal to Jellicoe and Beatty which was despatched at 12.30 p.m.: 'No definite news of enemy. They made all preparations for sailing early this morning. It was thought Fleet had sailed but Directionals place flagship in Jade at 11.10 a.m. GMT. Apparently they have been unable to carry out air reconnaissance which has delayed them.' Jellicoe received this signal at 12.48.

Hope, Denniston, Clarke and the rest of the staff in Room 40 did not learn that the signal had been sent until much later, when they were both horrified and furious that such gross misinformation had been sent to the Commander-in-Chief and to Beatty. It had two serious results. Firstly, Jellicoe, conscious of the need to conserve fuel, was steaming at an economical speed. Oliver's signal naturally persuaded him that there was no particular urgency, and precious time was wasted in examining neutral ships; the destroyers detached for this purpose (and the destroyers' fuel supply was most critical of all) did not rejoin at high speed. As a result, he was later than he intended in arriving at his rendezvous with Beatty, the distance between the main body of the Grand Fleet and the battle cruisers was increased and an hour or two of daylight, which might well have made a great difference to the outcome, was lost. Secondly, when Beatty first sighted Hipper's battle cruisers just under three hours had elapsed since both he and Jellicoe had been told that the *Hochseeflotte* was still in port! Both Jellicoe's and Beatty's faith in Intelligence supplied by the Admiralty was severely shaken. As Beatty remarked, 'What am I to think of OD [Operations Division] when I get that telegram and in three hours' time meet the whole German Fleet well out at sea?'

In fact the first contact between Beatty's and Hipper's light forces was made at 2.20 p.m. Beatty was some sixty-nine miles ahead of Jellicoe and the Grand Fleet, and Hipper fifty miles ahead of Scheer and the *Hochseeflotte*. Beatty had six battle cruisers with him and was supported by four of the latest fast dreadnoughts of the *Queen Elizabeth* class, the 5th Battle Squadron having been temporarily placed under his command. They were, however, slower than the battle cruisers and were soon left behind when Beatty started to chase Hipper to the southward. Hipper had five battle cruisers (although, as noted above, Beatty at first thought he had six against him). Hipper's task was to draw Beatty after him into the arms of the *Hochseeflotte*, whereas that of Beatty was not only to attempt to destroy his adversary but to establish, for Jellicoe's benefit, whether Hipper was operating on his own or as the advanced force of the main fleet. Hipper had the best of this 'run to the south'. Due to the superiority of the German fire control system, to the advantage of the light which the Germans enjoyed, to the weakness of the side armour of the British battle cruisers and lack of flash protection of their magazines, Beatty lost two of his ships, the *Indefatigable* and the *Queen Mary*, which were blown up with very heavy loss of life. The Germans, however, also suffered considerable although no fatal damage, particularly when the 5th Battle Squadron managed to get within range.

At 4.30 p.m. Commodore Goodenough in the light cruiser *Southampton* sighted the German main body, and a few minutes later reported the fact to Beatty and Jellicoe. It was now time for the roles of the opposing battle cruisers to be reversed; Beatty, after confirming the accuracy of Goodenough's report, turned back to the north to lead the Germans towards the Grand Fleet, a task in which he was completely successful because Scheer was still unaware that the whole British Fleet was ahead of him. Although Jellicoe was therefore far better informed than Scheer, faulty British reporting left him unaware of the precise position of the *Hochseeflotte* and without the necessary information upon which to take the vital decision how to deploy the Grand Fleet from its cruising into its fighting formation. In the event, and after only a few seconds' thought, he intuitively made the correct decision, so that when, at about 6.30 p.m., the leading ships of the Grand Fleet were able to open fire, the British were performing the classical operation of 'crossing the T' of their opponents, the naval equivalent of Wellington's infantry deploying in line against Napoleon's attack in columns.

Although around 6.00 p.m. a German destroyer which had picked up survivors of the British destroyer *Nomad*, left sinking during the run to the south, reported to Scheer that these survivors had stated that '60 large ships were in the neighbourhood, including 20 new battleships and 6 battle cruisers', Scheer was taken completely by surprise, and at once ordered an emergency 'battle turn away'. This order was given by low power wireless and was immediately and faultlessly executed. He also ordered his destroyers to cover the move by a torpedo attack and a smoke screen. By this time, although the British had lost yet another battle cruiser, Hood's *Invincible*, the leading German ships were suffering heavily; the prospects for the *Hochseeflotte* must have seemed bleak. However, the battle turn away and the smoke screen caused Jellicoe to lose touch, and firing ceased. Visibility was deteriorating, and the hours of daylight almost over. Jellicoe, uncertain of exactly what was happening on the German side and conscious of the possible threat from the torpedoes of the German destroyers, did not press on through the smoke screen but contented himself with placing his fleet between Scheer and his base. The German Commander-in-Chief, on the other hand, was not only anxious to disengage but to get to the eastward of the British and so be able to shape a course for the safety of the Heligoland Bight. Just before 7.00 p.m. he turned 180 degrees to the north-east but, for the second time, found that the Grand Fleet was crossing his T. His ships, particularly Hipper's already battered battle cruisers, began to receive very heavy punishment, and the position became desperate. Scheer ordered Hipper to carry out a death or glory attack on the British in conjunction with his destroyers, who were again ordered to lay a smoke screen. Under this cover, he once more carried out an emergency battle turn away and succeeded in disengaging. In this he was aided by Jellicoe's decision to turn away from the German torpedo attack, the classic response but one which has since been much criticised. However, as this turn was to the south-east, Jellicoe maintained his position between the Germans and the Heligoland Bight. Scheer,

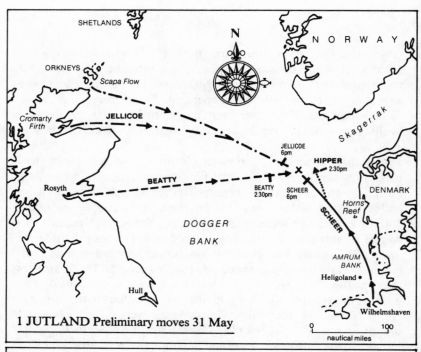

1 JUTLAND Preliminary moves 31 May

0 100
nautical miles

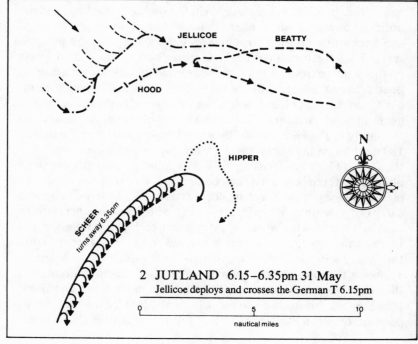

2 JUTLAND 6.15–6.35pm 31 May
Jellicoe deploys and crosses the German T 6.15pm

0 5 10
nautical miles

who had turned away to the south-west, now altered to the south and there was a further brief engagement between Beatty and Hipper, much in the former's favour, and the Germans were once more foiled in their attempt to break through for home.

The rival fleets were still only some miles apart, but daylight was now fading fast and Jellicoe, conscious that the British were not trained in night fighting and that he was still to the eastward of the Germans, decided to steer a course which would, he hoped, maintain this advantage and enable the Grand Fleet to resume the battle and administer the *coup de grace* on the following morning. Although, up to this point, the Germans had sunk three British battle cruisers without themselves losing a capital ship, they had suffered considerably more damage in the later stages of the action than had the British. They remained heavily outnumbered, and were handicapped by the presence of the slow and less powerful pre-dreadnoughts of their 2nd Battle Squadron. Scheer would have been foolhardy in the extreme to have accepted the British challenge for the following day; his only hope was somehow to get round or break through the rear of the Grand Fleet during the night, and to retreat as quickly as possible to Wilhelmshaven. He had four possible routes home but he chose the most direct, the one via the Horns Reef Channel by which he had come out. During the night, in a series of confused and bloody actions, he managed to force his way through the cruisers and destroyers screening the rear of the Grand Fleet; before first light the *Hochseeflotte* was clear of danger and on a course for home. In achieving this feat, he was greatly aided by two things. Jellicoe had decided that Scheer's most probable route would be by the Ems channel[1] to the south-west of the Horns Reef and so was steering a generally southerly course, ahead of but slightly diverging from that of the *Hochseeflotte* which, between 7.52 p.m. and 9.46 p.m. altered first to SSE ¼ E and then to SSE ¾ E. The paths of the two fleets were thus converging down the lines of a very narrow X. This would not have mattered greatly but for the well nigh incredible failure of any of the British forces engaged to realise what was happening or to report the facts to Jellicoe, who thus steamed steadily on further and further away from the *Hochseeflotte*. Next morning he swept an empty sea: Scheer was safely back in the Jade.

But despite all the British mistakes and misjudgements, Scheer's

---

[1] He had not been informed that in Room 40's view the Germans did not consider this channel free of mines.

escape was not inevitable; it need never have happened if only the information which, from 9.25 p.m. onwards came into Room 40's possession in an increasing flood, had been fully and promptly passed to Jellicoe and Beatty. Partly because of Scheer's use of low power wireless,[1] which was not intercepted by the British shore stations, and partly because even the best cryptanalysis can rarely be swift enough to have any tactical influence during the course of an actual engagement, Room 40 had contributed little during the afternoon. At 4.35 p.m. it had decoded the position of the German main force twenty-six minutes earlier, steering north-west at fifteen knots. This information was passed on to Jellicoe at 5.00 p.m., commendably quickly, if allowance is made for drafting and ciphering the signal. A further position report of 4.30 p.m. which was passed to Oliver at 5.00 p.m. was not, however, sent out by him for three quarters of an hour. Whether these two reports added much to Jellicoe's knowledge of the current situation at sea, is doubtful, although the second was received by him within only eight minutes of its official time of despatch. At 7.40 p.m. Room 40 passed to Oliver Scheer's instructions to three destroyer flotillas to attack the Grand Fleet during the night, but Oliver's out signal was not despatched for another hour and twenty-five minutes, an inexcusably long interval. Decodes ordering all U-boats to advance to the north and further instructions concerning the night destroyer attack, available at 8.40 p.m. and 8.31 p.m. respectively, were not sent to Jellicoe at all.

At 9.25 p.m. however, more valuable information began to become available when a signal from a German destroyer, giving the position and course of the rear battleship of the enemy fleet at 9.00 p.m., was passed through by Room 40. This was sent out at 9.58 p.m., but was not received by Jellicoe until 10.23 p.m. Unfortunately, the position seemed to Jellicoe obviously erroneous, although whether this was due to a navigational mistake on the part of the German destroyer making the report or to the fact that the *Hochseeflotte* was still in the process of taking up its new night formations, is not clear. Whatever the reason, Jellicoe was convinced that the position given was wrong.[2] Coming on top of the fatuous signal

---

[1]   It proved quicker and therefore more efficient than the British reliance on visual signalling.

[2]   The signal to Jellicoe was not an accurate paraphrase of the German message as it would have been in World War II; it stated baldly that the rear of the HSF was in such and such a position, thus giving no indication as to how it had been obtained or of its reliability.

around noon that the *Hochseeflotte* was still in the Jade, it destroyed what little faith he still had in the information being signalled to him by Oliver.

At 9.55 p.m. Room 40 provided an even more important piece of information, namely that at 9.14 p.m. the German battlefleet with its battle cruisers in the rear had been ordered home, course SSE ¾ E, speed sixteen knots. This signal was sent to Jellicoe at 10.41 p.m., and should have provided him with an unmistakable indication that Scheer was intending to use the Horns Reef swept channel. Jellicoe either chose to draw a different conclusion or, more probably, ignored it altogether because he had come to the conclusion that the information provided by the Admiralty was totally unreliable and misleading. Whatever his motives, he did not make the necessary alteration of course or alert his rear screen to the probability that a collision with the German Fleet was imminent.

Fifteen minutes after Room 40 had provided this invaluable clue to Scheer's intentions, at 10.10 p.m., Room 40 reported that at 9.06 p.m. Scheer had ordered the BdL, urgently, to provide Zeppelin reconnaissance of the Horns Reef. This at least should have settled all Jellicoe's doubts, but for some inexplicable reason this clinching intelligence was never passed out to him; Jellicoe did not even learn of its existence until some years after the war. The late Professor Marder quotes James as saying that when this vital decode was passed in to the Operations Division by Room 40, 'Oliver was taking the first opportunity since the fleet had sailed to retire for a badly needed rest . . . and that Captain A. F. Everett, the Naval Assistant to the 1st Sea Lord, was temporarily acting for Oliver.' This excuse simply will not hold water. Throughout the whole battle, Oliver drafted every single signal based on Room 40's decodes which was despatched to Jellicoe. Even if he had 'got his head down' for a few moments from time to time, it is obvious, from other signals which he himself drafted, that he must have been 'shaken' at intervals and shown the decodes that had arrived in the interval. If he was not woken, then Everett or Jackson or whoever was supposed to be in charge, was unfitted for the responsibility placed on him. A system which depended so entirely on the judgement and decision of one single man, was, as Beatty had already remarked, totally impracticable and unsound. But, the signal giving the possibly erroneous position of the rear ship of the German battlefleet was received in Operations Division at 9.25 p.m. and was not despatched to Jellicoe until 10.41 p.m. It was drafted by Oliver. The Horns Reef signal was in the hands of the Operations Division by 10.10 p.m. It seems highly unlikely that Oliver had already retired to the 1st Lord's bedroom,[1] only a few yards away, as early as this. Even if he had done so, why was he not woken, and why, when he was finally awake, which he most certainly was at the latest by 1.48 a.m. on the morning of 1 June (because he then drafted a signal), did he not look through the decodes which had accumulated while he was asleep and realise the significance of the information that should have been, but which had not been, passed to Jellicoe? Scheer was in fact late in reaching Horns Reef; had the information been passed out even as late as 1.15 a.m. on 1 June there would still at least have been time for Jellicoe to mop up some of Hipper's heavily damaged battle cruisers. Between 9.55 p.m. on 31 May and 3.00 a.m. on 1 June, no fewer than sixteen decodes, all of which would have added in some degree to Jellicoe's knowledge, were passed by Room 40 to Operations Division. Only three of them were sent to Jellicoe. It was a terrible indictment of the system which Churchill had originally devised, and which Oliver had entirely failed to modify in the twelve months since Churchill had left the Admiralty.

Despite all the British weaknesses in materiel and organisation at sea, Jutland would have been a crushing victory if only the inestimable advantage of superior intelligence had not been so needlessly dissipated by a faulty system. To the charge that this statement is being wise after the event, one can only point out that the existing arrangements for the analysis and dissemination of Room 40's information had been in force for seventeen months, and that there had been many examples, not unnoticed by those at sea, demonstrating that they were quite inadequate. For all this one must blame Oliver's conviction that only he, aided by the septuagenarian A. K. Wilson, was capable, afloat or ashore, of drawing the right conclusions and taking the necessary decisions.

Room 40 had certainly performed brilliantly. It had forecast the sortie of the *Hochseeflotte* more than a week before it occurred; it had given warning of its actual departure in time for Jellicoe and Beatty to get to sea before their adversaries had even sailed from the Jade. Indeed, it can be said, in the light of previous and subsequent experience, that but for Room 40, Jutland would never have been fought at all. If it had contributed little or nothing of tactical value

---

[1] Oliver had used the 1st Lord's bedroom and bathroom since Churchill's departure, because Balfour did not occupy Admiralty House.

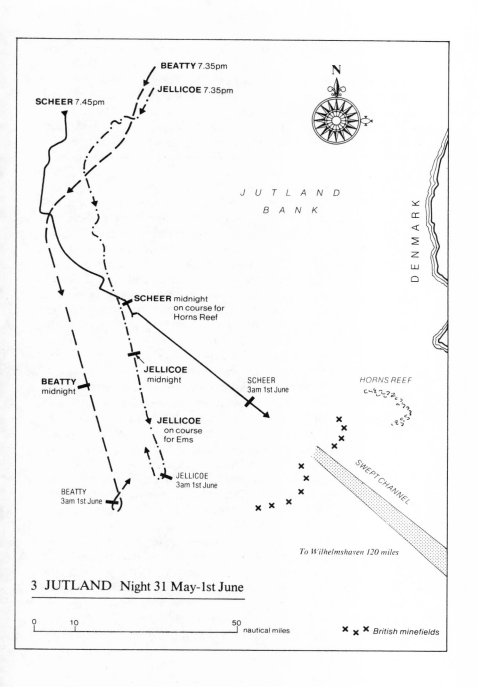

BEATTY 7.35pm

JELLICOE 7.35pm

SCHEER 7.45pm

N

JUTLAND BANK

DENMARK

SCHEER midnight
on course for
Horns Reef

JELLICOE
midnight

SCHEER
3am 1st June

BEATTY
midnight

HORNS REEF

JELLICOE
on course
for Ems

JELLICOE
3am 1st June

SWEPT CHANNEL

BEATTY
3am 1st June

To Wilhelmshaven 120 miles

3 JUTLAND Night 31 May–1st June

0   10   50
                                              nautical miles

× × × British minefields

during the afternoon of 31 May, it had provided all the information necessary to have enabled Jellicoe to renew the battle under highly favourable circumstances on the next day, if only it had been passed to him. By the evening of 1 June, Hope had compiled a list, almost entirely accurate, of the German ships involved, of those actually sunk and the damage, some of it very serious, which had been incurred by others. Within the very circumscribed limits of the responsibilities permitted to it, Room 40 had made no mistakes.

The Germans proclaimed, and still proclaim, that Jutland, or the battle of the Skagerrack, was a victory for Scheer. They had every reason to feel proud of the fighting performance of their ships and men. They had sunk three British battle cruisers, three armoured cruisers and eight destroyers against a loss to themselves of one battle cruiser, one pre-dreadnought, four light cruisers and five destroyers, 111,000 tons against 62,000 tons, and this against a considerably superior opponent, (although on the basis of serious damage to ships not acutally sunk the advantage lay with the British). But Scheer had failed completely in his primary object – to cut off and annihilate a detached portion of the Grand Fleet, and so radically reduce the disparity in strength between the two forces. British control of the surface waters of the North Sea was as complete after the battle as it had been before it. The Grand Fleet was anxious to resume the battle on 1 June; the *Hochseeflotte* was not. As one American commentator aptly put it, the German Fleet had assaulted its gaoler and was now back in gaol! Although, as we shall see, this was not the last sortie of the *Hochseeflotte*, and despite the immediate claims of victory, Scheer wrote to the Emperor on 4 July, 'Nevertheless, there can be no doubt that even the most successful outcome of a Fleet action in this war will not *force* England to make peace. The disadvantages of our military-geographical position in relation to that of the British Isles, and the enemy's great material superiority, cannot be compensated by our fleet to the extent where we shall be able to overcome the blockade or the British themselves . . . A victorious end to the war within a reasonable time can only be achieved through the defeat of British economic life – that is by using the U-boats against British trade.' If Jutland was no Trafalgar, it was nonetheless a strategic victory for the British and a strategic defeat for the Germans.

*

Jellicoe had reported at 9.45 p.m. on 2 June, only hours after the Fleet had returned to harbour, that it was again ready for sea at four hours' notice, and had received back all his damaged ships by the end of July, whereas the *Hochseeflotte* was not ready for further operations until mid-August and even then without two of its battle cruisers. One must therefore pay tribute to Scheer for at once planning a further operation with the same limited object – to whittle down the strength of the Grand Fleet by drawing it out with a bombardment of Sunderland, designed to lure it over carefully disposed U-boat patrol lines. To guard against the very unpleasant surprise which he had received on encountering the whole of the Grand Fleet at Jutland, Scheer relied on extensive reconnaissance patrols by his Zeppelins and on his U-boats. But once again he was betrayed by his own excessive use of wireless in the preliminary stages.

Hope's narrative of the events, ('The Stunt' as he rather engagingly called it), obviously compiled immediately afterwards, shows clearly that Room 40 was alerted to the possibility of some further move by the *Hochseeflotte* as early as 15 August, when it noted that 'two and a half flotillas of destroyers were detailed as outposts at Schillig Roads and none for Heligoland. This procedure, being unusual, presaged something.' It was also learned that the 1st and 3rd Battle Squadrons, at full strength, and the 2nd and 4th Scouting Groups plus two of the battle cruisers and the usual destroyer flotillas, were assembled in the Jade. All the usual portents followed – minesweeping, instructions to light vessels and, on the morning of 18 August the information that the 3rd Battle Squadron would pass the outer Jade at 10.30 p.m. that evening. Airships were given orders to take up prearranged positions.

So far as the U-boats were concerned, it was known that they had sailed and that they were divided into three groups off the north coast of England and some off Aberdeen, but their precise patrol areas were not revealed (in fact others were disposed in the southern North Sea). There was no final confirmation that the *Hochseeflotte* was actually at sea until the battleship *Westfalen* was torpedoed by a British submarine at 5.05 a.m. some sixty miles north of Terschelling. Her report was immediately D/F'd by the British shore stations and the position passed to Jellicoe, but he did not receive it until 7.00 a.m. However, the Grand Fleet had in fact been ordered to sea less than two hours after Room 40 had decoded the signal about the 3rd Battle Squadron on the morning of the 18th.

Once again Jellicoe and Beatty left harbour before the Germans. On this occasion, however, Scheer was rather better served by his U-boats, for just before 6.00 a.m. on 19 August one of them torpedoed and sank the cruiser *Nottingham*. Jellicoe at first thought that she had been mined and turned away to the north to avoid any danger of a possible minefield, until he was sure that the cruiser had been torpedoed. He thereby lost four hours. By this time Scheer was breaking wireless silence and his advance was being fixed by the British D/F stations, although the signals themselves were not decoded, because a change of key at midnight on 18-19 August had not then been broken by Room 40. Despite the delay caused by Jellicoe's fear of minefields, all might have been well for the British had not Scheer, in turn, been misled by a report from one of his Zeppelins guarding against a surprise attack from the south. L.13 mistook the Harwich force of light cruisers and destroyers for a squadron of battleships coming up from the south and Scheer, believing that at last he might catch an isolated portion of the Grand Fleet, abandoned his advance towards Sunderland and turned south-east towards this supposed quarry. This of course took him away from the Grand Fleet. He had also been confused by a report from another of his U-boats, U 53, which had sighted Jellicoe while he was still on a northerly course following *Nottingham*'s supposed mining. Had Scheer not reversed course in this way he would almost certainly have been brought to action by the Grand Fleet. The Harwich Force, having failed to find the Germans, also turned back to the south-east and so did not sight Scheer. At 2.13 p.m. Scheer received a further report from U 53 which had again sighted the Grand Fleet, but this time steering south and only about sixty-five miles away. Twenty minutes later Scheer decided that discretion was the better part of valour and turned to the ESE for home. At 3.46 p.m. Jellicoe learned from the Admiralty that he had no chance of catching Scheer and also turned about, losing a second cruiser to a U-boat before he reached Scapa. Tyrwhitt and the Harwich Force did sight the *Hochseeflotte* in the distance at 6.00 p.m., but were unable to overtake them before the rising of a full moon made a torpedo attack on such a superior force impossible. So, once again, through a series of mistaken reports and misunderstandings of the actual situation on the part of both commanders-in-chief, no general engagement took place.

Although Scheer was still anxious to continue with similar operations, and planned one for September which had to be postponed due to poor weather, the *Admiralstab* were by now even more convinced that a resumption of the U-boat war on commerce was necessary and this was ordered, although subject to the Prize Law. Scheer was thus deprived of one of the forces essential to his operations, and his last sortie was a limited operation on the night of 18 October to attack any shipping he could find east of the Dogger Bank. Room 40 gave the usual warnings, but the Grand Fleet was not ordered out. One of Scheer's cruisers was torpedoed, the weather was bad and his destroyers could not keep up, while Neumünster had already warned him that the British knew he was at sea and had diverted merchant ships and recalled light forces. He therefore turned back at 2.00 a.m. on 19 October. This was the last offensive sortie by the *Hochseeflotte* until April 1918.

The German strategy throughout 1916, indeed since the beginning of the war, had depended on achieving surprise. The commanders-in-chief of the *Hochseeflotte* had the advantage of being able to choose their moment for a sudden sortie and, at least for this purpose, the relative positions of the main bases of the two Fleets were more favourable to the Germans than to the British. It is unlikely that the Germans, given their inferiority in numbers, could ever have managed to get on equal terms with the Grand Fleet, but it is fair to say that they might well have inflicted some very unpleasant defeats on isolated British forces if their plans had worked out as intended. That the Germans never succeeded, in this period, in achieving the surprise for which they hoped must be attributed to the work of Room 40. The failure of the Grand Fleet to win the smashing victory which, after so many disappointments, seemed within its grasp at Jutland must be put down to the system under which Room 40 was compelled to work and on the incredible concentration of responsibility in the hands of one man, Oliver.

Jellicoe was not happy that he had been or would in the future be provided with all the intelligence available in the Admiralty. In November he wrote to the 1st Sea Lord, Jackson, to say so, pointing out also that information sent to him in documents often differed from that which he received in signals. Oliver was instructed to draft a suitable reply, which was then submitted to, and slightly amended by the 1st Lord, Balfour. Balfour once more stressed the paramount importance of preventing the 'Germans discovering our method'. If they did so, it would be 'a national disaster'. He pointed out that of the Board of Admiralty only the 1st and 2nd Sea Lords knew the secret, while the War Committee of the Cabinet had not been informed of it. He would nevertheless agree to a daily summary being sent to Jellicoe by hand of officer, but this was to be shown to no one except his Chief of Staff and was to be burned a few days after receipt. Should it ever be necessary to refer to these summaries telegraphically they were to be called 'the Japon returns'.

All this was fair enough. What was rather more questionable was Balfour's assertion that 'when the Grand Fleet has been sent out, the information is *the best and fullest* which we possess. You may (very naturally perhaps) have sometimes supposed that we possess information not supplied to you, and that you are asked to act in ignorance of the relevant facts which we have withheld from you. I can assure you that this is not so and that we always take you into our fullest confidence.'

Balfour may perhaps have believed what he wrote, but Oliver must have known that it was a long way from being the truth, the whole truth and nothing but the truth. One cannot but wonder what Jellicoe thought when, a few weeks later, he became 1st Sea Lord in place of Sir Henry Jackson and saw at first hand the extent of Room 40's knowledge.[1] He did not replace Oliver, but a number of changes did take place in the organisation and control of Room 40.

---

[1] According to Clarke, Jellicoe regularly visited Room 40 before he turned in for the night and chatted to the watchkeepers. He was the only 1st Sea Lord to do so.

CHAPTER ELEVEN

Ewing Departs

There was at least one officer of the Naval Staff who recognised the faults in the handling of Room 40's information, which had culminated in the failure to send Jellicoe the Horns Reef decode on the night after the Battle of Jutland. Blinker Hall saw that these faults stemmed from Oliver's conception that Room 40 was merely his private cryptographic bureau rather than a fully fledged Intelligence centre, but, as James remarks, 'the time was not yet ripe for making such a radical proposal to the Naval Staff, and Hall could do nothing until next year.' Put more brutally, this meant so long as Ewing was responsible to Oliver for the work of the Room, and so long as Oliver continued to regard the staff of Room 40, from Hope downwards, as incapable of appreciating the operational significance of the German signals which they decoded and which, in fact, they alone fully understood.

On 6 May, just before Jutland, Ewing had been offered the Principalship of Edinburgh University, vacant because of the death of the previous incumbent. Ewing at first replied that he was engaged on secret war work which he could not and would not abandon, but the approaches were renewed and it was suggested that an arrangement might be made which would permit Ewing to carry out both functions. It so happened that Balfour, still 1st Lord, was also Chancellor of Edinburgh University, and Ewing discussed the problem with him. Balfour pointed out that the supervision of Room 40 was a temporary job whereas the academic post was a relatively permanent one. Ewing was sixty-one, with a wife and family to consider and he decided to accept the University's offer. He took up residence there in October 1916, although officially retaining his post as Director of Naval Education and some supervisory responsibilities for Room 40. This was obviously an impossible arrangement, and in May 1917 Ewing finally handed over the complete control of Room 40 to Hall. One can only conclude that his far from happy relationship with the DID had some influence on his decision. It is also reasonable to speculate whether Balfour, one of the most intelligent of politicians, was as satisfied with the previous arrangements as he led Jellicoe to suppose at the beginning of November.

It is not easy to assess Ewing's real contribution to Room 40's success. His son tells us that 'In the discovery of enemy ciphers Ewing took little direct part, except during the first year, for, as the staff grew from a zero beginning, it came to comprise members whose faculty for that kind of inspired guessing and quick inference was far greater than his own; and it must be remembered that the problems themselves had by this time become much harder. His chief function now was to collect the staff and organise it, giving it such general direction as was necessary . . . As head, he did his best to co-ordinate the parts of the machine, supplying such drops of lubricant as might be required by nerves jaded through over-work and lack of sleep.'

Oliver certainly thought highly of Ewing. In 1919 he ran into him in Edinburgh, and found that Ewing was deeply wounded by the lack of any official word of thanks from the Admiralty for his work. Oliver endeavoured to secure for him an OBE or at least an official letter from the Board but was unsuccessful; Ewing received nothing. Too much should not be read into this lack of official enthusiasm. Service chiefs, particularly when a war has ended, often quickly forget heads of their Intelligence departments on whose efforts so much previously depended.

Nevertheless, it does seem a little strange that at such a critical moment of the war Ewing should have wished to leave Room 40, and that Balfour should have permitted him to do so, if his presence was still really essential. The only member of Room 40 to express any definite views about Ewing was William Clarke, and his views were extremely unfavourable. He considered that Ewing contributed nothing to Room 40's success even in the earliest days. Clarke believed that Rotter and Hope were the ones to whom the credit was due. Clarke was not, of course, a member of Room 40 in the early months and worshipped Hope and greatly admired Rotter. His views may be unduly biased. Professor Bruford, although he did not actually work under Ewing, has written that, when he joined the organisation in 1917, he heard nothing against Ewing from his immediate superior, Faudel-Phillips, rather the contrary. But the absence of any tribute to Ewing by Denniston, who also left notes on the early period, and various remarks made by some of the leading members of the Room when Hall was writing his auto-biography, do tend to suggest that Ewing was not held in the highest regard.

It must, however, be pointed out that the brief given to Ewing by Oliver, confirmed by Churchill, was a restricted one and that, within these limits, he fulfilled it with considerable success. He was the first to recruit staff who eventually became masters of their trade. He almost certainly was responsible for the initial influx of talent from the universities and particularly from King's College, Cambridge. It was his friendship with Russell-Clarke which resulted in the estab-lishment in such a short space of time of the Y intercepting stations, the pre-requisite of any cryptographic success. If he was not 'The Wizard of Whitehall', as the Press subsequently dubbed him, if he did not recognise the necessity for, or could not initiate, the developments and reforms which Hall subsequently introduced, if he lacked Hall's personality and Hope's popularity, he did preside over Room 40's birth and guide its first faltering footsteps. Hall would probably have done better (had Oliver permitted it), but in fact it was Ewing who performed the task and for that performance one must pay him full tribute. He was a most successful Principal of Edinburgh University until he retired in 1929. He died in 1935.

Room 40's difficulties were twofold. In the first place, despite the increase in staff during 1915 and early 1916, numbers were still insufficient to cope with the ever growing work load, and much potentially valuable material was still, perforce, neglected. For example, although a copy of one of the Austrian naval codes had been received from the Italians quite early on, no attempt was made for two years to exploit it due in part to lack of manpower but primarily to lack of liaison with the Italian and French intercepting stations in the Mediterranean. Baltic traffic, which was essential to a full understanding of the organisation and procedures of the German Fleet and which, as was subsequently found, could often provide an easy clue to new cipher keys and to the reconstruction of new codes, was all too often consigned to the NSL box or even the wastepaper basket simply because no one could be spared to tackle it.

Hope had from the first attempted to take a broader view, to act as an analyst, to build up a comprehensive picture and to form appreciations of likely moves either of the *Hochseeflotte* itself, or of the U-boats, minesweepers or Zeppelins and was by now compiling a most useful card index system, assisted in these tasks by Clarke

and Birch. He also began to keep, but only for his own purposes, a
War Diary. It is also true that Dilly Knox, Bullough, Lytton, de
Grey, Rotter, Denniston and indeed all the 'old gang' had become
much more expert cryptanalysts. But far too much still depended on
far too few men, and was to continue to do so right up to the
Armistice. The Log still had to be written up, watches had to be
kept, there were no modern office aids and no typists. Rotter's
health broke down under the strain (although after a spell of sick
leave he was able to return to duty).[1] The pressure on everyone was
great, although it is fair to point out that the best results are often
obtained by small overburdened organisations, working under
great stress but with a dedication and singleness of purpose which
their members themselves did not previously realise they
possessed.

The second disadvantage was of course the system itself. Appreciations of the general situation by Room 40's amateurs were not
asked for and therefore not seen by Oliver, Wilson and Jackson.
These three were still forming their own views solely on the basis of
the more important decodes passed to them raw, and were thus
cutting themselves off from a great mass of superficially unimportant but, in total, vitally important information. The fact that Room
40 was not a part of the Intelligence Division and was deprived of
often useful information from ID's sections, and even more important, that those sections were totally cut off from the priceless
information available in the decodes, was an error of such magni-
tude that it is now almost impossible to explain. Oliver had, after all,
been Director of Intelligence himself and surely should have realised that Intelligence is indivisible. One of the subsidiary values of
cryptanalysis is the ability which it gives to Intelligence officers to
check and evaluate the mass of reports from agents, spies and
diplomats, mostly wildly inaccurate but occasionally containing a
gem of information if only if can be recognised amongst all the
dross. The Intelligence Division did its best with the material at its
disposal but it would have done far better if it had access to Room
40, as was to be shown from 1917 onwards. There can be no doubt
also that Room 40 then benefited greatly from the additional
sources available from ID.

The first major change, at the end of 1916, was the provision of a
War Diary, a copy of which was sent daily to the Commander-in-

[1] Rodger Winn, Head of the Admiralty's World War II Submarine Tracking
Room, had a similar breakdown in December 1942.

Chief Grand Fleet, now Sir David Beatty. Although this was inevitably twenty-four hours out of date, sometimes more, it must have provided Beatty with an invaluable background against which to assess and understand the brief operational information sent him by cable or wireless. Unfortunately, these reports continued to be prefaced by quite unnecessary euphemisms such as 'There are signs that' so and so is going to happen or 'It is possible', thus mixing up fact and inference in a way which Beatty himself told Clarke at the end of the war often left him in doubt as to the degree of reliability the Admiralty actually placed on a particular piece of information.[1]

Other changes followed gradually. Individual intercepts were no longer sent in raw to operations but were replaced by reasoned appreciations. The War Diary was circulated. Specialisation within Room 40 was carried further; the skilled cryptographers concentrated on crytography; sub-sections were set up to deal with particular subjects or areas – the Bight, the Baltic, minesweeping, U-boats, directionals, and so on. This of course required additional staff.

More university teachers were recruited, not classical dons, with the exception of Ernest Harrison, classical tutor of Trinity College Cambridge (and later University Registrar), and in 1918 J. D. Beazley from Oxford, soon to be *the* authority on Greek vases. The rest were all Germanists from the universities, some of the scholars who had replaced the German and Austrian professors who had until the War held the principal German posts in about twenty-three universities in Great Britain and Ireland. In 1916 Dr E. C. Quiggin, lecturer in German in Cambridge and Fellow of Caius College, followed his colleague Edward Bullough and did pioneer work on Austrian codes. In 1917 the watch in Room Forty was augmented by the Taylorian Lecturer in Oxford, L. A. Willoughby, and the Professor of German from Trinity College, Dublin, G. Waterhouse; from Birmingham came F. E. Sandbach and from Leeds the lecturer (later Professor), C. E. Gough. Through Dr Quiggin two of his best recent pupils, unfit for service abroad, were also appointed, W. H. Bruford and C. W. Hardisty, both to help Faudel-

---

[1] Hall's World War II successor, Godfrey, overcame this problem quite simply. He laid down that such papers and signals should be divided into two parts; the first containing the facts, the second, headed 'Comment' containing any inferences which the Intelligence Division felt should be drawn from those facts. He also introduced a simple system for grading the reliability of information; A to E for the information and 1 to 5 for the source.

Phillips with the Madrid traffic. In mid-1918 the Professor of French
at Belfast, D. L. Savory, was somehow also appointed.

To these academics were added a number of other individuals
who subsequently became well known to the public, such as Patrick
Curwen, the actor, Desmond McCarthy the author, Gerald Lawrence, another actor, G. P. Mackeson, a caricaturist, Father Ronald
Knox, Dilly's younger brother,[1] Francis Toye, the musical critic and
author, and Edward Molyneux, the couturier. Molyneux, like
Lionel Fraser and a number of others, was an invalided Army
officer, of whom quite a number found their way to Room 40. These
non-academics were mostly employed as 'Tubists' and junior watchkeepers, receiving, sorting, recording, distributing and filing the
rapid flow of intercepts discharged with a rattle and a bang into the
wire box at the bottom of the pneumatic tube. It was essential work
which freed the experts for more specialist duties. Another City
man was Frank Tiarks, from the bankers Schroeders, who became
the Direction Finding expert, and who had started life in the
Navy.

Whatever their backgrounds – and they continued to be varied –
the new recruits quickly felt themselves to be members of an
important team, a happy 'band of brothers', proud to serve the
Royal Navy.

At long last the need for secretarial help was recognised, and a
number of very carefully selected young ladies, mostly university
graduates and personally vouched for by some existing member of
the staff, were recruited. Not many of them had previously been
taught to type, but they soon learnt. Clarke lists some of 'Blinker's
Beauty Chorus' as follows: 'Miss Tribe, secretary to Hope, Welsford who insisted on joining up again in 1939, Jenkin now [1953]
famous in the BBC programmes, Nugent who went to Chatham
House, Mrs Denniston, Spears, Henderson, daughter of Willie
[later Admiral Sir Wilfred Henderson and one of the organisers of
the convoy system], Mrs Bailey, who rather upset things with her
love affairs, Hudson who came as my secretary and used to embarrass us by her early arrival [when the night watch were still bathing],
and was a sister of Hudson, later in the Conservative government
and daughter of the soap king, Lady Hambro, as efficient as her
husband in the City, who startled Hope at one of our dinners by

---

[1] Subsequently a well-known Catholic divine, he in fact served only a short time in
Room 40, and confessed that he never really understood what he was supposed to be
doing!

smoking a large cigar, Curtiss who in my view was the most useful of them all, Joan Harvey, daughter of the Secretary to the Bank of England . . . Surprisingly there was only one romance . . . Miss Reddam, who spent most of working time in a bathroom, which we had with some difficulty persuaded the authorities to install. She married Dilly Knox [she was his secretary and shared his somewhat bizarre office!].'

Reggie Hall was adored by the opposite sex, an adoration of which he was by no means unaware, and which he was not averse to using to further his own ends. An elderly, but rich, admirer not only lent him her limousine for the duration of the war but the services of her chauffeur as well. Ella Lee (now Mrs Cochrane), a niece of Captain (later Admiral Sir) Gilbert Stephenson, joined the Intelligence Division when just eighteen in 1915. She said that one could not refuse Hall anything he asked for, no matter how tired one was or how inconvenient the request might be. She added that this was not the whole story, because he had a frightening temper, but, such was his charm, he was immediately forgiven and his slightest wish was law. Marjorie Napier, another young girl who joined ID, and returned to serve under John Godfrey in World War II, testifies that 'he inspired loyalty and devotion in his staff in whom he took a personal and stimulating interest. Normally friendly, he could be terrifyingly stern. He had a schoolboy delight in pulling off a coup . . .' Men reacted in the same way. Lionel Fraser wrote: 'Those of us who served Admiral Hall all revered him. We knew we would be his slaves, come what may, such was his magnetism and our blind devotion.' Even that severe critic of the staff of Room 40, William Clarke, fell under Hall's spell. 'I do not think,' wrote Clarke, 'that anyone who ever served under Blinker will ever forget his keenness, his energy or his kindness to us all, I certainly never shall . . . Towards the end of the war when things were very strenuous and conditions exacting, he would come into our workshop and say 'Look here, some of you want a little relaxation, my car is outside the North door, you and you are to go out in it for a breather' . . . When one of our more brilliant cryptographers had solved a very complicated problem, Blinker asked him what he would like as a reward and gave him the easy chair for his room which he asked for . . .' Claud Serocold became a great personal friend and after the war helped Hall considerably by securing company directorships for him. Hall's charm was quite unforced and quite genuine, but, consciously or unconsciously, he derived enormous benefit from it.

It should not be supposed that all these changes in organisation came about at once – they were still taking place up to the time of the Armistice. One important change in staff did take place early in 1917. Hope, who was a regular naval officer with his career to look to, obtained a sea appointment in command of the cruiser *Dartmouth*, then stationed in the Adriatic. He did very well, being awarded the DSO and, after the war, promoted Rear-Admiral. He was not an easy man to replace. Despite his difficulties with Oliver, he was certainly responsible for much of Room 40's early success and was, in practice if not in name, the real head of Room 40. He had neither the temperament nor the seniority to push his own views forward, but his judgement was always sound and his kindness and refusal to 'pull his rank' on his largely civilian and (from a naval point of view) undisciplined staff, endeared him to them all and obviously helped to produce the happiest of ships.

After two unsuccessful experiments Hall determined to secure 'Bubbles' James, who had been his executive Commander in *Queen Mary*. In 1917 James was serving on Sturdee's staff in the Grand Fleet and Sturdee, backed up sharply by Beatty, refused to let him go. Hall, however, managed in the end to get his way and James took over the day to day responsibility for Room 40. He was a very different type from Hope. A fine sea officer, it apparently took him some time to come to terms with his new 'crew' who resented his brisk and breezy quarterdeck manner, and what they felt was his inability to understand the esoteric details of their work. He never made any great attempt to do so, regarding himself as an administrator and the manager of the team rather than as a member, if the most senior, of it as Hope had done. In fact, this was probably just what the circumstances demanded and the staff gradually reconciled themselves to the loss of their beloved Hope and came to recognise the increased authority and prestige which James secured for them. He very soon decided that all those not already in uniform should receive commissions as Lieutenants in the RNVR. Curiously this was not at first welcomed by some of the senior civilians of the Old Gang, who felt that it was ridiculous to dress them up as sailors when they had no nautical knowledge or training. The Reverend Montgomery, something of a fighting parson, was not one of them. He wrote to Hall expressly disassociating himself from the protesters, saying that he was not one of those who believed that clerics should not take part in war and that his only regret was that he could not get to sea. He accepted his appointment as a naval padre with considerable pride. Whether it was a silent protest, or just absent-mindedness, some others, unnamed, certainly made rather odd naval officers; several never remembered to put on their caps when outside the Admiralty in uniform, and one, it is said, invariably wore his back to front.

Although the general opinion, to judge by Birch's *Alice in ID25*, was that James did not have enough to do and could rarely be found when he was wanted, he was an undoubted asset, and much more capable of pressing Room 40's views effectively on the Naval Staff than had been the modest and retiring Hope.

Another major and most important change for Room 40 was its official incorporation into the Intelligence Division in May 1917; it became ID 25, or section 25 of the Division. This did not, unfortunately, mean that all the watertight doors which had hitherto prevented the interchange of information were suddenly opened; even by the Armistice this had not been fully accomplished. It did, however, have the result that Fleet Paymaster E. W. C. Thring, who for the past three years had been trying to the best of his ability to track and record the movements of U-boats from 'open' evidence, was at last admitted to the Mystery. Thring, who in 1939, when he was sixty-four, returned to re-form the Admiralty's Submarine Tracking Room, was an ideal choice for this job. He spoke German well and had a careful, sceptical and analytical brain; he was not to be seduced by optimistic reports of U-boats destroyed from enthusiastic officers at sea or brow-beaten by senior officers in the Admiralty whose preconceived notions he outraged. This new combination of knowledge and expertise was only one of the signs that Hall's wish to turn Room 40 into an Intelligence Centre instead of a mere cryptographic bureau, was being realised. With the resumption of the unrestricted U-boat campaign in February 1917, it did not come a moment too soon.

One certainly does begin to see from mid-1917 onwards some signs of decentralisation and delegation. Signals which previously would only have been drafted and signed by Oliver, were sometimes originated by James or even one of the staff of Room 40 (although such signals were of course purely informatory, never containing operational instructions). Jellicoe, who had become 1st Sea Lord at the end of November 1916, created a new Anti-Submarine Division of the Naval Staff under Rear-Admiral A. L. Duff. He was put on the circulation list for Room 40's decodes and also began to send out information and instructions which until then had been left to the COS or A. K. Wilson.[1]

Some relief may have been provided by the despatch of the ineffable Thomas Jackson to Alexandria, where he attempted to reverse the reforms introduced by Admiral Wemyss, until suppressed by Wemyss's successor, Gough-Calthorpe.

Room 40 certainly needed all the additional strength and expertise with which it could be provided. The introduction of the FFB in May 1917 coincided, for the first and only time, with a complete change in call signs, while key changes were being made every twenty-four hours and the grid squares used to indicate latitude and longitude were disguised by a transposition code, which was also changed at intervals. Nevertheless, Birch and Clarke state that Room 40 reached its peak of success in the last few months of 1917. Given the improvements in German codes and the considerable reduction in the use of wireless by the *Hochseeflotte* itself, if not by light craft and U-boats, this judgement can only be taken as justification for the changes which Hall at last managed to introduce and, indirectly, as criticism of the previous state of affairs.

Perhaps another result of Hall's assumption of full control of Room 40, was the despatch of a British team of cryptographers in the late spring of 1917 to Italy. This followed a tour by Hall to Malta, Rome and Alexandria, and the realisation that both the French and the Italians were intercepting a great deal of German and Austrian Mediterranean wireless traffic, but were only having moderate success in decoding it. The party was headed by Nigel de Grey and consisted of seven or eight members of Room 40's staff, one of whom was Lord Monk Bretton, and a number of officers and ratings trained by Russell Clarke to erect and man additional Y stations, which were sorely needed. Established first at Taranto but later moved to Rome, de Grey's little band worked very closely with the Italian Director of Naval Intelligence, principally on Austrian codes in which the Italians had made considerable progress. Distrust of Italian security seems to have prevented the same interchange of information about German U-boat traffic, much of which was handled in Malta at least from the interception point of view, undecoded messages being cabled back to London.

By the end of 1917 the supply of information about Austrian and German activities in the Mediterranean, Adriatic and Aegean had improved out of all recognition, a situation which, sadly, could

[1] A. K. Wilson retired from his unpaid advisory work at the beginning of 1917.

easily have been reached in 1915 had the necessary steps been taken then. The moment was of course right for the change. With the withdrawal of the Royal Navy's most powerful and modern ships to the North Sea at the end of August 1914, the Mediterranean, apart from the Dardanelles, had become largely a French responsibility. The entry of Italy into the war on the side of the Entente in 1915, although ensuring massive superiority over the Austro-Hungarian Fleet, had not really improved the situation; the French were concerned to protect their own major interests – their supply lines to Algeria and their army at Salonika. They distrusted the Italians, while the Italians would not serve under a French commander-in-chief and had no intention of conducting active operations at sea, except the defence of their own coastal waters, preferring instead to safeguard their battlefleet as a bargaining weapon at the peace conference. The defence of trade, of which a great deal was British, engaged not only in supplying Imperial forces in Egypt, Mesopotamia, Salonika and Italy, but also in providing both France and Italy with the sinews of war and the necessities of life such as coal, fell largely on the British commands at Gibraltar, Malta, Taranto and Alexandria. Their ill co-ordinated attempts met with little success until, in 1917, with a face saving arrangement for the French naval supremo, a British Commander-in-Chief, Mediterranean, was once more appointed, convoys introduced and Intelligence reorganised. Without these measures the German U-boat campaign, which had never been called off in the Inland Sea, would not have been mastered.

It is difficult to establish how much co-operation there was with the French or indeed how successful the French themselves were in the naval field. The Head of the French Army cryptological section, General François Cartier, paid tribute to the help given by Hall in connection with Austrian codes, but this help was almost certainly given in 1917, and Cartier also complained that when he had appealed to Hall for help with German naval codes, the DID had suggested that the French leave this side of things to the British. Robert M. Grant's careful analysis of French records for 1916 and 1917 suggests that the main source of French success in establishing the position of U-boats, was direction finding rather than code-breaking. James claims that co-operation with the French was close and that information was sent to them by bag every night to Paris. This may have been true in 1917 and 1918, but James does not make it clear whether the information supplied was purely cryptographic,

to help the French decoders, or, as is much more probable, merely a
form of War Diary such as was sent to the Commander-in-Chief,
Grand Fleet. Such successes as the French did achieve were probably the results of captures from the few U-boats they themselves
sank, and were of value only so long as they were able to break the
daily changes of cipher key. Birch and Clarke suggest that by the
end of 1917 co-operation in the Mediterranean was good, and
resulted in a considerable lessening of the efforts of the E. Dienst to
supply information to U-boats. The French were certainly au fait
with the wireless messages sent between Berlin and Madrid in the
VB code by the end of 1917, and Hall was on good terms with
Admiral de Bon, Commander-in-Chief of the French Navy. There
is also evidence of a considerable exchange of information through
Commodore Heaton Ellis, the British Naval Attaché in Paris, and
of frequent visits by Claud Serocold to France. But this does not add
up to proof that the secrets of Room 40's expertise were given to the
French, and the weight of evidence and probability is that they were
not. Information that would, in Hall's opinion, help the Allied
cause, bearing in mind the very small part played by the French
Navy outside the Mediterranean, yes, but the wholesale handing
over of cryptological secrets, unless the French were able to recipro-
cate, no; that, in the absence of any evidence to the contrary, must
be the present verdict.

It is however possible that some of the difficulty may have arisen
through lack of co-operation between the *Ministère de la Guerre*
and the *Ministère de la Marine* (a state of affairs the British DNI
Godfrey found even more marked in America in 1941 and 1942). In
1916 a certain Colonel Cartier[1] invented a system for jamming
enemy wireless transmissions. The French pressed the British to
join them in the development and application of Cartier's idea, but
when the proposals reached the Admiralty via the Foreign Office,
the response of Their Lordships was unfavourable in the extreme.
The Foreign Office reactions were rather plaintive. 'I suppose we
must do this,' ran the first minute, 'but I cannot help feeling that the
Admiralty have been rather unreasonable throughout this business.' Not so, ran the second opinion; 'So far as I can remember the
beginning of this business, the Admiralty made out a very strong
case in opposition to the proposed jamming, and I entirely agree
with them.' The next writer had the last word: 'They have always
said they had a strong case, but have never, so far as I know,

[1] Perhaps the same officer as the General François Cartier just mentioned.

condescended to explain it. But we must assume that they know their business, and can only support their view.' The French proposal was duly rejected. The days when the Foreign Office would languidly accept that the Lords of the Admiralty knew their business, no matter how condescending they might be, are sadly gone for ever!

With the Russians, on the other hand, there was a continuous flow of information in both directions, and this was understandable in view of Room 40's debt to the Russians for the *Magdeburg* signal book. Frequent appeals were received from the Naval Staff in St Petersburg for help in breaking new keys, and information about the movements of the *Hochseeflotte* were regularly supplied by Room 40. An example from mid-1917 is the following, sent by cable via Alexandrovsk: 'Clear the Line. From North Sea messages it is clear that owing to three ships of the [German] Third Battle Squadron being badly damaged, both Divisions of the First Battle Squadron are not to be in the east Baltic at the same time, but perhaps the two Divisions will relieve each other from time to time.' Then again, Birch and Clarke remark in connection with *Fall Albion*, the second German attack on the Gulf of Riga, that 'Every step in the preparations, every movement of the squadron was known at once in the British Admiralty, whence the information was loyally forwarded to the Russians.'

In December 1916 Commander Przyleneki had visited Room 40 (and there is no evidence of officers of any other nation ever having done so), and left a note on the advantages which cryptanalysis had provided for the Russians; it had reduced the number of ships which had to be kept at sea as scouts; it had disclosed the routes followed by German warships; it had given advance warning, although often of only a few hours, of German operations; it had greatly assisted in Russian minelaying operations, which, because the Russians never broke wireless silence, were not detected by the Germans; Russian security was ensured by the universal use of one-time pads for the transmission of signals to ships at sea.[1] Anglo-Russian co-operation continued during the Kerensky regime and right up to the Bolshevik revolution. Both the Russians and the British of course had a great deal to offer each other. From the British point of view anything which would assist the operations of the Russian Fleet and so detain more German ships in the Baltic was as good as a direct reinforce-

---

[1] One-time pads, as the name implies, are codes that are used only once and thus unbreakable. The Russians had come a long way since Tannenberg and Lemberg.

ment of the Grand Fleet, while there was certainly no point in pretending that Room 40 knew nothing about the SKM! The outbreak of the October revolution naturally caused Hall particular concern and he cabled his opposite number on 4 October 1917, 'In view of present situation I earnestly beg you to burn all documents and papers connected with our mutual work. Should situation improve I can replace everything and will keep you advised.' No reply can be traced, but there is no evidence that the Germans learned anything important about the lack of security of their own codes from the Russians, so perhaps Hall's plea was answered. The Germans did learn in the middle of 1918 from a refugee Russian naval officer that the Russians had captured and made good use of the *Magdeburg's* signal book. Even the *Admiralstab* must have accepted the fact by this time but their informant did not mention, probably because he was ignorant of the fact, that the British had received one of the copies of the SKM. Towards the end of November Hall again cabled but this time his fears were for his former allies and colleagues; 'Am perturbed as to safety of Russian officers in the event of the Revolutionary Committee surrendering ships to Germans. Suggest you consider proposition of officers bringing all latest type of destroyers to south end of Sound on given date and time. Arrangements could be made to have forces to distract enemy and assist vessels through Sound to England. Please reply through same channel. Your Friend.' But events were now moving too fast and nothing came of this suggestion. Hall's subsequent involvement in the events of the Russian Revolution through the Naval Attaché, Commander Crobie, Bruce Lockhart and others are unlikely ever to be fully revealed and, in any case, fall outside the scope of a book dealing with Room 40. But at least one member of the Russian cryptographic team, E. Fetterlein, was brought out of Russia and joined Room 40 in June 1918. He stayed on with GC&CS, and will be remembered affectionately by some of Bletchley Park's World War II staff.

Looking at the changes and developments which took place from the end of 1916 onwards, one can see a greater realisation of Room 40's real potential, a definite attempt to transform the organisation into a true Intelligence Centre (although the process was still not complete by the time of the Armistice), recognition of the need for increased staff numbers and for the provision of elementary aids to office efficiency such as typewriters and for secretaries to use them. The driving force was undoubtedly Hall's, the actual execution to some extent James's. Room 40 had changed up into top gear, even if there was not quite sufficient time by November 1918 for it to attain the maximum speed of which it was truly capable.

CHAPTER TWELVE

Cloak and Dagger

Hall was something of a maverick; he was certainly not typical of the naval officers of his generation. He was fascinated by 'The Great Game', the world of spies and agents, deception, bribery, disinformation, destabilisation, all that side of Intelligence now stigmatised as the 'Dirty Tricks' department. Such activities of course had nothing to do with the painstaking, methodical if nonetheless thrilling work of Room 40, except that the two sources of knowledge did from time to time supplement and illuminate each other.

One of Hall's very first forays into this murky world, one to which he devoted a whole chapter in his autobiography, was the 'Cruise of the *Sayonara*'. Ireland had been on the verge of civil war in 1914 but on 4 August the vast majority of Irishmen, whether from the North or the South, decided to bury the hatchet, at least until the Germans had been defeated. The ranks of the British Services were filled with Irish volunteers who were driven to enlist not by the Press Gang or hunger, as so often in the past, but by the conviction that, on this occasion, Britain's cause was their own. But the hard core of the Sinn Fein movement, and their far more numerous supporters in the USA, did not agree and willingly accepted German offers of arms, men and money in order to carry on the struggle against the English. The activities of Americans like Judge Cohalan and John Devoy in New York, fostered by the German Military Attaché von Papen and the Naval Attaché, Captain Karl Boy-Ed, in assisting the Irish Nationalist, Sir Roger Casement, a former member of the British Consular Service, were well enough known to the British authorities. Late in 1914 Casement had left New York and had managed to reach Germany, where he endeavoured, with very scant success, to form an Irish Legion from among the Irish prisoners of war. Plans were made to land arms, and men too, if possible, from a neutral steamer in some remote spot on the south or west coast of Ireland where sympathy for the Sinn Fein movement remained strongest and active cells were still in existence. As was the case in 1939, rumours began to reach the British of U-boats being refuelled in lonely Irish bays, although just how supplies of diesel fuel in any worthwhile quantities were to be accumulated, let alone actually transferred to a U-boat, never seems to have been sensibly considered on either occasion!

The Royal Irish Constabulary, a most efficient force entirely Irish in composition, and Basil Thomson's Special Branch of Scotland Yard, are generally supposed to have had a pretty shrewd idea of what was going on and who was involved. However, Hall was not entirely satisfied, and in conjunction with Basil Thomson conceived the idea of chartering an American steam yacht, manning her with a Royal Navy crew disguised as Americans, with a pseudo-American owner and skipper, to cruise along the south and west coasts to investigate reports of U-boat refuelling centres, to make contact with Sinn Feiners, to discover where Casement was going to land and to seize him and his ship when he did so. Hall soon obtained an introduction through Mr Shirley Benn, MP for Plymouth and Mr Almeric Paget, later Lord Queenborough, to the American millionaire, Mr Anthony Drexel, owner of the steam yacht *Sayonara*. Drexel agreed to charter her to the British and Hall found a skipper, Lieutenanct F. M. Simon RNR, who had served under him in *Queen Mary*. As 'owner' he selected a soldier of fortune, Major Wilfred Howell, son of a Chamberlain to the Pope, born in France and educated in Austria, who had served as a volunteer in British colonial forces and been awarded the DSO. He became Colonel McBride of Los Angeles, a rich American of pronounced pro-German sympathies, but with his Homburg hat and up-turned moustaches looking more like a caricature of Kaiser Wilhelm II than the Yankee he was supposed to be. The naval ratings were carefully selected and were delighted to exchange their bell bottoms for suitable yachting gear, to chew gum and talk in what they believed to be American accents. It is unlikely that they would have deceived any genuine American, but they certainly deceived the rest of the Royal Navy, including Admiral Coke at Queenstown, Hall's old friend Captain le Mesurier of HMS *Cornwallis*, who placed the *Sayonara* under arrest, from which the yacht was only released on the intervention of the DID, and Lord Sligo, an Anglo-Irish landowner, who rushed to London in a paroxism of patriotic rage to compel Hall to take action against these Sinn Fein-loving Yankees whom he had observed with his own eyes laying mines in Westport Harbour. How far the local Sinn Feiners were taken in is hard to say. Colonel McBride met plenty of them, including a local leader with the same name. Hall claims that the information obtained was of great value during the Easter Rebellion in 1916, but one does wonder whether the Irish were (or are) quite as simple as English comedians like to pretend. Of course, nowadays, the whole idea of a yacht belonging to a neutral cruising round the coast of a country at war in the middle of winter (this was December–January 1914–15), seems so preposterous as to be laughable, but attitudes were different then.

Hall was so pleased with the results he obtained that he repeated the ruse a little later when he sent the Irish baronet, Sir Hercules Langrishe (no pseudonym, this) to cruise in another yacht under British colours in Spanish waters.[1] Of course *Sayonara's* main purpose was to intercept Casement whom the Germans planned to return to Ireland with a load of arms. On 4 January Hall wrote to Simon, 'It is anticipated that C. will arrive in the Danish steamer *Mjolnir* of Copenhagen – 580 tons. She is due to leave Christiansand on 9th and should be off the west coast of Ireland between 13th and 15th. With C will be Adler Christiansen, age 24, height 6 ft, strongly made, clean shaven, hair fair, gap in front teeth, wears thick double-breasted greatcoat and soft dark hat. Speaks English fluently but with Norwegian-American accent . . . I hope to get rendezvous, but it is doubtful, but I feel that you are at just about the best place round the coast from Cashel to Achill . . .' In the event, the Germans decided that an attempt to raise a revolt in Ireland would be premature, and the plan was postponed for fifteen months.

By early 1916 Hall was well aware that the Germans and Sinn Fein were intending to move. Count Bernstorff, the German Ambassador in Washington, had cabled Berlin that an armed uprising was planned for 23 April, Easter Sunday. He had further requested that 25,000 to 50,000 rifles, with machine guns and field guns should be supplied to the Nationalists. The General Staff had replied that arms would be sent in a small steamer, and gave details of codewords to be broadcast by Nauen to indicate that the expedition had started, or alternatively that it had been postponed. During

---

[1] Sir Hercules' mission was part reconnaissance for U-boat refuelling points, part propaganda to persuade the Spaniards that Britain was still a land of plenty. For the latter purpose he was supplied with a liberal quantity of the best champagne, a master stroke, because a German yacht engaged on a similar mission, which allegedly dared not put to sea for fear of British submarines, was only able to offer its Spanish guests beer!

the first three years of the war, Room 40 intercepted at least thirty-two messages dealing with German assistance for Sinn Fein which were exchanged between Bernstorff and his Government, but it is not now clear how many of them were made or decoded before the Easter Rising, or that all of them were decoded contemporaneously. Hall certainly had enough information to follow the main developments of the plot, and to cause the necessary countermeasures to be taken.

The gunrunner was the 1,400-ton *Libau*. She sailed from Lübeck on 9 April with a German naval crew, but was disguised as the Norwegian *Aud*. She carried 20,000 captured Russian Mausers, ten machine guns, a million rounds of ammunition and a quantity of explosives. Her departure was betrayed by a signal from Nauen on 15 April enquiring '. . . whether German auxiliary cruiser vessel, which is to bring weapons to Ireland has actually . . .' The last groups were corrupt, but the message was sufficient. The *Libau* reached Tralee Bay on the west coast of Ireland on 20 May, but having failed to make contact with the Sinn Feiners was intercepted by a British warship and scuttled herself while being escorted to Queenstown.

In the meantime Casement had also set out for Tralee. He subsequently claimed that it was his intention to call off the rising because he realised that it was doomed to failure, but in view of the *Libau's* mission this statement seems open to doubt. Casement and two companions had left Wilhelmshaven in U 20 on 12 April, but the U-boat's rudder was damaged and she had to return to Heligoland and transfer her passengers to U 19, which sailed on 15 April and landed the three conspirators at Tralee just after the *Libau* had departed. Casement was arrested on 22 April and his two companions two days later.

It is unlikely that the Easter Rising could ever have succeeded, given the lack of support for Sinn Fein at the time. Nevertheless, with Casement's leadership and *Libau's* cargo, the fighting might have been a great deal more serious than, in the event, it was. Although the British authorities in Dublin appear to have been taken by surprise, the Royal Navy was fully prepared for the uprising. Additional ships had been sent to Ireland, and marines and seamen landed to protect naval installations and coast guard stations, and to assist the Royal Irish Constabulary, which they did most effectively. Perhaps more had been gleaned from the cruise of the *Sayonara* than one would otherwise suppose. Casement's trial was a *cause célèbre* throughout the world. There could be no doubt that as a former servant of the British Crown, from whom he had accepted a knighthood, he was guilty of treason, but there was much sympathy for him in certain quarters both in Britain and the United States, and pressure was put on the British Government to commute the death sentence, which was inevitably passed on him on his conviction.

Hall had rather old-fashioned ideas about those whom he considered spies and traitors; he thought they should be hung by the neck until they were dead. On 1 July, the opening day of the Battle of the Somme, nearly 20,000 British soldiers, including a large number of the Ulster Division had been killed. The 141-day battle resulted in appalling slaughter; the United Kingdom of Britain and Ireland, indeed the whole British Empire, was fighting for its life. Hall had scant sympathy with those who pleaded for clemency for Sir Roger. Of that we can be quite sure. How far he was responsible for leaking the so called 'Black Diaries'[1], the record of Casement's undoubted homosexual activities, is hard to prove, but there is some evidence that Hall and Thomson leaked portions of the diaries to the British and American press and to Members of Parliament; this put an abrupt end to the 'Save Casement' campaign. He was hanged in Pentonville Gaol on 3 August.

In December 1916 the Germans renewed their attempts and informed Bernstorff in Washington that arms would be landed between 21 and 25 February 1917. Hall exchanged a series of signals, code-named 'Skal' with Bayly at Queenstown. On 15 February Hall cabled: 'Cannot definitely identify landing places but they appear most probably to be Galway and Tralee. Pilots apparently to be waiting between Kerry Head and Blaskets. Also to west of Barrel Shoal, north of Slyne Head. Names are problematical but above is nearest interpretation at present.' A light cruiser and a destroyer were sent to Queenstown, but on 27 February Bayly was told that everything pointed to the scheme having been abandoned.

A last attempt was made in April 1918, when U 19 landed a Sinn Feiner in Galway Bay, but, forewarned by Hall, the RIC quickly arrested him. The U-boat, however, escaped.

However efficient the Special Branch and MI5 may have been in contra-espionage operations in Britain and Ireland, it must be remembered that the Secret Service had only been formed in 1912

---

[1] One of Hall's staff, Fleet Paymaster Lloyd Hirst later wrote that Hall had given him his personal assurance that the 'diaries were undoubtedly kept by Casement.'

and had little time to build up a British spy network abroad. There was no Special Operations Executive to undertake sabotage in Germany or encourage resistance in German occupied territories, no Double Cross Committee to 'turn' enemy agents and supply false information, no Political Warfare Executive to conduct propaganda. These gaps in the Intelligence underworld were filled by men and organisations procured by Hall. According to Marjorie Napier: 'One example of the many pies into which he put his fingers [was] the organising and running of the Arab Bureau in Cairo – Mark Sykes, Hogarth and Lawrence all in his pocket.' Birch and Clarke remark that, 'In the Near East wireless was largely employed in operations, and to the successful interception and solution of wireless signals much of General Allenby's success is said to have been due', although they do not actually claim that Room 40 was responsible. Hall sold a fake edition of the Naval War Emergency Code to the Germans, and did not forget to supply a revised edition (for a good price) when the need arose. He planted false rumours, such as the story that a large shipment of gold was being made from America, in the hopes that this would attract a German commerce raider;[1] he arranged, by bribery, for copies of German cables to be extracted from South American cable offices and forwarded to him; and he created his own secret service where the official organisation failed to produce results.

One such country was Spain. Spain's sympathies were divided; impressed by Germany's power, she was cut off by land and sea from contact with the Central Powers; to some extent anti-French, a portion of public opinion was pro-British, but German commercial influence remained strong. Like other neutrals, Spain's main desire was to avoid becoming involved on one side or the other, at least until it was clear which of them was going to emerge the victor. Madrid, with access to and influence in the Spanish American countries from the Rio Grande down to Cape Horn, was a centre for espionage for both the Entente and the Central Powers. Nationalist movements in French North Africa naturally took the opportunity to try to cause the maximum embarrassment to their colonial masters, something encouraged by the Germans and by no means frowned on by the Spanish, anxious to extend their own sphere of influence in Morocco and Tangier.

Above all, the German Embassy in Madrid with its wireless link to

---

[1] It did not, and Hall was confronted by an angry Governor of the Bank of England demanding the surrender of the mythical gold.

Berlin provided a means of communication for the Wilhelmstrasse with the overseas world and this link, from mid-1915 onwards was increasingly at the mercy of Room 40. Even letters to the Fatherland sent by Germans overseas via Spain had either to be forwarded through France or by ships which had to call at British ports, where they ran the risk of interception by the British censorship. Hall could see that knowledge of what the Germans were doing in Spain, what they were doing in the Americas, and what the Spanish Government itself was thinking, was of great importance and that Room 40's surveillance of these matters needed to be supplemented by some men on the spot. Perhaps Sir Hercules Langrishe's foaming champagne was not entirely wasted! Hall appears to have selected two men to build up an organisation in Spain. One was the author and playwright A. E. W. Mason. Although already aged forty-nine he had enlisted in the Manchester Regiment on the outbreak of war, and by early 1915 had attained the rank of captain. Hall then 'cut him out' and obtained a commission for him in the Royal Marines, and sent him to Spain either with Sir Hercules or possibly in yet another yacht. He wrote a number of fictional short stories about his work there, in the Balearics, North Africa and Mexico, to which country Hall transferred him in 1917. He is sometimes dismissed as a bit of a charlatan, but Hall certainly regarded him as one of his star turns and at least one of the coups he claims to have pulled off, the destruction of a clandestine German wireless station at Ixtapalapa, in Mexico, in 1918, is perfectly true.

The head of Hall's Spanish organisation was a regular Marine officer, Colonel Charles Thoroton, always known as Charles the Bold. His headquarters were at Gibraltar and he eventually controlled an extensive organisation throughout Spain, the Balearics, North Africa and Greece. Records of his achievements are disappointingly scanty, no doubt because, as he wrote to Hall in 1932, he had destroyed all his papers except 'those which I thought necessary to defend myself in case of an attack being made on me for some of my more questionable activities.' One of Thoroton's agents was a Majorcan tobacco smuggler, Juan March, who by 1939 had become a millionaire and offered his help and influence to further the British cause to John Godfrey, a valuable offer which was gratefully accepted.

At the end of the war, Bell, of the US Embassy in London, in a report to Washington stated that Thoroton's organisation in Spain 'became immensely powerful and used frequently to give information to the Spanish Government of disaffection and strikes in Spain itself, and when a few months ago Admiral Hall started to cut down his organisation . . . the Spanish Government actually requested him not to do so on the grounds that his organisation was to them a far more reliable source of information of what was going on in the country than their own police and civil authorities . . .'

If Thoroton's work remains largely shrouded in mystery, there does survive at least one fully documented account of how Hall made full use of the combination of the information obtained from Room 40's Diplomatic Section and the reports of Thoroton's men in north Spain; this is the romantic and at times rather farcical story of the brigantine *Erri Berro*.

By mid-1917 the stringent Allied blockade was having very serious effects on the German war economy. Wolfram, the ore yielding tungsten, was in desperately short supply, one of the main providers being the Basque region of Spain. The Germans felt that it was worth almost any effort to smuggle wolfram past the Royal Navy's ever watchful patrols, and the British were prepared to go to great lengths to frustrate them. The small wolfram mines were kept under close if covert surveillance by a network organised by Commander Maurice Mitchell, RNR, with headquarters in Bilbao, with the help of Lieutenant Dawson, RNR, a Newcastle shipowner at San Sebastian, keeping in touch with the resident British Naval Officer Lt Commander G. H. Pierce, RNR, over the French border at St Jean de Luz, and through him with the head of the British Naval Mission in Paris, Commodore Edward Heaton-Ellis. In London the strings were pulled on Hall's behalf by his personal assistant, Lord Herschell, whom he had put in charge of Spanish and Spanish American affairs, and Paymaster Lloyd Hirst, the Intelligence Division South American expert.

The story of the *Erri Berro* really starts on 15 September 1917 when Mitchell wrote Herschell a long letter dealing with the wolfram problem, voicing his suspicions of a Spaniard, one Lauriano Diaz, who had previously been Krupp's agent in Bilbao and still had a German assistant named Morse, and another undoubted agent Pasch. Mitchell had been keeping in close touch with Thoroton, and he was satisfied that between them they would quickly discover any moves by the Germans to smuggle wolfram out of Spain, or to effect a break out by any of the German merchant ships interned in Spanish Atlantic and Mediterranean ports. The next piece of the puzzle to fall into place was provided by the *Admiralstab* in Berlin, courtesy of Room 40's diplomatic section. On 2 October Room 40 decoded a message to the German Naval Attaché, Madrid, which read as follows: 'The Ambassador informed me recently that there is a possibility of shipping wolfram ore in a submarine. The execution of the plan is perhaps possible in November in the neighbourhood of the Canary Islands. Report in detail as to the proposal.' The Ambassador was the aged and aristocratic Prince Ratibor, and the Naval Attaché, from 1916, Korvettenkapitän Krohn. Krohn was only a reserve officer and, moreover, had a French mistress, Marthe Regnier. If Krohn made himself unpopular with the Spanish authorities by his unneutral and illegal activities in organising espionage and sabotage, his relations with his ambassador and the rest of the Embassy were even worse. Prince Ratibor, when approached by Krohn denied all knowledge of any such suggestion, but the Naval Attaché liked the idea and on 16 October informed Berlin, and incidentally also Room 40, that it might be possible to make a transhipment in the Bay of Biscay, but the Canaries presented greater difficulties. He also considered that something could be achieved in the Mediterranean. Within three weeks Mitchell was able to report that he had discovered where the Wolfram was stored in Bilbao; one of his agents had got into the warehouse on the pretext of trying to recover a dog which had run away from its blind owner! Mitchell asked if he should inform the French, as it seemed obvious that an attempt was going to be made to ship the ore in fishing boats and transfer it to a U-boat. Hall at once telegraphed him to use every endeavour to prevent the ore leaving, and to report all developments immediately.

Four days after this, however, on 7 November, the *Admiralstab*, ignoring the alleged difficulties of getting a ship from Bilbao to the Canaries, signalled their Naval Attaché that, 'U-cruisers 156 and 157 can be at the Canaries on (group corrupt, ? 24 November). Each can take about 40 tons of wolfram ore. If you are still certain that the plan can be carried out safely, please report details and meeting place can then be settled.'

Hall at once saw the possibilities not only of capturing the wolfram but of sinking two U-boats as well, and urgently cancelled his previous orders to Mitchell; he was now to do nothing to prevent the wolfram leaving but should report the name and time of departure of the ship carrying it. The whole matter was discussed with Oliver and the 1st Sea Lord and consultations held, through Heaton-Ellis, with Admiral de Bon, Commander-in-Chief of the

French Navy, who was content to leave matters to the British. It is possible that the French were also reading the Naval Attaché traffic; if they were not, de Bon was certainly kept fully informed by Hall. On 19 November Hall assured the 1st Sea Lord and Oliver that Mitchell's reports could be relied on absolutely, and that agents were watching the warehouse where the wolfram was stored. This, combined with Room 40's expertise, obviously satisfied Hall's superiors because immediate orders were sent to Admiral Bayly at Queenstown to make two E. Class submarines with experienced commanding officers available for a special operation, on the understanding that two replacements would be supplied by the Grand Fleet. They were to sail for Gibraltar as soon as possible. Not content with this, Oliver, who as usual drafted every signal personally, ordered the Commander-in-Chief Mediterranean, despite his anguished protests, to send two more E. Class boats from the Adriatic to Gibraltar. A collier was also provided to act as mother ship. To deal with the capture of the ship carrying the wolfram to the Canaries, Commander-in-Chief Devonport was ordered to sail the ocean-boarding vessel *Duke of Clarence* to St Jean de Luz, where arrangements had been made with de Bon to provide a stock of coal. A second boarding vessel *Woodnut* was to be stationed at Lisbon. *Duke of Clarence* was to be provided with a prize crew of two RNR officers and eight hand-picked ratings accustomed to handling small sailing vessels, and with a hemp or manilla towing hawser suitable for sailing vessels of up to 200 tons. All these measures show the importance attached to the operation and Hall's confidence in being able to continue to supply the necessary information.

In the meantime, Mitchell had reported that it seemed likely that the wolfram would be shipped in the *San José*, 'a staunch wooden brig', capable of carrying 400 tons. He was, however, worried about maintaining communications with San Sebastian and St Jean de Luz because it was almost impossible to obtain petrol for his Lancia car, and he begged for the urgent supply of 500 gallons.

Excellent as were Mitchell's arrangements, it is doubtful whether the British would have been able to achieve much had it not been for the unwitting co-operation of the *Admiralstab* and the German Naval Attaché. On 15 November Krohn reported as follows: 'The carrying out of the plan is assured. The sailing vessel will receive sealed instructions concerning recognition signals. When sighting a U-boat at the rendezvous she will lower and furl her sails and hoist a Spanish flag as well as blue and yellow pennants under one another.

At night she will show a blue and yellow light . . . Request immediate instructions concerning the rendezvous and whether further
particulars are necessary.'

Two days later Mitchell telegraphed that he believed the sacks of
wolfram would be concealed inside sacks of saw dust. He was
continuing to watch the re-packing of the wolfram carefully.
However, all this proved to be something of a false alarm, as on 18
November he had to report that *San José* had sailed with only iron
ore on board. It is not clear whether the Germans had ever intended
to use her, or whether, for some reason, a second vessel had to be
substituted for her. In any case, all doubts were resolved on the 19th
when the ever helpful Krohn signalled, 'The sailing vessel is a
brigantine of 170 tons, both mast-heads of equal height painted
white. Fore and aft the Spanish flag is painted on both sides and
between it the ship's name *Erri Berro*. In front of the main mast a
large red water tank. I propose if necessary the further disting-
uishing mark: a Spanish flag sewn on the schooner's sails. Vessel will
put to sea about 26 November. Please let her bring the post and
German newspapers.' Presumably, the last request referred to her
return passage after her meeting with the U-boats.

Two further pieces of information were required by the British if
they were to make a successful attack on the U-boats – the exact
position and date of the rendezvous. Within a week the always
accommodating Germans had supplied the missing links. On 24
November the *Admiralstab* informed the Naval Attaché that 'two
U-cruisers will be at U.Platz 30 about 25 December'. But where *was*
U.Platz 30? Neither the British nor the Attaché knew! *Admiralstab*
once more obliged with the information; it was on the south-west
side of Ferro Island (Hierro), the most south-westerly of the Canary
Islands. To this Krohn suggested that a safe time for the meeting
would be from 31 December onwards, a somewhat vague suggestion which did not please Berlin, who signalled back that he was to
report immediately what date could be fixed with certainty. This
was all very well, but small sailing ships were subject to the vagaries
of the weather, a fact the gentlemen in Berlin seemed to ignore.
With a favourable wind the 25 December might still be possible, but
what, asked the harrassed Krohn, was the latest date that could be
arranged?

In the meantime, Mitchell and his minions had located the *Erri
Berro* and had reported that she had sailed from Corunna for Bilbao
on 30 November, and that the stevedore engaged to load her with

115 sacks of 'cement' for the Canaries was being paid over the odds, and estimated that the work would take two days. Arrangements were being made to notify *Duke of Clarence* in St Jean de Luz, whose endurance was limited and so had to keep her coal bunkers full. The four E. Class submarines, now at Gibraltar, could also only stay on patrol for a limited period, and there were some doubts about the range at which they would be able to receive and transmit wireless messages. Fortunately, the wireless transmitting sets of British submarines had been considerably improved in the last two years, and a trial run showed that reception was now possible up to at least six hundred miles. Two submarines were kept on patrol off the Canaries, while the other two rested and refuelled at Gibraltar. All seemed to be ready on the British side.

But the Germans were not ready. The captain of the *Erri Berro* was unfit or for some other reason unsatisfactory, and had to be replaced. A German supercargo also had to be found, but this was not particularly difficult as a considerable number of Merchant Navy officers were living on board one of the interned merchant ships in Bilbao. Johann Haberstock, formerly 1st Officer of the Hamburg America steamer *Phoenica*, had not seen his wife and children in Hamburg for three and a half years and was anxious to get back to the Fatherland, although he was apparently not informed that he would have to be rather more than just a passenger in order to do so. The next delay was caused by a decision that a further sixty tons of wolfram should be loaded, but in reporting this on 12 December, Mitchell warned that this might merely be a ruse to disguise an earlier departure. On the same day Berlin wirelessed that the *Erri Berro* was to be at the rendezvous from 20 January onwards. From the British point of view it was vital to have accurate information as to when she did sail, and even more vital that this information reached the *Duke of Clarence* promptly. The chain of communication between Bilbao, San Sebastian and St Jean de Luz does not seem to have been too reliable, but Mitchell had got his petrol and arrangements were made for Bilbao to inform Dawson at San Sebastian by telegram, and for the information then to be rushed across the border by car to St Jean de Luz. Dawson was an officer who was not afraid to act on his own initiative and, in case *Duke of Clarence* was at sea when the news came, he detained a British merchant ship, the SS *William Ball*, in order to be able to use her wireless to send the code word 'All's Well' to *Duke of Clarence* to indicate that *Erri Berro* had finally sailed (a very sensible move which aroused the anger of the ship's owners and for which he was subsequently required by the Admiralty to 'submit his reasons in writing'!)

On 15 December Mitchell reported to Hall that he had 'telegraphed *Duke of Clarence* that the brig [she was in fact rigged as a brigantine] should complete loading at midday. Anticipate she will sail today. No reliance can be placed on the original description of her painting. Also she may cross a foreyard after leaving here. Up to date the flag has disappeared and the hull is black. Two narrow white lines above and below letters of name and one yard square. Grey paint either side of stern.' Everyone, German, Spanish and British, must have been keyed up, but on the next day Mitchell had to report that defects had been found in *Erri Berro*'s lower masts' rigging (she does not seem to have been a very well found ship) and these would have to be made good. Mitchell deduced from such unusual fussiness that the rendezvous, of which he was of course quite unaware, must be a distant one and was worried about *Duke of Clarence*'s limited endurance.

The repairs took some days, but on 26 December Mitchell was able to tell *Duke of Clarence* that a tug had been ordered to tow *Erri Berro* out of harbour, but that owing to a gale she had not been able to put to sea. He suggested that, when intercepted, gear should be thrown overboard to give the impression that she had foundered in heavy weather. A very smart idea, but one which filled Hall with horror. He immediately wired Mitchell to 'Do nothing on lines suggested. It is important that Germans should think brig has safely sailed with every prospect of arriving at destination.'

And then, on the last day of 1917, *Erri Berro* finally got to sea. She sailed at 4 p.m. and by 6 p.m., thanks to the speedy Lancia, the news had reached St Jean de Luz and *Duke of Clarence* had been unleashed after her unsuspecting prey. It was now up to those at sea. Krohn also reported *Erri Berro*'s departure to the *Admiralstab*, adding, perhaps rather irritably, 'arrangements cannot be altered. Vessel will be at rendezvous on 20 January.' What, of course, he did not know was that *Erri Berro* had only been under way for a few hours when, at 0030 on 1st January, she was intercepted and boarded by *Duke of Clarence*. The crew were taken off, a tow line secured and a course shaped for Plymouth.

Hall was delighted and, such was the importance attached to the capture, that instructions were immediately issued for four destroyers to sail forthwith from Devonport to bring her in under

conditions of the utmost secrecy. Then, after all these careful and so
far successful plans, came the first setback. In manoeuvring to get
the tow line secured, *Duke of Clarence*, according to the Spanish
captain, struck *Erri Berro* a glancing blow. With a better found ship
it might not have mattered, but as it was, unknown to the prize crew,
the brigantine sprang a leak and by the evening the prize crew had to
be taken off and the already sinking vessel despatched with a few
rounds of gunfire. Hall was bitterly disappointed. It was a triumph
to have deprived the Germans of their wolfram, but he had wanted
to cap that by securing this valuable booty, without cost, for the
British. Whether it was poor seamanship, or as the British believed,
because Haberstock had scuttled the ship (which seems very doubtful), Hall was highly critical of the final outcome.

However, there were still the two U-boats. Obviously the Spaniards and Haberstock must be held incommunicado for the time
being; the *Erri Berro* carried no wireless and therefore no anxiety
would be experienced either by the crew's relatives, or, much more
important to Hall, by the Germans for the next two or three weeks.
He therefore requested the Commander-in-Chief Devonport to
'send the five Spaniards under friendly escort to London to be
handed over to the Commandant Cromwell Gardens Barracks [a
Prisoner of War detention centre off the Brompton Road in Lon-
don], care being taken that they have no communication with their
consul or anyone at all. The German should be sent to the same
address under separate [but apparently not necessarily "friendly"]
escort'. There they remained for the time being, the Spaniards, at
least, very satisfied with their treatment.

In the meantime, E 48 and E 35 sailed from Gibraltar for the
Canaries. One submarine in turn was to maintain diving patrol at
the rendezvous while the other kept well out of sight of land to
charge her batteries and rest her crew. U 156 had left Germany on
18 November and had occupied the time while waiting for the
arrival of *Erri Berro* by bombarding Funchal, Madeira, and sinking
merchant ships, but, by 17 January, had arrived at U.Platz 30 and
lay peacefully and all unsuspecting on the surface. The first news of
subsequent events was a short despatch from Tenerife to *The Times*
reporting an engagement between a 'British warship and three
German U-boats'. Two German sailors had managed to swim
ashore but claimed that their boat had escaped. Both Hall and the
Germans must have been on tenterhooks, because no report from
either submarine was received. It was not until 4 February, when

the British submarines returned to Gibraltar that Hall learned that E 48 had fired three torpedoes at a U-boat at the rendezvous on 17 January; two had missed and one had hit but had failed to explode! The U-boat had crash dived, leaving some of her men on deck. No other U-boat had been seen or heard on W/T, and it is still not clear what U 157 was doing at this time (for U 156 was the boat attacked). Both U-boats eventually returned safely to Germany, U 156 in March and U 157 in April.

Hall was bitterly disappointed that after all his efforts the coup had miscarried and this may have been the occasion, recounted by his daughter, when he displayed one of his fits of blinding bad temper. Returning early from the Admiralty and anxious to blow off steam to his wife, he found her entertaining a number of ladies to tea. Hall usually charmed and was charmed by the opposite sex, but on this particular occasion, he glared furiously at the assembled company for a moment and then, deliberately kicking over one of the tea tables on his way, strode out of the room banging the door behind him. Few wives, even in those days, would have put up with such an outrageous display of male chauvinism, but Lady Hall adored her husband (and he her), and this squall, like so many others, quickly blew itself out.

In any case, there was now a good deal of tidying up to be done. The Senior Naval Officer Gibraltar, who had made good use of his four submarines while they were waiting there, was told sharply that they must be returned to their former commands, and the fate of the Spaniards had to be settled in a way that would avoid an international incident, and allay any suspicions which might have been aroused in German minds about the security of their arrangements. This latter task did not prove too difficult. On 25 February Krohn had signalled Berlin that he was 'expecting a written report from Las Palmas in a few days by special messenger as I do not consider the ordinary post reliable. The two shipwrecked men are quite certain that U 156 escaped. Their statement before the Spanish judge was not compromising in my opinion; an interpreter who was friendly to us having been engaged. The grounds for lying at anchor were on account of repair to machinery. The ore sailing vessel according to news received was stopped by the English on her return journey, but before she could be searched she had been sunk by her crew. The English appear to be very badly informed. At the suggestion of the ship-owner, who was not inimical to us, the Government effected the release of the crew in England. The vigorous campaign of our local Press misled the English and veiled the affair.'

It is true that when rumours of the fate of the *Erri Berro* first began to circulate in Spain, there was something of an outcry against the British, but Hall was prepared for this. The crew had been closely interrogated, and the captain had made a sworn statement admitting that he had been working for the Germans in an attempt to smuggle contraband. The Foreign Office, however, had to be informed and placated, and Hall wrote to Lord Hardinge, explaining incidentally that all the information leading up to *Erri Berro*'s arrest had been obtained from his agents in Bilbao and that the planned transhipment to a German submarine 'has been confirmed from a French female source'. Marthe Regnier at least provided a good cover story: a typical Hall touch! On the 21st he blandly informed the Spanish Consul-General in London that five Spanish seamen had been rescued from *Erri Berro* by one of His Majesty's ships and were now lodged at the Military Barracks at Cromwell Gardens 'at the expense of HM Government'. It was desired to repatriate the shipwrecked mariners, and he begged to enclose his cheque for fifty pounds which he understood would cover the costs, if the Consul-General would be good enough to make the arrangements. The Consul-General was delighted and forwarded to Hall a receipted bill from Thomas Cook & Son Ltd as follows: 'Inclusive arrangements London to Irun with travel, Hotel and Meals. 5 @ £5.8.6 = £27.2.6 + Telegram @ 5 shillings. Total £27.7.6.' The Consul-General added that he had taken the liberty of handing the balance to the men to cover the cost of their travel from Irun to their homes.

The arrival of the crew in Spain quickly changed the tune of the Spanish Press. The men not only made clear the circumstances of their capture but expressed themselves very pleased with their subsequent treatment. It was the Germans who now came under attack for their activities in a neutral country. Doubts began to arise even in the mind of the Naval Attaché, and he reported on 2 March: 'The investigation into the matter concerning this affair has as yet yielded no certain data for undoubted betrayal nor in connection with the fight on 17 January.'

Poor Krohn. He was now in real trouble with everyone; the Spanish authorities, Prince Ratibor and the *Admiralstab*. He was recalled in disgrace, and left Spain. Two days later, Bell, 2nd Secretary of the American Embassy in London wrote to his superior, 'I understand that at the Spanish frontier an anti-German demonstration took place when he passed through. My friends in the Admiralty cannot understand how this occurred, and deplore such an outburst of popular feeling against a worthy and gallant officer. (Oh Yes, they do!)'

There we must leave the files on the *Erri Berro*, which have distinct echoes of Hornblower and Jack Aubrey,[1] combined with a foretaste of Hillgarth and Gomez Beare[2] twenty-five years later.

The story of the *Erri Berro* may have had its comical side, but it was nonetheless a serious episode in the constant war waged by Hall to ensure the total economic blockade of Germany. The Germans, for their part, strove ever more desperately to strike back at Britain and her Allies. Having been the first to resort to poison gas as a weapon against men in uniform, it was scarcely to be expected that they would refrain from attacking animals which, either as beasts of burden or as a source of food, were serving the Allied cause. If Britain prevented fodder and fertilisers reaching German farmers, Germany would retaliate by the use of germ warfare against livestock in neutral countries. Sometime in 1916 the General Staff decided to attack three targets which they thought they could reach; the reindeer which were sledging British arms from North Norway to Russia; the Roumanian sheep being supplied to southern Russia; and the Argentine sheep, beef and mules (the last named for the use of the Indian Army in Mesopotamia) which were shipped every week from Buenos Aires. The animals were to be infected with glanders or anthrax in tiny ampoules concealed in cubes of sugar beet.

These plans were, however, betrayed; betrayed as usual by German overconfidence in the security of their communications. The glanders germs to be used against the reindeer were sent to Christiania (Oslo) in the German diplomatic pouches, but this was detected by Room 40. Hall informed the Norwegian Government, which, unlike that of Sweden, was not prepared to act as a German stooge. Ignoring diplomatic protocol, the Norwegians seized a German diplomatic bag, opened it and confronted an embarrassed German Minister with yet another example of his Government's abuse of neutrality.

When Roumania suddenly, but rashly, declared war on Germany in August 1916, the German Military Attaché in Bucharest had to

---

[1] C. S. Forester's and Patrick O'Brian's legendary heroes.
[2] British Naval Attaché and Assistant Naval Attaché, Madrid, in World War II.

get rid of his incriminating evidence in a hurry; he buried it in the Legation's garden. Unfortunately, he was seen in the act by the Roumanian under-gardener who told the American Chargé d'Affaires, Brand Whitlock, as soon as the Americans took over German interests in Roumania. Intrigued to find out just what the Germans had been trying to conceal, Whitlock had the gardener dig up the airtight container and a large supply of ampoules and papers, making clear the purpose for which they were to be used, were revealed.

Hall was well aware of German ideas about germ warfare. On 7 June 1916 Madrid had cabled Berlin as follows: 'In order to close the Spanish-Portuguese frontier and to make communications difficult between Portugal and the Allies. I [Krohn or Prince Ratibor?] suggest contaminating at the frontier, with cholera bacilli, rivers flowing through Portugal. Professor Kleine of the Cameroons considers the plan to be perfectly feasible. It is necessary to have two glass phials of pure culture, which please send when safe opportunity occurs.' To be fair, Berlin replied the next day declining the proposal, but if the German authorities still had some scruples about employing germ warfare against humans, they had none about attacking animals in this way.

However, to supply germs to South America was less easy. It was decided to ship them by U-boat from Pola to Cartagena in Spain where the luckless Krohn would arrange for their onward transport to the Argentine. The U-boat concerned was almost certainly U 35. In June 1916 she is known to have reached Cartagena with a personal letter from the Kaiser to the King of Spain (although to Prince Ratibor's annoyance she did not bring him the new codes which he had requested). Four months later U 35 was back again to collect Leutnant zur See Wilhelm Canaris, the future head of Hitler's *Abwehr*, who had been trying to establish U-boat fuelling points in Spain. We do not know if U 35 carried supplies of anthrax and glanders germs on these two trips, but on 14 February 1918, when she landed two agents off Cartagena, she almost certainly did so. Hall had alerted the Cartagena Chief of Police, who was pro-British, and the consignment was seized, but had to be sent up to Madrid. However, the policeman arranged with Hall's men that one of the twelve cases which contained the sugar and the germs, should be thrown off the train at a given point. It reached Hall not long afterwards, and when he considered the moment most suitable he sent Herschell with some of the sugar cubes to show them personally to the King of Spain. Hall claims that this led to the recall of Prince Ratibor, but it is more probable that it contributed to the downfall of the wretched Krohn, whose responsibility it was. Paymaster Lloyd Hirst, head of the Intelligence Division's South American desk, recounts that Krohn, who could not take his French mistress with him to Germany, persuaded her to carry a supply to Buenos Aires; she sailed in the Spanish liner *Reine Victoria Eugenia*, but Krohn must have reported the arrangements by wireless to Berlin before he left. Hall knew exactly what was happening and even the lid of the particular trunk in which the germs were concealed. Unfortunately, although HMS *Newcastle* was detailed to intercept the Spanish ship, she missed her in a fog, and Marthe Regnier was able to hand over her lethal consignment safely to Herr Arnold, Germany's most dangerous agent in South America. Arnold lost no time; he managed to infect two hundred mules which were being shipped on board the SS *Phidias*, and they all died. A second shipment was similarly lost. Sir Reginald Tower, the British Minister, took a sample cube to the Argentine President, Hipolito Irigoyen, and dissolved it in a cup of water before the President's eyes to reveal the ampoul. Irigoyen refused to take any action, with the specious excuse that the British could not prove that the mules had been infected on Argentine soil rather than at sea. Arnold and his merry men were therefore able to continue this clever if very unpleasant campaign for some time longer, until finally checkmated by combined British and American action.

The generally pro-British attitude of the Norwegians also enabled Hall to gain an insight to Swedish opinion. At the beginning of February 1917, he obtained a reply to questions he had asked about Swedish reactions to a possible invasion of Denmark by Germany. The Norwegian General Staff, who worked closely with that of Sweden, were unwilling to supply all the information requested, but did make it clear that in the event of a German attack on Denmark the Swedes would refuse all co-operation and would adopt a posture of armed neutrality. Any request for the passage of German troops through Sweden would be resisted by force if necessary. It is interesting to note that Hall's agent had to promise that he would not repeat this information to the British Legation in Oslo. Further evidence of Norway's partiality for Britain, to be shown again so gallantly in World War II, was the suggestion that a Norwegian coastwatching organisation be set up to follow and report on the use made by U-boats of Norwegian coastal waters. This suggestion, made in January 1918, was to depend on the supply to the Royal Norwegian Navy of the latest British hydrophones and other equipment, but was in the end rejected by the British in favour of recruiting more and better trained agents. This too is interesting because, again in World War II, it was found that even the bravest amateur could not supply accurate reports about naval and mercantile movements without thorough training in recognition techniques. In World War II, however, agents could report by means of small wireless transmitters; this was not possible twenty-five years earlier, and all reports had to be sent by cablegram. The Germans, taking a leaf from *Telconia's* book, more than once cut the Norwegian-British cables, but, lacking command of the sea, were unable to prevent their repair.

It would require a whole book to chronicle all the exploits of Hall and his private network of agents which ranged from India to America and back to Europe. Unfortunately, the British authorities still seem to regard the release of all the records which survive (and many, like Thoroton's, have doubtless been destroyed) as likely to endanger the security of the nation in the 1980s, and so they remain locked away. Perhaps enough has been said in this chapter to give some idea of Hall's ingenuity and the exceptional sources of information which he organised and used to such great advantage.

CHAPTER THIRTEEN

'Alone I did it.' The Zimmermann Telegram

I am not likely to forget that Wednesday morning, 17 January 1917. There was the usual docket of papers to be gone through on my arrival at the office, and Claud Serocold and I were still at work on them when at about half-past ten de Grey came in. He seemed excited. 'DID,' he began, 'd'you want to bring America into the war?' 'Yes, my boy,' I answered. 'Why?' 'I've got something here which – well, it's a rather astonishing message which might do the trick *if* we could use it. It isn't very clear, I'm afraid, but I'm sure I've got most of the important points right. It's from the German Foreign Office to Bernstorff.'

This is Blinker Hall's account of how he first saw the famous, or infamous, Zimmermann Telegram – the telegram from the German Foreign Minister to his Ambassador in Washington, which dragged a somewhat reluctant America into World War I. It is very doubtful if any single Intelligence coup has ever had such profound consequences.

The partially decoded message which de Grey showed Hall that morning read as follows:

Berlin to Washington.　　　　　　　　W.158.　　16 January 1917.

Most Secret for Your Excellency's personal information and to be handed on to the Imperial Minister in (?) Mexico with . . . by a safe route.

We propose to begin on 1 February unrestricted submarine warfare. In doing so, however, we shall endeavour to keep America neutral . . . (?) If we should not (succeed in doing so) we propose to (?Mexico) an alliance upon the following basis:
(joint) conduct of war
(joint) conclusion of peace
. . .

Your excellency should for the present inform the President [of Mexico] secretly (that we expect) war with the USA (possibly)

(. . . Japan) and at the same time to negotiate between us and Japan . . . (Indecipherable sentence meaning Please tell the President) that . . . our submarines . . . will compel England to peace within a few months. Acknowledge receipt.

Zimmermann.

Hall could not remember a time when he was more excited. 'Yet, as de Grey pointed out, the telegram was only of importance if we could make use of it. Could we? At the moment nothing must be done except to take all possible precautions to keep the news to our three selves. I thanked de Grey, and asked him to bring me the original telegram in cipher. 'This,' I told him, 'is a case where standing orders must be suspended. All copies of this message, both those in cipher and your own transcripts, are to be brought straight to me. Nothing is to be put on the files. This may be a very big thing, possibly the biggest thing in the war. For the present not a soul outside this room is to be told anything at all.' A little later the original message was locked away in my desk, and I sat down by myself to evolve a plan of campaign.'

Blinker Hall was confronted with the most difficult decision of his whole career. Although it would be an exaggeration to have said, at the beginning of 1917, that victory for the Entente could only be secured by an immediate American declaration of war on Germany, such a position was rapidly approaching. If Passchendaele, the mutiny of the French army, the abdication of the Czar and the Bolshevik revolution still lay in the future and could not be foreseen, there were certainly no obvious signs of Germany's defeat. Asquith's government had fallen and Lloyd George, a man Hall did not admire, had become Prime Minister. There seemed no end in sight to the dreadful slaughter on all the land fronts, and there were signs of war weariness in Britain, as indeed in all the belligerent countries. Britain's finances were rapidly being exhausted and food shortages becoming serious. Now the unrestricted U-boat campaign was about to be renewed and not with three or four dozen ocean-going boats but, Hall feared, with upwards of two hundred.[1] The involvement of the United States on the side of the Entente would be worth almost any sacrifice – any sacrifice, Hall felt, except the betrayal of the existence of Room 40; somehow or other the German goose must be kept alive to go on laying its golden eggs.

[1] The official Admiralty estimate was exaggerated, due to inflated ideas of the rate of U-boat construction.

That was the first problem which had to be solved; the eternal problem for all Intelligence chiefs – how to make use of most secret information without imperilling the source.

It was not much easier to predict what American reactions would be on 1 February when the German announcement of unrestricted U-boat warfare was to be made. Despite dire warnings by President Woodrow Wilson after the sinking of the *Lusitania*, and notwithstanding renewed and even more serious admonitions thereafter, the Germans had so far always managed to avoid pushing America over the brink. Wilson, that most pedagogic of Presidents, seemed to regard both sides as juvenile delinquents who were disturbing the peace and quiet of the playground and were equally deserving of a sharp reproof. Although at heart more favourable to Britain and France (if not to Czarist Russia) than he was to Germany, the President wanted peace, but peace on his terms, 'peace without conquest' as he was soon to proclaim. He had already declared himself 'too proud to fight'.

Would he change this attitude when the U-boats were unleashed in all their fury? Wilson was, above all, a politician and he had just been re-elected on a pledge to keep the United States out of the war and free from foreign entanglements. If some Daughters of the American Revolution were now disposed to forgive King George and his Redcoats and others remembered Lafayette with gratitude, the sympathies of more recent arrivals from Ireland and Germany lay in the other camp. Their votes could not be ignored, nor those of the inhabitants of the Middle West and the West Coast, who, conscious of America's vast size and wealth, cried 'a plague on both your houses'.

Perhaps, thought Hall, the U-boats would this time go too far even for Wilson; perhaps he would declare war within days of 1 February. If so, there would be no problem; the Zimmermann Telegram would not have to be disclosed. But, supposing that, once again, the President, whether from personal conviction or for domestic political reasons, did no more than issue another schoolmasterly reproof? Then some way would *have* to be found to convey to Wilson and the great American public the true facts of international life. Any suggestion that Germany was proposing an alliance with Mexico to wage war on the United States, and that Japan was in some way to be associated with this scheme, would surely convince the most isolationist inhabitant of Texas, California or even Illinois that it was time to take the gloves off and teach the Germans and everyone else with similar ideas that the Great Republic could not be treated in such a manner with impunity. Moreover, Wilson himself was extremely sensitive about Mexico. The country had been in a state of revolution for years – Diaz, Villa, Huerta, Carranza (the current President) were each as bad as the other in Wilson's opinion; the Mexicans really had to be brought to see reason; they must be made better pupils even if the American headmaster had to use the cane. No, Wilson would not take kindly to Herr Zimmermann's plans.

But, to convince Wilson and the American public would require more than a partially decoded telegram, open to various interpretations, all of which would be promptly denied by the parties involved. It was essential to have a complete and unimpeachable. text. Reconstructing a difficult code takes time. Would Room 40's diplomatic section be able to produce the answer quickly enough?

Hall, therefore, had four problems to solve. The first was whether to make use of the Zimmermann telegram at all. The second, if its disclosure did seem essential, was to obtain a complete and accurate text. The third was to protect Room 40. The fourth was to find a way of presenting the information to the President which would not only convince him but also the American public of its authenticity. A lesser man, or a man with less confidence in himself, would have passed the buck – to Oliver, to Jellicoe, now 1st Sea Lord, to Carson the new 1st Lord, or to Balfour, whom Lloyd George had moved from the Admiralty to the Foreign Office. It was, after all, not something of purely naval interest; it concerned relations with foreign powers, and was so important that the Prime Minister himself would finally have to be involved. But Blinker Hall was not a man to shrug off his own responsibilities on to others; his whole training as a naval officer had taught him to make his own decisions and accept the consequences. He did not trust anyone, least of all the politicians (although he had a great admiration for Balfour) to act both wisely and boldly. No, it was up to him and to him alone to work out solutions to his four separate problems so that, if in the end the Zimmermann telegram had to be used, the matter could be handled both effectively and securely. He still had a few days of grace; nothing need be decided until President Wilson's reactions to the German declaration became clear. Hall decided to keep his own counsel for the time being.

Herr Zimmermann had despatched his telegram to Bernstorff in a new code transported to the United States in November 1916 by the cargo U-boat *Deutschland*. Room 40 had no copy of this code, and de Grey and Montgomery, the 'Padre', were trying patiently to reconstruct it by purely cryptographic methods. They had made enough progress to be able to put a very incomplete text before Hall on 17 January, but how quickly would they be able to fill in the gaps and produce a full and definitive version?

For some months past (exactly how many is hard to establish, but see Chapter 8) Room 40 had been reading without difficulty many messages in another German diplomatic code, No. 13040, which had been issued to a number of German embassies and legations at least ten years before the war. It is quite clear that, sometime in 1915, Room 40 had broken 13040, used principally, it was at first thought, for written, postal communications between the Wilhelm-strasse and its overseas diplomats. This slow, and by no means secure method had been forced on the Germans by the *Telconia's* severance of almost all cables which did not pass through Britain. The letters from overseas were sent, usually in duplicate, to various accommodation addresses in neutral countries such as Holland, Switzerland or Sweden whence they were forwarded to Berlin; but they had to be conveyed to Europe by ships all of which were compelled to call at British ports for examination. As British censorship methods improved and as the liaison between the censors and Room 40 became closer, an increasing number of letters were intercepted and decoded. Although it was Hall's policy to allow such letters to go on to their destinations so as to keep open a valuable source of information, the Germans must have become conscious of the risks they were running. They prevailed upon Sweden, whose Government and many of its people were distinctly pro-German, to convey official German messages between Washington and Berlin for them. Some of these messages were carried in Swedish diplomatic pouches; others, in German code but then re-encoded into Swedish codes, were despatched in Swedish diplomatic cables. This was, of course, a flagrant breach by the Swedes of the immunity always accorded in peacetime to all diplomatic correspondence and even in the war time to that of neutral powers. This Swedish double-dealing became known to the British and, in 1915, a very sharp protest was made to Stockholm. The Swedes expressed sincere regret and gave firm assurances that the practice would cease. They fulfilled their promise to the extent of refraining from conveying German messages directly to and from Washington, transferring the traffic instead to their Embassy in

Buenos Aires, whence the messages could speedily be re-routed by mail or telegraph lines over which the British had no control to German embassies and legations throughout the Americas. For a time Hall was deceived by this subterfuge, but he could see well enough that Bernstorff was somehow still able to communicate fairly quickly with Berlin. At the beginning of May 1916, Hall wrote to Captain Guy Gaunt, the British Naval Attaché in Washington,[1] 'We have traced nearly every route and I am really reduced to the following: he sends them down to Buenos Aires, thence across to Valparaiso. From there I cannot make out where they are sent, whether via China or Russia through the connivance of a netural legation or not?' One can hazard a guess that the protest to Sweden which had cut off the flow of information previously available, was made without consultation with Hall or at least against his advice, and that this was one factor in his initial reluctance to disclose the secret of the Zimmermann telegram to any other officer or official.

However, the mystery of Bernstorff's secret means of communication was not destined to remain secret much longer. Soon after Hall had written to Gaunt, de Grey brought Hall an intercepted letter which had reached him from the Censorship. It was in code, 13040, and was, says Hall, 'written on a double sheet of blue foolscap from the German Minister in Mexico [von Eckhardt][2] to von Bethmann Hollweg [at that time the German Chancellor]. It was dated 8 March 1916 and ran as follows:

The Swedish Chargé d'Affaires here, Herr F. Cronholm has, since he has been here, made no concealment of his sympathies for Germany and placed himself in close connection with this Legation . . . he is the only neutral diplomat through whom information from the enemy camp can be obtained. Further, he arranges the conditions for the official telegraphic traffic with your Excellency. In this connection he is obliged every time, often late at night, personally to go to the telegraph office to hand in the despatches . . . Herr Cronholm has not got a Swedish decoration but only a Chilean one. I beg to submit to your

[1] Although officially based in Washington, Gaunt spent most of his time in New York.
[2] This is the generally used spelling of the German Minister's name, but David Kahn has pointed out to me that in a letter he received from the German Foreign Office of 10 January 1964, it was given as Heinrich J. F. von Eckardt. This is probably correct, but I have used the accustomed spelling to avoid confusion.

Excellency, if your Excellency approves, that Herr Cronholm should be recommended in the proper quarters for the Kronenorden of the 2nd Class . . .

It was somehow fitting that Swedish duplicity should be revealed as the result of the vanity of a Swedish diplomat. 'It was clear,' Hall goes on,

that steps would have to be taken to have all Swedish Foreign Office cipher telegrams brought to us for examination. Arrangements were soon made for this to be done, and in many cases it was found that after a few Swedish groups our old friend 13040 would appear. Our excitement, moreover, may be imagined when through this means we discovered the route by which Bernstorff was communicating with his Government. Now we knew which Legation was responsible and as a result we were in a short time reading all the essential parts of Bernstorff's despatches and the replies of his Government. In this way we found ourselves in full possession for all practical purposes of the enemy's every move in the diplomatic game of the moment, and knew from the Ambassador's admirably clear despatches the points of greatest importance in Mr Wilson's fluctuating policy. In addition to that, it afforded us an insight into some of the devious ways of German agents all over the American continent.

Needless to say, no protest was made to the Swedish Government on this occasion! Hall was only too grateful for what Room 40 dubbed 'The Swedish Roundabout'. But what was also needed was knowledge of German cables passing over American lines between Washington and the lesser legations in Mexico, the Caribbean and South America. How were these to be intercepted? We have already seen that at the time of the Falkland Islands battle in 1914, the British had means of securing copies of German cables emanating from Valparaiso and Montevideo. What could now be done in Mexico City? The British Chargé d'Affaires there, Tom Hohler, had long had his suspicions of von Eckhardt and Cronholm and had reported them either to the Secret Service or to the Foreign Office. But no attention had been paid to his warnings. Hall, however, had lent him a more sympathetic ear and kept in touch. Hohler was friendly with two English brothers in the Mexican capital; one was a printer and the other employed in the Telegraph service. The country had been plagued for years by revolutions and coups, and the first step of each new conqueror was to cancel the currency of his predecessor and issue his own, in the shape of small cards, '*cartones*', rather like railway tickets. They were mostly of very little value but easily forged; counterfeiting had become almost a national pastime. President Carranza had decreed that counterfeiters, if caught, would be summarily tried and shot.

One day the English printer returned unexpectedly to his small works when his workmen were out at lunch. To his horror he found on one of the benches a whole pile of forged *cartones*, obviously a profitable sideline for one of his men. Hastily locking them up in his safe, the printer dashed off to consult his brother, but the guilty workman, returning and immediately guessing what had happened, decided to save his own skin by denouncing his employer to the authorities. The printer was arrested, compelled to open his safe, and immediately tried by court martial. He was found guilty and sentenced to be shot at dawn in thirty-six hours' time. The brother, meanwhile, had sought the help of his friend Hohler, who, with great difficulty managed to secure the printer's release and eventual acquittal. What happened to the workman is not recorded; presumably he was duly shot. But the two brothers were naturally more than grateful to Hohler, and declared that if there was anything they could do to repay the debt they owed him he had but to name it. The brother who worked in the Telegraph service, was only too ready to agree to Hohler's request for copies of all cables despatched to or received by von Eckhardt and Cronholm, which Hohler then forwarded to Gaunt to send on to Hall.

The intercepts were not at first of great importance – it seemed that Herr Cronholm was unlikely to get his *Kronenorden*, that he feared that the frequency of his telegrams would arouse English suspicions and therefore, suggested Eckhardt, should be permitted to drop his 'reports about ships'. Hall did, however, learn that Eckhardt now considered 'Carranza openly friendly to Germany [and] willing to support if necessary German submarines in Mexican waters to the best of his ability.' On 12 November Bernstorff cabled Eckhardt that

The Imperial Government proposes to employ the most efficacious means to annihilate its criminal enemy, and since it designs to carry its operations to America with the object of destroying its enemy's commerce, it will be very valuable to have certain bases to assist the work of its submarines both in South America and in

Mexico, as, for example in the State of Tamaulipas.[1] Accordingly, the Imperial Government would see with the greatest pleasure the Mexican Government's consent to cede the necessary permission for the establishment of a base in its territory, on the understanding that any arrangements completed will not involve the slightest damage to the dignity or integrity of Mexico, since that country will be treated like the free and independent nation which it is. The Imperial Government being perfectly acquainted with the special circumstances through which Mexico is passing at the present time – in the period of reconstruction in which being a young nation she finds herself – would like to know what advantages Mexico would find suitable on her part, especially in the financial and economic crises through which she is passing, if she agrees to the desires of the Imperial Government.

That U-boats were now quite capable of crossing the Atlantic had been demonstrated not only by the cargo-carrying *Deutschland* but by U 53, which on 7 October had spent twenty-four hours in Newport (to the intense embarrassment of the US Navy) and then sailed off to sink five ships within a few miles of the Nantucket Lightship before returning safely to Germany. There was nothing which the neutral Americans could do about it.

The incomplete decode of Zimmermann's telegram of 17 January cannot therefore have come as any great surprise to Hall. It had, in fact, been encoded in a new code, 0075, but German diplomats were no more alive to the simple rules of code security than were the *Admiralstab*, and for some inexplicable reason the *Deutschland* had only carried one copy of 0075 for Bernstorff's use; no additional copies had been supplied for him to forward to Eckhardt or any of the other legations in the Americas. They had to continue to use 13040, and so did Bernstorff if he wished to communicate with them. Hall, of course, could not be sure of this, but as Eckhardt was continuing to use 13040 in his communications with Germany, it seemed a strong probability. Blinker began to see a possible solution of all his difficulties. If a copy of the cable from Washington to Mexico City could be procured, and if it proved to be in the old code, which Room 40 had largely solved, the full text would almost certainly be revealed. Moreover, it was bound to contain certain differences in preamble and numbering from the cablegram sent to Bernstorff by Zimmermann. It might therefore be possible to

---

[1] On the east coast just south of the border with the USA.

suggest that the communication had been compromised by treachery or theft in America or Mexico, and so to divert all attention away from the Berlin-Stockholm-Washington connection. Perhaps it could even be represented as a purely American coup in which the British were in no way involved.

In the meantime, Hall was following with great attention the despairing efforts made by Bernstorff to persuade his Government to cancel or at least postpone the announcement of the U-boat campaign. Either Bernstorff was still using the old code or de Grey and Montgomery were making good progress with the new one, because on 28 January de Grey brought Hall part of the Ambassador's second protest, which included a request for a reply by wireless because 'cables always take several days'. He was quite right; Hall had read Zimmermann's instructions two days before Bernstorff had received them!

The Germans were of course quite capable, thanks to their high power Nauen transmitter, of communicating with America by wireless. The only trouble was that this had to go through the US Government wireless station at Sayville on Long Island, and, by international usage be either in plain language or in a code provided to the US Government. Thanks to President Wilson's *eminence grise*, Colonel House, a way round this difficulty had easily been found. House considered himself, and, more importantly was considered by Wilson, to be an expert on foreign affairs, and was used by the President as his personal representative in negotiations at the highest level with the belligerents in connection with Wilson's continual efforts to bring about peace. House short circuited Ambassador Page in London and Ambassador James Gerard in Berlin and often communicated direct with the President in a rather childish code of their own devising. This was very probably broken by Room 40 as also were normal American diplomatic codes. However, the Germans had, during negotiations in 1916, persuaded House that, as a result of British interference, the necessary communication between Washington and Berlin could only be carried on with reasonable celerity if the Americans themselves would transmit messages between Bernstorff and the Wilhelmstrasse for them, naturally in a code which the State Department could not read. No hard headed American business man would have accepted the German assurances that such misuse of normal diplomatic procedure would be confined strictly to the subject of the peace negotiations. But House and Wilson, those innocents abroad, were happy, despite the anguished protests of Ambassador James Gerard and the State Department, to provide the Germans with a second string to their Swedish bow. The Wilhelmstrasse could not believe its good luck, but hastened to make full use of it. The Zimmermann telegram was so important that it was despatched not only by the Swedish Roundabout but by wireless to Sayville and by cable from the American Embassy in Berlin as well, a truly unparalleled piece of effrontery.

Bernstorff's protests proved unavailing against the conviction of the German General Staff that the only way to bring England to her knees was by unrestricted U-boat warfare; the Ambassador had to carry out his orders and notify the American President of his Government's decision.

All round the world people anxiously awaited Wilson's reactions. Would it be war, something short of war or just another expression of pious disapproval? A man who was almost as anxious as Hall that it should be war, was Ambassador Walter Hines Page. For the past two and a half years he had been trying to persuade his good friend Woodrow Wilson that the only right and honourable course of action for the United States would be to join the Entente powers and crush Imperial Germany. He had not only failed entirely in his aim, but had lost the confidence and interest of the President: of this he was sadly very well aware. But surely, now at last, the President would have to act decisively? Surely, he would now declare war?

Hall had made it his business to establish the most cordial relations with Page, no difficult task because the Ambassador immediately appealed to all Englishmen, not only because he was an Anglophile but because of his great personal charm. On the evening of 1 February, Hall received a cable from Gaunt, 'The Barber gets his papers at 2 p.m. today. I will probably get soused.' (Gaunt and Hall used code names for personalities; Wilson was 'Aaron', House 'Beverly', while Gaunt had chosen 'Barber' for Bernstorff from 'The Barber of Seville' who sang so loudly and so much.) Gaunt had obtained this highly secret information from his friend 'Beverly', before even poor 'Barber' had been officially informed by the State Department. Hall hurried round to Grosvenor Square to give his friend Page the good news, and together they toasted it in champagne. But next day the euphoria evaporated; it seemed likely that the President would go no further than armed neutrality. Wilson's instinctive aversion to war, combined with his acute political awareness of the continuing isolationist sentiments of the bulk of the American electorate, had prevailed; he might prepare for war but he would not declare it.

Page was not the only one to be disappointed. Hall saw that he could delay no longer; he would have to disclose his secret to others. At least he had now some sort of a plan in his mind, and de Grey and Montgomery had made a little more progress. On 5 February Hall went to see Lord Hardinge, the Permanent Secretary at the Foreign Office, to enlist Mr Balfour's support. Balfour was, Hall thought, the one British politician whose integrity the American Administration would not question. Hardinge was 'his usual cool self, interested but cautious'. He promised to put the whole matter before Balfour and agreed that, in the meantime, Hall should take the further step that would be essential if his proposals were finally approved. This step was to obtain a copy of the Bernstorff-Eckhardt cable from Mexico. It so happened that Tom Hohler had left at the end of 1916 to go to Washington, but his successor, Edward Thurston, who had previously been Consul-General in Mexico City, had been fully briefed about the procedure for obtaining copies of German and Swedish cables, so no difficulty was anticipated on that score. On 6 February Thurston was instructed to obtain copies of all cables sent by Bernstorff to Eckhardt since 18 January and forward them to Gaunt. Gaunt was similarly ordered to recode the messages when received from Thurstan, and cable them immediately to the DID. The full text of Bernstorff's cable to Eckhardt, which contained Zimmermann's instructions, was received by Hall on 19 February exactly one month after its despatch.

In the meantime, a telegram from Zimmermann, which had been sent on 8 February direct to Eckhardt, had been intercepted and solved. It read: 'Most Secret. Decipher personally. Provided there is no danger of secret being betrayed to USA you are desired without further delay to broach the question of an Alliance to the President [Carranza]. The definite conclusion of an Alliance, however, is dependent on the outbreak of war between Germany and USA. The President might, even now, on his own account, sound Japan. If the President declines from fear of subsequent revenge you are empowered to offer him a definitive alliance after conclusion of peace providing Mexico succeeds in drawing Japan into the alliance.'

Hall was still waiting for a decision from the Foreign Office, but, possibly with the intention of pre-empting it, came to the conclusion that he would now put the American Embassy in the picture.

Despite his excellent relations with the Ambassador, Blinker opted
for a lower level first approach – through the 2nd secretary, Ned
Bell. Bell, a career diplomat, had been with the Embassy since
September 1913 and had become the link with the British Intelligence services. He was on very close terms with Hall and with
Herschell and Serocold, and had been the recipient of much confidential information over the past two years. With the receipt of
Thurstan's copy of the Zimmermann message, a complete and
accurate text was at last available. That same day, 19 February, Hall
asked Bell to come to see him. Within half an hour Bell was sitting in
the DID's room, staring with disbelief at the decoded and translated
message which Hall had handed to him. It read as follows:[1]

Washington to Mexico.   19 January 1917
We intend to begin on 1 February unrestricted submarine war-
fare. We shall endeavour in spite of this to keep the USA neutral.
In the event of this not succeeding we make Mexico a proposal of
alliance on the following terms:-
Make war together.
Make peace together.
Generous financial support and an undertaking on our part that
Mexico is to reconquer the lost territory in Texas, New Mexico
and Arizona. The settlement in detail is left to you.
You will inform the President of the above most secretly as soon
as the outbreak of war with the USA is certain, and add the
suggestion that he should on his own initiative invite Japan to
immediate adherence and at the same time mediate between
Japan and ourselves.
Please call the President's attention to the fact that the ruthless
employment of our submarines now offers the prospect of compelling England in a few months to make peace.

This really was dynamite – the prospect of another Alamo,[2] of a
latter day Santa Ana riding into Tulsa, of the Japanese landing in
San Francisco – this would cause a rush of blood to the head of even
the most isolationist American. It was unbelievable, it must be a
hoax, Bell exploded. Hall managed to convince him that it was
entirely genuine, to which Bell replied, '"But, DID, this means

---

[1] The text given is as finally published.
[2] The 1836 American equivalent of the British defeat at Dunkirk in 1940.
Sometimes referred to as the American Thermopylae. Santa Ana was the Mexican
Commander.

war." "*If* it is published," ' Hall told him, and went on to explain that although he had no hesitation in showing him the despatch privately, his hands were tied until he could obtain a decision from the Foreign Office. What he wanted Bell to do was to tell the Ambassador what he had seen, but to persuade him to make no move at all until Mr Balfour had made up his mind exactly how the matter should be handled. Bell was confident that Page would agree to these conditions, but he begged Hall not to delay a moment longer than was essential.

For the past fortnight Hall had been having daily consultations with Hardinge and Campbell in the Foreign Office, but to every suggestion he put forward they raised an objection. They certainly did not wish to give the impression that there was anything so ungentlemanly as 'a "Cabinet noir" in the Foreign Office, or that the British Government was endeavouring to influence a neutral state in its favour'! But matters were coming to a head on the Rio Grande, even if Hardinge and Campbell could not make up their minds. President Wilson had, some months previously, sent American troops under General Pershing into Mexico to suppress the bandit-hero Villa who was raiding indiscriminately on both sides of the border. Now, in an effort to appease Carranza, Pershing had been ordered to withdraw. Carranza was not appeased; he refused to recognise Wilson's right to interfere in any way in Mexican affairs, and rejected the proposal for joint policing of the frontier. A fresh rising by a nephew of Porfirio Diaz had taken place in the South, and German reservists[1] in Mexico were reported to be mobilising to prevent any American or British landing designed to safeguard the oil fields of Tampico. Something, Hall felt, must be done at once or the opportunity would be lost for ever.

Campbell and Hardinge were now debating whether it would be best for Herr Zimmermann's plans to be disclosed officially through the Foreign Office, which they felt would give the affair too official a character, or whether it might perhaps be preferable for the DID to tell Mr Bell privately (which, be it noted, he had already quietly done). Bell could inform the Ambassador who would see to it that the information reached the President. 'Hall,' wrote Campbell, 'has given the Embassy a considerable amount of information useful to them in this way, and they place considerable reliance on it.'

---

[1] German citizens resident in Mexico who had performed their compulsory military service in the Fatherland but had been unable to rejoin the colours because of the British blockade.

Alternatively, perhaps, Hall could arrange to leak the news to the American Press 'without any indication that HM Government or any British Official was at the bottom of the exposure. Whichever plan is adopted Captain Hall is confident that he can so arrange things so as to prevent any risk of the source of his information being compromised.' Hardinge expressed the view that it was 'difficult to say which course would be best', and feared that it might be hard to convince Bell of the authenticity of the telegram. Balfour, however, was one of the most intelligent politicians of his day, and he knew Hall well from his time as 1st Lord. On 20 February he minuted to Hardinge, 'I think Captain Hall may be left to clinch this problem. He knows the ropes better than anyone.'' Blinker Hall could not have asked for more; he had been given an entirely free hand. He felt rather less inhibited in the discussions which, completely without authority, he had already been having with Page and Bell.

Page was a very old friend of the President; he had no doubt that the effect on Wilson would be far greater if he, Page, could inform the President that the document had been handed to him personally by the Foreign Secretary. Balfour raised no objection, but Hall was still not absolutely sure that he had devised adequate cover for Room 40. Bell assured him that the American security agencies would be perfectly, no doubt happily, capable of assuming full responsibility for the discovery and exposure of the telegram. But although Bell and Page were by now completely convinced of its genuineness, others might take a different view. There could be no question, Hall decided, of handing over the German code to anyone else, even a friendly power whom it was hoped to transform into an active ally. Suddenly, the last piece of the jigsaw fell into place. The Americans could easily obtain their own copy of the coded cable from the Washington cable office, so the President could truthfully claim that it had been obtained on American soil. If, in addition, Ned Bell, under de Grey's guidance, were to decode the cable in the American Embassy, technically also American territory, Wilson could announce with a clear conscience that the whole process had taken place on American ground. Such legalistic scruples and subterfuges may seem a little absurd to modern readers, always prone to disbelieve the official announcements of their elected representatives, but, at that time, it can only be described as 'good thinking'. As to the German reaction to the disclosure, that would have to be played by ear when the time came. Hall, Page and Bell were now agreed. The fuse to cause the explosion of the dynamite could safely be lit. As one member of Room 40 remarked long afterwards, 'We gave the cards to Reggie to play, and he played the hand at his own time and in his own way but damned well.'

It was Friday, 23 February and that afternoon Page went to see Balfour at the Foreign Office in order to receive from him copies of the coded and decoded texts of Herr Zimmermann's telegram. He returned to the Embassy and began the task of drafting a cable to his President. It was not easy to find the right words which would explain the background (as agreed with Hall), and at the same time convince that starry eyed idealist, Woodrow Wilson, that he was not dealing with men of his own kind but with the government of a nation fighting for its life and prepared to use any weapon, no matter how ruthless or devious to attain its ends. Page worked throughout that long night, and at eight o'clock on the morning of 24 February warned the State Department that in another three hours he would be sending a cable of 'great importance to the President and Secretary of State'. However, what with revisions and coding, the fateful message was not finally despatched until 1 p.m. It read as follows:

> Secstate Washington. 5747 February 24th 1 p.m. My 5746 February 24th 8 a.m. Confidential for the President and the Secretary of State.
>
> Balfour has handed me the text of a cipher telegram from Zimmermann, German Secretary of State for Foreign Affairs, to the German Minister in Mexico which was sent via Washington and relayed by Bernstorff on January 19th. You can probably obtain a copy of the text relayed by Bernstorff from the cable office in Washington. The first group is the number of the telegram 130 and the second is 13042 indicating the number of the code used.[1] The last group but two is 97556 which is Zimmermann's signature. I shall send you by mail a copy of the cipher text and of the decode into German, and meanwhile I give you the English translation as follows:

There then followed the text quoted on page 216.

Page continued:

The receipt of this information has so exercised the British

---

[1] According to Kahn the same code was indicated by any number from 13040 to 13049, so 13042 meant the same thing as 13040.

Government that they have lost no time in communicating it to
me to transmit to you in order that our Government may be able
without delay to make such dispositions as may be necessary in
view of the threatened invasion of our territory. *The following
paragraph is Strictly Confidential.*
Early in the War the British Government obtained possession of a
copy of the German cipher code used in the above message and
have made it their business to obtain copies of Bernstorff's cipher
telegrams to Mexico amongst others which are sent back to
London and deciphered here. This accounts for their being able
to decipher this telegram from the German Government to their
representative in Mexico and also for the delay from January 19th
until now in their receiving the information [!] This system has
hitherto been a most jealously guarded secret and is only divulged
now to you by the British Government in view of the extraordinary circumstances and their friendly feeling towards the United
States. They earnestly request that you will keep the source of
your information and the British Government's method of
obtaining it profoundly secret but they put no prohibition on the
publication of Zimmermann's telegram itself. The copies of this
and other telegrams were not obtained in Washington but were
bought in Mexico.
I have thanked Balfour for the service his Government has
rendered us and suggest that a private official message of thanks
from our Government to him would be appreciated.
I am informed that this information has not yet been given to the
Japanese Government but I think it is not unlikely that when it
reaches them they will make a public statement on it in order to
clear up their position regarding the United States and prove
their good faith to their Allies.

Page's message reached Washington on the evening of Saturday,
24 February, and when it was shown to the President he displayed
'much indignation', but the Secretary of State, Lansing, was away for
the weekend and Wilson needed time to adjust his mind to this
unprecedented situation. Moreover, it was necessary to obtain the
original of the Bernstorff/Eckhardt cable from Western Union, and
the company at first insisted that they could not surrender it. So
those in London had to possess their souls in patience, and wait.
Page was depressed; 'This would precipitate a war between any two
nations,' he confided to his diary. 'Heaven knows what effect it will

have in Washington.' Bell was confident that all would be well, but Hall, who had staked everything, his reputation, his career, his country's future on the gamble that his plan would work, confessed that he spent the next three days in 'a kind of a nightmare'.

In the meantime, in Washington, the cable had at last been secured from Western Union, and Lansing had returned. He, like Page, had long come to the conclusion that the United States must join the Entente, but had not been able to move his President. He had felt sure that sooner or later the 'blundering Germans' would deliver themselves into his hands, and now they had done so with a vengeance. On Tuesday, 27 February, when he went to see the President, he was armed with 'an exceptionally long message of some one thousand groups', transmitted from the Wilhelmstrasse to Bernstorff via the American Embassy in Berlin and the State Department on 17 February; it could only be another version of Zimmermann's message, proposing an attack on the United States conveyed, thanks to arrogance and contempt on one side and simple minded trust on the other, by means of the victim's own communications system. Even Wilson was reduced to near profanity (for him) when shown it. 'Good Lord! Good Lord!' he is said to have exclaimed.

Wilson was taking his time to decide just how he would handle matters, but Guy Gaunt in New York, who kept his ear very close to the ground, soon became aware that something was in the wind. On Monday, the 26th, before Lansing had returned from his weekend, Gaunt cabled Hall in London, 'Urgent. Very Secret from Naval Attaché. Aaron has got hold of a cable to Barber from his employer directing him in the event of a break at once to conclude an alliance with Mexico. This information will most likely become public property by Wednesday morning. Can you send me any information which would make information fuller and more decisive.' Hall replied the next day: 'Germany guarantees assistance to Mexico if they will reconquer Texas, New Mexico and Arizona; also proposes alliance with Mexico to make war together. Do not use this till Aaron announces it . . . Premature disclosure fatal. Full details in possession of Aaron. Alone I did it.'

Hall was by now more confident that his ploy had worked. But secrecy was essential. Next day he wired Gaunt, 'It is imperative that knowledge of this affair shall never be traced to British sources.'

Hall's confidence was justified, because on the day of his first

jubilant message to Gaunt, Page had told him that the President had
instructed him to convey his personal thanks to Balfour for 'information of such inestimable value', *and* that it would be made
public on 1 March. A little later, however, came the coded text of
three other cables which had been discovered in the Western Union
files. 'Please endeavour,' wired Lansing, 'to obtain copy of German
code from Mr Balfour . . . Effort will be made to secure copies of all
German code messages as far back as possible and if the Department were in possession of the code, it would be a great saving of
time and expense. Contents of messages decoded here would of
course be communicated to the British Government . . .'

Hall had foreseen this request and had already decided that he
could not and would not accede to it. According to Hall, Page and
Bell privately agreed with him but 'had to press the point'. Next day,
1 March Page telegraphed Lansing that 'The three messages were
deciphered today and are practically identical. They contain instructions [from Bernstorff to German legations in Central and
South America] to use a certain variation of the cipher book when
communicating with Berlin. The question of our having a copy of
the code has been taken up, but there appear to be difficulties. I am
told that the actual code would be of no use to us as it was never used
straight, but with a great number of variations which are known to
only one or two experts here. They cannot be spared to go to
America. If you will send me copies of B's cipher telegrams the
British authorities will gladly decipher them as quickly as possible,
giving me copies as fast as deciphered . . . Neither Spring-Rice [the
British Ambassador in Washington] nor Gaunt knows anything
about this matter.'

While Hall was providing Page with this only partially true
information, Wilson had communicated the Zimmermann telegram
to E. M. Hood, of Associated Press, the dean of the Washington
Press Corps. without disclosing how it had been obtained but
vouching for its authenticity. The story hit all the headlines on
Thursday, 1 March. Not surprisingly it caused a sensation, not least
on the West Coast. Isolationist sentiment vanished almost over-
night except among a small minority of pro-German or truly pacifist
Senators. They at once demanded to know the source of the story;
had it come from the British? If so, it was surely a forgery designed
to trap America into a war it did not want and in which it still had no
reason to be involved.

Fortunately, Lansing's plan to get round this problem coincided exactly with that already prepared by Hall for such a contingency. Lansing telegraphed Page urgently on 1 March that:

> Some members of Congress are attempting to discredit Zimmermann message, charging that message was furnished to this Government by one of belligerents. This Government has not the slightest doubt as to its authenticity but it would be of the greatest service if the British Government would permit someone in the Embassy to personally decode the original message which we secured from the manager of the telegraph office and then cable to Department German text. Assure Mr Balfour that the Department hesitated to make this request but feels that this course will materially strengthen its position and make it possible for the Department to state that it had secured the Z note from our own people . . .

De Grey was now working solely on the new code, 0075, while Montgomery was dealing with messages in 13040. When Hall sent for him to come to the DID's room (because it was no longer thought necessary for Zimmermann's telegram to be decoded in the American Embassy), de Grey in his excitement took with him the book in which he was reconstructing the new code, not Montgomery's copy of the old one in which, of course, Bernstorff's cable to Eckhardt had been made. Fortunately, by this time de Grey knew the telegram off by heart and was able to coach Bell without giving away his mistake. In a few hours the German plain language text, set out by Ned Bell, was on its way back to the State Department, but to everyone's astonishment the authenticity of the telegram was actually confirmed by no less a person than its author – Herr Zimmermann himself. At a press conference on the morning of 2 March, the Foreign Minister was asked by the Hearst correspondent in Berlin (W. B. Hale, who was also in receipt of German pay) to deny the story. Zimmermann replied that he could not do so; it was true!

Although there was still some political manoeuvring on the part of the Administration and Congress, the die was now cast. On 21 March Wilson recalled Congress for 2 April, and on the afternoon of 6 April 1917 America was at war with Germany.

War had gradually been getting closer for months. With the resumption of the unrestricted U-boat campaign it was virtually inevitable. Sooner or later some further act of German folly or brutality would have driven even Wilson to move from armed neutrality to active belligerency, but the final break might well have been delayed for months. The Zimmermann telegram was important, not so much for what it did, but for when it did it. The United States was totally unprepared for war and the subsequent build up of the American Expeditionary Force in France was unbelievably slow. It took almost a year before even five divisions,[1] largely provided with British equipment, were in reserve and still unready for action behind the Western Front. Château Thierry was not fought until the end of May 1918, and Belleau Wood not won until the end of June. But everyone, British, French and Germans alike, had known since April 1917 that the Yanks *were* coming. The dark days of the German March offensive in 1918 would have been even darker without that knowledge. What would have happened if there had not then been a single US soldier in France? Would the line have held? Would a compromise peace, if not an abject surrender have been made? That such things did not happen is why the disclosure of the Zimmermann telegram can truly be said to have been the greatest Intelligence coup in history, and why Blinker Hall's name is never likely to be forgotten. There was a good deal of substance in his boast to Gaunt, 'Alone I did it.'

---

[1] Six British Divisons were in action within six *weeks* of the outbreak of war in 1914.

CHAPTER FOURTEEN

A Special Relationship

Edward Bell joined the United States Foreign Service at the age of twenty-seven in 1909. A New Yorker and a graduate of Harvard (1904) he had first spent some time in a stockbroker's office, but was obviously ideally suited for his new profession. After only one year his superior reported that 'Mr Bell is exceedingly intelligent, ambitious and painstaking. He is all that he should be. I have never met . . . a more efficient Secretary, whether in the Chancery or in Society. He is, in my opinion, the exact type of what a Secretary in our Service should be.' In September 1913 he was posted at his own request as Second Secretary to the London Embassy, crossing from the United States, as it happened, in the *Lusitania*. He thus arrived three months after his Ambassador, Walter Hines Page. Both Britain and America were to benefit immeasurably from the appointment of these two men. Page, a convinced Anglophile, won the hearts of all the 'great and the good' in London, but the extraordinary friendly and close relations which Bell established with Hall and his staff, produced results of almost equal value. Bell, Eddie to his British friends, Ned to his American ones, was a man of great tact and discretion with a quiet sense of humour which must have appealed to Englishmen like Serocold and Herschell. He never betrayed any of the confidences with which he was entrusted, and as a consequence was able to extract a great deal more secret information from Hall and the Intelligence Division than would otherwise have been possible.

At the beginning of the war much of the work of the American Embassy had been concerned with the repatriation of American citizens stranded in Europe to the States, and with securing the release of under-age Americans who had enlisted in the British Forces without parental consent. In addition the United States had taken over the representation of German interests in Britain, a task which Ambassador Page did not find particularly congenial but one which he performed most conscientiously. Even less pleasing to him was the duty of delivering the sharp protests of his own Government at the detention of American ships and goods resulting from the increasingly stringent enforcement of the blockade of Germany by the Royal Navy. Page frankly believed that such protests were ill-judged and more than once toned down their angry language (or at least accompanied them by more conciliatory verbal explanations) before presenting a note officially to Sir Edward Grey, the Foreign Secretary. Although Grey was, in the end, always willing to give way (much to the fury of the Admiralty) rather than to allow Anglo-American relations to become too bitter, there were several incidents which nearly provoked a crisis.

One such occurred early in 1915 when an American industrialist purchased a German steamer, the *Dacia*, interned in the States, and announced his intention of sailing her with a cargo of cotton, regarded by the British as contraband, for Germany via Holland. The Foreign Office made it clear to Page that if the ship sailed, she would be intercepted and her cargo condemned. American opinion, forgetful of the Federal Government's blockade of the Southern States during the Civil War, would have been outraged at yet another infringement of the sacred principle of the Freedom of the Seas – one of the causes of the War of 1812. Page produced a solution: let the French Navy intercept the *Dacia*. Franco-American friendship would survive such action by the descendants of Lafayette. Grey's advisers in the Foreign Office were against the idea, and officially Grey agreed with them, although he did add, with a touch of sophistry, that if, in the event, the *Dacia were* to fall into French hands, she and her cargo would have to go before a *French* Prize Court. Blinker Hall, however thoroughly approved of Page's plan; indeed it is more than probable that it was he who first suggested the idea to Page. Ignoring the Foreign Office view, Hall persuaded the Admiralty to transfer two Armed Merchant Cruisers to the French to enable them to make the interception. It all worked out as he hoped. The *Dacia* sailed; the Royal Navy kept carefully out of the way; the French Navy seized her; there was no crisis.

American anger with the blockade lessened as the British adopted a practice of purchasing all condemned cargoes and as American trade with Germany was increasingly replaced by extensive Allied orders. The sinking of the *Lusitania* also greatly influenced American opinion in favour of Britain. But Page's consistently pro-British attitude gradually irritated Wilson to such an extent that, by 1916, the President was seriously considering replacing him, while Page himself was determined to resign. Fortunately, neither of these things happened.

Bell, of course, although he shared his Ambassador's views, did not operate at this exalted level, but by mid-1915 he was already on the best of terms with Hall. It may at first seem strange that the DID should be dealing with a diplomat, and not the most senior one at that, rather than with the US Naval Attaché, Captain Powers Symington with his five Assistant Naval Attachés. There were a number of reasons for this. In the first place, Symington, as the representative of a neutral navy, albeit a friendly one, could not reasonably expect to be admitted to the innermost secrets of British Naval Intelligence. His duty was much more to collect information about wartime technical and operational developments, and in this field the Royal Navy was prepared to co-operate within limits. In fact, the British were ready to receive USN officers as observers on board their warships, but this was vetoed by the American State Department. Another factor, which cannot have been unknown to Hall, was that, in 1914, the US Office of Naval Intelligence was at a very low ebb and was in no position, even if it had been permitted to do so, to trade secrets of German activities either in the Fatherland or overseas with its much better organised British counterpart. It was, moreover, information of a largely non-naval sort that Hall was prepared to divulge, information from which he might expect that Britain would obtain a return. The State Department had more to offer than the Office of Naval Intelligence, and Bell was the ideal channel of communication.

The British Secret Service was very slow to organise any effective organisation in the Americas and, as we saw in Spain, Blinker Hall was not prepared to wait – if there was a vacuum he would fill it himself. He very quickly saw that there was a need, not to spy on the Americans themselves, but to counter German activities in the States and in Central and South America. These activities were controlled and financed by the German Embassy in Washington, by the Military Attaché, Franz von Papen, and the Naval Attaché, Karl Boy-Ed. Despite his post-war denials, Ambassador Bernstorff was fully aware of what his subordinates were doing and indeed he directed them. Money for propaganda was funnelled into German language American papers and some leading English language papers as well. Large orders for military or semi-military supplies were placed with American firms to prevent them accepting similar orders from the Entente powers. Anti-British German-American

and Irish-American organisations were subsidised. Indian nationalists were taken on to the pay roll to stir up trouble in India, just as
Casement was helped to organise revolt in Ireland. All this was an
abuse of American neutrality, but even more serious violations
were the attempts, organised by the Embassy, to cut the Canadian
Pacific Railway, to sabotage American factories working for the
Allies and to plant bombs on British merchant ships sailing from
American ports. Nor were these latter activities confined solely to
the United States. German representatives everywhere did their
best to fish in muddied waters, in Cuba, in Mexico and throughout
South America, not only to frustrate the British but to embarrass
and confuse the American Government. These were not activities
which President Wilson's administration, intent on maintaining the
most impartial neutrality, and particularly sensitive about events in
Mexico, could possibly tolerate. Unfortunately, the American
security services were ill-equipped to deal with the problem. Hall
was not the man to miss such an opportunity.

British Naval Attachés served two masters – the Ambassador to
whose staff they were appointed and the Director of Intelligence.
Hall was fortunate, when he came to the Admiralty, in finding
Captain Guy Gaunt already installed in Washington. Born in
Australia and educated at Melbourne Grammar School, he had
started nautical life as a cadet in HMS *Worcester*, the British
Merchant Navy Training ship. He went to sea in a windjammer from
the age of sixteen to nineteen and then transferred to the Royal
Navy. After an adventurous career in the Pacific he had risen
rapidly in rank. An outgoing, likeable man, a fine horseman and a
keen yachtsman, he soon had a host of American friends, including
both Teddy and Franklin D. Roosevelt, Edward Stettinius, a
partner in the banking firm of J. P. Morgan, General Lionel Wood
of the US Army, and, as we have seen, Colonel House. Like his
chief, Blinker Hall, he took to the murky world of counter-
espionage like a duck to water. He is alleged to have been adept at
disguising himself and an expert at street fighting, and even to have
personally disposed of more than one German agent, (although
whether he had learned these skills in Australia or the Merchant
Service is not reported). It is unlikely that his Ambassador, Sir Cecil
Spring-Rice, was aware of these hidden talents. If the Germans
found natural allies in the Irish in America, Gaunt found the Czech
and Slovak subjects of Austro-Hungary equally helpful to him, and
through them he built up an extensive organisation which kept him

remarkably well informed of what was going on in the Austrian and German Embassies and in their Consulates-General in New York. One of the first results was that Gaunt was handed copies of documents which were being sent by the Austrian Ambassador, Count Constatin Dumba, and by Bernstorff and von Papen to Europe in the care of a young American journalist, Archibald. Forewarned by Gaunt, Hall had the Dutch liner, in which Archibald was travelling, searched on her arrival in the Downs in August 1915. The papers were found and brought to Hall. Short circuiting the Foreign Office, who wished to handle the case in their own leisurely way, Hall gave copies to Bell, who promptly cabled the contents to the State Department. Although they did not definitely implicate the Ambassadors or Papen in actual sabotage, there were references to fomenting strikes and disruption in American factories which caused a sensation in America when they were published. This was probably not the first occasion of collaboration between Hall and Bell, but it was a typical one.

Before this had happened, however, Papen had received a blow from his own side. Dissatisfied with the results which he and Boy-Ed had obtained, the General Staff had despatched their own representative to America to take charge of sabotage and subversion, and to introduce a little professionalism into the rather amateur efforts of the two attachés. This representative was Franz von Kleist Rintelen, a Reserve officer of the German Navy. Rintelen's account of his adventures in his book *The Dark Invader*, contain a wealth of embroidery, but there is no doubt that, in the four short months in which he was in America he managed to create a very effective sabotage organisation which survived his own departure and was responsible for causing a great deal of damage to British ships and American property.[1] He had arrived in Washington at the beginning of April 1915 from Mexico, where he had been fomenting trouble through General Huerta to keep American attention centred south of the border rather than over the Atlantic. He received a very frosty reception from Papen and Boy-Ed, which he rapidly turned into open hostility by his arrogant attitude. The two regular officers persuaded Bernstorff, without too much difficulty, to demand his recall to Germany. Hall may have learned of Rintelen's intended departure from Gaunt or from an intercepted letter on the Swedish Roundabout, or he may just have been lucky. Rintelen travelled in the Dutch liner *Noordam* with a forged Swiss passport in the name

[1] For example, the great Black Tom explosion in July 1916.

of Gasché. Accompanying him was a rather shady American arms dealer, Andrew D. Meloy, to whom Rintelen had confided his secret papers. When the *Noordam* called at Ramsgate on 13 August for the usual British inspection, the spurious Mr Gasché was hauled off the ship and interrogated by the police. He stoutly and quite convincingly maintained his innocence, and might perhaps have got away with it had his friend Meloy not decided to come ashore and lend a hand. This immediately focussed suspicion on Meloy, whose baggage was then searched and Rintelen's papers found. Both men were hurried up to London where Rintelen, when interrogated by Hall, saw that the game was up and, rather than face a firing squad as a spy confessed that he was a German naval officer. Meloy maintained that he was an entirely innocent party, and demanded the protection of the American Embassy. Unfortunately, his own papers showed that the purpose of his visit to Germany was to purchase arms for one or other of the factions intriguing for power in Mexico, not exactly a criminal offence, but not a mission calculated to endear him to the American Government. Rintelen's papers also disclosed his intrigues with Huerta, and a good deal more besides. On 23 August Hall wrote to Bell, 'My dear Mr Bell, I enclose a preliminary précis of Gasché's Mexican correspondence. It is fairly extensive and I hope to make some further additions to it in a short time. Yours sincerely, W. R. Hall.' These additions, and a good deal more about Rintelen's activities in the United States must soon have been passed on to Bell, because some weeks later he was writing to Hall that, 'if you were able to obtain a photo of Herr Rintelen, I shall be glad to send it to the proper quarter for identification – I cannot help thinking that we might be able to settle definitely the question of his identity by this method. From today's papers I see that my idiotic countrymen are gathering up some of the Fatherland's rising young dynamiters in New York . . .'

The next move seems to have been an American request that an official of the Department of Justice be permitted to interrogate Rintelen, to which Hall was only too ready to agree. Unfortunately, the custody of prisoners of war was a War Office responsibility, and the officer whom Hall consulted had very different views. On 25 November he wrote to Hall '. . . Closely as we as a nation are concerned in the question, I feel strongly that neither you nor I are in a position to institute such an enquiry on our own. We may land others – our Government possibly – in difficulties. The procedure suggested is, you will I hope pardon my saying, very questionable

when adopted towards a prisoner of war . . . In all the circumstances, therefore, I feel that I must decline to be a party to a
procedure which seems to me to be inadvisable, or to grant facilities
for the visit to Rintelen – unless, of course, I receive orders from
higher authority.' Poor man. He evidently did not know Blinker
Hall very well. On 11 December Mr Siegel of the Department of
Justice arrived to carry out the interrogation. American bureaucra-
cy did not move very fast even in those days, but on 27 June 1916 the
United States made a formal request for Rintelen's extradition on
(considering all they then knew) the rather minor charges of forgery
and utterance of forged papers. To the fury of Bell and Hall, it was
rejected. However, when America came into the war, the request
was renewed, although not through official channels. Bell wrote to
the State Department in 1918 pointing out that Rintelen had not
been *extradited* in 1917 but had been sent to the States 'without legal
proceedings, by Admiral Hall at my request and in opposition to the
wishes of the British Military authorities.' Rintelen was most
apprehensive when he learned that he was to be handed over to the
Americans, but his protests were unavailing. To add to his humilia-
tion he was tried as a common criminal and sentenced to four years
in an Atlanta penitentiary, not at all the sort of treatment a German
officer expected! In the late twenties and early thirties when Amos
Peaslee[1] was trying to prove the responsibility of the German
Government for the Black Tom explosion and other acts of sabotage while America was still neutral, Hall, at Peaslee's request, got in
touch again with Rintelen and they became quite good friends.
Rintelen believed that the German Government were pursuing a
vendetta against him, and supplied a good deal of information
useful to the American case. The old admiral was not, however,
without some doubts about the former spy, because, when his much
loved daughter, Faith, was in Paris, where Rintelen was living, he
gave her strict instructions never to go out with him alone! He was,
however, a guest at Faith's wedding. So much for the self-styled
Dark Invader.

To return to Washington in 1915. The Archibald and Rintelen
affairs had opened the eyes of the American authorities to some of
Papen's and Boy-Ed's more questionable activities, a process which
was certainly hastened by Gaunt. Gaunt had found an ally in the
Editor of the *Providence Journal*, John R. Rathom, like himself
Australian born. The Naval Attaché supplied Rathom with a great

[1] See *Three Wars with Germany*, Hall & Peaslee, Putnam, New York, 1944.

many stories of the un-neutral behaviour of the Germans, which appeared simultaneously in the *New York Times* and so attracted much attention. The crunch came in December when the *New York Times*, primed by the Administration as well as Gaunt, carried banner headlines about German plots in Mexico and named Papen and Boy-Ed, together with Rintelen as chief instigators. Despite their denials, the two Attachés were declared persona non grata and had to be recalled to Germany. As diplomats they of course enjoyed immunity from capture by the British, but Hall did not consider that this immunity extended to the baggage of enemy diplomats. When Papen's ship called at Falmouth on 3 January 1916, his person and possessions were subjected to the most rigorous search. Papen[1] had expected this and had taken care not to bring with him anything incriminating – or so he thought. On the contrary; he had most foolishly kept the stubs of his cheque books from 28 August 1914 to 21 December 1915. Careful analysis soon showed disbursements to German agents already known to have been involved in sabotage in the United States and Canada. Hall must have thought that this might at last persuade President Wilson to move, because on this occasion he went to Page, who gladly sent the details on to Lansing, the Secretary of State. Lansing at once asked for copies of all papers seized, because he felt that details which might seem of no importance to the British would be of use to the American Department of Justice. Lansing was by now fully converted to the idea that Germany was America's enemy and that war was the only answer, but nothing would deflect Wilson from his self-appointed role as arbiter of world peace. It needed another twelve months and the Zimmermann Telegram to change his mind.

Hall took particular trouble to keep all his naval attachés well informed, writing personally to them at frequent intervals. It is therefore unfortunate that the correspondence he exchanged with Gaunt is not available, nor that with Mr (later Sir) William

---

[1] Von Papen was of course allowed to continue his voyage back to the Fatherland. If no great shakes as a spy master he was certainly a survivor. Later in the war he obtained a post on the staff of the German General von Falkenhayn in Palestine. In Nazareth in 1918 he had to run for his life, and once again left valuable papers behind him. He survived the revolution in Germany, ingratiated himself with Hindenburg in the thirties and was Chancellor of Germany in 1932, was Hitler's Vice-Chancellor in 1933, survived the Night of the Long Knives, managed to get himself appointed German Ambassador in Ankara, and so survived the plot against Hitler in 1944, in which he was involved, was tried at Nuremberg as a war criminal and survived that. A very slippery character.

Wiseman,[1] the business man who became head of the British Secret Service in the United States. Until the new route for the Swedish Roundabout was discovered in the middle of 1916, Hall must have depended largely on Gaunt's reports. The occasional item of interest did, however, continue to emerge from intercepted letters. An amusing, if not very helpful, sample was a letter which Hall forwarded to the Foreign Office in October 1916; this gave the salaries of all German diplomatic and consular staff in the United States, showing that Bernstorff was in receipt of $6793.36 per month, paid in advance, while Hossenfelder, the Consul-General in New York, was paid only $1421.66 a month. Bernstorff's salary was equivalent to about £1,200 per month at the then current rate of exchange – a pretty fabulous salary.

*

Before dealing with the immediate aftermath of the Zimmermann telegram and the developments which took place after the American declaration of war, we must introduce Bell's superior and contact in the State Department, Leland Harrison. Harrison was a year younger than Bell, but he had joined the Foreign Service two years before him. He was also a New Yorker. He had received part of his education at Eton (yet another old Etonian!) and had graduated from Harvard three years after Bell. He had served as 2nd Secretary in the London Embassy from 1910 to 1912 before being promoted to 1st Secretary in Bogota. He was assigned for duty in the State Department in March 1915. He was thus fully au fait with the London scene and also had a good insight into South American affairs. He, too, was a man of the greatest discretion. Herbert Yardley, the future head of the US Army's Cryptographic bureau, described him as 'positively the most mysterious man and secretive man I have ever known . . . He was almost a human sphinx, and when he did talk his voice was so low that I had to strain my ears to catch the words.'

The Germans were naturally most anxious to establish how and where the Zimmermann telegram had been compromised. On 12 March a certain Dr Göppert, who had amongst other duties assumed charge of the diplomatic cipher bureau in 1911, submitted a report detailing the codes in use by the Service and the steps which

---

[1] Just as Hall gave the World War II DNI, Godfrey, a great deal of help and advice in 1939, Wiseman was still in New York when William Stephenson arrived in New York in 1940 to assume similar responsibilities.

had been taken to render them secure. These had included the withdrawal in 1912 of older codes and their replacement with code 5950, and the supply of 13040 to those missions in the Americas which did not already possess it. 13040, although an older code, appeared, because it had not been much used, to be perfectly secure. In addition, Washington had been supplied with reciphering tables for use with its existing codes in communicating with the other posts in the Americas. It could not be established at the time of the report whether Bernstorff had used a recipherment for 13040 when transmitting the Zimmermann telegram to Mexico, but it seemed likely that he had not done so.

Suspicion at first fell on lack of security on the part of Eckhardt and his fat secretary, Herr Magnus, and the Minister was instructed to report how the message had been decoded by him and where the originals and plain language copies were kept, as 'various indications suggest that treachery was committed in Mexico.' Eckhardt replied indignantly on 30 March that 'Greater caution than is always exercised here would be impossible . . . The text is read to me at night in my dwelling house by Magnus in a low voice . . .' His servant, who did not understand German, slept elsewhere and only Eckhardt and Magnus knew the combination of the safe in which the telegrams were kept. He went on to throw suspicions on the security arrangements in Washington, and ended up by demanding to be informed immediately that 'we are exculpated, as we doubtless shall be; otherwise, I insist, as does Magnus also, on a judicial investigation . . .' This bold counter-attack had immediate effect. On 4 April Berlin cabled that 'after your telegram it is hardly conceivable that betrayal took place in Mexico . . . No blame rests on you or Magnus.'

Back in the Wilhelmstrasse Dr Göppert was pursuing his investigations, and he by no means ignored the possibility that 13040 could have been compromised. Unfortunately for him, he was thrown right off the right scent by Hall's low cunning. Although Göppert did mention the possibility that the American Government might have received some help from the British, he was obviously convinced from the outset that the betrayal had resulted from American not British action. Accepting this theory, he concentrated on an examination of how this could have happened. He pointed out that the message had been handed to the American Ambassador in Berlin, who had transmitted it via Copenhagen to the State Department (which he would not have done had he been aware of its contents), and that the State Department had immediately passed it on to Bernstorff. The fact that the American Government were so obviously surprised at the announcement of the U-boat campaign showed that they could not, on 19 January, have had any knowledge of the contents of the message to Bernstorff. Then there was the long delay before the telegram was made public, and added to this was the absence of any reference to the cable sent to Eckhardt direct on 8 February, instructing him to open negotiations with Carranza at once without waiting for an American declaration of War. Then there was the difference between the text[1] of the telegram to Bernstorff and that sent on by him to Eckhardt. All this convinced the good doctor that compromise of code 13040 was most improbable. Ignoring entirely the Swedish Roundabout, he concluded that the only possible explanation seemed to be that the Americans had obtained a plain text copy of the message by some means or another, possibly by the treachery or carelessness of some member of the Chancery staff in Washington. Reassured by Dr Göppert's long, and careful report, the Wilhelmstrasse continued, for the time being, to use 13040 for communications with their representatives in America south of the United States. They did, admittedly, have great difficulties to overcome if new codes were to be supplied; in the end they had to rely, as we shall see, on the naval VB code. The extraordinary feature about this is that, on 5 February Berlin had asked Eckhardt if he was au fait with the new ciphering method for 5950 used by Bernstorff, and had apparently received an affirmative reply. Not only that, but on 4 March Eckhardt was told by Berlin 'that cipher 13040 is compromised and must not be used for secret communications. Please inform Minister at Havana of the foregoing by means of secret ciphering method. Report by telegraph when this has been done.' The Wilhelmstrasse must have felt that the reciphering process rendered an insecure code secure whether it was 5950 or 13040. It is a curious fact that although Göppert was a little more open minded than the *Admiralstab* had been when confronted with the suspicion that the SKM might have been compromised, and proof that the HVB had been, the Germans preferred to attribute their misfortunes to spies or

---

[1] The main differences were the preamble, the date and the number of the telegrams. It was typical of Hall's genius that he had foreseen that such discrepancies would be found, and that they would persuade the Germans that the telegram had been compromised between America and Mexico rather than between Berlin and Washington.

traitors rather than to admit to themselves that their own technical arrangements could be to blame. They made exactly the same mistake in World War II over their naval Enigma. In all three cases the investigations were carried out by the very experts who were responsible for the real failures.

It was no doubt purely a coincidence that Hall was promoted Rear-Admiral in April 1917, but the award of a KCMG six months later was undoubtedly recognition of his faultless handling of the situation. Herr Zimmermann was less fortunate; he had to resign. Page hastened to congratulate Hall and to pass on a message from President Wilson, assuring Hall of his 'very great appreciation of what he has done and of the spirit in which he has done it.' Colonel House wrote personally saying, 'I cannot think of any man who has done more useful service in the war than you, and I salute you.' Although the KCMG is now bestowed exclusively on the recommendation of the Foreign Office, this was not the case at that time, and many naval officers received this honour. We have it, however, on the authority of James, that the Admiralty had nothing to do with Hall's award. 'It was made,' says James, 'on the recommendation of authorities other than the Admiralty.' When Hall retired Lord Hardinge wrote to the Admiralty to 'express our appreciation of the ever-willing and valuable help which he has always given me. It goes without saying that over so wide a field as that in which foreign relations and naval intelligence have a common demominator, there have been differences of opinion, but it is due to the DNI's[1] personal charm and loyalty that they have left no ill-feelings on either side; in the far more numerous matters in which there has been complete agreement his advice and co-operation have been as useful as his resourcefulness and energy have been encouraging. He will be a great loss to the many friends he now counts within these walls. I have written these few words because they voice not my own feelings alone but those of the Foreign Office as a whole.' It is probable that Hall's KCMG was proposed by the Foreign Office, and that Arthur Balfour, who may well have sensed that the Admiralty would do nothing, had a hand in it. Certainly, the promotion and the decoration added to Hall's prestige both inside and outside the Admiralty.

In Washington, Harrison had taken steps to obtain copies of all

---

[1] It is not clear when Hall's title was changed from Director of Intelligence, (DID), to Director of Naval Intelligence, (DNI), but it apparently occurred towards the end of the war. To Blinker's own staff he always remained their DID.

Bernstorff's cables, and a stream of them were despatched to Bell with the request that he obtain decodes from Hall. The majority of them were messages to the German representatives in Buenos Aires, Bogotá, Montevideo, Port au Prince, Santiago, Lima, Havana and Guatemala and had been sent in January and February. At first Bell passed these personally to Hall, but after a time the matter became one of routine and Bell dealt either with Serocold or Herschell. Montgomery was kept busy, and Bell must have met him as his papers contain more than one reference to 'the Padre'. Bell's relations with 'our friends', as he called Hall and Room 40 in his reports to Harrison, became very close. Hall could see that, with the United States as an ally much material which had previously escaped his net could be secured with American co-operation, and that counter-measures in Mexico and South America could often be undertaken more easily by the Americans than by the British. This was especially valuable because the British Secret Service was not very effective throughout Latin America, and Hall's own men were stretched to the limit. Nor was the Foreign Office particularly interested; indeed they relied, according to Bell, very largely for information from Hall even on political matters. Lloyd Hirst was Secretary of the Mexican Committee which met fortnightly under the chairmanship of the Foreign Secretary. Lloyd Hirst states that he supplied the Committee with most of its information. There were, therefore, obvious mutual advantages in increasing the interchange of information about German propaganda and sabotage activities in North, Central and South America. This interchange, however, stopped short of the supply of any cryptological expertise. It was not only Hall's main bargaining weapon but enabled him to exert considerable influence on the way in which the State Department handled the intelligence which was passed to Bell.

After the American declaration of war, the Germans redoubled their efforts to involve Mexico and to stir up trouble in South America by propaganda and sabotage of all sorts, including the planting of bombs on ships carrying supplies for the Allies, by infecting stored grain and spreading disease among cattle, horses and mules. Carranza was upset by the revelations of the Zimmermann telegram, but nevertheless remained hostile to President Wilson and rejected his attempts to improve relations. In the Argentine and Brazil, however, where German influence had been strong, public opinion reacted adversely to the unrestricted U-boat campaign. Count Luxburg, the German Ambassador in Buenos

Aires, although contemptuous of the Argentinians (he referred to them in one telegram decoded by Room 40 as being 'under a thin veneer, Indians'), was anxious to prevent Argentina from following the American example and pressed his Government to relax the U-boat campaign so far as Argentine ships were concerned. One Argentinian ship, the *Toro*, had been sunk and although the German Government paid full compensation, they cabled Luxburg that 'The proposed sparing of ships must absolutely remain secret, otherwise submarine war would be endangered. As blockade area rests on principle of retaliation, not on international law, the note must contain a limitation in this sense. Full compensation is guaranteed in regard to the *Toro* but, in view of the precedent involved, this is to be attributed, not to liberality, but to the circumstances that this course is justified by the facts.'

On 19 May Luxburg cabled the Wilhelmstrasse, by the Swedish Roundabout: 'This Government has now released German and Austrian ships in which hitherto a guard has been placed. In consequence of the settlement of the *Monte (Protegido)* case, there has been a great change in public feeling. Government will in future only clear Argentine ships as far as Las Palmas. I beg that the small steamers *Oran* and *Guazo*, 31 January [meaning, which sailed on that date], 300 tons, which are now nearing Bordeaux with a view to a change of flag, may be spared if possible, or else sunk without a trace being left ['*spurlos versenkt*'].'

Luxburg took a more cynical or tougher line than Bernstorff had done. On 3 July he cabled, 'I learn from a reliable source that the Acting Minister of Foreign Affairs, who is a notorious ass and an Anglophile, declared in a secret session of the Senate that Argentina would demand from Berlin a promise not to sink more Argentine ships. If not agreed to, relations would be broken off. I recommend refusal and, if necessary, calling in the mediation of Spain.' He followed this up the next week with a further telegram: 'Without showing any tendency to make concessions postpone reply to Argentine Note until receipt of further reports. A change of Ministry is probable. As regards Argentine steamers, I recommend either compelling them to turn back, sinking them without leaving any traces, or letting them through. They are all quite small.'

There is no particular reason to suppose that these telegrams, made in 13040, presented any very great difficulties to Montgomery and his colleagues in Room 40's diplomatic section, but once again Hall seems to have held his hand until he judged the moment ripe to disclose them. He has left no record of the episode, but he must once more have had to weigh the advantages – perhaps an Argentinian declaration of war – against the risk – even greater this time – that the Germans would realise that their codes were compromised. There was also the question of the Swedish Roundabout; had the time now come when it would be better to sever this means of German overseas communication, or was the information it disclosed to Room 40 of such importance to Britain that the line should be kept open?

By the end of August 1917, the decision had been taken and on 31 August Page informed the President in a Most Secret cable that 'Admiral Hall . . . has given me a number of documents comprising German cipher messages between German diplomatic officers and the Berlin Foreign Office, chiefly relating to the Argentine and definitely implicating the Swedish Government. In view of the negotiations now going on between Germany and the Argentine, the British Government hope that you will immediately publish these telegrams asking that their origin be kept secret as in the case of the Zimmermann telegram. I have the cipher originals and am sending them to you by a trustworthy messenger [William Wiseman] who will deliver them into your hands about 12-15 September. These telegrams also prove that Sweden has continuously used her legations and pouches and her code to transmit official information between Berlin and German diplomatic officers . . .' Page then gave the English text of the telegrams of 19 May and of 3 and 19 July. He also, for the first time, gave the text of Eckhardt's plea that Cronholm be awarded the *Kronenorden*.

Hall had decided that it was now time to 'come clean', or at least a little 'cleaner' with the American Government. He provided Page with an explanatory memorandum, describing exactly how the Swedish Roundabout had been used by the Germans since the outbreak of war. The statement concluded, 'Nothing but the most urgent Allied reasons can justify the exposure of this system and the loss of supremely valuable intelligence thereby entailed. At the present time, the immediate objects to be achieved are:

1. Entry of Argentina into the war on the side of the Allies, or at least severance of diplomatic relations with Germany.
2. Discrediting the pro-German party in Sweden and thereby aiding in the election of Mr Branting to power at the forthcoming general election.

3. Effect upon Austria at the exposure of German methods which would be greatly accentuated if Argentina joins the Allies.
4. Effect in the remaining neutral countries – Spain in particular.
5. Effect in Bulgaria and Turkey at the further exhibition of German clumsiness.
6. Effect in Germany at the advent of further enemies, should Argentina break with Germany.'

Lansing and the President were agreeable to releasing the telegrams to the American Press in the same way that the Zimmermann telegram had been disclosed, but once again required Bell personally to decode them in the Admiralty. The effect on public opinion both in the United States and in Argentina was predictably enormous. Nor did the Germans attempt to deny the authenticity of the messages, but the cynical phrase '*spurlos versenkt*' was something the Germans found hard to explain away. Luxburg was given his passports, but there was considerable delay in arranging his safe passage back to Germany. He complained bitterly of the humiliating conditions in which he claimed he was compelled to live. He had previously cabled Berlin, 'Whether it is a case of theft of documents or betrayal of a cipher I am unable to say with certainty. I infer the latter.' 13040 seems to have gone out of use, and where communications could be established – because at last the Swedes had to stop acting as postmen and telegraph boys for the Germans – the *Verkehrsbuch* had to be employed.

Having taken the decision to destroy the Swedish Roundabout, Hall was anxious to convince the US Government of Stockholm's complete co-operation with Berlin, and for the first time disclosed to Bell the precise channels by which Zimmermann's telegram had reached Eckhardt – via the Swedish Legation in Buenos Aires, thence to Luxburg and so to Bernstorff, and also showed him for the first time the telegram of 8 February instructing Eckhardt to make an immediate approach to Carranza. In his cable to Harrison of 17 September, Bell reported that Lord Hardinge had stated that all telegrams to and from the Swedish Foreign Office were being held in London with the exception of those of the Swedish Legation in London. There had been no reaction from the Swedes.

Argentina did not declare war but did sever diplomatic relations with Germany. Brazil, however, formally joined the Allies. The

Swedish General Election resulted in replacement of the right-wing, pro-German Government by a pro-Ally Liberal/Social Democrat Coalition under Eden and Branting.

Hall also supplied Bell with details of the activities of Chakravati and other Indian nationalists in the States, but was somewhat put out when the conspirators were all arrested. He had never taken them very seriously, having formed the opinion that their reports to Berlin contained more fiction than fact and were designed solely to secure handsome German subsidies. Nevertheless, some useful information had been gleaned from them and Hall would have preferred to have kept the line open for this reason.

German agents were another matter, and the activities of a certain Dr Delmar, a naturalised US citizen but in fact a representative of the German General Staff, who had reached Madrid en route to Mexico, were followed with considerable interest. The Germans refused to abandon their ideas of involving Mexico, convinced that this would prevent the United States from taking any active part in the war in Europe. Delmar had plans for running arms to Mexico in four blockade runners and for the supply of equipment for a wireless station, which was essential after the collapse of the Swedish Roundabout. It was also hoped to sabotage the Mexican oil wells and to organise extensive sabotage in the United States by Irish-Americans. All this came to light because Delmar's subordinate in Mexico, Dr Gehrman, managed to get to Spain in a Spanish ship. He requested onward transport to Germany by U-boat, but this could not be arranged, and a great deal of information flashed to and fro between Berlin and Madrid by wireless in the VB code, the only available code now believed to be safe by the German Embassy in Madrid. There were frequent alarums and excursions on the British and American side concerning the proposed movements of the two Germans, including the information that Dr Gehrman had 'concealed about his person or baggage one or more phials containing germ culture for the purpose of poisoning cattle or human beings.' In the end it all came to nothing. Dr Delmar died of influenza before he could put his rather grandiose plans into operation.

German communications with the Western Hemisphere became increasingly difficult, but they did manage to gain control of a wireless station at Ixtapalapa in Mexico which was capable of receiving messages from Nauen, although it is not now clear if it could also transmit. By this time Hall's 'star man', A. E. W. Mason was established in Mexico under the disguise of an eccentric British lepidopterist (he hated butterflies and knew nothing about them!). In July 1918 he managed to put the station out of action by destruction of its audion lamps, which could not be replaced. Bell, commenting on this, reported to Harrison that it was not clear how Jahnke, the principal German agent in Mexico, would be able to keep in touch with Berlin.

This is, however, anticipating events, and we must return to the autumn of 1917, and another example of Hall's constant concern to protect his source, Room 40, and yet to extract the maximum value from its information. He had little faith in the ability of politicians to keep their mouths shut; whatever he may have felt about security in the French Navy, he rated French politicians even lower, if that were possible, than English ones. The French Army had suffered devastating casualties from the very first day of the war. For two years it had had to bear the greater share of the fighting on the Western Front. It had fought with tremendous courage, but the failure of the Nivelle offensive in April 1917 was the last straw. In May virtually the whole of the French Army was in a state of passive disobedience if not open mutiny. Lloyd George correctly remarked that 'The British Army was the one Allied Army in the field which could be absolutely relied on for any enterprise', which does a great deal to explain the agonies of Passchendaele. Defeatism was widespread in France. The French Government took the most energetic steps both in the Army and on the Home Front. Pétain, the victor of Verdun, managed, by standing strictly on the defensive, to restore discipline in the Army, and Clemenceau, who became Premier, tackled the traitors among the journalists and politicians. Monsieur Caillaux, an ex-Prime Minister was arrested as was Monsieur Malvy, the Minister of the Interior. One of the other individuals arrested was a certain Bolo Pasha, a shady individual of Egyptian extraction. He was in German pay and mixed up with *Le Bonnet Rouge*, a defeatist left-wing paper heavily subsidised by the Germans.

Room 40's attack on old material now paid dividends. Intercepted messages from Bernstorff showed that Bolo had approached Bernstorff, almost certainly with Caillaux's backing, in Februray 1915, for a loan of $1,700,000 to bring about peace – obviously peace on terms satisfactory to Germany. Hall could see that, by October 1917, the Allied cause depended on Clemenceau, 'The Tiger', extirpating all traces of defeatist, pro-German elements in

Rear-Admiral Sir Reginald Hall, Director of Intelligence 1914—18. Sketch by Louis Raemaker

Commander Lord Herschell RNVR
and unknown French Officer, Paris
1919

Commander Claud Serocold RNVR

Commander Alastair Denniston
RNVR

**Paymaster Lieutenant-Commander
William Clarke RNVR**

Lieutenant-Commander Nigel de Grey RNAS

Lieutenant Walter Bruford RNVR

Herr Arthur Zimmermann, German
Foreign Minister, 1917

Captain 'Bubbles' James RN, *c.* 1920

Programme cover of ID 25 Concert, 11 December 1918

'The *Seydlitz* is in Scapa Flow'. The famous battle cruiser and other units of the *Hochseeflotte* in internment, 1918

Surrendered
German U-boats
at Harwich, 1918

France. The Bolo-Bernstorff messages, if made available to the French authorities, would be of considerable assistance in achieving this object. This would, however, mean disclosing secrets of Room 40's success to the French. Whether because of fears of French security, or because he was unwilling to let the French cryptanalysts know how much had been achieved, Hall did not hand the incriminating messages to the French, but decided, instead, to follow the precedent, which had worked so well, of the Zimmermann and Luxburg telegrams, and pass the information to the Americans. On 2 October Bell forwarded the relevant decodes to Harrison, and on the following day Page cabled the President that 'The British authorities have not communicated these telegrams to the French as to do so would divulge the source of information which for reasons of their own they wish to avoid. They would however be glad if you would do so. As it is quite possible that, for internal political reasons, the French may not find it desirable to make public the contents of the telegrams or the fact that they have received them, the British authorities ask that they may be informed when the telegrams are handed to the French Government so that they may know for certain that the French have the information.' All this was duly done. Bolo Pasha was convicted and executed in February 1918.

We cannot be sure that Hall had information about Monsieur Caillaux at this time, because it was not until January 1918 that he showed Bell a series of telegrams from Luxburg in Buenos Aires disclosing evidence of treasonable activities by Caillaux during a visit to the Argentine in February 1915. These telegrams had of course reached Germany via the Swedish Foreign Office. Bell cabled them to Harrison on 9 January 1918, with a covering request from Hall that they be given to the French Government in the same way as those concerning Bolo had been. Bell went on, 'To save time and to ensure this most important information reaching the proper quarters, they venture to suggest that it be not handed to the French Ambassador at Washington but telegraphed to Sharp [US Ambassador in Paris] with instructions to place it himself in Clemenceau's hands in order that it may be certain to reach him directly without the possibility of its existence becoming known to Caillaux's friends.' Once more the Americans were prepared to play ball, and the incriminating telegrams were discreetly used by the prosecutor in Caillaux's trial. This was, however, a very protracted affair, even by French standards, and was not concluded until 1920 when

Caillaux was sentenced to a short period of imprisonment and ten years' loss of civil rights.

Hall was, however, less successful in getting the Americans to play his game in the case of the Irish. The harshness with which the British authorities had suppressed the Easter Rising in Ireland in 1916 had transformed the general apathy of the Irish public towards the Sinn Fein into a degree of support. In May 1918 the Lord Lieutenant of Ireland, Field Marshall Lord French, an Irishman himself but not the most intelligent or stable of British generals, decided to arrest all the Nationalist leaders. This was obviously going to cause a crisis in Anglo-Irish and possibly in Anglo-American relations. Room 40 had by now decoded thirty-two communcations between Bernstorff and his Government between 1914 and 1917, showing conclusively, in Bell's words, that the German Government 'was involved both in the insurrection of Easter 1916 and in a similar outbreak planned for February last year [1917] and later postponed. In order to give the appearance of consistency in respect of previous disclosures of German telegrams, all of which have been made by our Government, Hall would, in communicating the documents to higher authority for publication, have to intimate that after inter-changing information with the American secret service for a period of over a year he is now in a position to decipher German messages himself . . .' Hall attempted to put the pressure on the President by indicating that he might be compelled by higher British authority to publish the documents before they reached the President, but said that he would do his best not to do so. He added that three of the messages from Bernstorff were appended, without the American Government's knowledge, to cipher telegrams sent for him by the Department of State. This combination of cajolery and blackmail failed. The President took eleven days to reply. He then stated that the American Government, believing that disclosure would create difficulties both for the British and US governments, was 'not prepared to publish these documents at this time and is not willing publicly to sanction their publication.' Hall's bluff had been called. Whether he had really approached Bell before discussing the question fully with the Home Secretary is not known, but it is quite possible. The incriminating documents were never published.

Nor was Hall any more successful in persuading the American authorities to adopt his Old Testament views on the punishment of Americans convicted of treachery. In a considerable number of cases, Hall was able to supply Bell with information about German agents in the United States which sometimes was the prime cause of their arrest and in others gave proof of their guilt. One such case was that of Heinrich Bode, a spy and bomb expert who had been apprehended by the US Immigration authorities. Bode was a naturalised American, had deserted from the US Army and had also served in the German Army. Hall asked for Bode to be shipped to England, where he would have received very short shrift, but this was refused. Hall then pressed Bell to ensure that, if convicted, Bode should be sentenced to death. In passing on this request, Bell wrote to Harrison in September 1918, 'I know you will give every consideration to what Hall says, for this is not a mere matter of his interfering in our internal affairs. It is largely on the information he has been able to supply that we have kept track of Bode and others . . . The other authorities in the US probably have no idea to what an extent our Government is indebted to Hall, but as you do know I hope you will do what is possible to see that his views are properly presented in the right quarter . . .' Bode was very lucky to get away with a sentence of ten years' hard labour for desertion from the US Army.

One of the most successful German agents in South America went by the name of Arnold. Bell described him as 'a nice quiet fellow who for the past two years has been engaged in the Argentine in sabotage work against shipping; introducing fungus in stored grain; innoculation of mules with glanders; and the promotion of strikes harmful to Allied interests . . .' Thanks to Anglo-American co-operation, Herr Arnold's activities were brought to a halt.

That Bell was by now on intimate social terms with Herschell, in charge of the Intelligence Division's Spanish and Spanish-American desk, is evidenced by this note to Harrison when the latter was attending the Peace Conference, 'He is the most genial soul but unfortunately on the water waggon at the present moment!' He was also very friendly with Serocold, and was addressing his letters to Hall, 'Dear Hall'.

Of course, all matters of purely naval interest were dealt with by Admiral William S. Sims. Sims had been sent to London immediately after the American declaration of war to assume command of all USN forces in the European theatre. The Royal Navy took him to their hearts at once. He and Jellicoe became firm friends, and there were no secrets between them. His relations with Hall were also excellent, and he was made fully aware of Room 40's

naval work. Hall briefed him daily and in addition any information
from decodes affecting the American eastern seaboard, was passed
to Washington, although without disclosing its source. Sims, like
Page and Bell, was the soul of discretion, but although in overall
charge of the US Navy in Europe, he did not have operational
control. USN detachments, whether they were Admiral Rodman's
battleships with the Grand Fleet, the destroyers and escorts at
Queenstown or Gibraltar or elsewhere, were fully integrated into
the appropriate Royal Navy command. There could therefore be no
question of Sims or of anyone else sending USN officers the fruits of
Room 40's work. Nor is this in the least surprising, when one
remembers the very limited number of most senior British officers
who received this priceless information. The 'need to know' theory
was not invented by Admiral Ernie King in World War II.[1] Indeed,
it is clear that the Assistant Secretary to the Navy, Franklin D.
Roosevelt, who visited London in 1918 and who was greatly
interested in Intelligence and met and formed a great admiration for
Blinker Hall, was totally unaware of the existence of Room 40. Sims
was certainly kept very fully supplied with all the relevant naval
information which he required, which put him in a strong position
vis à vis the Director of Naval Intelligence in Washington, Captain
Roger Welles, who was doing his best to make bricks without straw.
The relations between the two were not good.

Although Sims received all the naval information he wanted, he
was not aware of the work of Room 40's diplomatic section, and this
led to an amusing contretemps at the beginning of 1918. Sims had
insisted, against Welles' wishes, that US Naval Attachés in Europe
should send their reports to him so that they could be checked
against the much better British information before being forwarded
to Washington. It was humiliating for Welles, but in fact a sensible
proposal. On one occasion, however, Sims slipped up. The Naval
Attaché in Madrid, Captain Benton C. Decker, was energetic if
nothing else, and reported that the Germans were sending wireless
messages from every important town in Spain. On 16 February Bell
cabled Harrison urgently that he had 'just learned that on 31
December Admiral Sims informed the American Embassy at Madrid that wireless messages in cipher were being transmitted from
Spain to Berlin and requested that 'this grave matter be taken up
seriously with the Spanish Government.' Please discreetly take such
steps as may be necessary to prevent the occurrence of any such

[1] Commander-in-Chief US Fleet, 1942–45.

catastrophe.' It would indeed have been a catastrophe if Sims had got his way; the Berlin-Madrid link was now Germany's only means of communicating with the outside world, and the 'Lord Mayor' and his staff in the Diplomatic Section would have become immediately redundant if it had been severed. Fortunately, the calamity was averted.

Captain Decker caused other difficulties. He had been endeavouring to build up his own network of agents in competition with Colonel 'Charles the Bold' Thoroton, Royal Marines, a rather forlorn task. Decker accused Thoroton of being a 'loose liver', (he was apparently living with a woman to whom he was not married and was certainly no teetotaller). The feud caused a certain amount of acrimony, but Hall expressed the most complete confidence in Thoroton; he was not interested in morals, only in results, and these Charles the Bold was producing in full measure. Decker got no support from his superiors. The Office of Naval Intelligence in Washington was making enormous efforts to catch up with its British counterpart, but in Spain, as in Holland and Scandinavia, the British had established too great a lead. It was better to eat humble pie, and learn from veterans hardened by the bitter experience of more than three years of war.

Hall was very willing to share his secrets whether diplomatic or naval with the Americans, where he could see that it was to the advantage of the Allied cause. What he would not do, despite continual requests both from the Office of Naval Intelligence and the State Department, was to impart to them any cryptographic expertise or to assist them in any way to establish their own cryptographic bureau. America, like Britain, had started the war without any such organisation. By June 1917 the War Department had begun to create a cipher bureau under Major Van Deman of the General Staff's Military Intelligence Branch. Almost his first recruit was a brash young cipher clerk from the State Department, Herbert O. Yardley, a born cryptologist who became the first head of MI8, the Army's Cipher Bureau. But Yardley had to start completely from scratch without any of the 'pinches' which had enabled Room 40 to make an initial breakthrough. He was, moreover, also preoccupied with work on devising new American codes, and so made little progress for many months in attacking German ones. The US Navy also attempted to set up a code-breaking unit, but with even less success. Quite early on the Navy agreed to turn over this work to the Army, a clear indication of how hopeless they thought the task was! In November 1917 Harrison asked Bell to obtain a copy of the second edition of the HVB code, and this Hall did supply, pointing out quite truthfully that it was no longer being used and would be of no value to the Americans.

In the meantime, the Americans continued, through Bell, to supply Room 40 with copies of coded messages which they had secured and which were immediately passed to Herschell for the Padre's attention. Many of them were old messages but some were new ones obtained in Stockholm and elsewhere in neutral countries. The decodes were returned to Bell with little delay. Nauen was continuing to send messages to agents in Mexico and South America, some of which were intercepted by US Y stations and passed by the Navy to Yardley's MI8 section, but he was not able to make any real progress with them. In July 1918 Harrison told Bell that what he was 'working for is, if possible, complete co-operation and exchange of information . . . for our cipher bureau with Britain and France.' Although he expected that 'the Bureau will shortly be in a position to do good work . . .' he had to admit that 'We are unfortunately in the position where we have much to learn and perhaps nothing to offer.' A Transatlantic Radio Conference was being held in Paris, and Bell had to report that Hall 'is absolutely opposed to any definite arrangement for the general pooling of this class of information because he feels certain that it would end in the source becoming compromised through leakage, particularly if certain Allies were in regular receipt of it. Hall sees to it that our naval authorities here receive information from this source, and our Military Command in France is doubtless in close touch with the French who also have access to this source . . .' From a later message it is clear that Hall was anxious about Italian security. He told Bell that he hoped to be able to make arrangements with the French to avoid duplication of information supplied to the Americans. Bell concluded his report by saying that Hall had assured him that the United States would receive 'all necessary information. 'This,' said Bell, 'is the best I can do at present.'

While it was perfectly true that Hall was worried about cryptographic security if too many people of different nations were made privy to the secret, it must be pointed out that he had been in close contact with the Russians from October 1914 up to the time of the Bolshevik Revolution, and that for the past year at least he had been working with the Italians on Austrian, though not German, codes, and that there had been a considerable interchange with the French.

The hard fact was, as Harrison had stated, that the American cipher bureau had really nothing, at this stage, to offer in exchange. Hall was not prepared to give away Room 40's immense lead and the power and influence which it conveyed without a substantial quid pro quo. To decode German messages obtained from American sources was one thing; to disclose the process by which this was achieved was altogether a different kettle of fish.

Even in obtaining coded messages, the Americans still had something to learn from the British. Harrison ruefully cabled Bell in June 1918 that the American Intelligence officer attached to the Legation in Stockholm had been offered ten German telegrams, but while he was consulting the Minister, the agent had gone off and sold them to the British. Bell was asked to try and obtain copies from Hall in order to complete the American files!

In August 1918 Yardley paid a visit to London and was introduced to Hall by Bell. The mission was not a success. According to Yardley, Hall refused to give him the VB code so that he could begin to tackle the Berlin-Madrid traffic, but did give him copies of a neutral government's code (which may have been Swedish) and promised to forward a two-volume German naval code to Washington for his personal and unofficial use. It is, in fact, improbable that he achieved even this measure of success, because in May 1919 Harrison wrote to Bell from Paris, concerning two red bound code-books which Bell had obtained many months before. These had been sent to Harrison on the strict understanding that they never left his office, and Harrison had religiously observed these conditions. Now MI8 wished to borrow them. Harrison felt that the situation had changed. The war was over and 'our friends have refused to come across with certain information . . .' (presumably decodes of the sort so regularly passed to Bell previously). Harrison asked Bell if he could see any objection to the Cipher Bureau borrowing the books, as the Bureau 'may properly be considered part of my office . . . on the strict understanding that copies are not to be made, and that no use whatsoever or distribution is to be made of any decodes which they may secure by this manner?'

Moreoever, at the end of 1918 and the beginning of 1919 Yardley had been making persistent attempts, which obviously irritated Bell, to obtain the German naval code (almost certainly the VB code). On 21 January he had written to Bell, 'I feel very certain that if you can get the verbatim German decipherment of the two enclosed messages [Berlin/Madrid] I shall be able to reconstruct the entire German diplomatic code and thereby accomplish myself that which the British and the French have refused to accomplish for me.' Bell had to report that 'Yardley's name was anathema at the Admiralty.' It is scarcely surprising that the aggressive and pushing Yardley failed where the charming Bell, with four years of close and friendly contact behind him, could not succeed.

But Bell had achieved a very great deal for his country. Despite Hall's close relations with Ambassador Page, one cannot help feeling that the solid groundwork upon which confidence was built up between British Naval Intelligence and the American Embassy, was done by Bell. Personalities count for a great deal in all walks of life, but in none more than in the Intelligence field. Bell won the complete confidence of Hall, Serocold and Herschell, and was almost certainly entrusted with more secrets from Room 40 than was the British Foreign Office. He was undoubtedly fortunate in having Leland Harrison behind him, and tribute must be paid to both Harrison and to Secretary of State Lansing for the complete discretion and loyalty with which the information which Bell obtained was handled in Washington. It is sad to have to record that Ned Bell, who would surely have gone to the top in the US Foreign Service, died from a fall in 1924 when serving as Counselor at the American Embassy in Pekin. He was only forty-two.

Ambassador Page barely survived the end of the war. His health broke down and in August 1918 he had to resign and return to the United States. His departure from London was marked by many official tributes to his work for the common cause and by expressions of affection for him personally. He died on 21 December 1918 in North Carolina, aged sixty-one. He had at least seen the realisation of his dream – America standing shoulder to shoulder with the Western Allies to achieve victory over those whom he considered barbarians. Perhaps if Wilson had listened to his advice earlier the world would now be a happier place; it would certainly have been very different.

Leland Harrison was appointed Secretary of the US Commission to Negotiate Peace in 1918. In 1922 he became Assistant Secretary of State, but left the Foreign Service in 1930. In 1937, however, he was appointed to what was to be a vitally important position, Minister to Switzerland, a post which he held throughout World War II. On his death in 1951, Dean Acheson, then Secretary of State, paid him the following tribute: 'During his long term of duty in Switzerland . . . he was frequently obliged to make exceptionally important decisions on his own responsibility, and through his good judgement was able to render valuable service to his country . . .' Those who had known him during World War I would have expected nothing less from this American ex-Etonian.

CHAPTER FIFTEEN

Unrestricted U-Boat Warfare

In the month of April 1917, 869,000 tons of British, Allied and neutral shipping was sunk by the Central Powers, 90 per cent of it by German U-boats.[1] This brought the total lost since the beginning of the year to 2,360,000 tons, compared to a total of 4,000,000 tons sunk in all the preceding twenty-nine months. The *Admiralstab* had promised to bring Britain to her knees within six months of the opening of the unrestricted U-boat campaign; they were well on their way to making good their boast. The world's shipping was being sent to the bottom far faster than it could be replaced, but the same could not be said of the U-boats. From the beginning of the war up to the end of 1916, the Germans had commissioned 170 new U-boats. During the same period they had lost only forty-eight, by no means all of them as a result of enemy action. In January 1917 two were sunk, in February five (one of which by one of its own mines), in March three (again one by a German mine) and in April only one. In the same four months over thirty new U-boats had been commissioned, a further nett gain of twenty. Moreover, these new U-boats were much more formidable craft than those with which Germany had started the war; they were larger, had a greater radius of action, could dive deeper, and carried a heavier gun and torpedo armament. It was not only Britain which was facing disaster; the whole Entente was dependent on the ability of the Royal Navy to staunch the haemorrhage which was bleeding the Alliance to death even more swiftly than the continuing slaughter in the trenches.

However much the British Admiralty may have underestimated

[1] A figure higher than that sunk in any single month in World War II. In March and June 1942, and again in March and June 1943, Allied and neutral shipping from all forms of Axis attack suffered just over 834,000 tons. In April 1917 the total operational U-boat fleet, that is excluding boats engaged in training or working up, was 128. Of these on average no more than 47 were at sea on patrol, or proceeding to or from their operational areas. This figure should be compared with the 125 U-boats *at sea* in all areas at the end of April 1943, when the Battle of the Atlantic reached its climax.

the U-boat threat to trade in 1915, by the end of 1916 they were well aware of the danger and were conscious of how this would be increased when the expected unrestricted U-boat campaign was unleashed. Balfour and Sir Henry Jackson (not to be confused with Thomas Jackson, the Director of Operations) had been replaced as 1st Lord and 1st Sea Lord by Carson and Jellicoe at the end of November 1916, largely as a result of the general dissatisfaction with the failure to bring the U-boat menace under control. Jellicoe at once attacked the problem with energy, but without any great conviction that he would swiftly achieve success. One of his first acts was to create an Anti-Submarine Division of the Naval Staff under Rear-Admiral Duff to supervise and co-ordinate the development of anti-U-boat weapons and tactics. The Division considered every suggestion, no matter how unlikely (as for example the training of circus sealions to detect U-boats). The great majority of proposals were, however, practical ones, such as improvements in hydrophones and depth charges, the wholesale adoption of the paravane,[1] and the placing of large orders for these and other weapons. Steps were at last taken to copy the excellent German mines and to produce the new type in adequate quantities. The net and mine barrier in the Strait of Dover was strengthened and extended when it was learned from Room 40 that in December 1916, the Germans had lifted the ban imposed in April 1915 on larger U-boats using this route to and from the Western Approaches. British minelaying in the Heligoland Bight was stepped up. British submarines were employed to hunt U-boats and a new class, the R class, specifically designed as hunter-killers.[2] Non-rigid airships and aeroplanes were employed to patrol coastal waters (their range was too limited for more distant patrols). Steps were taken to try to economise in the use of merchant shipping and to increase the output of the shipyards. Merchant ships were given heavier defensive armament, and virtually all ocean-going ships were armed. Four routes for merchant shipping approaching the British Isles were laid down, and explicit mandatory instructions concerning their use issued to all ships. Every available small warship was employed in patrolling these approach 'funnels' and in hunting for U-boats in the focal areas. There was no lack of effort or ideas.

[1] A device towed from the bows of ships to cut moored mine cables.
[2] Twelve were ordered in December 1917, but were not completed in time to see active service.

The U-boats were now operating much further afield, often 300 miles out in the Atlantic. Early in 1917, operations off the US seaboard or the coast of Africa were still a rarity, but the majority of losses of merchant ships was now occurring more than fifty miles from land. Although the arming of merchant ships had resulted in a marked drop in losses from gun fire, this had merely resulted, even before 1 February, in most attacks being made by submerged U-boats by torpedo and without warning, a procedure sanctioned by the *Admiralstab* in January if the vessel was thought to be armed. The four' approach routes – cone shaped funnels – to the British Isles, far from making it more difficult for U-boats to find targets, greatly simplified their task. British patrols entirely failed to drive the U-boats away, let alone to sink them; the U-boats merely waited submerged and undetected until the hunting craft had steamed on, and then surfaced to choose their next victim, conveniently directed towards them by the mistaken policy of the Admiralty and the geographical configuration of the British Isles.

Room 40's information about U-boats was still excellent, indeed better than it had ever been. The increase in the number of U-boats at sea, the improvements in their already efficient wireless sets, and the need of the U-boat command to direct its boats to the most profitable areas caused a rise in the volume of wireless traffic. This was of much assistance to Room 40's experts in breaking the changes in key, by now much more frequent, in solving the disguised grid squares in which positions were given, and in identifying changes in call signs which now took place every two months. Sailings and arrivals of U-boats were disclosed as before, although this applied more to the ocean-going boats based on Emden and Wilhelmshaven than to the smaller types operating out of Bruges through Zeebrugge and Ostend. Neumünster continued to broadcast via Norddeich what information it could obtain about British shipping, and to retransmit to boats at sea the experience and advice of those which had just returned to port. The British Direction Finding system was now extensive and efficient[1] and could often fill

---

[1] Just how efficient is hard to say. Based on World War II experience, it is unlikely that fixes were accurate to within a smaller radius than twenty miles from a central point even in the North Sea, while in the more distant areas, out in the Atlantic, a fifty mile radius was probably the best that could be given. A good deal no doubt depended on how recently a decode had given a definite position for the U-boat concerned, and whether it could be indentified by its call sign. Considerable claims were made for 'radio finger printing', the identification of a particular W/T operator by the peculiarities of his operating procedure. World War II experience also suggests that such claims were exaggerated, perhaps as a cloak for decodes.

in the gaps when delays in decoding did occur. The U-boats themselves were becoming more talkative. Although there was nothing like the stream of signals necessitated by the Wolfpack tactics employed in World War II, the more distant operations being undertaken by the beginning of 1917 did require more frequent reports from U-boats at sea and instructions from their shore Command. U-boat patrol areas were frequently designated by a letter of the alphabet. Thus, on 17 February, Hope noted in his diary that as U 67 had reported little traffic in Area B, U 50 had been ordered to go to Area A. He deduced in consequence that Area B was between Ushant and Finisterre. From January onwards U-boats passing outward bound through the English Channel normally reported the route they had taken and any problems encountered, as for example on 4 April when UC 30 reported that the Channel passage had been accomplished without difficulty. From on shore there were constant broadcasts for the benefit of inward-bound U-boats, about which of the swept channels to their bases were open or temporarily closed due to British mining.

Room 40 was therefore able to supply Oliver and Duff with a great deal of invaluable information, often of a detailed and up-to-date nature, and always sufficient to indicate the scale of attack to be anticipated in any particular area. But this was not quite the same thing as being able to pin-point the exact position of an individual U-boat with the degree of accuracy required by anti-submarine patrols to pounce and make a kill. With no radar to assist them and with sea/air co-operation in its infancy, destroyers, sloops and trawlers were almost always themselves sighted by their intended prey before they could sight a surfaced U-boat; despite the improvements in hydrophones, location of a submerged U-boat remained almost entirely a matter of guess work, and was to remain so until the end of the War when ASDIC[1] (named after the Anti-Submarine Detection Investigation Committee) was devised and produced.

A constant stream of signals were sent out by Oliver or Duff. On 1 January, for example, Gibraltar was warned that 'Enemy submarines may be expected to pass through the Straits going east during the nights of 1 to 6 January inclusive. Make every effort to intercept them.' On the same day Queenstown was told that 'An enemy submarine going south may be expected to pass 51 degrees 30 North tomorrow Tuesday.' On 3 January Dover was informed

[1] Sonar, in modern parlance.

that '. . . submarines pass under your nets near the Goodwin end at a depth of 20 to 24 fathoms in vicinity of 2A buoy. Deep mines laid near the bottom seem advisable', and then again, a month later, that 'There is no doubt that submarines are going along French side where there is no barrier.' The next day Dover was told that five minelaying submarines would pass the Strait of Dover to the westward during the next twenty-four hours. Admiral Bacon at Dover found it hard to believe that they had done so, and asked for more information. Oliver replied that there was none, but added that 'we believe route to be west of Sandettie and under nets close to second buoy. It is not clear whether the second buoy is near the Goodwins end or at the Elbow close to Sandettie.' Despite such detailed intelligence, Bacon's counter-measures proved totally in-effective. Yet another example of the accurate information which Room 40 could supply occurred in April. On the 4th Bayly, at Queenstown, was informed that 'An enemy submarine [UC 30] was in 49 degrees 30 North 6 degrees 46 West [some seventy miles south-west of Lands End] apparently with partially disabled en-gines. Will probably return northabout.' It was thought that the U-boat could not dive and could not make more than three knots even on the surface. The U-boat's progress was followed by direc-tionals and its own reports as it struggled north. By 13 April it had reached the vicinity of St Kilda, west of the Outer Hebrides, and ten Grand Fleet destroyers were hunting it despite a strong northerly gale. Four days later the Grand Fleet was told it would pass Muckle Flugga or south of the Shetlands. UC 30 was indeed sighted and unsuccessfully hunted throughout the night of the 16th south of Sumburgh Head. On the 18th, the Admiral commanding the 1st Battle Squadron was forced to report that the U-boat's 'diving qualities were apparently unimpaired and that there was little chance of catching her in the open.' Despite a tremendous effort by the anti-submarine craft lasting a whole fortnight, the crippled U-boat managed to struggle back to the Danish coast, only to meet her end there in a freshly laid British minefield.

Examples such as the above could be multiplied tenfold, but it would be tedious to do so. It was not so much good intelligence that was lacking, but the means of detection and counter-attack at sea. Nor were the efforts to reduce the calls on shipping or to increase the rate of shipbuilding any more successful. Apart from ships actually sunk, dozens more were damaged and the ports were clogged with vessels held up because of unswept mines (laid by

U-boats) or by the known presence of U-boats close offshore. No wonder Jellicoe's natural pessimism turned almost to despair. According to Admiral Sims, who saw Jellicoe on the day after his arrival in London on 9 April, the 1st Sea Lord said to him, 'It is impossible for us to go on with the war if losses like this continue.' He added that he could see no solution to the problem.[1]

There *was*, however, a very simple solution staring him in the face if only he and the rest of the Naval Staff would accept it – Convoy. Convoy – merchant ships sailing in company under naval protection – had been used since medieval times to defeat a '*guerre de course*', and it had, in the end, always done so. In the wars against Revolutionary and Napoleonic France it had been compulsory for all British ocean-going shipping; convoys of a hundred or more ships (sometimes as many as four hundred) had regularly and successfully been shepherded through danger areas by the frigates and sloops of the Royal Navy, such losses as were incurred never exceeding, overall, about a half per cent.[2] But when steam replaced sail both naval and mercantile opinion was that convoy was no longer either necessary or practical. There were many reasons advanced, but the rejection of convoy was certainly partly the result of the mistaken belief held by most naval officers that it was a purely defensive measure and so unworthy of the Royal Navy whose whole tradition was thought to be to seek out and destroy the enemy. This feeling may subconsciously have been strengthened by the dislike, inherited from their forbears, for the dull and unrewarding duty of the escorts, whose mission had been 'the safe and timely arrival of the convoy' rather than the glory of single frigate actions, let alone the chances of making a fortune out of prize money!

There was, nevertheless, a certain ambivalence in the attitude of the Admiralty, even in 1914. *All* troop convoys were then immediately given an escort. In the middle of September, the first Canadian troop convoy, consisting of thirty-one transports, was escorted from Halifax to England by the 12th Cruiser Squadron in which the World War II DNI, John Godfrey, was serving. 'In 1914,' he wrote, 'no naval officer had ever seen a convoy, or had met anyone who had ever seen one. No merchant captain had ever sailed in convoy or had steamed in formation close to other merchant ships

---

[1] Jellicoe later claimed that what he had said was that there seemed to be no *immediate* solution to the problem. There is no doubt, however, that Sims was greatly shocked by the picture Jellicoe painted.

[2] Statistical analysis of this sort was not thought of before 1917.

. . . When we assembled . . . opinion among the captains of the
transports was about equally divided as to the feasibility (as distinct
from the desirability) of convoy. But when . . . we dispersed . . .
everyone, even the most apprehensive, was converted to the idea.'
So, convoy *was* possible with steamships. Convoy was, of course,
intended to meet the threat of attack by surface ships. U-boats, it
was claimed, posed an entirely different problem. Nevertheless,
neither Jellicoe nor Beatty would take the Grand Fleet to sea
without an adequate escort (screen) of destroyers. We have also
seen how, in 1915, the *Lusitania* and other important individual
merchant ships were, on occasions, given destroyer escort.

Gradually, however, a number of British naval officers, including
Beatty, became convinced that the *only* answer to the U-boat
menace was a full scale convoy system. Those who at first opposed
the idea, and they included Jellicoe, Oliver, and Duff, did so not
only because of their mistaken belief in the efficacy of 'offensive'
hunting tactics,[1] but because, in the absence of any reliable statistics, they greatly overestimated the number of ships which would
have to be convoyed and the number of escorts which would be
required to do so. (The statistics which were available, included
every port of call by coasters as a 'safe arrival', thus greatly
understating the true percentage of losses suffered by ocean-going
ships.) Merchant Navy opinion was also said to be against it,
although those masters consulted cannot have been drawn from the
ranks of captains of troopers and others who had actual experience
of sailing in convoy. In the end, the pressure of events and the
limited experience with the Dutch, Scandinavian and French cross-
channel coal trade, in which a form of convoy was instituted at the
beginning of 1917, forced the hands of the diehards on the Naval
Staff. The entry of the United States into the war held out prospects
of additional destroyers becoming available, but there was certainly
strong pressure also from the Prime Minister, Lloyd George. Lloyd
George was primed by accurate statistics supplied surreptiously by
one of Duff's staff, Commander Reginald Henderson, enthusiasti-
cally supported by Mr Norman Leslie, of the Ministry of Shipping.
On 30 April Lloyd George visited the Admiralty, and subsequently
claimed that he had forced the adoption of convoy on a very
reluctant and obstructive Admiralty. In fact, Jellicoe had given his
approval for plans to be worked out for the introduction of an

[1] Why they should have maintained this view in the light of Room 40's accurate
knowledge of the U-boat losses, is inexplicable.

experiment with ocean convoy three days earlier, so the Prime Minister's famous confrontation was probably something of an anti-climax. On 10 May a trial convoy was run from Gibraltar to the UK. It arrived without loss and without having experienced any of the anticipated difficulties. The first eastbound Atlantic convoy sailed from Hampton Roads, Virginia, on 24 May; it lost only one ship. and that a straggler. It should perhaps be recorded that the US Navy (although not Admiral Sims) was as firmly opposed to the idea of convoy as was the British Naval Staff, and it was only due to Sims's ardent advocacy that the Americans finally supplied a modest quota of destroyers for mercantile, as opposed to troop, convoys.

Although driven in desperation to give convoy a trial, Jellicoe, Oliver and Duff – and indeed many other senior officers – were by no means fully converted to the idea, and the organisation and extension of the convoy system proceeded with lamentable slowness. At first only homeward-bound shipping proceeded in convoy; outward-bound and ocean-going ships moving around the British Isles, continued to sail independently. Large numbers of anti-U-boat craft were tied up, almost to the end of the war, on futile 'seek and destroy' missions, which, despite Room 40's excellent information about U-boat movements, continued to fail to find, let alone destroy, a proportionate number of the enemy. By July 1917 most eastbound North Atlantic shipping was sailing in convoy, but it was not until August that approval was given for westbound convoys to be started; it took even longer for convoys to and from West Africa (and U-boats were now operating as far south as the Azores) to be organised. The first through convoy in the Mediterranean did not start until October, while coastal shipping round the UK was not given escort until a few months before the end of the war. By the end of 1917, eight months after approval had first been given for mercantile convoy, only just over half of the UK's overseas trade was receiving this almost foolproof system of protection.

The results were, naturally, predictable. Losses of ships *in convoy* were reduced dramatically – to around one half per cent. But there were still targets in plenty sailing independently. Although tonnage lost in May fell from its April peak to 593,000 tons, it rose again in June to 683,000 tons and even in December still totalled 394,000 tons. Such monthly losses, which continued to exceed new construction substantially, were extremely serious. That the losses were almost all suffered by ships sailing independently, was either ignored or not fully realised by the decision makers in the Admiralty, who continued to be obsessed by the difficulties of providing escorts (without, that is, denuding the forces engaged in the fatuous 'offensive' operations), and who failed to understand the significance of the accurate statistics which were at last being provided. Nevertheless, merchant shipping losses *had* been reduced and sinkings of German U-boats *had* increased. Whereas only eighteen U-boats had been sunk in the first six months of 1917, German losses in the second half of the year amounted to forty-three, although, as Room 40 were well aware, fifty-five new boats had been commissioned during the same period. At least some sort of a tourniquet had been applied, and the loss of blood greatly reduced.

Why was convoy so successful? First, contrary to all expectations, the U-boats at once found it much more difficult to locate targets. A collection of one or two dozen merchant ships steaming in close formation was in fact less easy to find than twelve or twenty-four ships steaming independently. A convoy presented only a comparatively brief opportunity for attack by a single U-boat (for there were no co-ordinated Wolfpack onslaughts), and instead of being able to pursue one ship whose only defensive weapon was a gun, the U-boats had to face immediate and aggressive counter-action by the escorts. To pick off an independent ship required skill, seamanship and hardihood, but was not unduly risky; to press home an attack on a defended convoy required even more skill and a great deal more courage. Such qualities were by no means lacking in the German U-boat commanders and their crews, but, as was the case in 1943, the rapid expansion of the U-boat arm caused personnel problems. Room 40 intercepted more than one signal calling for the transfer of officers from the surface fleet to the U-boats. A feature, also observable in World War II, was that a high percentage of sinkings were obtained by a small proportion of U-boat commanders; losses among these bolder spirits were heavy. For the British, convoy solved the problem, as it had done against French and American privateers one hundred years earlier, of locating the aggressors – convoy was not *merely* a defensive strategy, it provided opportunities for highly offensive tactics.

Karl Dönitz, who in 1918 was a young U-boat commander based on Pola and who was taken prisoner by the British when his boat, UB 68, was sunk by British convoy escorts in the Mediterranean on 3 October 1918, has this to say; '. . . the introduction of the convoy system in 1917 robbed [the U-boat] of its opportunity to become a decisive factor. The oceans at once became bare and empty; for long periods at a time the U-boats, operating individually, would see nothing at all; and then suddenly up would loom a huge concourse of ships . . . surrounded by a strong escort of warships of all types . . . The lone U-boat might well sink one or two of the ships, or even several; but that was a poor percentage of the whole. The convoy would steam on. In most cases no other German U-boat would catch sight of it, and it would reach Britain bringing a rich cargo of foodstuffs and raw materials safely to port.' The conclusion which Dönitz drew from this was that U-boats must be concentrated in sufficient numbers to overwhelm the convoy escorts – the Wolfpack tactics which he employed so successfully in World War II, until they were, in turn, defeated by the provision of adequate British and American sea and air escorts.[1]

The U-boats would, under any circumstances, have found convoys harder to locate than ships sailing independently, but their difficulties were greatly increased by the work of Room 40. At long last evasive routing of shipping based on fairly accurate knowledge of the positions of U-boats and merchant ships, became possible. Quite apart from the fact that in 1917 many merchant ships were still not equipped with wireless, the effective control of hundreds of independents was impossible. Their own positions could not be known ashore with any certainty while, for security reasons, the whereabouts of U-boats could not be signalled to them. But *every convoy* had a Commodore sailing in a ship equipped with wireless and supplied with naval codes and naval signal ratings. Convoys could be diverted at a moment's notice, and the Commodore and Senior Officer of the escort could be informed of the latest information not only about the U-boats themselves but about minefields which some of them had laid. It is impossible to calculate how many ships were saved by evasive routing either in World War I or in World War II, but in both conflicts the numbers must have been very significant. James subsequently wrote that he thought 'it is true to say that without the Room 40 information the defeat of the U-boats would have been far more difficult and more prolonged . . .', while the post-war Admiralty Monograph states that 'For the first time one could see the latest information as to enemy submarines side by side with the track of a convoy, and as the

---

[1] Submarine and anti-submarine tactics have changed immeasurably since World War II, but the currently fashionable idea that shipping can be protected by 'patrolled lanes' or hunter-killer groups is likely to prove as illusory in the 1980s as it was in 1800, in 1916 and in 1939.

Commodore's ship was always equipped with wireless, it was possible at once to divert a convoy from a dangerous area . . .' The defeat of the unrestricted U-boat campaign did not depend on the number of U-boats sunk; it did depend on the number of Allied and neutral merchant ships successfully escorted through the danger areas. James also claims that his and Henderson's exceptional promotion to Captain were proposed by Geddes (see below) because of his great satisfaction with the combined work of Room 40 and the Convoy Section.

Here it may be remarked that Direction Finding, whatever its degree of accuracy, often gave the swiftest clue to the position of a U-boat. Moreover, as the U-boats were, in 1917, operating entirely individually, scattered over the ocean like a chequer board, as opposed to being deployed on long patrol lines as they were in 1942 and 1943, there was less risk that a sudden alteration of course by a convoy away from one danger would merely direct it straight towards another.

There was another way in which Room 40 could help in defeating the U-boats, perhaps its greatest potential contribution; its very accurate knowledge of the overall situation should have enabled the operational authorities, and particularly the Admiralty, to allocate their anti-U-boat resources to the best advantage; to concentrate the maximum effort at the decisive points. To some extent this was done, but as long as naval opinion clung to the idea that convoy was only a defensive palliative and that the U-boats would only be finally mastered by an 'aggressive, offensive hunt and destroy' policy, whether in the Western Approaches, the Strait of Dover or those of Otranto, ships, aeroplanes and airships continued to be squandered on such futile tasks; the introduction of a full and interlocking convoy system was quite unnecessarily delayed; shipping losses continued at an avoidable and very damaging level almost to the end of the war. British, Allied and neutral shipping losses in 1917 totalled six and a quarter million tons, an average of approximately 520,000 tons per month. In the nine months up to the end of September 1918[1] they still totalled just over two and a half million tons, a monthly average of 281,000 tons. If only Jellicoe, Oliver and Duff – and many other senior officers – had been fully convinced from April 1917 onwards that convoy would beat the U-boats, precious resources of men and materials could have been freed to meet the terrible problems facing the British and French armies on

---

[1] The last full month of the unrestricted U-boat campaign.

the Western Front, caused by the collapse of Russia and the freeing of so many German divisions for their great March offensive.

The re-organisation of the Naval Staff started by Jellicoe did have good results, but decentralisation and delegation of responsibility did not go far enough in practice. Jellicoe himself dealt with innumerable matters of detail and he unfortunately felt that he could not do without Oliver's expertise and experience. The records show no diminution at all in the number of signals personally drafted and despatched by the latter. One great step forward was the appointment in May 1917 of Sir Eric Geddes as Controller, in charge of supply and administration. Geddes, aged forty-one, was an extremely able business man. A former director of the North Eastern Railway, he had worked wonders as Director-General of Military Railways in France. He was appalled by the inefficiency of the system he found when he arrived at the Admiralty. He was given the rank and wore the uniform of an Honorary Vice-Admiral in the Royal Navy, something which did nothing to endear him to the more hidebound members of the naval hierarchy.[1] Oliver was full of contempt for Geddes's attempts to deal with over-centralisation, and to introduce modern business methods into the Admiralty. 'We have been upside down here,' he wrote, 'ever since the North Eastern Railway took over the management, but manage to worry along somehow doing our job.' His Director of Operations, the dreadful Thomas Jackson, shared his views and was, according to Henderson, 'universally execrated as the source of all this inertia and opposition . . .' The Old Guard were not going to surrender even if the nation died! Oliver's ire was particularly raised by Geddes's introduction of Lt-Colonel Beharrell as Director of Statistics. His department at long last supplied accurate and sensible figures about shipping on which decisions could be based. 'Oliver's inability to see that foresight must be based on sound knowledge of the past, is very illuminating and it goes a long way towards explaining why the Admiralty were so slow in adopting and extending the convoy system,' was Marder's verdict.

Oliver's iron grip on Room 40 had been partially relaxed with the departure of Ewing and the transfer of full responsibility to Hall. Two immediate results can be seen. The first was Hall's trip to the

---

[1] Geddes had found in France that, as a civilian, he could make no headway against the equally hidebound military and had been given the honorary rank of Major-General. By 1939, Service attitudes had changed and it was probably an advantage to be a civilian in World War II.

Mediterranean and the much overdue attempt to tackle the problem of inter-allied Intelligence in that area. Additional Y and D/F
stations were set up and de Grey's party despatched to Italy. There
were constant requests to Colonel Lampen, the Royal Marine Staff
Officer (Intelligence) at Malta to intercept and forward the call signs
of German U-boats, information of much greater importance now
that the Germans were changing their call signs every two months.
Lampen was also instructed to cable the encoded texts of German
and Austrian signals using the codeword *Grey* (perhaps because of
Nigel de Grey), and Hall made arrangements to pass these messages
on to the French in Paris. In July Lampen forwarded a copy of an
Austrian code captured by the Italians from ULC 12. Lampen
commented that 'It is believed that both signal book and cipher
book are still in use. At any rate the Italians translate most of the
current messages with little difficulty and I have no reason to
suppose that they have any other book, as I have watched them at
work. They have, however, a very thorough familiarity with the
various ways of ciphering.' The code was the *Offsekt* code, a fairly
simple ten-letter one issued in 1911, but the ciphering system was
clever.

In home waters there was the same preoccupation with German
U-boat call signs. For example, on 4 May Hall cabled Bayly at
Queenstown who controlled the Irish D/F stations, that the call
signs had been changed and that the Germans were 'now apparently
using 3 letter call signs of which two letters are out of the following
combinations, FU, LU, SX, VM. Some of the submarines at sea are
using their old call signs. For the present all directional observations
of hostile submarines observed by Irish stations should be reported
to Admiralty by wire.' Two months later the call signs were again
changed, and both Queenstown and the Grand Fleet were told that
the 'FU bar [accented letter] class are apparently OK class, LU class
possibly now VA class. Further information will be sent as the new
call signs become established.'

All this was rendered possible by the re-organisation which was
taking place within Room 40 – the creation of specialist sub-
sections, the long overdue admission of Fleet Paymaster Thring to
Room 40, and the emergence of a Submarine Tracking Room
almost on World War II lines. Moreover, on 25 June a Convoy
Section under Fleet Paymaster H. W. E. Mannisty was set up in the
dining room of Admiralty House. It was connected by pneumatic
tube with Thring's U-boat section and with the direction finding

section under Tiarks. There was no longer the least delay in information from Room 40 reaching officers who could make immediate and efficient use of it.

By July 1917 a daily U-boat situation report was being sent out by Duff, although only to Beatty and Bayly, not to lesser commands or ships at sea. A typical example is that for 9 July: 'There has been great activity SW of Ireland where 5 submarines appear to be operating. Also 3 submarines are operating SW of the Scillies. Forecast. Outwardbound. One large minelaying submarine expected to be in the vicinity of Shetlands during next 24 hours. Homewardbound. Nothing definite.'

Redoubled efforts were made to recover papers from any U-boat sunk in water shallow enough for divers to operate. Divers were kept standing by, trained and instructed in what to look for and where it might be found; they received a bounty of £100, a considerable sum of money in those days, for any successes achieved. On 4 August UC 44 was sunk as the result of a clever ruse. Learning, through Norddeich's broadcasts of Neumünster's information, that the code in which the clearance of German minefields was reported by the British authorities was compromised, and aware that U-boats were laying mines off Waterford Harbour at regular intervals, Hall arranged with Admiral Bayly that the port should be secretly closed to all traffic for a fortnight. No minesweeping was to be undertaken although a fake clearance signal should be made. UC 44 duly reappeared to lay fresh mines and promptly blew up on one of those previously laid, which she erroneously believed to have been swept. Her commander, Teben-Johans, when interrogated by Hall, complained of the inefficiency of the British minesweepers! Bayly was immediately instructed to try to locate the wreck with the 'object of recovering all books and documents . . .' He was warned that it was most important that no information should get out as to how or where UC 44 had been destroyed. The wreck was quickly found, and valuable papers including her signal book were recovered. A month later UC 44's sister boat, UC 42, was mined off Queenstown, either on one of her own mines or perhaps from an unswept one of an earlier lay. On 6 November Bayly reported that the wreck appeared to be buoyant and enquired if he should try to raise it. He was immediately told by the 1st Sea Lord to do nothing, because the Admiralty had 'all the information we are likely to get and knowledge that we have recovered her might lead to a change of codes, etc. which it is desirable to avoid.' However, only four days later

German call signs were again changed and considerable difficulty was obviously experienced in identifying the new ones. On 18 November Hall enquired from Bayly if the wreck could still be located. He was told in reply that divers had already visited it but work on raising the boat, which was lying in twenty-five fathoms, had been stopped in accordance with previous orders. Presumably a fresh haul of papers was then retrieved from UC 42. There were many other examples of similar salvage from sunken U-boats.

The minelaying U-boats of course had to operate in comparatively shallow water, and most of the considerable haul of secret papers recovered during the second half of 1917 and in 1918 came from this class of boat. Thirteen of the twenty U-boats sunk in the first six months of 1917 and twenty-three of the forty-three sunk in the second half of that year, were minelayers. Only twelve minelayers were sunk in 1918 of which eight were in the first six months. Minelaying was highly dangerous work, and after such losses in 1917 it is not surprising that the German minelaying effort faltered, while their successes also shrank, thanks to the extension of the convoy system and the much better control which this gave to the British authorities.

A valuable source of information about U-boats was the interrogation of prisoners of war. Although this could never provide up-to-date operational intelligence, it did reveal many technical details, occasionally helped to disclose the cause of losses of U-boats otherwise unknown to the British, and gave some clues as to the state of morale in the U-boat arm. Interrogation of prisoners was a joint Army/Navy affair and the senior Naval Intelligence representative was Captain Trench, Royal Marines, who had no doubt learned some of the tricks of his trade when arrested by the Germans and imprisoned for espionage before the war. Trench, by then Colonel Trench, performed the same task in World War II and with equal success. Not surprisingly, his reports were prepared in exactly the same form as they had been twenty-five years earlier, and with the same red covers. The prisoners were amazed at the amount of information about their Service and its personalities possessed by their interrogators but, based on World War II experience, it is safe to say that none of this was derived directly from Room 40; there would have been far too great a risk of a prisoner managing to get information about the British code-breaking back to Germany.

Information from prisoners of war, particularly anything concerned with intangibles like morale, needs to be checked very carefully against the evidence provided by other sources. In both World Wars there was a natural tendency for interrogation reports to exaggerate a decline in the morale of the U-boat arm. On both occasions the U-boat men, despite proportionately far higher losses than the rest of the German Navy, remained ready to do their duty, and indeed full of fight, right up to the end.

In December 1917 just under 400,000 tons of Allied and neutral shipping was sunk, but in January 1918 the figure dropped by nearly 100,000 tons and thereafter, with one or two hiccups remained under 300,000 tons a month until September when only 188,000 tons was lost. Throughout this time 99 per cent of the ships sunk were independents or stragglers. The convoy system had mastered the threat from the U-boats; if only it had been extended more quickly and more completely it could virtually have eliminated these still serious losses. Moreover, escorts of convoys or single ships sank twenty-one U-boats out of the total of forty destroyed by surface ships during the last fifteen months of the war when convoy was in force.

The climax came, as it did again in 1943, in the month of May when fourteen U-boats were sunk, four each in the Atlantic, North Sea and Mediterranean and two in the English Channel. British submarines were responsible for the destruction of four of them, depth-charges and ramming accounted for three each and mines and gunfire two each. The cause of the loss of one U-boat could not be established; it may also have been a mine.

The greatest killer of U-boats during the war as a whole was the mine. Here again, Room 40 was able to make a notable contribution, but only when the prejudice against mining as a 'defensive' weapon had been overcome and efficient horned mines on the German model produced in adequate quantities.[1] Intelligence, on its own, cannot compensate for faulty strategy or insufficient or defective weapons. Although Room 40 did experience difficulties from time to time with the special keys used for U-boat codes, and with changes in the transposition system for disguising the grid squares, there was no difficulty in following the ever increasing efforts made by the Germans to keep open their swept channels in the Heligoland Bight. These were given colour code-names by the Germans – Blue, Yellow, etc., and street code-names by the British

[1] September 1917.

– Kingsway, Mall and so on. Two examples will suffice to demonstrate the extent of Room 40's knowledge and the effectiveness of the British mining campaign. On 19 January 1918, Beatty was informed that it was hoped that a recent minelaying operation would compel the U-boats to use the Kattegat rather than the Bight, and he was requested to arrange British submarine patrols accordingly. Before the day was out a further message stated that UB 22 and her escorting destroyer, S 16, had been mined and sunk just north-west of Heligoland. All inward U-boats had been ordered to proceed in through the Kattegat and the Sound, and German heavy ships were putting to sea to support the extensive minesweeping operations necessary to clear the channels in the Bight. Beatty then enquired whether it was intended to repeat the minelaying, and was told that minelayers should be kept ready to avoid any delay, because 'Orders have already been given to sweep Kingsway and the Mall and it seems evident that the enemy attaches much importance to clearing Kingsway.' By 5 February the Heligoland Bight was again closed due to mines and both inward and outward-bound U-boats were having to use the Kattegat, adding something like two days to the time taken to proceed to or from their operational areas. During 1918 the British laid over 21,000 mines in the Heligoland Bight, and the number of occasions when all routes were closed for forty-eight hours or more became increasingly frequent. Six U-boats were lost in the Bight minefields in 1917 but only one in 1918. However, the Germans were compelled to devote a tremendous effort to keeping their swept channels clear; they lost, in the two years, something like twenty-eight destroyers and seventy minesweepers and patrol craft in this area. In addition, their minesweepers had to work further and further out in the Bight and so required cruiser, battle cruiser or battleship cover.

In 1918 the Northern Barrage, a vast minebarrier, was laid, mainly by the US Navy, between the Orkneys and the coast of Norway. It was a great feat and accounted for between five and seven U-boats[1] and, despite its imperfections, would doubtless have claimed more victims if the war had lasted longer. During 1918 the Strait of Dover was also finally, if belatedly, made impassable to U-boats, sixteen being lost there, largely on mines, during the year. During the whole course of the war fifty-two U-boats were sunk by British or Allied mines and at least nine more by German ones, a

---

[1] I have accepted Robert M. Grant's figures, although other authorities put the figure lower.

total more than twice as high as that achieved by any other single weapon.

One last point should be noted about British minelaying, and it was an enormous bonus; it provided Room 40 with a great deal of information and considerable help in breaking keys and identifying call signs. Despite a marked reduction in the use of wireless by the *Hochseeflotte* itself, the reports from the minesweepers and the covering forces continued very much as before, while all outward-bound U-boats had to report when they had passed either the Northern Barrage or the Strait of Dover, exactly as they were to do again in World War II.[1]

Hall had no secrets from Admiral Sims; he briefed him daily on all German naval information, and supplied him with the most detailed intelligence available to Room 40 concerning the movements of the large U-cruisers which operated off the North American coast from early 1918 onwards. Such information was also passed to the British Commander-in-Chief of the North America and West Indies Station, but Sims cabled reports direct to the Navy Department in Washington, ascribing the source of the British knowledge to agents. In spite of Sims's care and discretion, Hall was more than once concerned about lack of security on the other side of the Atlantic, a concern which Sims fully shared and passed on to the Navy Department. Although Hall would never divulge Room 40's techniques, the Americans had no cause at any time to complain that they were not given every scrap of decoded information which could be of use to them. Nor did they – Sims was one of Hall's most fervent admirers.

Although the failure of the U-boat campaign to bring Britain to her knees may not have had a very serious effect on the morale of the U-boat men themselves, it did greatly depress the German public, in spite of claims of shipping losses being consistently exaggerated, at times by over 100 per cent. So confident of success had the *Admiralstab* been that, for most of 1917, the new construction programme was allowed to lag. One hundred and twenty new boats were finally ordered in December 1917 and 220 in January

---

[1] In February 1942 the Germans introduced a special variation of their naval Enigma cipher for their Atlantic U-boats. This defeated Bletchley Park for ten months, but throughout that period the Submarine Tracking Room remained well aware of which U-boats were at sea, thanks to signals from their escorts on the swept channels leading to and from the Biscay ports; the U-boats themselves had to report when they were in the open waters of the Atlantic by short stereotyped signals, which could be D/F'd even when they could not be decoded.

1918, but it was too late; none of them were completed in time to take part in operations before the Armistice, a situation almost exactly repeated with the delayed introduction of the new and revolutionary types XXI and XXIII in 1945. The German General Staff had recognised by the end of 1917 that Germany could not win the war at sea, and in consequence staked everything on the tremendous land offensives which started in March 1918, and which were to prove the death knell of the German Army.

From August 1914 to November 1918 nearly 13,000,000 tons of British, Allied and neutral shipping was sunk. Of this total just over 11,000,000 tons was sunk by U-boat and over one million tons by mines, mostly laid by U-boats. German U-boats themselves suffered 178 losses, of which the British were responsible for 133, the Russians six, and the French one. To these should be added the five to seven lost in the largely American Northern Barrage. Although the average monthly number of operational U-boats never exceeded 123 (1918) and the maximum monthly average actually at sea was never more than forty-five (also 1918), there can be no doubt that it was the U-boat arm which came nearest to securing Britain's defeat, nearer even than it did in March 1943. That adequate steps to meet this peril were not taken earlier was the fault of the Admiralty, and of the concentration of decision making in the hands of so few individuals. The greatest share of blame must surely be attributed to Oliver, Chief of Staff[1] from November 1914 to January 1918. His theoretical executive powers may have been limited, but, after serving an apprenticeship under Churchill, he remained the arch-centraliser, who, in practice, took most of the decisions and influenced all of them. He had Room 40's priceless information at his disposal and he failed to make the best use of it; for far too long, he refused to permit Room 40 itself to do so.

But the U-boats could not have operated without the strength of the *Hochseeflotte* behind them – to protect their bases, and the approaches to them and to prevent any landing on German territory whether in the North Sea or the Baltic. As long as the *Hochseeflotte* existed, undefeated if comparatively inactive, the Grand Fleet was needed to contain it. It is to the activities of the surface ships of the two fleets to which we must now return.

---

[1] Deputy Chief of Naval Staff from mid-1917.

CHAPTER SIXTEEN

The Last Sorties

1917, which had opened with high Allied hopes, ended in deep gloom. Kerensky and his well-meaning but ineffective Social Democrats had tried to carry on the war after they overthrew the Czar in March, but had in turn inevitably been routed by Lenin and the Bolsheviks in November.[1] Resistance to the Germans had then finally collapsed. Although the mutiny of the French Army had been suppressed, and Pétain was even able to attempt some small-scale and strictly limited offensives by the autumn, it had been the British and British Empire forces which had assumed, for the first time, the leading role on the Western Front; despite immense British sacrifices the German lines had remained unbroken, and it was clear that they would shortly be reinforced by German divisions transferred from Russia. In October the Germans and Austrians had almost succeeded in knocking Italy out of the war with their victory at Caporetto; and the situation was only saved by the hurried transfer there of British and French divisions, desperately needed on the Western Front. There were only two rays of comfort – the British capture of Jerusalem in December, and the fact that the United States was slowly bringing its immense resources of men and materials to the aid of the Allies. The question was, could Britain, France and Italy survive long enough for American aid to turn the tide?

At sea, as we have seen, the antidote to the unrestricted U-boat campaign had been found with the introduction of convoy, but even by the end of the year this fact had not been fully realised and shipping losses remained so serious that politicians, soldiers and sailors alike were asking themselves whether the Army could win the war before the Royal Navy lost it. More accurately, avoidance of defeat on land was dependent on victory at sea, a truism which applied no less to the Central as to the Western powers.

The British Prime Minister, Lloyd George, had never had much faith in Jellicoe or the Admiralty, but recognised that he would have

[1] The 'October' Revolution by the Russian Calendar.

to move slowly. His first step was to remove the 1st Lord, Carson, a strong supporter of Jellicoe; he replaced him by Geddes on 20 July. But Geddes was not prepared to get rid of Jellicoe without giving the Admiral an opportunity to prove that he could adapt to a new regime, and Jellicoe was not prepared to get rid of Oliver. In the next few months Geddes forced through a much needed reorganisation of the Board of Admiralty and the Naval Staff. Its principal effect was to separate the operational from the purely administrative functions and to give the Naval Staff the executive powers which it had previously lacked in theory, even if it had exercised many of them in practice. Jellicoe, the 1st Sea Lord became Chief of Naval Staff, with Oliver as Deputy Chief of Naval Staff with responsibility for surface operations, and Duff, as Assistant Chief of Naval Staff, responsible for the anti-U-boat war. Admiral Wemyss, the Commander-in-Chief East Indies and Egypt, was brought to the Admiralty as Deputy 1st Sea Lord, avowedly to relieve Jellicoe of administrative detail, but almost certainly to groom him to replace Jellicoe should the latter fail to satisfy Geddes and Lloyd George. A start on forming a Plans Division to look forward and consider schemes for offensive action, was at last made. This was a measure which found little favour with either Jellicoe or Oliver. All these changes, designed to introduce decentralisation and business efficiency into the salt-encrusted Admiralty machine, were steps in the right direction, and indeed the Admiralty began to take on a shape and appearance easily recognisable to those who knew it in World War II. But the new organisation could not hope to produce the best results unless the men at the top, and in particular Jellicoe and Oliver, could convince themselves that it was an improvement on the old, autocratic, centralised regime. They could not bring themselves to do so; they had both borne an immense burden of responsibility for more than three years; it was time for them to give way to others. At the end of the year Geddes dismissed Jellicoe abruptly, and in January 1918 Oliver was given a sea appointment in command of the 1st Battle Squadron. A fresh and invigorating breeze began to blow through the Admiralty with the appointment of Wemyss as 1st Sea Lord.

Anxiety about the measures being taken to defeat the U-boats, had of course been a major factor leading to Jellicoe's dismissal. His caution, not to say his pessimism, had greatly irritated Lloyd George. He had also begun to lose the confidence of Beatty and the 'Young Turks' in the Grand Fleet and in the Admiralty. Blinker

Hall was certainly one of the latter. Hall has left no record of his feelings or actions at this time, but Oliver, in his Recollections, has this to say: 'In December 1917 there was evidence to me that there was some underground work going on. One evening about 10.30 p.m. some officers were talking in my room about Admiralty affairs, and one of them referred to someone as "Judas Iscariot", and I asked him who he was, and was told it was Hall who was mixed up with political people in high places and did not support Jellicoe.' This may have coloured Oliver's views on Hall, because he must have known that he himself would not survive if Jellicoe fell. Elsewhere in his Recollections, Oliver states that Hall 'made a great reputation and expanded the Intelligence Division enormously; he was very energetic and excitable and used to dash about a great deal, and every month or two would have to go to a farm in the West Country for a few days' rest. In an air raid he would dash about all over London in a car; I never could understand why or what use it was.' Oliver did allow that Hall had done a 'good job' over Ireland, but his remarks as a whole savour of damning with faint praise. Oliver ignores the facts that he himself was in large measure responsible for Hall's appointment as DID, and that he was his immediate superior throughout; if he had not been satisfied with the performance of an officer holding such a key post he should, and undoubtedly could, have arranged for his replacement. Oliver was a dour, silent centraliser, Hall an ebullient individualist; they had clashed early over Ewing and it is surprising that Hall survived the Oliver regime.

An officer with very different views about Blinker Hall was Jacky Fisher. When rumours began to circulate that Jellicoe was about to be replaced, the old volcano began to show signs of another eruption. He intrigued violently and characteristically for his own return as 1st Sea Lord. Amongst others, he approached Hall through Tom Marlowe, the Editor of the *Daily Mail*, but Hall, convinced that Fisher 'was now a very tired old man, and his judgement was not what it had been . . .', refused to become in any way involved.[1] By the end of 1917 Hall may not have been Oliver's

---

[1] It is perhaps worth noting, that at the time of Fisher's resignation in 1915, and when he was still expecting to be called back on his own terms by Asquith, the old Admiral had compiled a list of appointments which he would make and had discussed them with his devoted Naval Assistant, Captain T. E. Crease. Crease asked the old man 'what he intended to do with Reggie Hall. He said that must be a secret for the present – then added that he was the only one with any guts who did not turn his other cheek to the enemy, and he meant to have him at the War Committee to help the Admiralty there in getting on with the war.'

blue-eyed boy, but he had his admirers, and these included those now in power, Geddes, Wemyss and Beatty.[1]

*

The *Hochseeflotte* had not attempted any major sortie since October 1916, contenting itself with providing covering forces for the minesweepers and outpost craft in the Heligoland Bight. The Grand Fleet, both under Jellicoe and Beatty, was almost equally unwilling to force the issue in the southern North Sea until at least some of the deficiencies in British shells and armour, which had been revealed by Jutland, had been remedied, although this did not mean that Beatty was not prepared to react energetically to any aggressive action by the Germans, if such a move could be detected. There was a good deal of anxiety on the British side that this would prove more difficult than it had been for the past two and a half years. This was because of the introduction of the FFB code in May 1917, and the complete change in all German call signs. Admiral Scheer was also beginning to be much more circumspect in his use of wireless, although we do not know whether Room 40 immediately realised this. Birch and Clarke deny that Scheer's caution was due to any conviction that his codes were compromised, a view supported by the continued excessive use of wireless messages in the AFB code to U-boats, patrol craft and minesweepers. It was almost certainly the result of German fears, based on their own experience, of the efficiency of British direction finding. In fact, thanks to their mastery of the AFB, the British were still able to follow much of what was going on across the North Sea and, by September 1917, were well on their way to reconstructing the FFB and the new Nordo cipher for the Flag Officers' version of the VB code. This is shown by the amount of information passed to the Russians at the time of the German offensive against the Gulf of Riga in that month.

Nevertheless, Room 40's task was now becoming more difficult. It was depending increasingly on the ability to draw the right conclusions from the information revealed by the movements of U-boats and small craft, without the clinching evidence of preliminary orders issued by wireless to the heavy ships, which had given warning of the Yarmouth Raid, the Dogger Bank and Jutland. Traffic analysis, the evaluation of changes in the type and volume of

[1] The considerable volume of correspondence between Hall and Beatty could not be traced when Hall was writing his autobiography, and still cannot be located.

German messages, the identification of call signs and direction finding, became of greater importance.

The Germans attempted to supplement the U-boats' attacks on commerce by sending out disguised merchant raiders, such as the *Möwe*, *Wolf* and *Seeadler*. These ships were provided with special keys and ciphers, but whether to the AFB or FFB codes cannot at present be established. They also used wireless very sparingly, so that Room 40 lacked the volume of traffic necessary to break the keys, and in fact never did so. Indications that a raider was outward- or homeward-bound could often be discerned from traffic analysis, and occasionally by orders to U-boats or patrol craft, but very rarely in time to be of operational value. Despite the tightness of the British blockade, disguised merchant raiders proved to be extremely elusive, as was found again in World War II. It is curious that the *Admiralstab* did not send out more of them. As it was, despite their successes, they were no more than an irritant.

Early in 1917 the Germans did attempt to attack the Dutch Trade, British shipping in the Downs, and the trawlers and drifters of the Dover barrage. Sometimes Room 40 could detect these movements in advance, as for example on the night of 22–23 January, when cruisers and destroyers were able to intercept a German destroyer flotilla on passage to Zeebrugge, and severely to damage three ships. On 25 February the Germans did manage to achieve surprise in an attack on the Dutch trade and shipping in the Downs but inflicted little damage. Another attack on 17–18 March was foreseen and driven off after only meagre success. On 20–21 April a more serious raid by twelve German destroyers was intercepted by HM destroyers *Broke* and *Swift*; two German ships were sunk, which seems to have discouraged the enemy from further raids for the next ten months.

In the North Sea, however, the Germans scored two distinct successes. British and Scandinavian (largely Norwegian) shipping was now proceeding regularly in convoy between Lerwick (in the Shetlands) and Bergen. The convoys usually consisted of up to a dozen merchant ships, escorted by a couple of destroyers and one or two trawlers. That these convoys were running a grave risk not only from U-boats but also from German surface ships, was of course obvious to the British authorities. With neutral ships sailing from and arriving at a neutral port, the timing and composition of the convoys could not be concealed from the Germans; British submarine and cruiser patrols could not guarantee to intercept a

German raiding force steaming up the Norwegian coast, unless Room 40 could provide adequate advance warning not only of its departure but also of its precise intention. If the Germans displayed even a modicum of boldness a disaster was bound to occur sooner or later, just as it did with the World War II North Russian convoys. The Grand Fleet therefore generally maintained cruiser squadrons at sea to cover the convoys, or at least to try to intercept possible raiders on their way home.

In July and August quite serious disorders occurred in several battleships of the *Hochseeflotte*. They were caused by very bad food, harsh discipline and a drop in morale due to the monotony of constant patrols in the Heligoland Bight, unrelieved by the excitement of any offensive operations. The best officers and men were being drafted into the U-boat arm, and very little effort was made to provide the ratings with opportunities for sport and amusement as was done in the Grand Fleet. At least one of the ringleaders was shot, and other draconian measures adopted to restore discipline. There is no evidence that Room 40 became aware of what was happening through decodes, but the facts were reported fairly quickly by agents in Denmark. Morale in the cruisers and destroyers was never affected and, although he may have had some doubts about the reliability of his battle squadrons, Scheer decided that, with the bad weather of the autumn in the North Sea providing some cover, he would strike at the Scandinavian convoys with his light forces.

Early on the morning of 17 October two German light cruisers, *Bremse* and *Brummer*, fell upon a westbound convoy of twelve ships about sixty-five miles east of the Shetlands. The escort consisted of two destroyers, *Mary Rose* and *Strongbow*, and two trawlers. The German cruisers were crack ships, fitted as minelayers and with a top speed of thirty-four knots, and more British than German in appearance. British recognition procedures failed again, and when, at last, an enemy report was made it was jammed by the *Brummer*. *Mary Rose* and *Strongbow* fought to the last, but were both sunk with heavy loss of life, as were nine neutral ships in the convoy; only one British and one Belgian merchant ship and the two trawlers managed to escape, thanks to the gallant defence of the destroyers. The news of the disaster did not reach the Admiral Commanding the Orkneys and Shetlands until 3.50 p.m. that afternoon, by which time it was far too late to intercept the Germans on their way home. *Brummer* did not repeat *Meteor*'s mistake of prematurely breaking wireless silence. She did not report until early on the following morning, when Room 40 decoded a signal from her announcing that her first task had been carried out but that the second task had fallen through, adding that her position and that of *Bremse* at 6.00 a.m. was off Lynwig Lighthouse.

The German operation had been well planned and executed with ruthless efficiency, but it should never have achieved the complete surprise which it did. At 4.23 p.m. on 15 October, Room 40 had intercepted and decoded a signal from *Brummer* reporting the postponement of Most Secret Order 71950 until 16 October. Her captain added that she would be leaving by way of Norman Deep due to the mining of Way Blue, and requested that minesweeping be carried out. One hour later Oliver signalled Beatty, 'Minelayer *Brummer* leaves via Norman Deep tomorrow 16 to northward probably for minelaying. She should be intercepted.' Soon afterwards further decodes became available which should at once have indicated that *Brummer*'s mission might involve more than minelaying. Neumünster gave instructions for strict and unusual wireless restrictions, and UB 64 reported having observed heavy convoy traffic off Lerwick. On the evening of the next day, 16 October, the cruiser *Regensburg* reported that she would be off List with accompanying destroyers in accordance with *Brummer*'s signal of the previous afternoon, and this was followed by orders to all U-boats not to attack small cruisers unless positively identified as British. Oliver had told Beatty that if any fresh information about *Brummer*'s position became available, it would be signalled to ships at sea. In spite of this no action was taken to signal the later decodes, or the obvious deductions to be drawn from them even to Beatty himself until the 17th, when the convoy had in fact already been decimated. At 2.20 p.m. Oliver personally sent the Commander-in-Chief the following appreciation: 'It is just possible *Brummer* may be accompanied by one or perhaps two light cruisers but if this is the case she has not yet left. Enemy has warned all submarines not to attack light cruisers unless certain they are hostile. This may indicate intention to operate on East coast or to attack Lerwick or other convoys. In order to be prepared it seems desirable to withdraw *Courageous* and *Glorious*[1] to Scapa to refuel and also 1st

---

[1] Two of three very large light cruisers displacing around 19,000 tons, armed with four 15-in. guns and capable of over thirty-one knots speed. They had been ordered by Fisher with Baltic operations in mind. They were very lightly built and were subsequently converted to aircraft carriers. *Courageous* and *Glorious* were lost early in World War II but *Furious*, the third ship, survived much arduous service.

Light Cruiser Squadron . . .' Fifty-five minutes after sending this signal, Oliver had second thoughts and told Beatty that it was 'practically certain that light cruisers are not with *Brummer* and are remaining in the Bight.' Had Beatty received even this rather vague warning that the Scandinavian convoys might be *Brummer's* objective as soon as the intercepts were decoded, i.e. on the evening of the 16th rather than eighteen hours later, he would most surely have redisposed the very considerable forces, including the *Courageous* and *Glorious*, which he already had at sea. It might well have been possible to save the convoy, and there certainly would have been every chance of intercepting and sinking the German cruisers on their return passage.

It really is difficult to find any excuse for this incredible delay in passing out intelligence at this late stage in the war. If Oliver was, for once, absent from the Admiralty throughout the sixteenth – and this we do not know – surely someone else should have been able to draw the right conclusions and have had the initiative to send them to Beatty without waiting for Oliver's return? Why not the Chief of Naval Staff himself, Jellicoe? James, who was of course in charge of Room 40, writing from memory in the sixties, claims that Room 40 knew that both *Brummer* and *Bremse* were involved from study of call signs and direction finding, but there is in fact no evidence that *Bremse* made any signals throughout the operation, so this at least is doubtful. On the other hand, the records show clearly that all the decodes were passed through from Room 40 to the Operations Division within, at the most, fifty minutes from the time of interception, an indication of the speed with which Room 40 was working. James also suggests that if only Room 40 had been permitted to keep plot of British ships, the danger to the convoys and the faulty positioning of the covering forces would have been at once apparent. This entirely begs the fact that Operations did keep such a plot and did have the benefit of all Room 40's information. Whether it was the man or the faulty system, which he had devised and apparently refused to modify in the light of all experience, the *Mary Rose* disaster was yet one more example of Oliver's many inexplicable failures to make proper use of the priceless intelligence at his disposal.[1] Beatty was furious, and the whole episode must have

---

[1] Possibly as a result of a visit which the angry Beatty paid to the Admiralty, Oliver introduced on 4 November an additional method of promulgating 'special secret intelligence' to six of the principal operational commanders in Home waters – Beatty and his second in command, Vice-Admiral Battle Cruiser Force, Vice-Admiral 3rd Battle Squadron, Vice-Admiral Dover, Tyrwhitt at Harwich, and Captain (Sub-

reinforced the determination of Lloyd George and Geddes that both Jellicoe and Oliver must be replaced as soon as possible.

Both the Germans and the British busied themselves with the possibilities of a repetition of the raid. As early as 20 October, Room 40 had intercepted instructions to UB 61 to proceed to the coast north of Bergen to try to discover the new route which it was presumed would be ordered for the convoys. Reports came in from agents in Copenhagen of an impending attack by seven light cruisers and thirty-six destroyers. Oliver told Beatty that the Germans had such forces available in the North Sea, and warned him that the use of battle cruisers could not be discounted. Reports from Christiania (Oslo) were even more alarming, and on 3 November Jellicoe told the Commander-in-Chief that he feared that 'Norwegian and Danish reports will be frequent but we cannot ignore them unless obviously untrue . . . I know reports cause you great difficulties and regret it but see no alternative but to inform you . . .' It was unfortunate that Foreign Office telegrams, often widely inaccurate, were circulated to the naval staff without reference to a checking by Room 40. The movements of the *Brummer* and *Bremse* were followed as closely as possible, and there was anxiety that other ships of their class would soon join the enemy Fleet. The strain on the Grand Fleet in providing protection to the convoys against attack by cruisers without offering a tempting target for the German battle cruisers, and at the same time in keeping the Grand Fleet concentrated and ready to deal with a sortie by the whole strength of the *Hochseeflotte*, was severe. The difficulties were not immediately resolved, with the result that a second disaster took place only two months after the first.

Before this, however, Beatty endeavoured to pay the Germans back in their own coin. Thanks to Room 40, he was well aware of the

marines) at Harwich. In order to enable telegrams conveying 'special secret intelligence' to be decoded by selected staff, they were, in future, to bear a special prefix. This prefix would consist of a Greek letter spelt out and sent *en clair*, 'e.g. *Alpha* or *Beta* which would be changed every fortnight', but this new system was only to apply to messages sent by landline; wireless signals would be sent by the 'special Z transposition' method. Circulation of the signals in the Admiralty was confined to the CNS, DCNS, ACNS, DOD and DID only. It did nothing, of course, to ensure that information available in the Admiralty was sent to those who could make use of it. It is, however, interesting to see that the Admiralty were using the term 'Special Intelligence' (and there are many other examples of this) in World War I to designate information obtained from decodes, a practice always followed in World War II. It is also worth noting that the use of the prefix *Ultra*, introduced by the DNI, Godfrey, on 13 May 1940 to replace a previous prefix *Hydro*, was merely a continuation of World War I practice.

efforts being made by the Germans to keep the swept channels in the Heligoland Bight clear, and of the fact that the minesweepers were always supported by a covering force of cruisers or battle cruisers. On 17 November Beatty sent a strong force under Vice-Admiral T. W. D. Napier into the Heligoland Bight, to attack and destroy these German formations and to withdraw again at high speed before the *Hochseeflotte* could put to sea. The daring operation failed to achieve any success and Napier was held to blame, rather unfairly, for failing to pursue the retreating Germans with sufficient vigour. Napier certainly made some errors of judgement, but faulty staff work beforehand added to his difficulties. Room 40 were very well informed about the location of German minefields and charts were available showing their positions and those of the British fields, which the Germans were endeavouring to clear. These charts had not been supplied to Napier, who somewhat naturally was reluctant to permit his ships to go too far into areas which, on the charts he did have, were shown as dangerous. Excessive secrecy had again robbed the Royal Navy of the chance to inflict a damaging blow to the Germans on their own doorstep. At least there was no failure on this occasion to supply Napier, and the other senior officers concerned, with operational intelligence, perhaps because of an urgent request made by Beatty to the Admiralty just after the various squadrons had sailed. The German light forces, when retiring ahead of Napier endeavoured to lure him towards the German battleships which were coming up in support. They had sailed at 8.30 a.m. and this fact was reported to Napier within an hour and a half. Information was also promptly supplied about the position of the German cruisers, including that of the only one to suffer severe damage, the *Königsberg*.[1] Thus, although, from the British point of view, the operation failed to achieve its object, Room 40 certainly contributed to the prevention of a sharp reverse.

On 12 December Scheer again boldly attacked another Scandinavian convoy, this time with four destroyers. For once the Germans seem to have arranged matters without giving Room 40 the slightest clue that anything was in the wind. The convoy of six ships, escorted by the destroyers *Pellew* and *Partridge* and four trawlers, was some twenty-five miles off the Norwegian coast near Bergen, when the Germans attacked. Once again there were failures in the British

---

[1] Not to be confused with the cruiser of the same name destroyed in the Rufigi River.

recognition and enemy reporting procedures; only the *Partridge* survived, thanks to a lucky rainstorm. British cruisers were to the west and to the south of the scene of the engagement. The southern force might have caught the Germans but for the fact that they returned through the Skagerrak. Like the previous attack it had been well planned and executed, and it is difficult to understand why the Germans did not risk more of these tip and run raids. Instead, the surface of the North Sea remained undisturbed for another four months. The British did reorganise the whole system of control of the Scandinavian convoys, shortened the route, reduced the frequency and increased, for a time, the strength of the covering forces; sensible measures and the best which could have been devised in the circumstances, but still depending, in the end, on the ability of Room 40 to give advance warning of any German move.

We must now return to the Strait of Dover and the U-boat war. The Admiral in command at Dover since Hood had been summarily removed by Churchill early in 1915, had been Sir Reginald Bacon. Although an able specialist, a student of naval history, and, in many ways a brilliant man, he was so convinced of his own rectitude and of the correctness of all his decisions, that he would not accept the incontrovertible evidence of Room 40 that U-boats were experiencing no difficulty in passing through the Dover Barrage. Marder implies that this evidence was not available until the recovery of documents from UC 44, but in fact reports from outward- and homeward-bound U-boats, intercepted and decoded by Room 40, had long provided all the proof that should have been needed. Duff, Oliver and Jellicoe must have seen these reports, and Jellicoe's faith in Bacon is hard to understand. Not everyone, however, was convinced by Bacon's almost insubordinate statements that what he was doing was right and that any other suggestions were wrong; he was quite sure that he was the only man in the regiment in step.

One of Bacon's most severe and persistent critics was Roger Keyes. Keyes was the antithesis of Bacon. He was certainly no intellectual; he longed for 'glory' and saw himself as a second Nelson. Commodore (Submarines) at the beginning of the war, he had then become Chief of Staff to Admiral de Robeck at the Dardanelles, and had been a most persistent advocate of attempts to force the straits at almost any cost. He was, nevertheless, conscious of his own limitations, and was more prepared than was Bacon to accept the advice of those whom he recognised as better qualified than himself. Keyes had been appointed Director of the newly formed Plans Division, and was chairman of the Channel Barrage Committee. The Committee's recommendations for extensions of the deep minefields and for the Barrage to be strongly patrolled and brilliantly illuminated at night in order to force the U-boats to dive, was violently rejected by Bacon. One third of British shipping losses were now occurring in the western English Channel, all caused by U-boats from the Flanders bases passing through the Strait of Dover. On 18 December Jellicoe at last gave Bacon a direct order to illuminate the Barrage as suggested by the Committee. On the very next night UB 56 was caught by the illuminations, forced to dive and blown up in the minefield. So far as the 1st Lord, Geddes, was concerned this was almost the last straw, and he was strongly supported by Wemyss. They shared the opinions of Keyes that such successes would not be repeated so long as Bacon remained in command. Jellicoe refused to agree. It was another nail in his coffin and when he was dismissed, Keyes replaced Bacon at Dover. Fourteen U-boats were sunk in 1918 by the Dover Command and the Strait became virtually impassable. The last U-boat to make the passage was U 55 in February.

The Germans reacted quickly, and on the night of 14-15 February launched a heavy destroyer raid on the trawlers and small craft patrolling and illuminating the Barrage. Once again they achieved surprise; once again British recognition and reporting procedures failed. Seven small ships were sunk and another seven severely damaged. British destroyers actually sighted the raiders as they were returning, but, uncertain that they were hostile, did not engage them. It was an astonishing failure and a sharp reminder of the difficulties of defending a barrage so close to the enemy's advance bases.

Keyes then revived and revised plans prepared by Bacon, which had been approved by Jellicoe, for an operation to block the Belgian ports of Zeebrugge and Ostend, which were connected by canals to Bruges, the base for the Flanders U-boats and an advance base for destroyers. The outcome was the famous raids on the two ports, which finally took place on the night of 22-23 April (St George's Day). They were both failures. At Ostend the block-ships were unable to get into position at all, while at Zeebrugge, despite the tremendous gallantry displayed by all concerned (eight Victoria Crosses were awarded), the gap in the channel was not completely closed. Small destroyers were able to leave the port within twenty-four hours and U-boats within forty-eight hours; only the larger

U-boats were compelled, and that only for a short time, to use Ostend. These facts were known to Room 40 at once, but Keyes, like Bacon before him, refused to accept them and continued to maintain that the Zeebrugge operation at least, had been a resounding success. The raid was greeted rapturously in the British Press, and was a tremendous boost to the nation's morale at a time when the news from the Western Front was still of massive German offensives. At last the Royal Navy seemed to be taking the offensive and doing something effectively to support the hard pressed soldiers; the far more valuable though less spectacular results achieved by the blockade of Germany and the mastery of the U-boats, was ignored or forgotten. The Admiralty, perhaps understandably, did nothing to dispel these illusions. Zeebrugge, in spite of its almost complete practical failure, was probably well worth all the effort and sacrifice which it had involved.

We must now examine the last occasion during the war when Admiral Scheer took the whole strength of the *Hochseeflotte* out into the North Sea, thus providing the Grand Fleet with its final opportunity to achieve the decisive sea victory for which it was still striving. Eighteen months of almost total inactivity on the part of the German main fleet had not lulled either Beatty or the Admiralty into ignoring the possibilities of some sudden move by the enemy. On the contrary, all concerned were constantly on the lookout for signs of a renewed attack on the Scandinavian convoys, for a serious attempt to disrupt the cross-Channel traffic during the March and April land offensives, or even for that hoary old bugbear, an invasion of the East Coast. The surprising thing is that Scheer did not move sooner.

Early on 23 April he finally took the *Hochseeflotte* to sea to cover an attack by Hipper's battle cruisers on the Bergen convoys. He was ill-served by his Intelligence Department, because he was unaware of the recent transfer of the whole of the Grand Fleet from Scapa to Rosyth or of the changed convoy cycle. He apparently relied on reports from his U-boats about convoy sailing dates, which were inaccurate, instead of obtaining precise details from the German consul at Bergen, which he could easily have done. On the other hand, his own signal security had been considerably improved. In the first place all orders to the Fleet itself were issued in writing, and also, on this occasion, orders to light vessels and minesweepers. Second, strict wireless silence was imposed on the *Hochseeflotte*. Third, although Room 40 had completely mastered the AFB code and largely reconstructed the FFB one, key changes were now being made every seven to ten days, and were taking Room 40 two to three days to crack, depending on the amount of traffic on which to work. Fourth, the Germans were making even greater use of 'damped wave', low power, transmissions, which were more difficult to intercept fully and accurately. Finally, in order to warn U-boats already at sea that German surface operations were in progress, they had, for some time past, been issued with a series of short code-words, 'catchwords', which could be broadcast by Norddeich when the need arose; even if the signal giving a catchword could be decoded by Room 40, it in no way revealed the nature of the operation ordered. For example, on 18 January the Admiralty explained to Beatty that references to a catchword had been passed on by the outpost commanders of the Jade and Weser. The only clue to its meaning was the fact that destroyers had left the Jade at 7.00 a.m., and that they had not been detailed for escort work. The Admiralty anticipated some operation was under way but had no further evidence of its precise nature. The new 1st Sea Lord, Wemyss, the DCNS, Rear-Admiral Sir Sydney Fremantle, who had replaced Oliver, and Hall made great efforts to keep Beatty primed with every scrap of information available, and to explain to him just what Room 40's difficulties were. Daily reports of the weather in the Heligoland Bight, a factor of some significance in estimating the likelihood of any operation (derived of course from the Germans' own reports), were supplied and each evening, around 8.30 p.m. a signal was sent about signs of activity or the absence of activity in the Bight. Those on the 22 and 23 April read 'No sign of activity in Bight.' The Germans had taken the first trick.

The *Hochseeflotte* had in fact sailed at 5.00 a.m. on the 23rd. Unfortunately for Room 40, not only had there been a recent change in all German call signs – and the process of identifying the new ones was still far from complete – but a change of key[1] had been made on the 21st and was not apparently broken until early on the 24th. In the event, due to fog, the *Hochseeflotte* had to anchor near Heligoland at about 10.00 a.m. on the 23rd. Scheer made a signal in the Flag Officers' code, and Hipper reported that his 1st Scouting Group was anchored. It is improbable that Hipper's signal was decoded immediately, but it was accurately D/F'd by the British. This was not, however, sufficient evidence that the Germans were doing any more than carrying out one of their frequent exercises in

[1] From Gamma Alpha to Gamma F.

the Bight. But, in all, five signals were intercepted, although not decoded, between 10.00 and 11.00 a.m., and this should have made the British more suspicious than it appears they were. Moreover, during the forenoon Hunstanton, one of the British Y Stations, reported that there had been a change of W/T control, a very definite pointer to the start of a major German operation. Room 40's subsequent private 'inquest' remarked that 'the various small craft protecting the route were very nervy, frequently imagining an enemy air raid. Owing to their protection the Fleet was able to proceed without [further] signalling. The outpost craft had been strictly ordered to make no reference to the passing Fleet.'

It is easy, with hindsight, to criticise Room 40's failures to detect immediately what was going on, but, as those of us with personal experience of similar situations in World War II can confirm that, what, in retrospect, can clearly be seen as significant, is clouded at the time by all the other flow of information, both routine and important. It must be remembered that at this very time, the attack on Zeebrugge was at its height.

The British had, however, been well aware of the possibility that Room 40 might not be able to give advance warning of any sortie, and had therefore stationed four submarines in the approaches to the Bight to report, and attack, any such move by German forces. One of them, J 6, actually sighted the leading German ships, including five battle cruisers, when the Germans finally got under way again in the late afternoon of 23 April. Convinced, for some incredible reason, that the ships were British, the submarine commander made no report. After all the failures to make proper enemy reports throughout four years of war, including Jutland and more lately during the attacks on the Scandinavian convoys and in the very recent German raid in the Channel, there can really be no charitable excuse for this failure on the part of both the officer immediately responsible or of the senior officers concerned with issuing instructions about the vital necessity of making enemy reports. The commander of J 6 compounded his mistake by taking an hour and a half to report his sighting of Hipper's forces on their return passage! There was something very wrong with the Royal Navy's system of training and staff work that such mistakes could be repeated again and again.

Nevertheless, although the Admiralty's evening signal on 23 April (8.15 p.m.) had, as we have said, reported all quiet in the Bight, four hours later (0.24 a.m. on 24 April) the first faint alarum was sounded when an Urgent Priority message was sent to Beatty that 'Today April 24 5 Zeppelins will be stationed between (a) 59 North and 1.30 East and (b) 54 North 3 East [down the central North Sea]. Also two Zeppelins between (a) and the Naze [Harwich].' The last Zeppelin patrol line perhaps suggested a raid on the east coast. At 1.54 a.m. another message was sent to Beatty which read as follows: 'Not quite certain but believe catchword made to submarines', and shortly after that the Harwich Force was ordered to have steam at one hour's notice by 5.00 a.m. Then at 4.20 a.m. the temperature dropped a little. It had been learned that the Zeppelin reconnaissance had been abandoned because of high winds. If Room 40 and Operations Division had missed some faint clues, which indeed they had, they had not done badly, given the very vague information available. At 8.48 a.m. by which time one would imagine that Wemyss and Fremantle had appeared on the scene, the following appreciation was sent to Beatty: 'Measures of an elaborate and unusual nature have been ordered for Regent [one of the German swept channels in the Bight] at 1.00 p.m. Our wireless signalling is being observed and reported on. [Neumünster were reporting nothing unusual in the character and volume of British W/T traffic.] All flying stations have been ordered to attempt reconnaissance. Indications point to some enemy operation.'

There was very little for the British to go on, but it had at least been obvious, and had indeed been realised since 2.00 a.m. on that morning (the 24th), that some move by the Germans was either imminent or actually in progress. The Harwich Force had been brought to one hour's notice; why were similar instructions not issued to the Grand Fleet at the same time? It is true that there were no firm indications that the *Hochseeflotte* was on the move, or if it was, in what direction; it was also known that there was dense fog in the Bight – and also at Rosyth – but surely the Grand Fleet should have been brought to the same state of readiness as the Harwich Force.

Up to this time the German operation had gone well, but there then occurred one of those comparatively minor mishaps which, in war if not in peacetime manoeuvres, so often disrupt an admiral's best laid plans. Just after 5.00 a.m., when Hipper's 1st Scouting Group was approaching Bergen, the battle cruiser *Moltke* suffered a severe mechanical breakdown. Hipper ordered *Moltke* to return – by visual signals – but a little later the trouble got worse and at 6.43 a.m. *Moltke* reported the situation to Scheer by wireless. She followed this up, at 7.45 by a further report, upon which she was taken in tow by the battleship *Oldenburg* and ordered back to Wilhelmshaven.

These signals were intercepted by the British direction finding stations, but, perhaps because of the low power on which they were made, did not give a very accurate fix. It was also unfortunate from the British point of view that the change in call signs made it difficult to be sure of the identity of the sender; nor could the signals, at that moment, be decoded. At 7.58 a.m. this urgent signal was sent to Beatty: 'Call sign believed to be *Moltke*, also unknown call sign located by directional in 58 degrees 30 North 6 degrees 20 East at 7.00 a.m.' The position given was some twelve miles inland from Bergen, and both the Admiralty and Beatty were stupid in not respectively stating and accepting that it indicated the presence of an important German unit close off the Norwegian coast. Instead, it took nearly two hours before Beatty's query and the Admiralty explanation made this clear.[1]

One can well imagine the debate that went on in the Admiralty War Room. Was this a raid on the East coast, or was it a move against the Scandinavian convoys, or was it a German reaction to the Zeebrugge operation? Apparently, at least one German battle cruiser was off the Norwegian coast, but although *Moltke*'s call sign had tentatively been identified, that of *Baden*, Scheer's flagship, whose signals had also been intercepted had not, nor had there been any sign of Hipper's flagship. How many German formations were at sea and where were they? If only J 6 had made a report some at least of the uncertainties would have been resolved.

Then, at 9.55 a.m., Beatty was informed that, 'Enemy W/T procedure shows important operation in progress. Neumünster reports British unaware that German forces are at sea.' He immediately gave orders for the Battle Cruiser Fleet to raise steam, and followed this half an hour later with similar instructions to the rest of the Grand Fleet. At 10.47 a.m. the Admiralty ordered the Grand Fleet to sea; despite a dense fog, its 31 battleships, 4 battle cruisers, 26 cruisers and 85 destroyers had all cleared the Firth of Forth by the early afternoon – a great feat of seamanship, but far too late to afford, in the event, any hope of intercepting the Germans.

Despite the mishap to *Moltke*, Scheer had been reassured by

[1] Professor Marder rather curiously remarks that the 'error was in *Moltke*'s signal, not in Room 40.' This is of course quite wrong because the signal was not decoded, merely D/F'd.

Neumünster's reports and therefore decided to continue with the planned operation. At 1.40 p.m. Neumünster informed both Hipper and Scheer that convoys 'leave Bergen and Haugesund on 24 and 27 respectively.' Hipper swept up as far as Bergen, but found nothing for the good reason that German Intelligence was at fault and no convoys were at sea. He rejoined Scheer and the *Hochseeflotte* turned south for home.

By this time Room 40 had broken the current key and were able to signal Beatty at 4.25 p.m. the position of Scheer's flagship (although without being able to identify her by her call sign), and the fact that she was on SSE'ly course, speed ten knots. A little later, at 6.09 p.m. the Admiralty sent the following signal by the specially secure method devised for such purposes; 'Enemy submarine [U 19] reports as follows; Begins. Apparently 11 old enemy cruisers in 58 degrees 50 North 3 degrees 55 East Course South East. Speed 18 knots. Ends. This may be enemy [i.e. German] force.' British submarines were not the only ones to make recognition mistakes! By early on the 25th, a tentative identification of *Baden*'s call sign had been achieved, and it was sadly clear to the British that the Germans were nearing port. *Moltke* was in fact torpedoed by the British submarine E 42, but survived.

If only Scheer had received more reliable information about the sailing dates of the convoys, he might have secured a spectacular success not only against the merchant ships and their close escorts but against the covering forces as well. So, to this extent, the British were lucky. Room 40 held its own private enquiry to determine whether clues, which should have given earlier indications of the German intentions, had been missed. James wrote in 1936 that the only failure was in not appreciating the proper significance of the catchword order (*Spannkraft* = full force) to U-boats. He also sent a rather breezy apologia to Beatty's staff officer immediately after the fiasco, pointing out the difficulties caused by the W/T silence maintained by the Germans, by the changes in call signs and so on. He claimed that 'Our intercepting and D/F stations did very well indeed and it is a good augury for the future as they picked up all the signals that were made . . .' This was really cold comfort, and in any case was putting a gloss on things. Room 40's staff themselves admitted that, with hindsight, clues had been missed; it should have been realised earlier than it was, that this was not just another exercise in the Bight but the opening moves in a major operation. Marder concludes that, to have had any chance of intercepting

Scheer, Beatty would have had to have sailed before midnight on the 23rd. Whether he could have done so in the prevailing weather conditions is doubtful. Room 40 felt, whatever James may have said, that they ought to have realised from the events on the forenoon of the 23rd, that a major operation was under way. Perhaps it was an over-critical judgement and even had they done so, one cannot be sure that the Operational authorities would have accepted such insubstantial evidence as sufficient to order the Grand Fleet to sea.[1] On the other hand, it is hard to see why the Grand Fleet was not brought to short notice at least six hours before it was.

It is salutary, if depressing, for lovers of the Royal Navy, to remember that there were only five occasions throughout the four and a quarter years of war when the Grand Fleet – or a part of it – might have inflicted a severe defeat on the Germans. These were the Yarmouth Raid, the Dogger Bank action, Jutland, the August 1916 and the April 1918 sorties. On only two of them, the Dogger Bank and Jutland, was there any contact between the main forces and in neither was the result as satisfactory for the British as it should have been. On this last occasion Room 40 itself must share at least some of the blame, because they were now being consulted and Operations were beginning to pay attention to their opinions. The basic fact, however, was that the *Hochseeflotte* had failed, and it was now too late to expect the U-boat arm to retrieve the situation.

Within two months of this final sortie of the *Hochseeflotte*, the tide had turned on the Western Front. The last of the German offensives had been held and the British and the French, and, at last, the Americans were going over to the offensive. The might of the German army was no longer sufficient to sustain its allies. No amount of propaganda could conceal the fact that the war at sea was lost, and that nothing could prevent the arrival of over-powering reinforcements from the United States. The boast of the *Admiralstab* that the U-boats would bring Britain to her knees in six months had patently failed; the *Hochseeflotte* could do nothing; the Royal Navy's blockade (so similar to old General Winfield Scott's 'Anaconda Plan' during the American Civil War) had slowly but surely reduced the will of the civil populations and the ability of the General Staffs of the Central Powers to carry on the war much longer. It had been slow, and it could not, by itself, defeat a

[1] Compare the attitude of Admiral Pound during the disastrous North Russian convoy, PQ 17, in 1942.

Continental power; only the soldiers could do that. Napoleon was not defeated until ten years after Trafalgar, but he might well have established himself in an unassailable position in Europe but for his failure to overcome the Royal Navy. So it was again in World War I and in World War II. The British Army may not have been just a 'projectile to be launched by the Royal Navy', as Jacky Fisher thought, but British sea power despite mistakes and so many missed opportunities, had been a major factor in ensuring the defeat of Imperial Germany.

CHAPTER SEVENTEEN

The War must be Ended

There had been signs even in 1917 that all was far from well with the Central Powers, and that Austro-Hungary, that 'corpse' to which Germany had so long been 'fettered', was anxious to make a deathbed repentance. The old Emperor, Franz-Joseph, had died at the age of eighty-six in November 1916. He had been succeeded by his great nephew Karl, a well-meaning and intelligent young man of twenty-nine. Karl was, from the first, convinced that the survival of the Hapsburg dynasty and of the Austro-Hungarian Empire depended on the conclusion of an early peace. In April 1917 he made secret approaches to the French but the negotiations broke down because, on the one hand the Germans were still confident of total victory and of obtaining their goal of German hegemony in Europe, while on the other, Italy and Roumania, who had been bribed into the war by Franco-British promises of territorial acquisitions, were not prepared to forego the loot which they had been promised. By this time, of course, President Wilson's high minded ideas about a 'peace without conquest' were being tempered by the harsh realities of actual involvement in war. Karl's sub-rosa schemes came to nothing.

However, in January 1918 President Wilson (without consulting his Allies) issued his famous Fourteen Points for peace, and Karl seized on them as the last chance to extricate his Empire from total disaster. On 20 February Quiggin, Room 40's Austrian expert, decoded a message from Count Czernin, the Austro-Hungarian Minister of Foreign Affairs to Count Fürstenberg, his Ambassador in Madrid, requesting the King of Spain, Alfonso XIII, to pass a personal message from the Emperor Karl to President Wilson. Karl proposed a secret meeting between his own representatives and the President's to 'clear up the situation to such an extent that no further obstacles would stand in the way of a world peace congress . . .' This was not news which even Hall could keep to himself. He went at once to Geddes, and the two of them rushed off on what Hall called

'our mad journey' to Manchester, where Lloyd-George had been speaking. Before he left, Hall had given Bell a copy of the Austrian message for Ambassador Page to cable to the President. Thus it came about that both the British Prime Minister and the American President knew the exact contents of the Austrian proposals before the Spanish Ambassador was able to present them officially in Washington. 'The President,' Colonel House cabled Balfour, 'had difficulty in composing his face and in trying to look surprised . . .'
In London, Balfour discussed the situation with Page; he could not see that Karl's proposals would lead to anything; what he described as the 'regrettable' secret Anglo–French Treaty with Italy had promised her territorial gains at Austria's expense; if Italy, still reeling from the disaster at Caporetto, thought she would not in the end receive them, she would 'quit the war'. Wilson was so impressed with the need for secrecy that he typed all his own replies! The Germans had got wind of this further attempt at back-sliding by their principal ally and, as Room 40 discovered, informed their Ambassador in Madrid, Prince Ratibor, that they did not approve of Karl's efforts and did not think that they would succeed. Hall told Bell that he thought that the German Government was lying to Ratibor, as it had done on more than one occasion in the past. The Germans, like Balfour, were correct; the negotiations soon broke down as the Austrian attitude hardened with the initial success of the German March offensive.

But the collapse not only of Austro-Hungary, but of Bulgaria and Turkey, and with them of Imperial Germany itself, could not be long delayed. By the end of July the Allied armies were everywhere on the offensive. On 8 August the British struck on the Somme, and the Germans suffered what their official history describes as 'the greatest defeat the German Army had suffered since the beginning of the war . . .', or, in Ludendorff's words, 'the black day of the German Army . . .' Three days later, he submitted his resignation to the Kaiser. It was not accepted, but Wilhelm II recognised that, '. . . we must strike a balance. We have nearly reached the limit of our powers of resistance. The war must be ended.' The Austrians stated bluntly that they could not continue resistance during the coming winter. On 29 September Bulgaria signed an armistice, and shortly afterwards Turkey opened negotiations for peace. On 4 October the new German Government under Prince Max of Baden decided, under pressure from the General Staff, to approach President Wilson to try to arrange terms. On 5 October Bell cabled

Harrison for the President as follows: 'I learn from the usual unimpeachable source that the new German Government intends making a peace offer to the President.' Thanks to the Berlin–Madrid link and to a series of wireless messages sent by the German High Command to their generals in (Russian) Georgia, Room 40 were able to follow every move in the negotiations which finally led to the end of the fighting at 11.00 a.m. on 11 November 1918. Officially it was an armistice; in practice it was capitulation.

But until almost the eleventh hour of the eleventh day of the eleventh month, it looked as if the Imperial German Navy was determined to go down fighting rather than in tame surrender. Beatty, for one, hoped fervently that he would at last get his chance; neither Wemyss nor Hall could believe that the *Hochseeflotte* would refuse to make one last challenge, however forlorn the hope, for the honour of the fleet and the flag.

In August Scheer had become Chief of the *Admiralstab*, and Hipper had taken over command of the *Hochseeflotte*. Both moves were interpreted by the British as likely to herald more aggressive action. Scheer in fact believed that only the U-boats offered any hope of decisive success, but it was of course now too late to reinforce their numbers to the point where there was in fact any likelihood of this being achieved. On 14 October President Wilson demanded as a condition for continuing negotiations, that the Germans abandon all attacks on passenger ships. Prince Max of Baden had no option but to accept. Scheer regarded such a measure as so restrictive that on 20 October he issued orders for attacks on *all* merchant ships to cease and for U-boats on patrol to return to port. Ostend and Zeebrugge had just been evacuated in the face of the advancing Allied armies, and so the whole strength of the U-boat arm was becoming available to co-operate with the surface fleet. Scheer did indeed feel that the Germany Navy must make one last desperate effort against the Royal Navy, no matter what the cost. Even a Pyrrhic victory might alleviate the increasingly stringent demands which the Allies were now making. On 22 October Hipper received verbal instructions from Scheer that 'the forces of the *Hochseeflotte* are to be employed to strike a blow against the English Fleet.'

Room 40, despite a further change in all German call signs, 'on an entirely new principle', in the middle of September, were on the whole able to follow what moves were taking place *at sea*; but they could not be sure what these moves really signified, nor could they know of any instructions not issued by wireless. The Admiralty were reluctant to divert destroyers from the Grand Fleet to hunt the returning U-boats (from the Atlantic, the Channel and the Mediterranean), because they considered that the chance of a sortie by the *Hochseeflotte* 'is unaltered by the present circumstances.' A very close watch was still being kept on the dangerous *Brummer* and *Bremse*. However, on 22 October Beatty was informed that U-boats had been ordered to concentrate in the middle of the North Sea and only to attack men of war by day. Beatty at once asked for the Admiralty's ideas of the significance of this order. The Admiralty appreciation was that British mining of the U-boat swept channels required returning U-boats to wait until the latest information was available, and that this waiting position was chosen so as to give opportunities for attacks on the Grand Fleet. 'A co-ordinated movement of the High Sea Fleet is not necessarily intended.' However, in a further appreciation on the next day the Admiralty concluded that there was some connection with the future move-ments of the German Fleet, but that this conclusion was not sufficiently certain to justify the abandonment of North Sea and Channel escorts. The Admiralty were, however, anxious to set free all the Grand Fleet destroyers to accompany the Fleet as soon as the situation became clearer.

On 23 October the Admiralty reported no further signs of German activity, but on the 24th became alarmed at 'an unusually large number of messages in a most secret cipher on the night of 23–24 October, but purport unknown.' The anxiety lessened a little during the next four days, because Hipper's flagship and his 4th Battle Squadron had departed for the Baltic. On 28 October, however, orders to five U-boats to take up patrol positions were decoded and to the 3rd Battle Squadron to coal at Wilhelmshaven. On the same day it was, incidentally, learned that all U-boats had been instructed to leave the Mediterranean if fuel permitted, and if not to seek internment in a Spanish port.

Just before midnight on 28 October, Fremantle and Hall sent Beatty an appreciation which started, 'Dispositions of enemy sub-marines combined with position of their large minefield recently laid and now clear constitutes fairly decisive evidence of his desire to draw the Grand Fleet out . . . No evidence as to how he proposes to achieve his object but evidence that no move of battlefleet can take place before . . . tomorrow night. No objective for enemy is apparent which will not involve great risk to him. Therefore he may confine himself to emerging from the Bight and returning after making us aware of his exit by W/T signals. Unlikely that enemy will risk fleet action until Armistice negotiations are settled one way or another. Press reports of German submarines proceeding home via the Norwegian coast probabably emanate from Germany and are intended to conceal existence of submarine trap.'

This appreciation erred in underestimating, for once, the boldness of the Germans. Bearing in mind the *Admiralstab*'s cautious policy over the past four and a quarter years, Fremantle and Hall may be forgiven. What is noticeable, is the change in the Admiralty attitude to promulgating intelligence. Beatty was being taken fully into the Admiralty's confidence, and was being given the Admiralty's best guess and the reasons behind it. The Chief and Deputy Chief of Naval Staff were at last consulting Hall and his experts before coming to conclusions. The Operations and Intelligence Divisions were working in concert instead of in separate watertight compartments. It was very much overdue.

The tension mounted, as well it might. Hipper's plans had been approved by Scheer, and a major operation was planned to start on 30 October and last for three days. It was to involve the whole of the *Hochseeflotte* and all available cruisers, destroyers and U-boats. Attacks were to be made on British traffic off the Flanders coast and in the mouth of the Thames, designed to provoke the Grand Fleet into a hurried dash to the southern North Sea over freshly laid minefields and across U-boat patrol lines. On the evening of 29 October, Fremantle told Beatty that the battle cruiser *Moltke* had returned to the North Sea, that the 4th Battle Squadron and three battle cruisers were at anchor in Schillig Roads and that the Fleet Flagship had left Wilhelmshaven at 4.00 p.m. to join them. Early on 30 October, the Admiralty warned that there were indications that the *Hochseeflotte* would carry out evolutions in the Bight that day, but at 8.33 a.m. it was learned that the German Fleet was to remain at anchor for the time being and then, at 1.12 p.m. that the exercises had been postponed until the following day. Fremantle then told Beatty that the cancellation was probably due to fog, and that the whole of the *Hochseeflotte* remained in readiness in Schillig Roads. He warned the British Commander-in-Chief that it would probably not be possible to obtain any news of the Fleet's actual sailing, though he had every hope of getting some indications of its intentions. However, shortly after this Beatty was informed that tasks for all submarines up to 4 and 5 November had been cancelled, and that they could leave their waiting positions at their own discretion. This made it obvious that the planned operation had at least been postponed for several days.

That morning Hall had discussed the situation with Ned Bell, and had warned him that a source in Berlin had reported to his government[1] that the recent cessation of attacks by U-boats on passenger ships was dependent on the conclusion of an armistice, and that they would be resumed if negotiations broke down. Reports from Scandinavia that U-boats had been ordered to return to base, were untrue and that in fact a large concentration was taking place and that Admiral Sims was being kept fully informed. 'Finally,' Bell cabled Harrison, 'Admiral Hall informs me that he has learned from an absolutely sure source that at a recent Council in Berlin the German Emperor said: "During the peace negotiations, or *even after peace* [Author's italics], my U-boats will find an opportunity to destroy the English Fleet." Hall asked to be excused from divulging the source of this astonishing piece of information, but he assures me that it is as certain as the wireless to Madrid and he dictated what I have quoted as being the exact words used by the Emperor.' Bell added a handwritten note to his file copy of the cablegram, 'I am satisfied that the source was the same one as that from which previous info. was obtained, i.e. W/T from Berlin to Madrid, but in this case in Spanish cipher.' Hall did not in fact dictate the words quoted – he wrote them down on a scrap of paper which Bell carefully preserved. It *was* an astonishing piece of information! Did the Kaiser use these actual words? Were the words so precisely written down by Hall for Bell exactly those quoted by the Spanish source? Hall was adept at planting false information on the enemy but, although he had not always told Ned Bell the *whole* truth in the past, he had never given him any information which was not, basically, true. One is inclined to believe that Hall was telling the truth so far as he knew it, but only a sight of the original decode would confirm this.

The Allies were already beginning to disagree about the terms of the armistice. Foch and the French politicians were insistent that the German Army should be rendered incapable of renewing the war on land, but were anxious that the final conditions should not be so humiliating that the Germans would refuse them and renew hostilities, which the French nation, after all its sacrifices, would be in poor shape to meet. They therefore were opposed to the British

[1] Bell's telegram referred to 'Polo', possibly a code-name for the Swedish Minister.

demand that the German Navy must, equally, be rendered impotent. The Anglophobe American Chief of Naval Operations, Admiral W. S. Benson, and the Secretary of the Navy, Josephus Daniel, supported the French, but for different reasons; they did not wish the Royal Navy to emerge from the war with even more preponderant power than it had entered it. Wemyss and Beatty (the latter did not think that Wemyss was taking a strong enough line) would settle for nothing, even under the armistice terms, but the surrender of every single U-boat as well as the emasculation of the German surface fleet. True or false, the Kaiser's alleged remarks greatly strengthened the Royal Navy's case. Nor can they in any way have lowered the excitement and tension in the Admiralty or on board Beatty's flagship.

The oracle, Room 40, could, for a few more days, only produce Delphic utterances. Early on 31 October, Beatty was told that the key had not changed, as expected, that minesweeping had been cancelled due to fog, that certain other measures had also been cancelled and there were no significant signs of activity. That afternoon it was learned that the 3rd (German) Battle Squadron had proceeded into the Baltic. For the next few days the usual situation report sent to Beatty each evening, disclosed no signs of activity except routine minesweeping and outpost duties. The intended operation was obviously postponed if not definitely cancelled – but why?

In fact, mutiny had broken out. The orders to the *Hochseeflotte* to assemble in the Schillig Roads on 29 October had been interpreted by the crews of the big ships as meaning that 'the Fleet was putting to sea to seek a glorious end off the English coast.' The first sign of disaffection was that large numbers of men failed to report back on board after shore leave and had to be rounded up at gun point. On the night of 29–30 October ratings in several battleships assembled on the forecastle shouting and cheering for peace. The rot began to spread, and Hipper realised that he must call off the sortie and order the heavy ships to disperse to Wilhelmshaven and Kiel. The destroyers, minesweepers and above all the U-boats, however, remained largely unaffected and continued to do their duty and obey orders.

On 1 November Room 40 intercepted a number of signals from the battleships *Ostfriesland*, *Heligoland* and *Schwaben* with references to courts martial and deserters, and on the following day a message, only partially decoded, concerning leave for the crews of

the *Derfflinger* and *Von der Tann*. There were also a number of
signals from Hipper which could not be even partially decoded at
the time. By the evening of 4 November it was evident that
something was amiss; whether it was a full scale mutiny or disturb-
ances which could, like those in 1917, be suppressed was still not
clear. By the 5th it seemed more likely that the situation was
serious. Hipper sent out an order for all key tables to be locked up
immediately and for signals to be decoded by officers only. Half an
hour later FdU (Senior Officer, U-boats) informed U 139, 'Revolution and Soldiers' Council in Kiel.' The U-boat was to await further
orders and keep its wireless transmitter permanently in the hands of
officers. That evening Wemyss cabled Beatty that there were
'indications of a revolution at Kiel. It does not appear to have
affected the 3rd Battle Squadron which has moved to Lübeck Bay
. . . Submarine Headquarters has not yet been affected by mutiny.'

At 2.26 a.m. on the 6th, FdU (Captain Andreas Michelsen),
signalled all U-boats giving instructions to five specific boats then in
the Baltic to 'fire without warning on ships with the red flag. The
whole of Kiel is hostile. Occupy exit from Kiel harbour.' He
followed this up with instructions to his boats to blockade Kiel and
allow no ship to proceed. 'Use all means to break down resistance.'
As late as that evening Hipper, too, was hoping to restore order.
'The *Admiralstab* in conjunction with the Government has ordered
that resistance is to be broken with all available forces. Red Flag is
to be treated as enemy.'

From then onwards, however, the situation deteriorated rapidly.
Although Michelsen and his U-boats continued to breathe fire and
thunder against the mutineers, even those cruisers whose crews had
hitherto remained loyal began to be infected. Soldiers' Councils
were in control at Cuxhaven, Kiel and Heligoland. The staff of
Room 40 followed these developments with great excitement, but
also with a curious feeling of regret, of sympathy, almost, for their
opponents. They had come to know the German Navy intimately,
more intimately indeed than their own. After more than four years
it was hard to believe that it was all ending, not with a ride of the
Valkyries, which had seemed inevitable less than a week ago, but in
shameful mutiny.

Not so Beatty. He felt unjustly denied his triumph. He was kept
completely informed by frequent appreciations from Fremantle or
Wemyss, who was in Paris. On 7 November the British felt that it
was 'inconceivable that the crews of vessels which are still believed

to be loyal are not affected to a certain extent', but on the 8th it appeared that 'the revolt is at an end. This result has been obtained by means of negotiations in which the Government appears to have met the mutineers more than half way . . .' Next day, the 9th, Beatty was told that the German Commander-in-Chief had resumed control but was working with the Soldiers' and Workmen's Council at Kiel. The small craft were still on the whole carrying out their normal duties, and the Soldiers' Council at Heligoland enquired what should be done in the event of a British attack on the fortress. Similar queries were raised by the forces responsible for the defence of the Jade and the Ems.

Hall, of course, had not failed to try to spread alarm and confusion in the enemy camp and to encourage the mutineers. He arranged for photographs of British ships flying the Red Flag to be distributed in Kiel and the North Sea ports from Denmark and Holland. The Royal Navy, Hall suggested, was also mutinying, and would soon join its German comrades in overthrowing the old order everywhere. Michelsen actually told his U-boats on 6 November that a British squadron wearing the Red Flag would arrive that very day; but *he* had no intention of welcoming it with anything but salvoes of torpedos.

As late as 9 November BdL (Senior Officer, Airships) reported that the Zeppelin Station at Nordholz was 'under the orders of the officer corps in complete and unchanged understanding with all crews and their representative council.'

But, in reality, the revolution was sweeping all over Germany. The Kaiser had abdicated to go into exile in Holland. Just before noon on 10 November a joint order from Hipper and the Soldiers' Council ordered all ships at sea to return to port immediately. By then it was known that the Armistice would come into force in twenty-four hours' time.

British naval officers simply could not bring themselves to believe that the enemy's power was broken, broken by the blockade, by inaction, by bad food, by a feeling that they could *never* defeat the Royal Navy. On the afternoon of 11 November, Fremantle sent Beatty the following appreciation of the 'present position in the German Fleet. Fleet remains fully mobilized with officers at their posts under the joint control of the Commander-in-Chief and Soldiers' Council . . . Naval armistice terms are of a severity unexpected by the enemy and may provoke reaction . . . General conclusions are that no offensive action need be anticipated but

Fleet is still powerful for defensive action. Submission of remainder
of submarines to Revolution is not assured so isolated action against
men of war by them is still possible.' That afternoon U 70 had
refused to enter Emden unless given an assurance that she would
not be put under the Red Flag. The Soldiers' Committee gave her
permission to wear the Naval Ensign.

It is easy to understand why Beatty and Wemyss had been
insisting that the naval terms of the armistice should be no less
severe than those which would be included in the ultimate peace
treaty. In the end they more or less got their way. All Germany's
submarines capable of crossing the North Sea were to be interned at
Harwich. It had originally been intended that the major German
surface ships should be interned in neutral ports, until a peace treaty
was signed and their ultimate fate settled. No neutral power was
willing to take on the responsibility, and on 21 November the whole
Grand Fleet including Admiral Rodman's US 6th Battle Squadron
put to sea to escort the *Hochseeflotte* to Rosyth before internment in
Scapa Flow. At 9.30 a.m. contact was made with the leading
German battleship. She was followed by eight other battleships, five
battle cruisers, seven light cruisers and forty-nine destroyers. At
11.00 a.m. Beatty made his well-known signal: 'The German flag
will be hauled down at sunset today, Thursday, and will not be
hoisted again without permission.' When, that evening, the order
was executed, there was a storm of cheers from the men of his
flagship, HMS *Queen Elizabeth*. Beatty turned to them and said
with a smile, 'I always told you they would have to come out.' For
him it was no armistice; it was surrender. Room 40 had a representative on board *Queen Elizabeth* – Lieutenant Commander Alastair
Denniston RNVR, hurriedly sent up to act as the C-in-C's interpreter. He commented afterwards that 'Sir David Beatty is a very wilful
man, and has no mercy on a man or a nation he despises . . . I
confess I did feel sorry for the [German] Senior Officers there. They
were keen, efficient men, who had learnt their work and made the
German Navy their career, and this was the end of it.'

Not quite the end. That came seven months later when, on 21
June 1919, Vice-Admiral Ludwig von Reuter gave orders to all
German ships at Scapa Flow to scuttle themselves. Fifteen of the
sixteen capital ships, four of the eight cruisers and thirty-two of
the fifty destroyers succeeded in doing so. One cannot blame von
Reuter, but it was a sad end for one of the mightiest fleets the world
has ever seen.

CHAPTER EIGHTEEN

Heroes and Monsters

On Wednesday, 11 December 1918, ID 25 gave a farewell party. Frank Birch saw to it that there were recitations, poems and songs. There was a programme with a picture on the cover showing a delighted looking Blinker Hall, concealed behind a screen with his hand to his ear, listening to two angry and gesticulating German admirals. Some verses of one of the songs summed it all up;

While some say that the Boche was not beaten by Foch
But by Winston or Ramsay Macdonald
There are others who claim that the coup de grace came
From the Knoxes (our Dilly and Ronald)
It was Tiarks and Thring who with charts and with string
Gave the U-boats their oily quietus
Yet without the Lord Mayor in his Diplomats' lair
The Huns *might* have managed to beat us
    Peace, Peace, who gave us peace?
    And how was our victory won?
I know scores who aver it's through him (or through her)
On the strictest QT it's entirely through me
That the war is all over and done.

There is one little scene, would look well on the screen
Or it might suit the brush of a cubist
It's the hour before dawn, when there's no time to yawn
'Cause a paper storm's drowning the tubist.
There are Zeppelins about, the key isn't out
And Lord knows what's afoot in the Bight now
When the tube basket's crammed and each message is jammed
Operations want all the news right now.
    Peace, Peace, oh for some peace
    Is the cry of the night-watch each one.
Dichter Nebel[1] at sea is the weather for me

[1] Thick Fog.

Till the war is all over and done
But they're all Cock a Hoops when a U-boat is YŪPS[1]
And its cruises all over and done.

Peace, Peace, now we've got peace
Our Benny the Lord Mayor's napoo[2]
There's horrid dejection
In Political Section
For he's taken his chocolates too
Peace, Peace, *Oh* for some peace
Miss Roddam says Knox does not please her
When instead of a mat he makes use of her hat
And knocks out his pipe on the geyser.

Peace, Peace, we don't get much peace
The tubist is ne'er left alone
The monotony palls of replying to calls
From Miss Welford's young man on the phone.
Peace, Peace, now you've got peace
There's nothing much left for the IO[3]
Let C-in-C wait if the War Diary's late
For the *Seydlitz* is in Scapa Flow.

Room 40, or ID 25 as it had been renamed, had been a happy ship. Its crew had all spoken the same language[4] even if it was not always as nautical as the Royal Navy would have liked. Some had been to Scapa, others to Harwich, others to Kiel or Wilhelmshaven; others were to go to the Peace Conference in Paris. But all that was a bit of an anti-climax. Most of them wished to return as speedily as possible to their old careers – to the Stock Exchange or the City, to the universities, to literature or antique furniture, to haute couture or to the stage. But for a few Room 40 had become a way of life, something they could not give up. Denniston, Clarke, Dilly Knox and one or two more were 'hooked'. They would all have earned much more by returning to civil life than the five or six hundred pounds a year which they were paid in Intelligence, but not one of them had ever, or could contemplate ever having in the future, a

---

[1] Missing.
[2] WWI soldiers' slang from the French *il n'y en a plus*, 'there is no more of it.'
[3] IO. Intelligence Officers, William Clarke and Frank Birch.
[4] The disproportionate number of Old Etonians among the staff of Room 40 is remarkable, but then Eton has always had a well-deserved reputation for making the very best out of generally unpromising material.

career which would give the fulfilment and satisfaction they had experienced in Room 40. They decided to stay on with the Old Firm. Thank God they did; they were soon to be disillusioned by Government apathy and Treasury parsimony; there was no longer the same excitement and constant pressure sending the adrenalin racing through their veins as there had been before *Seydlitz* was swinging to a buoy in Scapa Flow. But somehow they managed to keep the torch burning so that Britain did not enter World War II without any code-breaking expertise; it was not the least of Room 40's achievements that it gave birth to Bletchley Park. Nor were Denniston and his colleagues without immediate reinforcements when the time came. Clarke and the Lord Mayor had kept old associations alive with annual gatherings at Faudel-Phillips's lovely country house. When the call came, first at the time of Munich in 1938 and then, finally in September 1939, the former crew, or such of them as were still able, promptly reported back on board for duty. Times had changed; the enemy had learned some lessons; machine ciphering had revolutionised cryptology. But like Room 40, Bletchley Park attracted some extraordinary and extraordinarily talented men. The problems *were* solved. I suggest that this would not have been achieved so successfully without the initial 'lift off' provided by the old hands.

Hall himself did not attend the Peace Conference. He had set his heart on it. He knew everyone; the politicians, the admirals, the generals and the pressmen. He would have been in his element. But Wemyss, that very rare bird among British naval officers, a 1st Sea Lord who could deal with his own and other Services *and* with kings, presidents and prime ministers, would have none of it. Hall, he must have known, had played a part in the drama of Jacky Fisher's resignation. Oliver had described him as Judas Iscariot when Jellicoe was unshipped. He was a friend of David Beatty who, regrettably and on the whole unjustifiably, had quarrelled bitterly with Rosy Wemyss. The fighting at sea might be over, but the 1st Sea Lord had some tricky problems to settle with his country's allies and with his own people. One could hardly blame him if he had, perhaps, felt that Hall had succumbed to the occupational disease of so many Intelligence chiefs – intrigue – and that he might prove a Brutus if not a Cassius.

Hall could not in any case expect to remain much longer on the Active List; he had never flown his flag at sea and was, indeed, unfit for sea service. He offered his resignation and was placed on the

Retired List on 3 February 1919, being succeeded as Director of
Naval Intelligence by his deputy, Captain H. F. P. Sinclair.[1] Bell
reported the change, rather sadly, to Harrison. 'While the Admiralty are cutting down their work in the Intelligence Division . . . they
intend, I am glad to say, to keep up the work on the source you know
of, although with a somewhat reduced staff. There was some talk of
an inter-departmental organisation . . . but the Foreign Office have
declined to have anything to do with it so it is going to remain
entirely in the hands of the Admiralty. I shall of course try to get in
proper touch with the new DNI, and Hall, and certain others who
will remain behind, assure me that this will be alright. I am rather
doubtful, however, of my ever being able to accomplish in the
future what we have been able to do in the past, but I shall do my
best.'

Some in the Admiralty were glad to see Hall go. He had trodden
on a number of toes and, like the soldiers who wished to get back to
'proper soldiering' once the war was finished, there were staff
officers and civil servants in the Admiralty who looked forward to a
return to the old ways and to splicing the red tape through which
Blinker had so often ruthlessly hacked his way. But there were
others who felt that Britain could ill afford to dispense with the
services of a man like Hall. Geddes wrote to him that 'I do not think
that I have been in closer relationship with any officer in the
Admiralty than yourself during my tenure of office, and I would like
to let you know how very much I have appreciated your help,
assistance and unvarying loyalty and keeness throughout. It has
been a great pleasure to me to work with you and to experience your
great mental acumen. Everybody in the country owes you a great
debt of gratitude in my opinion, for what you have done in the war,
so little of which can be told . . .

Beatty wrote even more warmly:

> My dear old friend, . . . I was fortunate indeed to have had under
> my command one who embodied the very best ideas and princi-
> ples of the Service both during the year immediately preceeding
> the war when we endeavoured to fit ourselves for the struggle we

[1] Sinclair, always known as 'Quex' because his nasal way of talking suggested
the quacking of a duck, later took over as 'C', the head of the Secret Service, a post he
occupied until his death at the end of 1939. There was, therefore, yet another link
between Room 40 and Bletchley Park, since the code-breaking organisation, now
inter-departmental and called the Government Code and Cipher School, had by then
become part of the Secret Service under the suzerainty of a reluctant Foreign Office.

knew was coming, and during the first months of the war when so much had to be done to settle into our stride and meet the new conditions. Your advice and assistance was a tower of strength and as you know I hated your leaving for the far more important office which you have filled with such unparalleled success. Goodbye, old friend, and good luck to you in your new venture. I know that you will still be a tower of strength and support to the Navy and I shall never hesitate to call upon you for advice and assistance when I need it. Your old friend and comrade, David Beatty.

Lord Hardinge's views have already been given, and they were echoed by the Ambassador in Rome, Sir Rennell Rodd, who wrote to Balfour on 14 November, 'At a moment like the present when one is rejoicing over great results and must think of those who have assisted in bringing them about, I feel an impulse to record an unsolicited testimonial to the valuable work which Sir Reginald Hall did here in organising with the Italian Naval Authorities a special secret information service. During the last week or two it has been of great value to us to obtain rapid and sure information of what was going on on the other side of the Adriatic, and I don't think either we or the Italians should have had much if it had not been for the system which he devised and induced the Italians to work. Probably very few people know of this or would give him credit for all he did . . .' Ernest Mayse, the Consul General at Rotterdam, said it was his 'genuine and honest conviction, after more than three years' work in connection with your Department, that your personality is practically irreplaceable . . . However, I cannot let the opportunity pass without thanking you most heartily and most warmly for the strong and permanent support you have afforded me when I have been in great difficulties with other Departments . . . I feel that I am losing, not only a friend, but a very strong support by your departure . . .'

Hall, unlike the Directors of Military Intelligence, did not figure in the post-war Honours List. Perhaps it was felt that the KCMG he had received a year before on Foreign Office recommendation was sufficient – rather shabby treatment which his 'old friend and comrade', David Beatty might, one would have thought, have done something to rectify when he became 1st Sea Lord in November 1919 after special promotion to the rank of Admiral of the Fleet, the conferment of an earldom and the grant of £100,000 by Parliament.

Hall was at least luckier than his brilliant World War II successor, Godfrey, who was the only officer of his rank to receive no recognition of any sort at all for his immense services.

Hall went into politics, first as Conservative General Agent, and then, for a time, as a Member of Parliament. Thanks partly to Claud Serocold, who was devoted to him, he secured directorships on the boards of a number of leading companies. He led a full, active and enjoyable life but he never again found the outlet for his great talents which the Directorship of the Intelligence Division had provided. Early in 1939, when war with Germany again seemed inevitable and John Godfrey was appointed DNI, Reggie Hall saw an opportunity to serve his country, if only at second hand. He was at this time nearly sixty-nine but as alert and full of vitality as he had been twenty years earlier, when he had sat in Godfrey's chair in the same room in the West Block of the Admiralty overlooking the Horseguards' Parade. 'He very unobtrusively offered me,' wrote Godfrey, 'full access to his enormous store of knowledge, wisdom, cunning and ingenuity . . .' Hall warned Godfrey that the job had 'more kicks than halfpence', but, although the situation had changed greatly, and Hall told Godfrey to develop the Division along his own lines – and Godfrey indeed did so – there can be no doubt that the new DNI benefited enormously from Hall's advice and experience. 'When in doubt,' Godfrey said, 'I often asked myself what Hall would have done.' In 1940, when the Blitz started to make life uncomfortable for Londoners, Hall offered Godfrey the use of his own flat, 36 Curzon Street, an offer which was most gratefully accepted.

The old Admiral was himself then commanding a platoon of the Home Guard near his home in the New Forest, and refused all offers from his friend Amos Peaslee to come and stay with him in warmer, easier surroundings in the United States, despite warnings from his doctors that winters in wartime England would place an unendurable strain on his chronically weak chest. By the summer of 1943 the end was in sight. Two operations were unsuccessful, and he died on 22 October 1943. His daughter Faith tells this story of his last days, which were spent in the comparative comfort of Claridges Hotel rather than in a wartime hospital. Something went wrong with the plumbing of the bathroom of his suite, and the Hotel management sent a plumber up to put matters right. He proved to be a tall rather lugubrious looking individual, clad, as it was Claridges, in an impeccable black suit, white shirt and black tie. He was somewhat startled to hear a sharp remark from the death-bed, 'If you're the undertaker, my man, you're too early.'

Oliver survived Hall, indeed he survived all his contemporaries. He retired after commanding the Home Fleet from 1924 to 1927 and was promoted Admiral of the Fleet in 1928. On his hundredth birthday on 22 January 1965, he was presented with an illuminated scroll by the eleven of his successors as Director of Naval Intelligence still alive. Oliver died shortly thereafter.

Bubbles James went on to become Deputy Chief of Naval Staff in 1936. With the storm clouds of another World War already threatening, James feared that the Naval Intelligence Division, which had been greatly run down since he had last been a member of it, would not be able to cope with hostilities. He gave directions for the formation of what became the Admiralty's Operational Intelligence Centre. Thanks to his foresight, and to the practical work of the young Norman Denning and the guidance of John Godfrey, the OIC was able to make better use of the work of the code-breakers than Clarke, Birch, Thring and Tiarks had been permitted to do until the closing months of World War I. James died in 1973.

*

It is time to sum up – to try to strike a balance. What had they all achieved – Oliver, Ewing, Hall and the rest of them? Could they have done better? What contribution to victory had Room 40 made? The defeat of Imperial Germany, despite the odds against her, was by no means inevitable. In April 1917 her U-boats came within weeks, if not days, of winning victory for her at sea; twelve months later her army seemed almost as nearly within reach of success on land. Perhaps her only real chance of achieving the sort of result which she desired had vanished with the Battle of The Marne in September 1914. But it had not seemed like this to her opponents on many occasions during the next four years. The war had, like the Battle of Waterloo, been 'a damned nice thing, the nearest run thing you ever saw in your life',[1] so that even comparatively minor factors exerted a quite disproportionate influence on the final outcome. But first class intelligence is never a minor factor; it is an absolute prerequisite to victory in war, (unless one side is so overwhelmingly powerful that it is bound to win no matter how many mistakes it makes). Britain's wars have, in the end, all been won or lost on land, but no British army has ever been able to fight

[1] The Duke of Wellington's verdict.

without first being put ashore and then maintained by the Royal
Navy. Britain did not lose the American War of Independence
when Cornwallis surrendered at Yorktown, but when Admiral
Graves failed to drive de Grasse's blockading fleet away from
Chesapeake Bay. The invasion of Normandy in 1944 would have
been unthinkable if the second Battle of the Atlantic had not been
won in 1943. So what did Room 40 contribute to the eventual victory
of the British, British Empire, French, Italian, Belgian and American armies in 1918? The answer must surely be a very great deal, for
without the Royal Navy's control of the sea routes throughout the
world, the European armies of the Entente could never have held
out and the British and eventually American armies could never
have reached the fields of battle. But, without Room 40, it is very
doubtful whether the Royal Navy could have performed its task as
successfully as, in the end, it did.

The Imperial German Navy started the war with certain marked
disadvantages, but equally some definite advantages compared with
its opponent on the other side of the North Sea. The disadvantages
were that it was seriously outnumbered in most classes of ship, and
particularly in battleships, by the Royal Navy. It lacked its rival's
long tradition of victory. Denning's verdict on Hitler's navy in 1942
was that 'The discipline and morale of officers and men continues to
be exceptionally high, but on proceeding to sea is tempered by the
fact that they believe their chances of operating successfully against
the British naval forces are slight, and they are mainly imbued with a
spirit of determination to fight and die in accordance with the
highest traditions of the German Navy.' These words might equally
have been applied to the *Hochseeflotte* and its leaders fom 1914 to
1918. The policy of maintaining a 'fleet in being', rather than of
risking losses to achieve big results, dominated German naval
strategy more than it should have done and contributed largely to
the eventual loss of morale and to the final mutiny. On the other
hand, the *Hochseeflotte* was extremely well built and trained, and its
senior officers did not suffer to the same extent from the rigid
centralised control exercised by the British Admiralty (and by
Jellicoe) over the Grand Fleet. But the Germans' greatest asset was
that they held the initiative; they could choose their moment for a
sortie. In the absence of British aerial reconnaissance or the ability
to maintain a close blockade by surface ships or submarines of
German ports, they could reasonably hope to achieve surprise. The
policy of attempting to whittle down the strength of the Grand Fleet

by sudden raids and ambushes was not, on the face of it, without prospects of success. Who can say what the result would have been if German raids on the East Coast of England or on shipping in the North Sea had been repeated more often, with defeats of isolated British battle cruiser or cruiser squadrons? The Germans would have been encouraged to become bolder and, perhaps, make a serious attempt to interfere with the vital flow of British supplies and reinforcements across the Channel to France, or even to risk a powerful raid into the Atlantic. That these things did not happen, that the world wide commitments of the Royal Navy were not, in the event, ever stretched quite to breaking point, was due almost entirely to one factor – the superiority of British naval Intelligence. It was Room 40, despite its imperfections and despite the Admiralty's repeated failures to make the best use of its information, which enabled the Grand Fleet to meet every German move and which confirmed the German High Command in its essentially defensive, unenterprising use of the *Hochseeflotte*. Room 40 robbed the Germans of the advantages of surprise.

It is less easy to be so precise about Room 40's contribution to the defeat of the U-boats. Both the British and the Germans underestimated, for far too long, the real potential of submarine warfare. To be fair to both sides, it was a very new and entirely untried weapon. It would be wrong to criticise either British or German attitudes in 1914 or even in 1915 because of events in 1917 (let alone in 1943). The facts, however, are that the Germans failed, until it was too late, to devote sufficient effort to U-boat warfare, while the British equally were slow to recognise the seriousness of the situation with which they were confronted and only took the necessary steps to counter it at one minute to midnight. In the U-boat war, the British did not start off with the in-built advantage which they possessed in the Grand Fleet; both the British and the Germans began virtually from scratch and on an equal basis. Only with the introduction of convoy and an offensive mining campaign could Room 40's accurate information be put to effective use. Neither in World War I nor in World War II did British Intelligence win the U-boat war, but in both cases it certainly shortened it.

Room 40 itself had its failings, but these were almost entirely the result of the system imposed on it from above. Here again, one must try to avoid the temptation to be wise after the event. There was no precedent for the situation which arose, almost by chance in the early months of the war, when the British Naval Staff – or rather the

1st Lord, the 1st Sea Lord, and the Chief of the War Staff – were suddenly presented with the ability to read a large number of their enemy's operational signals. One must pay tribute to Churchill's immediate realisation of the enormous advantage which this placed in his hands, and of the vital importance of maintaining secrecy so as to prevent any German suspicions being aroused. The existence of 'Special Intelligence' was concealed from the enemy as successfully in World War I as it was in World War II (although the secret was not maintained for nearly so long once the first war was over). But secrecy was carried far too far, and this very mistaken policy stemmed from Churchill's original charter for Room 40. 'The effect,' state Birch and Clarke, 'was suicidal . . . Every section [of the Intelligence Division] worked in isolation in a watertight compartment . . . the section at work on the most direct and vital form of intelligence conceivable, that is on the enemy's wireless traffic, was not until May 1917 part of the Intelligence Division at all! . . . This amazing policy of divorcing from the ID for nearly three years its most vital member was an error as fatal as it is still inexplicable.'

Of course it is not inexplicable – it was due to the personalities of the decision makers at the top. Winston could no more leave the details of intelligence to the Director of the Intelligence Division and his staff than he could restrain himself from taking operational decisions out of the hands of the 1st Sea Lord and the Operations Division.[1]

But Churchill had departed from the Admiralty in May 1915. Sufficient experience had by then been gained which should have shown the need for modifications and improvements to the system imposed by the man who was now serving on the Western Front as a Lieutenant Colonel of the Royal Scots Fusiliers. And here we come to the nub of the thing. The reader will by now have realised that I do not share Professor Hinsley's 'feeling for the appropriateness of Flaubert's recipe for the perfect realistic novel: *Pas de monstres, et pas de héros*.'[2] Room 40's 'monster' was undoubtedly Dummy Oliver. An arch centraliser and a 'workaholic', to use the modern jargon, he just could not conceive that anyone except Henry Francis Oliver could be entrusted with interpreting and promulgating the

[1] He acted no differently in World War II. When Special Intelligence again became available, he insisted on seeing a selection of the original decodes raw, that is before those most competent to do so could produce reasoned appreciations of their true significance. The results were not always happy.

[2] *See* his Preface to Volume I of *British Intelligence in the Second World War*, HMSO, 1979.

fruits of Room 40's work. Although he had been Director of Intelligence for just over a year before he became Chief of War Staff and should, therefore, have gained some insight into intelligence problems, this experience had merely confirmed him in his conviction that he must continue to act as Pooh Bah, and Lord High Everything Else.[1]

Oliver simply refused to delegate at all; the volume of signals which he drafted in his own hand is staggering. How he managed to accomplish so much is amazing. He himself says that he only left the Admiralty for an hour or two in the evening when he went home for dinner. He made virtually no use of the staff of either the Operations or the Intelligence Divisions – and for most of his time there was no Plans Division. He was contemptuous of other people's efforts; he did *everything* himself. On the very rare occasions when he was not 'in the chair', the Admiralty came to a halt.

But effective use of intelligence, by reasoned appreciations of the enemy's intentions, by prompt promulgation of those facts which can be ascertained so that those at sea can act on them, cannot be achieved by one single individual studying only the isolated and more important items of information placed before him. Good intelligence depends, not just on a few brilliant coups, but on the patient study of an accumulation of small, often dull and seemingly unimportant facts; on the establishment of norms so that any deviation from the standard pattern of behaviour immediately sets the alarm bells ringing for the expert. Such a system requires that Intelligence, Plans and Operations should work together in the most complete harmony, sharing each other's secrets, trusting each other's judgements, testing each other's opinions and accepting each other's decisions. Such a concept was entirely foreign to Oliver's nature, to his training, and, it must be said to that of practically every other senior British naval officer of his time. Nor was it realised by Oliver that *Operational* intelligence, the information about the day to day, hour to hour movements of the enemy, *must* reach those at sea, i.e. those who, in the end, have to bear the final responsibility, with the minimum of delay – that minutes, not hours, count in this game. This is only possible if those who in the first place receive and understand the information, are permitted to pass it at once to those at sea. Oliver and his ilk did not consider that

[1] The character in Gilbert and Sullivan's *Mikado* who was First Lord of the Treasury, Lord Chief Justice, Commander-in-Chief, Lord High Admiral, Master of the Buckhounds, Groom of the Back Stairs, Archbishop of Titipu, and Lord Mayor.

Room 40 were capable of performing this function, nor did he trust Jellicoe to take the right decisions, except in a purely local and tactical sense, even when he, Oliver, had finally decided what information should be passed to the Commander-in-Chief.

There is no record of Oliver ever visiting Room 40 or of his ever having consulted any member of its staff. His Director of Operations, Thomas Jackson, did no better. As Birch and Clarke commented later, '. . . we have noticed errors of commission due to faulty organisation and errors of omission due to lack of breadth of view and foresight. The results of both had this much in common – Intelligence of an important nature was either not forthcoming or was not available to the fullest extent in the right place at the right time.' Sufficient examples of delays in passing information to the Fleet, or of failures to pass any information at all, have been given in these pages to substantiate the charge that proper use of Room 40's information was not made until Oliver left the Admiralty. I am convinced that things would have gone better for the Royal Navy, perhaps far better, if Oliver had been given command afloat in 1915 rather than in 1918. What, for example, would have been the effect on the general fortunes of the war if the Grand Fleet had been able to renew the battle on the day after Jutland and had achieved, as it should and probably would have done; a really decisive victory over the *Hochseeflotte*?

How then, does one assess Blinker Hall? He was, like Oliver, a fine seaman, a successful sea officer. In all other respects he was completely different. Is he our 'hero'? Hall had the capacity to inspire intense admiration, affection, even devotion, in those who worked for and with him. Men and women, Service and civilian, would exert themselves to an extent they had not thought previously possible, to meet his demands. He knew how to get the best out of everyone with whom he came in contact; he had a fascination and charm which he used, consciously or not, with devastating effect. He did not attempt to do everything himself, to master all the intricate details of the great web of the Intelligence organisation which he built up. He chose his people, he tested them, he trusted them and he recognised that in time they would know more about their own particular functions than he would. Birch, in *Alice in ID 25*, maliciously portrays the DID as a turkey, the 'DIND'. '"Please," began the White Rabbit, "I believe I've got the hang of this now"', and he held out a piece of paper on which a lot of letters were written backwards and a lot of numbers upside down. "You see, it seems to be a chi on an anagram, followed by transposition and substitution." "Transsubstantiation! That's it," cried the DIND. "Exactly! I knew it. I said so all along."'

Well, Hall may not have been exactly au fait with the esoteric mysteries of code-breaking, but he certainly knew how to make the best use of the results. One cannot imagine Oliver displaying the patience and finesse with which Hall handled the Zimmermann Telegram. Hall did not despise civilians; he welcomed their advice and help. He told John Godfrey in 1939 that 'the DNI is entitled to enlist the help of anyone inside or outside the country from the Archbishop of Canterbury and the General of the Jesuits downwards, and that they would all be delighted to help . . .' Hall revelled in the shadier side of the Intelligence world and I have, at times, asked myself whether he did not neglect the hard slog of administering Room 40 in favour of the excitement of coups like the cruise of the *Sayonara* or the capture of the *Erri Berro*, the high stakes of bribing Enver Pasha to desert the Central Powers, or the byzantine manoeuvres to publish the Luxberg Telegram, or unmask von Papen and Rintelen. He did these things superbly; his sense of timing was impeccable, his judgement of the reactions of others, friend and foe alike, almost faultless. He saw the gaps in Britain's Intelligence armoury – and there were many in 1914 – and he filled them, instinctively and brilliantly, on his own initiative and without reference to higher authority.

As to Room 40, he did not, officially, have any control of it until the end of 1916. Up to that time it was the responsibility of Sir Alfred Ewing and, in a vague and ill-defined way, of the COS, Oliver. Neither of them could see that, if it was to realise its full potential, it must be developed from a cryptographic bureau, pure and simple, into an active Intelligence Centre. Denniston and Birch and Clarke are extremely critical of the failure to recruit sufficient staff in the early days, of the unbusinesslike methods and routines imposed upon them and of the absence of secretaries, clerical help and office appliances. To Oliver, such things would no doubt have savoured of the methods of the North Eastern Railway, but Ewing, surely, should have had more understanding and insight.

Hall obviously tried to remedy some of these deficiencies early on, but all he got for his pains was to be hauled over the coals by Oliver. When he set up the Diplomatic Section he was careful to keep it under his own control. It is notable that in this field, he managed to extract the last possible ounce of value out of Room 40's information, without ever endangering his sources. Oliver was so obsessed with the need for secrecy that he failed to realise that a secret is not worth keeping if you cannot make use of it. As soon as Ewing left, and when the whole of Room 40 became officially a section of the Intelligence Division, we can see a change in the handling of purely naval intelligence. More staff were recruited, including many girls – a daring innovation in the ultra conservative Admiralty. Specialisation was introduced, the work load more sensibly divided, an attempt made to create an Intelligence Centre. The watertight compartments were gradually broken down and officers, experts in their own fields, however junior in rank and whether regular or reserve, at last permitted to use their initiative and even themselves originate certain signals to the Fleet. If this process was slow, one must remember that Oliver's stultifying and autocratic influence was not finally removed until January 1918. No, it would not be fair to blame Hall for the failures to make the best use of Room 40's naval information. If he had been given a free hand in 1914 things would have been very different.

Perhaps Hall did develop a taste for intrigue. For a comparatively unknown Captain (he was not promoted to Rear-Admiral until October 1917), he quickly established astonishingly close relations with politicians, with diplomats, with the Press and with the City. It is also remarkable that, after only just over six months in the Admiralty, the 2nd Sea Lord should have asked him to ensure that Fisher's resignation was accepted – a task which Hamilton and his colleagues on the Board were unable or unwilling to undertake themselves. If Hall did not support Jellicoe in December 1917, who is to say he was wrong? There are rare occasions when the traditional naval virtue of unswerving support for senior officers must be sacrificed to the overall good of the Service and the nation: this was surely one such occasion.

Hall had all the qualities of a great leader; courage, imagination, initiative; the ability to inspire his subordinates and the charm to gain acceptance from his equals; the good sense to delegate and then to stick by his staff through thick and thin, but equally the inspiration to see when he himself must take personal charge. Above all, he had that flair which is impossible to describe but which every great Intelligence chief (and there has never been a greater) must possess. Hall, like Nelson, had some indefinable quality which impressed everyone the moment they met him. He won no Trafalgar, but perhaps he deserved almost as well of his Service and country as that other little admiral whose 'immortal memory' is still toasted on 21 October each year.

Intelligence chiefs cannot expect the same public recognition as those commanders on sea or land or in the air, whose victories they have done so much to make possible. Their fate is usually to remain unknown and unsung. Hall has been more fortunate than most, thanks to his handling of the Zimmermann Telegram, the greatest intelligence coup in history. He may be forgiven his boast, 'Alone I did it' – it would certainly never have been done without him – but perhaps the true verdict on this and so much of his work was that of his staff: 'We gave the cards to Reggie to play and he played the hand at his own time and in his own way, but damned well.'

In the course of writing this book, I believe that I have got to know the characters described in it. A few I actually met, briefly, before or during World War II, but now, at the end of my story, I have the feeling I am saying goodbye to *all* of them as old friends. I have shared with them the life and excitements of Room 40; the frowsty atmosphere of the night watches, the desperate desire to put one's head down and sleep, which vanished the instant a fresh intercept rattled down the pneumatic tube; the doubts, the frustrations, the moments of elation; the feeling that, however humble one's role, one was taking part in great events and, no matter how mistakenly, that one's own part in it all had to be performed to the full if the British Empire was to survive and victory was to be won. Herschell and Serocold, Blinker's confidantes, moving in a rare and mysterious world; Hope, 'our beloved chief'; Rotter who first solved the key to the SKM; the quiet hard-working Denniston, and Nobby Clarke with his love of the Navy and lawyer's brain; Dilly Knox, that most brilliant and extraordinary code-breaker, and Waterhouse, Willoughby, Bullough, Quiggin and all the other dons and professors; Frank Birch with his sharp wit and George Young, so anxious to see action; the Lord Mayor, Nigel de Grey and the fighting Padre; Ernest Thring, that patient, wily U-boat tracker and Frank Tiarks, the D/F expert; Russell Clarke, Hippisley and Lambert, whose Y stations made it all possible; Lionel Fraser and all the tubists; Bubbles James, that breezy Commander, so puzzled at first by his motley crew; Ned Bell, the American, who was almost an honorary member. These, and many others, have become as real to me as those with whom I served in World War II. Perhaps it is the staff of Room 40 who are the real heroes of this story.

APPENDIX I

List of Abbreviations

Admiralstab	German Naval Staff or Admiralty.
AFB	*Allgemeinefunkspruchbuch*. Replaced the HVB in 1917.
AMC	Armed Merchant Cruiser.
ASDIC	Anti-Submarine Detection Investigation Committee, which was responsible for the production of the ASDIC or Sonar used in World War II.
BBC	British Broadcasting Corporation.
BCF	Battle Cruiser Force, later Battle Cruiser Fleet.
BEF	British Expeditionary Force, British Army in France, 1914–1918.
BP	Bletchley Park. World War II home of Government Code and Cipher School, Britain's inter-Service code-breaking organisation.
CID	Committee of Imperial Defence.
CNS	Chief of Naval Staff, a position held by the First Sea Lord (1917 onwards).
COS	Chief of War Staff (H. F. Oliver, 1914–17).
D.Day	The day on which an operation commences. Now often used to designate the day on which the Allies landed in Normandy in 1944.
DF	Direction Finding.
DID	Director of the Intelligence Division of the Naval Staff. *c*. 1918 renamed DNI, Director of Naval Intelligence Division (Hall, 1914 –18).
DNI	*See* DID.
DOD	Director of Operations Division of the Naval Staff (Thomas Jackson, 1914–17).
DSO	Distinguished Service Order.
DTD	Director of Trade Division of the Naval Staff.
E. Dienst	*Entzifferungsdienst*. German naval decoding service.
FdL	*Führer der Luftischiffe*. Senior Officer Airships.
FdU	*Führer der U-boote*. Senior Officer Submarines.
FFB	*Flottenfunkspruchbuch*. Replaced the SKM code in 1917.
GC & CS	Government Code and Cipher School. The inter-Service cryptological organisation which incorporated Room 40 in 1922. *See also* BP.
GMT	Greenwich Mean Time. Standard British Time.
HMS	His Majesty's Ship.
HMAS	His Majesty's Australian Ship.
HSF	*Hochseeflotte*. The High Sea Fleet, the principal German fleet, equivalent to the British Grand Fleet.
HVB	*Handelsverkehrsbuch* (Imperial German Navy/Merchant-Navy Code).
ID	Intelligence Division of the Naval Staff.
ID25	Official designation of Room 40 from 1917 as section 25 of ID.
KC	King's Counsel. A senior barrister.
KCMG	Knight Commander of St Michael and St George.

MI5	Department of British Security services responsible for contra-espionage within the UK.
MI6	The British Secret Service responsible for security and espionage services outside the UK.
MI8	US Army Cipher Bureau.
NID	Naval Intelligence Division. *See also* ID.
NO	Naval Officer.
NSL	Box in Room 40 into which were thrown all intercepts which were neither sent into Operations Division nor entered in Room 40's log.
OBE	Order of the British Empire.
OIC	The Admiralty's Operational Intelligence Centre in World War II.
PRO	Public Record Office, Kew, London.
QC	Queen's Counsel. *See* KC.
Q-ship	Disguised and armed merchant ship manned by RN crew to deceive and attack U-boats.
RAN	Royal Australian Navy.
RN	Royal Navy.
RNR	Royal Naval Reserve formed from officers and men of the Merchant Navy.
RNVR	Royal Naval Volunteer Reserve, formed from yachtsmen and other volunteers.
SKM	*Signalbuch der Kaiserlichen Marine* (Principal German Naval Code).
SO	Senior Officer. A naval officer usually of Captain's or Commander's rank.
SS	Steam ship (merchant vessel).
U-boat	*Unterseeboot*. Submarine.
UK	United Kingdom of Great Britain and Ireland (now Northern Ireland).
US and USA	United States of America.
USN	United States Navy.
VA	Vice-Admiral.
VB	*Verkehrsbuch*. Imperial German Navy code used for communication with Naval Attachés, overseas warships, consuls and, with special recipherment, Flag Officers.
WSC	Winston Spencer Churchill.
W/T	Wireless Telegraphy.
Y Stations	Wireless stations to intercept and record enemy wireless messages.

APPENDIX II

List of Staff Identified as Serving in or Closely Connected with Room 40/ID25, 1914–18

Adcock, F. E.
Allington, A. H.
Anstie, W. H.
Bailey, Mrs
Beazley, J. D.
Birch, F. L.
Boulton, H. E.
Bond, D.
Bruford, W. R.
Bullough, E.
Bush, ?
Buxton, ?
Christie, S. K.
Clarke, W. F.
Cooper, J.
Curtiss, Miss
Curwen, P.
Denniston, A. G.
Denniston, Mrs
Dummett, ?
Ellis, C. R.
Eves, ?
Ewing, J. A.
Faudell-Phillips, B. S.
Fetterlein, E.
Forbes, N.
Ford, H. R.
Fraser, W. L.
Fremantle, ?
Godfrey, C.
Gough, C. E.
Grant-Duff, E.
Green, E. J. C.

de Grey, N
Haggard, ?
Hall, W. R.
Hambro, Lady
Hanley, ?
Hardisty, C. W.
Harrison, E.
Harvey, Miss
Henderson, J. B.
Henderson, Miss
Herschell, Lord
Hippesley, B.
Hirst, L.
Hope, G. L. N.
Hope, H. W.
Hudson, Miss
James, W. M.
Jenkin, Miss E.
Knox, A. D.
Knox, R.
Lambert, L.
Lawrence, G.
Lawrence, H. W.
Le Blanc Smith, ?
Lee, Miss E.
Lock, ?
Lytton, Lord
Mackeson, G. P.
Marlowe, ?
McCarthy, D.
McGinn, P.
Molyneux, E.
Monkbretton, Lord

Montgomery, W. L.
Morrah, H. A.
Norton, R. D.
Nugent, Miss
O'Connor, Miss
Ould, R.
Parrish, A. J.
Peile, F. S. G.
Quiggin, E. C.
Rawson, G. C.
Robertson, Miss M. E.
Roddam, Miss
Rotter, C. J. E.
Round, ?
Russell Clarke, E.
Sandbach, ?
Savory, D. L.
Scrine, Miss R.
Serocold, C. P.
Somers-Cocks, C. S.
Spears, Miss
Talbot, G. F.
Thring, E. W. C.
Tiarks, H.
Toye, F.
Tribe, Miss
Waterhouse, G.
Welsford, Miss
Willoughby, L. A.
Winthrop-Smith, Miss
Woods, ?
Young, G.

IN ADDITION TO ROOM 40, ID25 probably also occupied Rooms 41, 42, 43 and 44 and certainly occupied Rooms 45 to 56. The numbering of the rooms has been changed more than once since 1919. The original Room 40 can be positively identified. Rooms 45 to 56 would appear to have been those on both sides of the first floor of the northern one of the two wings which run out from the main entrance of the Admiralty to Whitehall.

Sources and Select Bibliography

Official Papers

The first of Room 40's own files seem to have reached the Public Record Office sometime in 1976, apparently as a result of requests made by John Light. Their reference numbers are ADM 137/3956 to 3962. No further releases were made until the end of 1980 when I persuaded the authorities to resume the process of declassification. The first batch have reference numbers ADM 137/4057 to 4189. Releases have continued steadily, but at the time of writing a considerable number of files which I have been able to examine have not received their PRO reference numbers.

Special Telegrams made by Admiralty to C-in-C Grand Fleet and other naval authorities which were based on Room 40's information are to be found in the series which start with PRO reference ADM 137/203. Special signals received by C-in-C Grand Fleet and some special signals made by the C-in-C start in the Grand Fleet In Signals, PRO reference ADM 137/1779, although the first one containing the fruits of Room 40's work is ADM 137/1802.

Another valuable source is the *Contribution to the History of German Naval Warfare 1914–1918* by Birch and Clarke, at present in the Naval Historical Branch of the Ministry of Defence. This account was compiled between 1919 and 1922. It is not a history of Room 40, but contains a good deal of incidental information about that organisation and about German naval codes. It consists of three volumes, of which the third is an index of all the Room 40 files upon which the history was almost entirely based. It lists every single one of Room 40's files, which Birch and Clarke carefully collected and bound, and gives a brief description of each one showing what it contains, whether it was a strictly contemporary document or whether it was compiled later in the war or even after it, which files are duplicates, and so on. The index has hitherto been classified, but extracts from it are likely to be released to the PRO shortly or incorporated into the PRO's own index of the papers released.

The Edward Bell correspondence is in the Office of Counsellor files of the Diplomatic Section of The National Archives, Washington DC. The Military Section holds under reference SRH 030 *A History of the Code and Cipher Section during the First World War, prepared in 1919 by Major Herbert O. Yardley*, and *A Brief History of the Signal Intelligence Service* by William F. Friedman, June 1942, SRH 029.

Information about the capture of the HVB code, the code book itself and Dr Wheatley's papers are to be found in the Australian Archives under reference 1921/0614 and 15/021 and in the Australian War Memorial Archives, under reference 311.1.

Korvettenkapitän Kleikamp's paper, *Der Einfluss der Funkaufklärung auf die Seekriegsführung in der Nordsee*, 1914–1918, Kiel 1934, was made available to me by the Bibliothek für Zeitgeschichte, Stuttgart.

Richtlinien für die Entwicklung der Marine-Geheimschrift-Verfahren, 1916, is in

Bundesarchiv RM5/1709, as is the original fair copy of Schwieger's log (only an excerpt is available in the PRO). Dr Göppert's report on the Zimmermann Telegram is in the Politisches Archiv of the Bundesarchiv.

Private Papers

The Clarke, Denniston, Hall and Lloyd Hirst papers are (or in the last case shortly will be) in the Churchill College Archive Centre, Cambridge, as are copies of some of John Light's earlier notes and correspondence about his *Lusitania* researches.

Admiral of the Fleet Sir Henry Oliver's *Recollections* are in The National Maritime Museum (OLV 12).

Published Books and Articles

Although a number of books refer incidentally to the work of Room 40, only three, so far as I know, deal specifically with it. The first is H. C. Hoy's *40 OB. How the War was Won*, Hutchinson, 1932. This must be treated with the very greatest reserve. Hoy was not, as he claimed, Hall's Private Secretary but a confidential typist and he had no access to Room 40. Admiral Sir William James's *The Eyes of the Navy*, Methuen, 1955, is in quite a different class. But James was refused permission to examine the records and had to rely largely on memory, his own and other people's. He did have access to Hall's not very extensive papers, including a number which can no longer be traced, but his account is, considering when it was written, necessarily discreet. A. W. Ewing's biography of his father *The Man of Room 40*, Hutchinson, 1939, in fact contains only a single chapter on Room 40.

For the general background to my story I have relied on the published works of the late Professor Arthur Marder and on those of Captain Stephen Roskill, which, in addition, contain much incidental information about Room 40.

The following is a short bibliography.

C. Andrew, *The Mobilisation of British Intelligence for Two World Wars*, International Security Studies Programme, Woodrow Wilson International Centre for Scholars, 1980.

Bailey and Ryan, *The Lusitania Tragedy*, The Free Press, New York 1975.

Beesly, P., *Very Special Intelligence*, Hamish Hamilton, 1977.

Beesly, P., *Very Special Admiral*, Hamish Hamilton, 1980.

Benckendorff, *Half a Life*, The Richard Press, 1954.

Bonatz, H., *Die Deutsche Marine-Funkaufklärung 1914–1945*, Wehr und Wissen, 1970.

Churchill, W., *The World Crisis, 1911–1918*, Revised Edition, Thornton Butterworth, 1931.

Clark, R. W., *The Man who Broke Purple*, Weidenfeld & Nicolson, 1977.

Dorwart, J. M., *The Office of Naval Intelligence*, Naval Institute Press, 1977.

Fitzgerald, P., *The Knox Brothers*, Macmillan, 1977.

Fraser, W. L., *All to the Good*, Heinemann, 1963.

Gaunt, G., *The Yield of the Years*, Hutchinson, 1940.

Gilbert, M., *Winston S. Churchill*, Vol. III, Heinemann, 1971.

Grant, R. M., *U-boat Intelligence, 1914–1918*, Putnam, 1969.

Green, R. L., *A. E. W. Mason*, Max Parish, London, 1952.

Gregory, R., *Walter Hines Page*, University of Kentucky Press, 1970.

Hall, W. R. and Peaslee, A. J., *Three Wars against Germany*, Putnam, 1944.

Hendrick, B. J., *The Life and Letters of Walter Hines Page*, Heinemann, 1922.

Hickling, H., *Sailor at Sea*, Kimber, 1965.

Jones, R. V., *Alfred Ewing and Room 40*, Royal Society, July 1979.

Kahn, D., *The Codebreakers*, Weidenfeld & Nicolson, 1973.
Kahn, D., *Codebreaking in World Wars I and II*, Historical Journal, 23.3.80.
Marder, A. J., *From the Dreadnought to Scapa Flow*, 5 vols, Oxford University Press, 1961–1970.
Marder, A. J., *From the Dardanelles to Oran*, Oxford University Press, 1975.
Pitt, B., *Coronel and the Falkland Islands*, Cassell, 1960.
Roskill, S. W., *Admiral of the Fleet Earl Beatty*, Collins, 1980.
Roskill, S. W., *Churchill and the Admirals*, Collins, 1970.
Roskill, S. W., *Naval Policy between the Wars*, Collins, 1968.
Roskill, S. W., *The Strategy of Sea Power*, Collins, 1962.
Simpson, C., *Lusitania*, Longman, 1974.
Taylor, E., *The Fossil Monarchies*, Weidenfeld & Nicolson, 1963.
Toye, F., *For What We Have Received*, Knopf, 1948.
Tuchman, B., *The Zimmermann Telegram*, Constable, 1959.
Waters, D. W., *The Science of Admiralty, The Naval Review*.
Yardley, H. O., *The American Black Chamber*, 1931, Ballantine Books, 1981.

Index

Index